The Triumph
of the
English Language

The Triumph
of the
English Language

A Survey of Opinions Concerning the
Vernacular from the Introduction
of Printing to the Restoration

By
RICHARD FOSTER JONES

STANFORD UNIVERSITY PRESS
STANFORD, CALIFORNIA

STANFORD UNIVERSITY PRESS, STANFORD, CALIFORNIA
LONDON: GEOFFREY CUMBERLEGE, OXFORD UNIVERSITY PRESS

THE BAKER AND TAYLOR COMPANY, HILLSIDE, NEW JERSEY
HENRY M. SNYDER & COMPANY, 440 FOURTH AVENUE, NEW YORK 16
W. S. HALL & COMPANY, 457 MADISON AVENUE, NEW YORK 22

COPYRIGHT 1953 BY THE BOARD OF TRUSTEES OF THE LELAND STANFORD JUNIOR UNIVERSITY
PRINTED IN THE UNITED STATES OF AMERICA BY STANFORD UNIVERSITY PRESS

Library of Congress Catalog Card Number: 52-6350

To
Margaret Williams Jones
and
Edward Hallaran Jones

PREFACE

SOME years ago I published in the *Washington University Studies* an article on Richard Mulcaster's view of the English language, which considered at some length Mulcaster's opinion of the vernacular in relation to the various efforts made at orthographic reformation in the sixteenth century, and most of which has been incorporated in the present study. Since that time I have maintained a lively interest in the general status of the English tongue during the sixteenth and seventeenth centuries, which has resulted in my noting from time to time opinions on the vernacular, until in the years preceding the recent war I enjoyed the opportunity, both here and in England, of examining a large part, if not most, of the English books printed before 1600, and an equally large number of books which appeared in the seventeenth century. The nature of the subject is such as to render a more restricted investigation inadequate and misleading, because during this period consciousness of the vernacular was so keen and widespread that it is manifested in all kinds of writing. Today, writers may well take their medium of expression for granted, but in the early stages of the development of Modern English the potentialities of the language were in large measure concealed.

I am by no means the first to explore the field covered by my investigations. In 1909 Wilhelm Prein in *Puristische Strömungen im 16. Jahrhundert. Ein Beitrag zur englischen Sprachgeschichte* examined the hostility to borrowed words in the sixteenth century, but his path was too narrow to furnish adequate explanations of the phenomena with which he was dealing. The next year J. L. Moore in *Tudor-Stuart Views on the Growth, Status, and Destiny of the English Language* surveyed both the sixteenth and seventeenth centuries, but so superficially that his findings cannot furnish sufficient grounds for generalizations, especially since he employed the statistical method, which is the least satisfactory and illuminating procedure and which requires the greatest amount of data to approximate accuracy. A much better treatment of the subject is found in Professor Albert Baugh's *History of the English Language,* which presents new material and shows that opinions concerning the nature and worth of a language find a legitimate place in its history. In various treatises the problem has been touched upon, either tangentially or as a subordinate part of larger views. In fact, it has reached that stage where a more comprehensive and ambitious study of it is a desideratum.

The present volume is neither a history of the language nor a history of style, though at times it skirts the fringes of one or the other. It aims at being a history of ideas concerning the English tongue—its nature, use, and improvement—during the period 1476–1660. There are various conceptions of the nature of this discipline, for so the history of ideas may be considered, though at present it occupies no place in the collegiate curriculum. It may approach a history of philosophy and deal with ideas on a purely intellectual level without thought of their influence on mundane affairs. Or it may deal with thoughts which dwell in the hearts as well as in the heads of men and so become social forces, which in the form of opinions, values, and attitudes pursue their way toward destined ends. In both types, however, the proper relationship between logic and history in determining the thought pattern of the past is of great importance. It is not enough to show that a pattern could have existed; it is necessary to prove that it did occur. It is hard to say who makes the greater mistake, the one who painfully collects an abundance of data over a wide field and then leaves them an unanalyzed, undigested mass, or the one who seizes upon a few random opinions and constructs a beautiful pattern logically sound but historically dubious. The latter is more interesting, but the former is more useful. Sir Francis Bacon looked upon the Copernican system as mathematically, or logically, satisfying, but he doubted that it was true in nature. May we not, to better purpose, ask of many a pattern imposed upon thought of the past, no matter how rationally attractive, if it is true to history? Sir Francis distrusted reason because its delight was in construction rather than in discovery, and because, enraptured with the beauty and regularity of its own compositions, it sought to impose them upon nature.

The temptation to organize past ideas in designs agreeable to our sense of order and regularity, to leave too soon the materials with which reason must work, and to which it must constantly refer, is responsible for most of the doubtful generalizations which not infrequently appear on the pages of literary history. It might be suggested that the more attractive and interesting an explanation of the thought of the past is, the less it conforms to historical truth, either because the human mind can create better designs than history can offer, or because "truth is a naked and open day-light, that doth not shew the masks and mummeries and triumphs of the world half so stately and daintily as candle-light."

If, then, we are to cast our patterns on the earth and not in the sky, we must dwell with our data. Since these data are not only definite ideas, but also opinions, values, and attitudes, expressed or implied, they present problems not found in factual evidence. They are less easily analyzed, interpreted, and evaluated. Furthermore, the reasoning involved differs in some particulars from scientific induction. In the natural sciences a single contradictory instance will invalidate a whole line of inductive reasoning, such is the uniformity of nature. But in dealing with ideas, contradictory instances, if not too numerous, are evidence for rather than against the patterns of thought which we wish to establish, such is the divergence and perversity of human minds. They may occasionally discourage an investigator or furnish a reviewer with a short-lived triumph, but when rightly considered, they frequently testify to the strength and importance of what they oppose.

To determine the prevalence and importance of a thought pattern in a climate of opinion, the first test is obviously the frequency with which it or its constituent elements occur. If, however, this test is carried too far, it degenerates into mere statistics which ignore the fact that repetition may evince conventionality only. In its life-cycle an idea may begin as a thought, proceed as an emotion, and expire as a habit. If we are concerned largely with the logical nature of our patterns, a relatively small amount of data suffices, but if we are interested in their historical reality a greater amount is necessary.

Another test of dominant patterns is the way they fit into the general thought of the times. If it can be shown that ideas from other fields have entered into and been integrated with them, that a logical connection has been established between them and the age, their significance becomes obvious. If we may call upon Sir Francis again, one of Bacon's most earnest injunctions was to study phenomena over a wider field than that in which they occur, a procedure clearly applicable to the history of ideas. To trace the complexes of religious thought only in the field of religion, of literary thought only in the world of literature, or of any other matter only in its own field, will inevitably result in an inadequate explanation. Ideally the scope of the study of almost any combination of ideas is beyond the powers of one individual, but practically much may be achieved by the conscientious following of the leads which we discover in analyzing our data. It is the complex rather than simple ideas that have been responsible for man's weal or woe. If we could only discover what combinations are beneficent and what are explosive, human progress might prove more real than it is. The discovery of the constituent elements, at any rate, would surely carry us beyond the limits of the field in which the pattern was first encountered. For example, the present study of opinions concerning the vernacular, however inadequate it may be, touches upon the Reformation, Humanism, Puritanism, antiquarianism, experimental science, and literary history.

In the study of ideas we are restricted for the most part to their expression in written or printed form. Today, ideas find much readier access to publication than in the past, so that the difficulty on the score of determining accurately thought patterns is not so great, though on the score of an overwhelming amount of data it is more considerable. In the past much more must have been thought and expressed than was written or printed. If ideas may be considered social forces, the various forms of social contact furnish a medium for their transmission. This element is now lost to us, so that we have to rely upon more enduring forms of expression for our data. Where possible, the analysis and interpretation of these should take into account the circumstances of expression such as a writer's sincerity, motives, and interests. In most cases, however, we must consider our data as sincere expressions of more or less objective ideas. While we can usually assume that the more important a thinker is in his age, the more weight particular ideas of his will carry, we must be on our guard not to ascribe to him too much importance. Ideas may be intrinsically valuable and yet not accurately expressive of the climate of opinion. Though we may detect in Milton's tractate on education the influence of the thought of his time, we cannot consider it as representative as numerous other educational treatises by obscure men. In the same way, it is a mistake to consider, as literary historians have frequently done in the past, Pope's *Essay on Criticism* as representative of the critical temper of the first quarter of the eighteenth century.

I trust that this explanation of the principles upon which I have tried to proceed may justify the large number of inconspicuous men whom I have considered, and the large amount of quotation found in the following pages. Honesty at least recommends the publication of the data upon which generalizations are based. Furthermore, quotations make possible a scrutiny of a writer's analyses either for a correction of his errors or a detection of significant points which he has missed. I am painfully aware of the fact that there is more in the material presented than I have educed. For the most part I have restricted my investigations to England, though there are many Continental parallels to English opinions, especially in France. It is a mistake, however, to place too much emphasis upon similarity alone as evidence of indebtedness; similar conditions give rise independently to similar phenomena. It was not feasible to follow strict chronological divisions in my discussions, though in general the first four chapters cover the last quarter of the fifteenth century and the first three quarters of the sixteenth century, and the fifth, the last two quarters of the latter. The sixth chapter is restricted to the last quarter of this century, and the next three chapters cover the first sixty years of the seventeenth century. The last deals for the most part with the twenty years of Puritan domination.

I have tried to follow the old spelling, though contractions have been expanded and "and" substituted for its unsightly symbol. I have restricted the use of "neologism" to verbal borrowing, and have been bold enough to retain the "uneloquent" of the sixteenth century, which possesses connotations the modern form lacks. Unless otherwise stated, when a date in parentheses follows the date given for a title, it refers to the first edition.

It is a very great pleasure to acknowledge my indebtedness to Dr. L. F. Powell, distinguished Johnsonian, who in full keeping with the generosity and humanity revealed so frequently by him to American scholars presented me with a whole sheaf of notes. I am grateful to Mrs. Cathryn Mahne Purnell, who read several weeks for me in the library of the British Museum, and to my friend and former colleague, Professor George B. Parks, who gave me a number of references. To another friend and former colleague, Professor Donald Bryant, I am indebted for assistance in English libraries. And to my many unnamed friends I am glad to express my appreciation for a suggestion or a reference casually given me. Professor Herbert D. Meritt read the entire manuscript, much to my profit, and Miss Dora George read the first two chapters with the same result. To the British Museum Library, the Bodleian Library, the Cambridge University Library, the Folger Library, and the Huntington Library I am indebted for the efficient service rendered us. To express indebtedness to my wife in any terms would be highly misleading. Besides performing most accurately the various mechanical tasks incident to scholarly work, she searched so widely and indefatigably for material as to justify her being considered as much the author of the substance of this book as the writer himself.

R. F. J.

STANFORD UNIVERSITY
December 20, 1951

CONTENTS

The Triumph
of the
English Language

CHAPTER I

THE UNELOQUENT LANGUAGE

THOUGH one seeks in vain for any significant body of literary criticism in England before the Renaissance, there did come down through the Middle Ages a very definite rhetorical tradition, based upon the postclassical writers and supported by the position of rhetoric in the university curriculum. It is not strange, then, that in the absence of a critical terminology, those who might wish to comment on poetry should use rhetorical terms, and that criticism should be primarily interested in that element which is common to both rhetoric and poetic, namely, style. Chaucer's relations with the rhetoricians have been thoroughly examined,[1] and his concern with rhetoric made clear. His disciple Lydgate reveals a similar interest. The depreciation of his own work, which characterizes the fifteenth-century poet, and which appears frequently in the writers of the next century, is expressed almost entirely in stylistic terms. When Lydgate laments that his pen is barren of "aureat lycoure" and that his translation of the *Troy Book* "stumbleth aye for faute of eloquence,"[2] he may perhaps be commenting on the only feature a translator can consider his own contribution, but when, in the same passage, he says that Guido illumined

> This noble storye with many fresshe coloure
> Of Rhethoryk and many ryche floure
> Of eloquence to make it sounde the bett,

[1] The late Professor J. M. Manly has shown how much Chaucer was influenced by medieval rhetoricians, how widespread the use of rhetoric was, and what great value was placed upon it. See "Chaucer and the Rhetoricians," *Proceedings of the British Academy*, 1926, pp. 95–113. Mr. J. W. H. Atkins speaks of "the absorption of poetic by rhetoric, the debasement of poetic (or rhetoric) to a mere study of style, and the limitation of style to ornamental details" as characteristic of the Middle Ages. *English Literary Criticism; The Medieval Phase*, 1943, p. 184. See also C. S. Baldwin, *Medieval Rhetoric and Poetic*, 1928.

[2] *The hystorye/Sege and dystruccyon of Troye*, 1513, Prologue.

he clearly shows that his critical vocabulary does not extend beyond rhetorical expressions applicable to style. Whether he is engaging in modest depreciation of his own worth or in compliments to those whom he admires, it is style, and particularly language, that limits his critical pronouncements. Chaucer, he says, rained golden drops of rhetoric "Our rude language onely tenlumine."[3]

This self-depreciation and exclusive emphasis upon style continue unabated throughout the fifteenth century, and in Caxton become even more pronounced. He had reason for his acute sensitiveness regarding the language of his compositions, for, as he tells us, French, the language of many of his originals, he knew only imperfectly, having never been in France; he learned his native tongue on the Kentish wold, "where I doubte not is spoken as brode and rude Englissh as in any place of England."[4] Also it is not improbable that the invention of printing impressed upon its early users a lively realization that their compositions would come under the scrutiny of many eyes, and thus made them all the more conscious of their expressions. At any rate, scattered through Caxton's prologues and epilogues are many apologies for his simple and rude style and his rude and common English, and he frequently laments his lack of the "art of rhetoric," "curious gay terms of rhetoric," "ornate eloquence," and

[3] *The hystorye . . . of Troye*, sig. K2^r. In the prologue to *The Falle of Princis*, Lydgate speaks of his rude language and lack of eloquence; and in the prologue to the *Lyfe of Seint Albon*, he prays to be spared the troublesome mist of rude, naked, and barren language. See also his *Minor Poems*, ed. H. N. MacCracken, 1911, pp. 18, 41, 173–74.

[4] See Caxton's translation of Raoul le Fevre's *The recuyell of the historyes of Troye* (1475?), Prologue. Mr. Atkins considers these expressions of self-disparagement as "little more than a fifteenth-century convention, designed to win the good-will of the reader, after the fashion of the epistolary device, *captatio benevolentiae*, of which to all appearances they are in some sort a revival." (*Op. cit.*, p. 177.) Certainly in some cases they are conventional. Yet if Caxton were merely observing convention, why need he go to the trouble of pointing out the reason for his "rude" diction? He evidently means what he says. Throughout the first three quarters of the sixteenth century we find innumerable examples of self-depreciation in vernacular writers, but since a clear explanation of most of them can be found in the demonstrably low opinion of English, we are hardly justified in disposing of them on the ground of conventionality. An age may find conventions a suitable vehicle for authentic ideas and feelings.

"the new eloquence." In addition to being afflicted with a sincere modesty, which expressed itself in confessions of rudeness and lack of rhetorical embellishments in his work, Caxton must have been aware of the difficulties presented by an unstabilized vernacular. He was keenly conscious of the confusion arising from dialectical differences[5] and also of the rapidly changing nature of English, which fact moved him to declare, a short time before his death, that the language of his youth was then unintelligible to him.[6] These considerations could hardly have failed to breed in him distrust of the mother tongue; and indeed, in spite of the stereotyped nature of the apologies for his rude language, one may detect in them a feeling of inferiority because of his medium of expression. When Caxton speaks of translating a Dutch tale "in to this rude and symple englyssh,"[7] and when he apologizes for reducing the original of *Blanchardyn and Eglantine* (*c.* 1489) "to rude and comyn englyshe," he is expressing his opinion of the vernacular as well as revealing his modesty.[8]

The absorption in rhetoric and the employment of rhetorical terms in comments on literature caused emphasis to be placed

[5] See the Prologue to the *Eneydos*. In *Here begynneth a treatyse of a galaunt*, sig. Aiv[r], Lydgate, if he be the author, attributes the confusion in his native tongue to the fact that five times strangers had invaded England, and each time had changed the language. In 1530 a translator, after speaking of the difficulty of translating Latin into English because of lack of words, adds: "There is also many wordes that haue dyuerse vnderstondynges/and some tyme they ar taken in one wyse/some tyme in an other/and som tyme they may be taken in dyuerse wyse in one reson or clause[.] Dyuerse wordes also in dyuerse scryptures: ar set and vnderstonde some tyme other wyse then auctoures of gramer tell or speke of. Oure language is also so dyuerse in yt selfe/that the commen maner of spekynge in Englysshe of some contre/can skante be vnderstondid in some other contre of the same londe." *Hereafter Foloweth the boke callyd the Myrroure of Oure Lady*, the second prologue.

[6] See *The Golden Legend*, ed. Alfred Aspland, 1876, Introduction, p. 11. (Holbein Society's Facsimile Reprints.)

[7] See the end of *The Historye of reynart the foxe*, 1481.

[8] In a work begun in 1477 and entitled *The Ordinall of Alchimy*, Thomas Norton finds it necessary to defend his use of "plaine and common speache" on the ground that he is writing for the unlearned multitude. No wise man, he says, should despise it, because it is "here set out in *English* blunt and rude" to please "Ten Thousand *Layman*" rather than "ten able *Clerkes*." (See Elias Ashmole's *Theatrum Chemicum Britannicum*, 1652, pp. 7, 106.) The use of English, free from classical expressions, required an apology.

on style, and considerations of style focused attention upon language, so that users of the vernacular became acutely conscious of their medium of expression. Since eloquence was the stylistic ideal,[9] and since it had traditionally been associated with the classical languages, it is not strange that it could not be discovered in the mother tongue. The aureate style confirms this view, for it represents an attempt to gain eloquence through the introduction of only slightly disguised classical words.[10] That as regards English compositions of the first half of the sixteenth century eloquence was largely confined to neologisms is revealed in numerous ways. In an interesting early collection of anecdotes entitled *A.C. mery Talys* (1525), one story reads as follows:

In the vnyuersyte of Oxonford there was a skoler that delytyd mich to speke eloquent english and curious terms/and cam to the cobler wyth hys shoys whych were pikid before as they vsyd that seson to haue them cloutyd and sayd thys wyse/Cobler I pray the set me .ii tryanglys and .ii semy cercles vppon my subpedytals and I shall gyue the for thy labor/Thys cobler because he vnderstode him not half well answerid shortly and sayd/Syr your eloquence passith myne intelligence/but I promyse you yf ye meddyll wyth me/the clowting of youre shone shall cost you .iii. pence.

By thys tale men may lerne that it is foly to study to speke eloquently before them that be rude and vnlernyd.[11]

[9] A good idea of the high honor paid eloquence may be secured from Caxton's Prohemye to Trevisa's translation of Higden's *Polycronicon*, 1482.

[10] In view of the attitude which Caxton and others who followed him maintained toward the vernacular, it is difficult to interpret Caxton's opinion of Chaucer. In the Epilogue to Chaucer's *Consolacion of Philosophie*, the printer calls the poet "the first foundeur and enbelisher of ornate eloquence in englissh . . . making the sayd langage ornate and fayr. which shal endure perpetuelly"; and in the Prophemye to the *Canterbury Tales*, he asserts that Chaucer "for his ornate wrytyng in our tongue may wel haue the name of a laureate poet/For to fore that he by hys labour enbellyshyd/ornated/and made faire our englisshe/in thys Royame was had rude speche." (See *Prologues and Epilogues of William Caxton*, ed. W. J. B. Crotch, 1928, pp. 37, 90. E.E.T.S., Original Series, No. 176.) These words seem to imply that English had been rendered an eloquent language and was enduring as such. Yet this certainly was not the view of the age. They may represent only a conventional mode of praise, or they may mean that Chaucer's poetry endures, but that it no longer represents the vernacular.

[11] See W. C. Hazlitt's edition of *A Hundred Merry Tales*, 1887. This conception of eloquence persisted to the end of the century. Angel Day tells of

Eloquence inhered not in the native elements in the language but only in the words introduced into it from the classics. That the English language per se was considered uneloquent may be easily deduced from the adjectives most frequently used to describe it: rude, gross, barbarous, base, vile. For the most part these terms did not possess the strong connotations for the Renaissance that they hold for us. "Vile," for instance, meant only of little or no worth,[12] and "base" was equivalent to "low," "common," "vulgar," "uncultured."[13]

The first three terms in the list are practically interchangeable, and their most frequent meaning is "uneloquent." In determining their meaning, one finds it necessary, because of the absence of English dictionaries, to rely on the definitions given their Latin equivalents. For instance, Thomas Thomas in his *Dictionarium* (1588?) defines "barbare" as "barbarously, vnmannerly, grossly, rudely, strangely, without eloquence"; and "barbarus," as "rude in doing or speaking . . . ignorant, rustical, churlish: without eloquence." Thomas Cooper defines "barbarus" as follows: "In olde tyme all people, excepte greekes, were called Barbari, proprely it be they, whyche doo speake grossely, without obseruyng of congruitee, or pronounce not perfectly, especially Greke or Latine. also they that abhorre al elegancy. More ouer it signifieth them that be fierce and cruell of maners and countenance: rude, ignorant, rusticall, churlyshe,

a doctor who, "intending to bee verie eloquent in wordes," began a dedicatory epistle with a passage replete with inkhorn terms. (*English Secretorie*, 1586, p. 38.) Three years later Nash says, "I am not ignorant how eloquent our gowned age is growen of late, so that euerie mæchanicall mate abhorres the english he was borne too, and plucks with a solemme periphrasis his *ut vales* from the inkhorne." See *Elizabethan Critical Essays*, ed. G. G. Smith, I, 307.

[12] Cf. the definition of "vilis" in Thomas Cooper's revision of Elyot's dictionary, *Bibliotheca Eliotae*. The lack of worth indicated by the term springs from "commonness." In one of Robert Recorde's works, after a teacher has explained how common the use of arithmetic is, his pupil replies, "This is the cause that I judged it so vile, because it is so common in talkyng euery while: for plentie is no deintie, as the common saieyng is." See *Grounde of Artes*, 1561 (1543), sig. Aiiʳ.

[13] See the preface to Thomas Morton's *Salomon*, 1596, which calls a popular proverb a base one. Thomas Becon says the Scriptures exercise the strong with dark meanings, "and flattereth the litle ones with base speach." *The thyrd parte of the Bookes*, 1563, fol. 469ᵛ.

without eloquence."[14] This relatively long definition indicates the importance Cooper attaches to the word. It is probably from this source that the author of *The Arte of English Poesie* (1589) derived his better-known definition. Characterizing barbarous speaking as "the foulest vice in language" he says that the term came from the Greeks and Romans, who considered all languages except their own rude and uncivil,

> So as when any straunge word not of the naturall Greeke or Latin was spoken, in the old time they called it *barbarisme,* or when any of their owne naturall wordes were sounded and pronounced with strange and ill shapen accents, or written by wrong ortographie, as he that would say with vs in England, a dousand for a thousand, isterday for yesterday, as commonly the Dutch and French people do, they said it was barbarously spoken.[15]

He goes on to say that the Italians with like arrogance called all other Europeans barbarous. Though there is evidence that this meaning was given to the term "barbarous," the other definition given by Cooper, "without eloquence," was more widely accepted. An anonymous work entitled *A proper dyaloge betwene a Gentillman and a husbandman* (1530) introduces an old treatise with the words:

> Though I am olde clothed in barbarous wede
> Nothynge garnyshed with gaye eloquency

where "barbarous" is equivalent to "uneloquent." In his *Alvearie* (1573) Baret defines "barbarously" as follows: "To speake barbarously, corruptly, not vsing piked and choyse woordes." *Riders Dictionarie,* as corrected by Francis Holyoke (1612), defines "barbarously" as "incompte, inconcinne, impolite, incondite, inquinate, georgice." The prologue to *A new and mery Enterlude called the Triall of Treasure* (1567) introduces the clause, "Though the style be barbarous, not fined with eloquence."[16] That "barbarous" retained its meaning of "un-

---

[14] *Bibliotheca Eliotae,* 1548.

[15] See p. 209.

[16] It is quite apparent that "rude" and "gross" are exact equivalents of "barbarous." John Bullokar (*An English Expositor,* 1616) defines "barbarism" as "rudeness in speech, or behaviour"; John Mauritius (*Lingua Linguarum,*

eloquent" until the next century, and that eloquence continued
to be associated with neologisms, is apparent from Samuel Rowlands' *Letting of humours blood* (1600), Satire IV:

> *Melfluuious* sweete Rose-watred elloquence
> Thou that hast hunted Barbarisme hence,
> And taught the Goodman *Cobbin*, at his plow,
> To be as eloquent as *Tullie* now.

irony

And the author makes it plain that by eloquence he understands
neologisms and figurative language.

eloquence

It may seem that too much attention has been paid to the
words discussed above. Yet clarification of their meaning is
necessary, for the chief key to an understanding of the sixteenth-
century attitude toward the English language is to be discovered
in the conception of eloquence. It is introduced so frequently
that at times one feels that literary excellence in general was
understood by the term, but the two definite elements that are
at this distance discoverable in the conception are classical neologisms and figurative language, the former being more prominent in the first part of the century, and the latter in the second.[17]
The first element, as has been noted, reveals a clear recognition
that the vernacular could attain eloquence only by borrowing
words from the ancients, and the art of figures of speech seemed
so restricted to classical rhetoric and classical authors that it was
not until the last quarter of the century, when numerous rhetorics in English appeared and the influence of Lyly, Sidney, Spen-

---

1621) defines "barbarous" as "rude"; Richard Huloet (*Abcdarium Anglico-
Latinum*, 1552) considered "barbarous" and "rude" synonymous. In the preface to *An exposytion in Englyshe vpon the Epistyll . . . to the Philippians*
(1550?) Lancelot Ridley says he composed the treatise "rudely" rather than
striving "for eloquence in wordes." In the prologue to *A Playne Demonstration
of John Frithes lacke of witte and learnynge*, 1557, John Gwynneth remarks:
"Some, yf they finde not the matter, sette out wyth paynted speeche accordinge
to theyr pleasure, streyght, they wyll say it is veri grose, and but rudely dunne."
"Rude," "gross," and "barbarous" possess, as their most consistent signification
relative to expression, the meaning of "uneloquent."

[17] "Exornation is a gorgiousse beautifiynge of the tongue with borowed
wordes." (Thomas Wilson, *The Arte of Rhetorique*, 1553, fol. 90.) "Rhetorick
. . . hath two parts, *Adornation* and *Action*. *Adornation* consisteth in the
sweetness of the phrase, and is seen in Tropes and Figures." John Barton, *The
Art of Rhetorick*, 1634, p. 1.

ser, and others was being felt, that the English language was thought fully capable of employing them. During the first three quarters of the sixteenth century, roughly speaking, the English language for the most part was considered rude, gross, and barbarous, but these terms meant little more than an absence of eloquence. The derogatory attitude toward the vernacular characteristic of this period has been frequently noticed, but the problem merits further elaboration.

In 1499 no less a person than the Bishop of Durham published a work, partly in English, for those who could not read Latin, and partly in Latin, "to gyue consolacyon in that byhalf to lettred men whiche vnderstande latyn," in which he declares that "our grosse natyue langage and specyally in dytement of meter can not agree in all poyntes with the perfeccyon of latyn."[18] The English language, however, was depreciated not only in connection with Latin, but also in comparison with other modern languages. The anonymous translator of a French treatise, whose spelling does not reveal any great familiarity with the English language, says, perhaps partly in extenuation of his own shortcomings:

loss of meter

> Remember clarkes dayly dothe theyr delygens,
> In to oure corrupte speche maters to translate.
> Yet betwene frenche and englysshe is grete deffens.
> Their longage In redynge is douse and dylycate.
> In theyr mother tonge they be so fortunate.
> They haue the bybyll and the apocalypys of devynyte,
> With other nobyll bokes that in Englyche may not be.[19]

---

[18] *The Contemplation of Sinners*, 1499, Prologus.

[19] See "The awtor" at the end of *The Kalender of Shepherdes*, 1506. The preface explains that the treatise was first translated into English in Paris so incorrectly that it could hardly be understood in England. It was later translated at the instance, cost, and charge of Richard Pynson, "into playn Englysshe." Some of the first version must have remained in the second. The anonymous author of another book published by Pynson speaks of

> The mater/that I purpose to declare
> In rude englysshe/in sentence grose and bare . . .

Of the tryumphe/and the vses that Charles themperour/and the most myghty redouted kyng of England/Henry the .viii. were saluted with/passyng through London (1520?).

It is interesting to note that the superiority of the French language over "corrupt" English[20] is discovered not only in its sweetness and refinement, but also in the fact that the Bible had been translated into it. Nearly a score of years before Tyndale's work, the English translator implies a desire for an English translation of the Bible, and the belief that the vernacular would be improved by containing it.

No one has expressed more clearly than John Skelton the idea that it is impossible to write eloquently in the mother tongue. In one of his poems, after a roll call of the famous poets of antiquity, the character Margery, who is but a mouthpiece for the poet, complains:

> For as I to fore haue sayd
> I am but a yong mayd
> And cannot in effect
> My stile as yet direct
> With englyshe wordes elect
> Our natural tonge is rude
> And hard to be ennuede
> With pollysshed tearmes lustye
> Oure language is so rustye
> So cankered and so ful
> Of frowardes and so dul
> That if I wold apply
> To write ornatly
> I wot not where to finde
> Termes to serue my mynde.[21]

Skelton makes it perfectly plain that he considers the vernacular lacking in the polished and ornate expressions which constitute eloquence, and which are nowhere to be found in the English vocabulary. Margery, indeed, goes on to suggest that a search for eloquent English words would have scant success in Gower, whose "englysh is olde/And of no value told," and she maintains

---

[20] The vernacular is called corrupt by Alexander Barclay in a translation of Mancinus' *Myrrour of good manners* (1523?), prologue.

[21] *The boke of Phyllyp Sparowe* (1545?), sig. cii^v. The poem was composed in the first decade of the century. In this connection see the first chapter of E. J. Sweeting's *Studies in Early Tudor Criticism*, 1940.

a similar attitude toward Lydgate. Chaucer's matter she calls
delectable, and his language "well allowed," even though men
bark at it, for his words, if not eloquent, are "pleasant, easie, and
playne." Having finished her unsuccessful search for classical
eloquence in the English language, she is forced to compose her
bird's epitaph in Latin.

A few years later we find more evidence of the distrust of
the literary value of English. In 1521 appeared a saint's life
translated from the Latin by a monk, Henry Bradshaw,[22] to
which one who is represented by the initials I. C. prefixed a
prologue imploring the saint to look with favor upon

> Henry Bradsha/sometyme monke in Chester
> Whiche only for thy loue/toke the payne and laboure
> Thy legende to translate/he dyd his busy cure
> Out of latine in Englisshe rude and vyle
> Whiche he hath amended/with many an ornate style.

[margin note: Perhaps an example of mixed pentameter & divided lines]

Bradshaw calls the author of the original a disciple of Cicero, and
he contrasts the Latin version, "flourisshyng in the flouers of
glorious eloquence" with the "rudenes all derke" of his translation, a contrast, whatever the modesty of the translator, between Latin and English. If, as I. C. states, Bradshaw amended
his mother tongue with an ornate style, it must have been
through the introduction of what one admirer calls his "pollished
terms," i.e., classical neologisms. At the end he says he translated the work for merchants and rude men who possess little
learning, and he commands his book to submit to the ancient
poets, flowering in eloquence, and to Chaucer, sententious Lydgate, pregnant Barclay, and inventive Skelton, but of their eloquence nothing is said.[23]

[margin note: new audience]

Down through the years the disparagement of the literary
qualities of the English language continues unabated. Not much
is said about what constitutes literary excellence, but all seems

---

[22] *Here begynneth the holy lyfe and history of saynt Werburge,* 1521. It
has been edited for the E.E.T.S., 1887.

[23] See "A balade to the auctour" and "Another balade" suffixed to the translation. Thomas Wyatt thought English could not reproduce the "grace" of
Greek because of the narrowness of its vocabulary. See the preface to *Tho.
wyatis translatyon of Plutarckes boke/of the Quyete of mynde.*

to be comprehended in the word "eloquence," and that, we may repeat, was generally thought to be secured through borrowed words. So strictly confined to and so universally associated with Latin and Greek was eloquence that each individual classical word retained its share. In spite of extravagant praise of past poets, especially Chaucer, and sometimes of modern writers, there was almost universal agreement in excluding the native tongue from the literary world. Sir Thomas Elyot, who did not disdain to use the vernacular in *The Gouernour* (1531), says that poets who write in Latin "do expresse them [good ideas] incomparably with more grace and delectation to the reder, than our englysshe tonge may yet comprehende."[24] He reveals the same attitude a few years later, when he remarks that a Latin sermon which he is translating "is verely elegante, and therfore the harder to translate into our langage."[25] Elegance seems to have been a quality beyond the abilities of the vernacular. In a book which, full of the nationalistic spirit, ridicules the aping of foreign customs and rings with praise of things English, Andrew Borde suddenly says, without the suggestion of a doubt or of the likelihood of contradiction, "The speche of Englande is a base speche to other noble speches, as Italion, Castylion, and Frenche; howbeit the speche of Englande of late dayes is

[24] *The boke named the Gouernour*, 1531, fol. 51ᵛ. In another passage he clearly states his opinion that rhetorical effects may not be secured in the vernacular. After saying that some attention is paid to eloquence in the training of lawyers in England, he remarks, "But for as moche as the tonge, wherin it is spoken/is barbarouse/and the sterynge of affections of the mynde in this realme was neuer vsed, therfore there lacketh Eloquicion and Pronunciacion/two the princypall partes of rhetorike." *Ibid.*, fol. 56ᵛ. Cf. also fols. 104ᵛ, 107ʳ.

[25] *A Swete and Devoute Sermon of Holy saynt Ciprian*, 1534, preface. In the same year, in the preface to his translation entitled *The Doctrinal of Princes made by the noble oratour Isocrates*, he says he undertook the translation "to thintent onely that I wolde assaie, if our Englisshe tunge mought receiue the quicke and propre sentences pronounced by the greekes. And in this experience I haue founde (if I be not muche deceiued) that the forme of speakyng, vsed of the Greekes, called in greeke, and also in latine, *Phrasis*, muche nere approcheth to that, whiche at this daie we vse: than the order of the latine tunge: I meane in the sentences, and not in the wordes: which I doubte not shall be affirmed by them, who sufficiently instructed in all the saide three tunges, shall with a good iudgement read this worke." Elyot is really claiming for English only the ability to render clearly the meaning of the original. He deliberately refuses to make any claims for the "wordes," or eloquence, of the vernacular.

amended."[26] Whatever strength the nationalistic spirit possessed at this time, it was not sufficient to raise English to a plane of equality with even modern languages. We are left in the dark as to how the vernacular has been improved, but we should not go far wrong in supposing the author had neologisms in mind. Likewise, another writer, eager to impart knowledge, especially astronomical and mathematical, in his native tongue, labors under no illusions regarding its eloquential characteristics as compared with Latin. "This sentence of Cicero," he says, "am I lothe to translate into Englishe, partly for that vnto your Maiestie [Edward VI] it needeth no translation, but especially knowing how far the grace of Tullies eloquence doth excell any Englishmans tongue, and much more exceedeth the basenesse of my barbarous stile."[27] It is eloquence in which the native tongue falls short.

It is significant that men like Elyot and Recorde, who effectively used the English language, and who seem to have been far removed from pedantic superciliousness, had nothing to say in behalf of the vernacular so far as eloquence was concerned. In the same class was Roger Ascham, whose employment of his native tongue must have contributed much to its prestige. In the dedication of *Toxophilus* (1545), addressed to the "Gentlemen of England," he admits that the use of Latin would have been much easier and would have redounded much more to his reputation, and he defends his employment of English against those who would blame him for it, not on the ground of the excellence of language but on the ground that the best men in the realm use it, and that he is willing to sacrifice his own interest to the good of the unlatined gentlemen and yeomen of England. He does not hesitate to reveal his opinion of the low state of the vernacular: "And as for the Latin or greke tonge, euery thyng is so excellently done in them, that none can do better: In the Englysh tonge contrary, euery thinge in a maner so meanly, bothe for the matter and handelynge that no man can do worse." This condi-

Ascham

A. Borde

[26] *The fyrst boke of the Introduction of knowledge*, 1548. (See Furnivall's edition in the E.E.T.S, 1870, p. 122.) The dedication is dated May 3, 1542.

[27] Robert Recorde, *The Grounde of Artes: teaching the worke and practise of Arithmetike*, 1575 (1543), "The Preface vnto the Kings Maiestie." The reference to Edward VI shows that the preface must have been written between 1547 and 1553.

Ascham

tion he attributes to the fact that the ignorant think it in their power to write in English, and that the learned had not condescended to do so. He has no comment to make on the language itself, except an attack on neologizing.[28] Later *The Scholemaster* clarifies the author's opinion of the mother tongue. Since

> the prouidence of God hath left vnto vs in no other tong, saue onelie in the *Greke* and *Latin* tong, the trew preceptes, and perfite examples of eloquence, therefore must we seeke in the Authors onelie of those two tonges, the trew Paterne of Eloquence, if in any other mother tong we looke to attaine, either to perfit vtterance of it our selues, or skilfull iudgement of it in others.[29]

Elsewhere he gives unmistakable evidence that the language he is using has no claim to eloquence. Latin and Greek, he says, are the only learned tongues, "Yet neuerthelesse, the rudenes of common and mother tonges, is no bar for wise speaking. For in the rudest contrie, and most barbarous mother language, many be found [who] can speake verie wiselie."[30] He concedes the lack of eloquence in English, among other modern languages, but he expresses the common view in upholding its adequacy so far as thought is concerned. The fact that Ascham employed the vernacular is no proof that he admired it. He speaks with enthusiasm of the unspotted propriety of Latin, and he says that "next to the Greeke and Latin tong, I like and loue [Italian] aboue all others."[31]

style distinct from wisdom or 'thought'

Italian

---

[28] In the dedication to Henry VIII, after stating that he wrote in English for the profit of the many, Ascham expresses the hope that the King will perceive that an English book is "a thinge Honeste for me to write, pleasaunt for some to rede, and profitable for manie to follow." The honesty and utility of the vernacular are consistently recognized throughout this period. Eloquence only is denied it.

[29] Cf. *The Scholemaster*, 1570, fol. 56ᵛ.

[30] *Ibid.*, fol. 46ʳ. A few pages farther on he speaks of the "fewe rude English wordes" which comprise one passage.

[31] *Ibid.*, fols. 23ʳ, 31ʳ. In a letter to Sturm at Strasbourg, which states that he wrote *The Scholemaster* in English for home consumption, Ascham speaks of being born in a barbarous island, and of English as a barbarous language. (See J. A. Komensky, *The Great Didactic*, tr. M. W. Keatinge, 1896, p. 117.) In the same letter Ascham says that *The Scholemaster* could have been written "floridly," if Cheke, Haddon, or Smith had undertaken it. John Strype, *Life of the Learned Sir Thomas Smith*, 1698, p. 27.

As viewed by Scotch eyes also, the vernacular left much to be desired. In the preface to his translation of the *Aeneid* (1553) Gawin Douglas speaks of his lewd barbarous tongue, the deficiencies of which have forced him to use some bastard Latin, French, or English. Though he tried to follow his original as closely as possible, yet sometimes he found it necessary to use three words for one.

> Besyde Latyne, our langage is imperfite
> Quhilk in sum part, is the cause and the wyte
> Quhy that Virgillis vers, the ornate bewte
> In till our toung, may not obseruit be
> For thar bene Latyne wordes, many ane
> That in our leid ganand, translation has nane
> Les than we mynnis, thare sentence and grauite
> And yit skant weil exponit, quhay trowis not me
> Lat thaym interpret Animal, and Homo
> With mony hundreth, other termes mo
> Quhilks in our langage, sothly as I wene
> Few men can tell cleirly, quhat thay mene
>
> .   .   .   .
>
> Bot yit twiching, our tongis penurite
> I mene vnto compare, of fare latyne
> That knawin is maist, perfite langage fyne.

Douglas attributes the inability of the vernacular to match the eloquence, or "ornate bewte," of the Latin to the inadequacy of the English vocabulary, but he also finds the vocabulary inadequate as regards meaning. He is more explicit than most of his contemporaries regarding the nature of the deficiency of his mother tongue, for he cites numerous specific Latin words difficult of translation into English.

In view of the high estimation of Latin and of the unflattering opinion of English as a literary language, we should naturally expect to find expressions of the latter in connection with translations of Latin works, especially of those authors most highly prized by the Elizabethans, for in translation the two languages involved almost coerce comparison. This expectation is fully realized in the translations from Seneca, in comments upon which we find definite evidence of distrust of the vernacu-

Seneca

lar, though we should not forget that the translator may partly be seeking an excuse for his own shortcomings. In the dedication to a translation of the *Troas* (1559), Jasper Heywood, at that time a student at Oxford, apologizes for his own limitations, and then adds the statement: "and also how farre aboue my powre, [it is] to keepe that grace and maiestie of stile, that Seneca doth, when both so excellent a writer, hath past the reache of all imitacion, and also this our english tong (as many thinke and I here finde) is farre vnable, to compare with the latten." Here, as usual, the deficiency seems to lie not in meaning but in the literary qualities of grace and majesty. The same is true of Alexander Neville's linguistic attitude, revealed in the dedication of a translation of the *Oedipus* (1563):

When first . . . I trauayled in the translation of this present Tragedie, written by the moste graue, vertuous and Christian Ethnicke (for so doubteth not *Erasmus* to terme him) *Lucius Anneus Seneca*: I minded nothynge lesse, than that at any tyme thus rudely transformed he should come into the Prynters hands. For I to no other ende remoued hym from his naturall and loftye Style to our own corrupt and base, or as al men affyrme it: most barbarous Language: but onely to satisfye the instant requestes of a few my familiar frendes.[32]

In the preface, Neville harps upon his rude and base translation and gross style, with the admission that the lesson contained in the play was the only reason that "I suffred this my base translated Tragedie to be publyshed: from his Author in worde and Verse far transformed, though in Sense lytell altred." Here again the usual view finds expression, namely, that the substance, but not the eloquence, of a work can be adequately expressed in the native language. Neville concludes with another derogatory statement regarding his mother tongue: "In fyne I beseche all

---

[32] In a postscript to *The seuen first bookes of the Eneidos of Virgil, conuerted in English meter*, 1558, Thomas Phaer bears witness to the wide disparagement of the vernacular, though he proposed his own work as an example of what could be done with it. "I have heard," he says, the English language "discommended of many, and estemyd of some to be more than barbarous." The translator of Ramus' logic anticipates objection to his use of the vernacular on the ground that "our tongue is barbarous," and Latin and Greek are eloquent. *The logike of the moste excellent philosopher P. Ramus Martyr*, 1574, p. 16.

Phaer

togyther (yf so it myght be) to beare with my rudenes, and consydre the grosenes of oure owne Country language, whiche can
by no means aspire to the hyghe lofty Latinists Stile."[33]

The opinion of the vernacular as uneloquent was so widely
accepted that expressions of it sound like truisms rather than
novelties, a situation which has already been noted in the case of
Andrew Borde, who, though praising all other matters connected with England, adds in a matter-of-fact way that the
language is base. That this attitude was all but universal is borne
out by Sir Thomas Hoby's "Epistle" prefixed to *The Courtier*
(1561), which ardently advocates translations from the classics,
"that we alone of the worlde maye not bee styll counted barbarous in oure tunge, as in time out of minde we haue bene in
our maners." In a letter to Sir William Cecil, 1562, Richard
Eden, in upholding the adequacy of English for purposes of
translation, says, "the Latin toonge be accompted ryche, and the
Englysshe indigent and barbarous, as it hathe byn in tyme past,
muche more then it nowe is, before it was enriched and amplified
by sundry bookes in manner of all artes translated owt of Latine
and other toonges into Englysshe."[34] In the two adjectives applied to the vernacular Eden touches upon the two aspects of it
which generally are noticed, meaning and eloquence. Opinion
on the adequacy of the language to express meaning was not
always consistent, as we shall see later, but as regards eloquence
it was nearly unanimous. Eden expresses the widely held view
that one gauge of the worth of a language is the amount of learning contained in it.

The Englishman viewed his language as plain, honest, and
substantial, but uneloquent. This view is clearly seen in some
of the figures of speech used to describe the vernacular. Nicholas
Haward, for instance, defends the practice of translation against

[33] In the preface to his translation of the *Agamemnon*, 1566, John Studley
speaks of the play as "but groslye, and after a rude maner translated," and in
the dedication to his translation of the *Medea* he comments on his "rude and
vnskilful pen," and on the translation as "rudely and symply" done. Though
these words obviously represent a modest recognition of his own limitations,
they also may suggest the limitations of his medium.

[34] Quoted in J. L. Moore, *Tudor-Stuart Views on the Growth, Status, and
Destiny of the English Language*, 1910, p. 95.

those who contended that it would hinder the study of Latin and Greek:

And where as some theyr be whyche obiecte that throughe these translatyons, the affectynge and desyre of the attaynynge of the Greeke, Latyne, Italian and other tounges dooth decay, and is the lesse soughte after, who seeth not howe friuolous and vaine that theyr saying is. For as it is very absonant that anye one who hath the perfect vse of corn and grain, and tasted the pleasauntnesse there of, woulde refuse the same to be fed with Acornes, so is it no lesse dissonant to say, that anye man hauing ones tasted the pleasaunte puritye of the Greke and Latine tounges, would (forsaking the same) fal to the barbarousnesse (in respect) of thys our Englyshe tounge. But lyke as Ceres hathe not so indifferently delt wyth all men, to instruct and shewe them the vse of corne, for whyche some muste of force content them selues to be fed with Acornes. So for that ech man hathe not attayned the knowledge of those languages, in whych notwythstandinge many thinges are worthy to be knowen, some must neades contente them selues to wade only in the troubled streames of Translators: for that they are not able to attayne to the well spryng it selfe.[35]

By a similar figure of speech Thomas Wilson justifies his translation of Demosthenes, at the same time admitting that the vernacular is incapable of expressing the eloquence of the original. He may have the Wife of Bath in mind when he replies to the opponents of translation: "But such as are grieued with translated bokes, are lyke to them that eating fine Manchet, are angry with others that feed on Cheate breade. And yet God knoweth men would as gladly eate Manchet as they, if they had it." In the next sentence he introduces a more popular comparison to express his opinion of English: "But all can not weare Veluet, or feede with the best, and therefore such are contented for necessities sake to weare our Countrie cloth, and to take themselues to harde fare that can haue no better."[36]

Frequently during this period the English language, represented as plain, serviceable, honest, and unadorned clothing, is

[35] See the preface to Nicholas Haward's translation of Eutropius' *A briefe Chronicle*, 1564.

[36] *The three Orations of Demosthenes*, tr. Thomas Wilson, 1570, "The Epistle."

contrasted with the rich fabrics of Latin. One persistent translator, Arthur Golding, when apologizing for his "rude and vn-
polished translation," admits that because of "the wante of fyne
pennynge and eloquent indityng" of "the hystorye in our language," his original has been "spoyled of hys Romayne Garment
and turned into a playne Englyshe cote."[37] Eloquent Latin has
been reduced to homespun English. He again makes use of the
simile in the preface to a translation of another historical work,
when, conscious of the humble nature of the language he is employing, he says,

in lyke maner as oftentymes beautifull and welfauoured persons, turned
out of their gorgeous apparell and costly attyre, into simple raiment, doe
lyke [i.e., please] the beholders as well as they dydde in theire gayest
garmentes: Euen in lyke wyse (I trust) it may so comme to passe, that
this my rude translation voyd of ornate termes and eloquent indityng,
may (as it were) in his playne and homely English cote, be as well accepted of the fauorable reader as when it were richly clad in Romayn
vesture: consyderyng that the valewe and estimacion of Thistory, is no
more abased thereby, then should the vertue of a precious stone, by setting
it in brasse or yron, or by carying it in a closur of Leather.[38]

The various figures of speech employed in this passage, and also
in the next to be quoted, indicate how earnestly vernacular writers were attempting to express their conception of the plain,
useful, homely nature of English. Golding also makes it clear
that thought rather than language is the really important element. Though this idea will be discussed later, we may introduce here one more passage which emphasizes content rather
than language, and which, though contrasting the homeliness of
English with the beauty of Latin, certainly suggests the adequacy
of the former as to thought. In the preface to a translation of a
Catholic treatise, one who signs himself A. P. says:

The third and last motiue which incouraged me to this labour, and ought
partly to moue thee to the reading, is the breuitie of the worke, the fine-

[37] *The historie of Leonard Aretine, concerning the warres betwene the
Imperialles and the Goths for the possession of Italy* . . . , 1563.
[38] *Thabridgment of the Histories of Trogus Pompeius, Collected and
wrytten in the Laten tonge, by the famous Historiographer Iustine, and translated into English by Arthur Goldyng,* 1564.

ness of the methode, the eloquence of the stile . . . Only I am to craue
pardon that my rough and rude English, nothing aunswereth his smoothe
and curious latin, and therefore I could wish thee, if skill serueth, rather
to common and parle with the Author him selfe, then to vse the helpe
of his rude interpretor, otherwise for such as be not of so deepe reading,
for whom especially I haue taken this paine, I am to desire that they
nothing dislike the soueraign medicine for the wooden box, nor the
exquisit and rare gemme for the course casket.[39]

The clothing comparison, however, is the most popular of
all. Thomas Newton, who, though himself translating Cicero,
advanced the latter's "incomparable sublymity and sappye eloquence" as an argument against translating his works into the
uneloquent English language, says, "I for lack of knowledge
haue racked [Cicero] from gorgeous Elegancie, and oute of
Romayne gownes more boldly I feare then wyselye chaunged
[him] into Englyshe Liuerayes."[40] Five years later he makes
use of the same comparison, when he says of his original, "I haue
aduentured to deuest him of his Latine weede, and after a
homely sorte forced [him] into barbarous English."[41] Though
translators often glance at their lack of ability and rudeness of
style, they give little indication that they think the English language capable of affording any beautiful raiment for an idea.
On the contrary, the implication seems to be that the rudeness of
their work is due to the rudeness of the medium used. Though
the quotations given above suggest at times a modest diffidence,
and that frequently conventional, none of those using the figure
of speech imply that the vernacular can be anything more than
homespun stuff. In the dedication to a translation of an Italian
grammar, Henry Granthan says, "Now suche as it is rudely
attired with this englishe habit, I betake vnto your fauorable ac-

---

[39] *The Golden Treatise of the Aucient and Learned Father Vincentius
Lirinensis* [St. Vincent of Lerins]. *For the antiquitie, and vniuersalitie, of the
Catholicke Religion: against the prophane nouelties of all Heresies* (1559?).
The spirit of the casket scene in *The Merchant of Venice* characterizes this
attitude toward the language.

[40] See the preface and dedication to *The Worthye Booke of Old age otherwyse entituled the elder Cato,* 1569.

[41] *A Direction for the Health of Magistrates and Students . . . Written
in Latin by Guilielmus Gratorolus,* 1574, dedication.

ceptance."[42] And in the dedication to one of his many translations, Abraham Fleming begs "that this my homelie handeled Expositor, a straunger borne and newlie arraied with course English cloth," may find favor.[43] Sometimes, the translator laments his own unworthiness, and in rare cases hints that there are greater possibilities in the mother tongue than he has realized,[44] but such instances are so infrequent as to prove the exception rather than the rule. In fact, John Lyly, who did much to inspire in his countrymen confidence in the literary possibilities of English, seems not himself to have felt that confidence. In enumerating the manifestations of fastidiousness on the part of his contemporaries he introduces the very things which had been figuratively employed to describe the language. "It is a world," he says, "to see how English men desire to heare finer speach then the language will allowe, to eate finer bread then is made of Wheate, to weare finer cloth then is wrought of Woll."[45]

Distrust in the literary qualities of the vernacular consistently dominated the greater part of the sixteenth century. Again and again we encounter it. Richard Shacklock, "M. of Arte and student of the Ciuill Lawes in Louaine," explains that he was not ignorant that "our base tounge coulde not atteine to the maiestie of *Osorius* his Laten," but "I regarde not so much the fines of wordes, as the diuynenes of the matter," and though the

---

[42] *An Italian Grammar Written in Latin by Scipio Lentulo a Neapolitan,* 1575.

[43] *The Epistle of the Blessed Apostle Sainte Paule, which he . . . sent in writing to the Ephesians . . . Expounded by Nicolas Hemminge,* 1581.

[44] One is afforded by the dedication of Joshua Sylvester's translation of one of Du Bartas' poems: "And withal I craue his [Du Bartas'] pardon for my presumtion, in that I maie seeme to haue spoiled these books (his lovely babes) of their rich and sumptuous French garments, to cloath them in so poore and base English weeds as my course wardrobe hath affoorded: as it were stripping them out of the robes of Salomon, to wrappe them in the rags of *Frus*: and robbing them of the riche mans purple, to couer them with *Lazarus* patches: Wherein (peraduenture) I haue not only wronged the worthy Frenchman: but also iniured some gentlemen of our own, in preuenting perhaps their liberalities, that are in preparing some more costly suites of better fashion, to intertaine them in: which when they shall be finished, I shall bee well content that mine be cast aside." Sylvester describes himself as a "Marchant Aduenturer," and perhaps consciousness of his unlearned vocation inspired his humility. See *The Triumph of Faith,* 1592.

[45] See the Epistle Dedicatory to *Euphues,* 1578.

language cannot effect eloquence, it is adequate for the expression of thought.[46] Shacklock persistently maintains this attitude. In the dedication to Queen Elizabeth of another translation of the same period he asserts that, although devoid of eloquence, the mother tongue can adequately express the meaning of an original, and can thus render important books a great benefit to those unversed in Latin. "No man," he says

is so wel indued with the knowledge of forren tongues, but when a matter of greate importaunce is tolde hym, the truthe of the which he is desyrouse to knowe certaynly, and to the which he is mynded to make an aunswer wysely, had rather haue it declared in his natural and mother tonge be it neuer so barbarouse, then in a straunge language be it neuer so eloquent, I thought that this boke intreatyng of so weyghtye and necessari an argument for all Christian men to knowe, shold be better welcome to your grace in oure owne countrye speche for profyt, then in any fyner forren language for pleasure.[47]

These words furnish a very clear picture of the contrast between the eloquence of Latin and the barbarousness of English. Greek also sometimes sustains the classical side of the antithesis. William Barkar, in speaking of Xenophon's life of Cyrus, which he had translated, says,

All these thinges which seuerallie be scattered and sparsed in other, be almost al in one gathered togither in this boke of Cyrus bringing vp, and going forthe vnder this title, is in deed a path way to wisedome, and for matter most fitte to be read and knowen of all Gentlemen, and for finenes of stile, most pleasant and perfect in his owne tong. And although herin I haue a goodly occasion to commend the writer, that in the moste eloquent and excellent tong hath written moste purelie, yet bycause it carieth the matter whole into an other tongue, and keepeth his own fines still in his owne tongue, and our grosse tongue is a rude and a barren tong, when it is compared with so florishinge and plentifull a tongue, I wil passe ouer this praise . . .[48]

---

[46] *An Epistle of the Reuerend Father in God Hieronymus Osorius* [Osorio da Fonseca (Jeronimo)] *Bishop of Arcoburge in Portugal, to the most excellent Princesse Elizabeth*, 1565, preface.

[47] See Stanislaus Hozyusz, *A Most Excellent Treatise of the begynnyng of heresyes in oure tyme*. Antwerp, 1565.

[48] See the preface, addressed to the Earl of Pembroke, of *The Bookes of Xenophon, Contayning the discipline, schole, and education of Cyrus* (1560?).

Yet Latin was the linguistic standard most widely accepted, and its excellence was so universally recognized that it is hardly necessary to cite specific instances, though a few representative testimonies may not be superfluous. "But aboue all how necessary," says Rudolph Waddington,

> the knowledge of the Latine tongue is to any of vs, that either desire to be entred into other bordering tongues, or to serch the depth of any Science, or the assurance of our saluation through the true vnderstanding of holy scripture, is so commonly knowne, and so generally agreed on, that happie seemes he that may attaine thereto, or procure and leaue it to his child as a sufficient heritage.

He continues to praise it as a language rich in words and adorned with many apt phrases.[49] Abraham Fleming expresses a similar view:

Sense of ambiguity in Latin

> The Latine tongue being so copious and plentifull, so darke and doubtfull, so necessarie and fruitfull, that no nation, no people, no trade, no vocation, but feele what discommodities issue from the ignorance of the same: what rewardes they deserue, what pension, what praise, which no lesse painfully, than skilfully, haue searched out the secrets of so singular a speech, I appeale to any of indifferent iudgement.[50]

The literary excellence of Latin occupied a height which the vernacular could not but despair of approximating. "If this woorke," says a translator of Ovid, "were fully performed with lyke eloquence and connynge of endyting by me in Englishe, as it was written by Thauthor thereof in his moother toonge, it might perchaunce delight your honour."[51] In the dedication to his translation of Apuleius' *Golden Ass* (1566) William Adlington speaks of his original as "beyng now barbarously and simply framed in our Englishe tongue." Another translator represents himself as "vnhable to expresse in Englishe, the sentences, of so

---

[49] Jean Veron, *A Dictionary in Latine and English . . . now newly corrected and enlarged by R. W.*, 1575, preface.

[50] See his "Obseruations of instruction" prefixed to the index of Baret's *Alvearie*, 1580 (1573). Cf. J. L. Moore, *Tudor-Stuart Views on the English Language*, pp. 7–8.

[51] *Fyrst Fower Bookes of . . . Metamorphosis*, tr. Arthur Golding, 1565, dedication.

manye Poets and aunt famous doctors of the church."[52] Indeed, the conviction of the literary inadequacy of the mother
tongue, especially when compared with Latin, is encountered
at every turn. It continues even into the last quarter of the century. "It would haue beene," says the author of a legal treatise,

much more acceptable, (peraduenture also to my selfe more commendable) to haue set foorth this Treatise in the Latine tongue, wherein the
Lawes Ciuill and Ecclesiasticall, as they be originally written: so are they
elegantly and sententiously compact; and now by the translation thereof
into our vulgar tongue, either loose something of their former vertue,
or of their naturall beauty and grace.[53]

A translator of Seneca asserts that he has done the best he could
to render clearly the meaning of the original "out of so meane
a stoare," evidently as his native tongue afforded him.[54] The history of Herodotus, "beeyng most sweete in Greeke, conuerted
into Englishe looseth a great parte of his grace."[55] Another
translator explains that Tacitus' histories have been translated
"with much losse of their lustre, as being transported from their
natural light of the Latin by an vnskilfull hande into a strange
language, perchance not so fit to set out a peece drawne with so
curious a pensill."[56] This list of witnesses could be further extended, but it has already come to resemble an Elizabethan roll
call. Those given are sufficient to indicate how conscious of their
uneloquent or unliterary medium were those who employed the
vernacular.

If during the first three quarters of the sixteenth century
Englishmen viewed their language in the light revealed above,
they looked upon the earlier stages of its development in an

[52] *The tranquillitie of the minde. A verye excellent and most comfortable
Oration. . . . Compyled in Latin by John Barnarde,* tr. Anthony Marten,
1570, dedication.

[53] Henry Swinburne, *A Briefe Treatise of Testaments and Last Willes,*
1590, preface.

[54] *Seneca His Tenne Tragedies Translated into Englysh,* 1581, preface
signed by Thomas Newton.

[55] *The Famous Hystory of Herodotus,* tr. B. R[ich], 1584, "To the
Reader."

[56] *The Ende of Nero And Beginning of Galba . . .,* tr. Henry Savile,
1591, dedication.

equally unfavorable light. The very strangeness of the earlier dialect, arising from the considerable extent to which the tongue had changed, and also the fact that it was the language of the Middle Ages, a period which did not stand high in the favor of most Englishmen of the sixteenth century, made for depreciation of the earlier language. Richard Pynson flatly asserts that the English tongue was rude in Chaucer's day,[57] and treatises written in the earlier dialect are characterized by another writer as rude, uneloquent, and lacking in "ornate speache set out curiously."[58] This in general was the attitude of the age.[59] And yet, as has been noted, the attitude toward earlier poets, Chaucer especially, was highly laudatory, and that, too, in a way that would indicate that with them the English language lost its rudeness. Pynson says that Chaucer "by his labour/embelyshed/ornated/and made fayre our englysshe."[60] Skelton, whose own verse discredits his judgment in things poetical, considered Gower the first that "garnisshed our englysshe rude," and he maintained that Chaucer "nobly enterprysyd/How that our englysshe myght fresshely be a mende," and that his polished eloquence "Oure englysshe rude so fresshely hath set out."[61] And yet the age considered its own language, as well as that of an earlier day, barbarous. One explanation of this apparent contradiction lies in the fact, stressed at the beginning of this chapter, that there were no critical terms available for praise except those appropriate to rhetoric, so that only style and language could be noticed. Certainly eloquence must have been restricted to the works

[57] Cf. the Proheme to his edition of *The Canterbury Tales*, 1526.

[58] See the anonymous *A proper dyalogue betwene a Gentillman and a husbandman*, 1530.

[59] Cf. the preface to Richard Whitforde's adaptation of a work attributed to Saint Bernard and entitled *Notabile Documentum . . . the golden pystle* (1530?); the title of *A Sermon no lesse fruteful then famous Made in the year of our Lorde God, MCCCLXXXVII . . . tholde and rude Englysh ther of mended, here and there* (1550?); and John Skelton's *A ryght delectable tratyse vpon a goodly Garlande*, 1523, sig. Bii[r].

[60] See the Proheme to his edition of *The Canterbury Tales*, 1526.

[61] *A ryght delectable tratyse*, 1523, sig. Bii[r]. Cf. the "Praefatio translatoris" of J. Walton's translation of Boethius' *De Consolatione Philosophiae*, 1525; the prologue to Sir Paul Bushe's *Extripacion of ignorancy* (1526); the prologue to Sir David Lindsay's *The complaynte and testament of a Popiniay*, 1538; and the dedication of Stephen Hawes's *Pastime of Pleasure*, 1509.

of Chaucer and other poets, and did not become, in the eyes of the sixteenth century, a possession of the language.

Just as the terms selected for praise derive from the rhetorical tradition, so do the expressions found in the self-criticism so prevalent in the English works of the century. For the most part writers touch only upon their style or language, and that in terms suitable to rhetoric and invariably derogatory. A list of these terms furnishes sufficient evidence: barbarous, rude, unpolished, base style, rude speech, "misorned" language, void or barren of eloquence, etc., etc. This self-depreciation, which goes as far back as Lydgate, and perhaps farther, though Chaucer in his serious moments seems free from it, dominated most of the sixteenth, and even lingers into the seventeenth century. In many cases it must have become only a conventional expression of modesty.[62] Certainly toward the end of the century, stereotyped expressions of it had been worn threadbare. In the preface to his translation of *Orlando Furioso*, the original and independent John Harington says, "Certainly if I shold confesse or rather profess, that my verse is vnartificiall, the stile rude, the phrase barbarous, the meeter vnpleasant, many more would beleeue it to be so, then would imagine that I thought them so." Yet there must reside even in a convention enough reality to inspire its use, and give it some significance. Men could hardly come so completely under the domination of a verbal charm as to lose all conception of the meaning of the words themselves, or to be unaware of the stylistic quality denoted by them.

It is possible to interpret this derogatory criticism as an expression of something like an inferiority complex on the part of those writing in the vernacular. At any rate, in the last quarter of the sixteenth century, when confidence in the eloquential potentialities of English begins to rise, the note of self-disparagement grows much fainter in English works. In the light of the numerous direct derogatory statements regarding the mother tongue which have been given above, the passages discussed below can be construed to indicate more than a conventional confession of personal lack of ability on the part of their authors. In

[62] Associated with the habit were conventional anticipations of hostile criticism and innumerable references to Momus and Zoilus.

the translation of a French treatise[63] Barclay renders the Prologue, which apologizes only for the "petite simplesse" of the
author, as follows:

> Thus in conclusyon who redeth this treatyse
> To the rude langage gyue none aduertence
> It is but wryten the tyme to exercyse
> Without studye/payne/or dylygence
> With style inornate voyde of eloquence.

At the end of the original is a passage headed "L'acteur," which
refers to the French work only as "ce simple liure," but which is
called "Actoris excusatio" in the English version. The latter
reads in part as follows:

> Go forth smale treatyse and humbly the present
> Unto the reders as indygne of audyence
> Exortynge them with meke and lowe entent
> To this rude langage to gyue none aduertence
> For many one hath parfyte dylygence
> Whiche by no meane his mynde can expresse
> The cause therof is lacke of eloquence
>
> . . . .
>
> So certaynly in suche case am I
> Somwhat asayenge yf I can ensue
> The steppes of them the which craftely
> All vyce of wrytynge vtterly eschue
> But ignoraunce ryght ofte doth me subdue
> And often I fall for lacke of exercyse
> This rude langage so on me doth renewe
> That I agayne vnnethes may aryse
>
> The cause why I folowe nat these oratours
> Is for lack of intellygence
> And that I haue nat smelled of the flours
> Spryngynge in the garden of parfyte eloquence.

Barclay injects into his original this long unfavorable criticism
of his work and himself, but certainly he is also thinking of his
uneloquent mother tongue, as the repeated reference to "this

---

[63] *The Castell of Labour. Translated from the French of Pierre Gringore
by Alexander Barclay. Reprinted in facsimile from Wynkyn de Worde's Edition of 1506 . . . and an introduction by Alfred W. Pollard,* 1905.

rude langage" indicates. Likewise when Skelton speaks of translating Diodorus Siculus "Out of fresshe latine in to owre englysshe playne," he is describing the vernacular in general as much
as his use of it.[64] In a dedication to Henry VIII, Richard Taverner says,

The selue prayers, no doubte, be excellent, pure, syncere, godly and
Christian. But my translacion, I feare, is rude, base, vnpleasaunt, grosse
and barbarouse. I feare, I saye, lest accordynge to the prouerbe I shal
render pro aureis ferrea, lest of good latine I haue made euil English,
lest I haue turned wyne into water.[65]

There is no doubt that he is referring to his own style, but since
"evil" is obviously introduced as an antithesis to "good," we may
give a wider interpretation to the passage, namely, that English
is as inferior to Latin as water is to wine. Consciousness of this
fact prompts him to apply the comprehensive list of uncomplimentary adjectives to his version. When Edmund Elviden says,
"I muste acknowledge my worke barbarous, rude and vnpol-
lished, yet I dare presume to say that it is necessary,"[66] he certainly considered it poor because of his own limitations; he may
also have thought it deficient because of his linguistic medium.
The widely held derogatory opinion of the English language
could hardly fail to impart a spirit of uneasiness to anyone using
it, and to create in him considerable doubt regarding the quality
of his work. Moreover, the very terms that are most frequently
applied to the vernacular—barbarous, base, rude, gross, vile—
are those usually applied to works composed in English.

The influence of the rhetorical tradition, together with the
absence of a critical terminology, caused criticism to emphasize
style. As a very important element of style, language received
marked attention, attention which the invention of printing may
have increased. So it is not strange that writers became acutely

[64] *A ryght delectable tratyse vpon a goodly Garlande,* 1523, sig. Fii[r].

[65] *An Epitome of the Psalmes, or briefe meditations vpon the same,* tr.
Richard Taverner, 1539.

[66] See the preface to *The Closet of Counsels . . . Translated and collected
out of diuers aucthors, into English verse,* 1569. Innumerable examples of self-
depreciation could easily be added to the few discussed above. In fact, this note
is so frequently sounded in English works that we come to look for it.

conscious of their linguistic medium. But so closely were rhetoric and literary excellence associated with the classics, though high tributes were paid to Chaucer and a few other poets, that eloquence, the daughter of rhetoric and the highest embodiment of literary art, was restricted to the classical languages, and the mother tongue was denied it. Indeed, classical words of all sorts were so encircled by an aura of learning and art that they became eloquent in themselves, and were capable of rendering the vernacular eloquent when introduced into it, a practice which today would merit only the stigma of pedantry. Until the last quarter of the sixteenth century the mother tongue was consistently considered devoid of eloquence. Consciousness of the unliterary nature of their medium of expression induced in those who wrote in English a kind of inferiority complex. This feeling was also, perhaps, stimulated by the knowledge that unlearned men could write in the same language. According to Ascham, the use of the English language by ignorant men, rather than by the learned, was the reason for its low state. But after all is said, the picture still remains vague. The key to the situation lies in the conception of eloquence, which unfortunately from the modern point of view seems decidedly hazy, though two elements can be detected in it—neologisms and figures of speech. Furthermore, those who comment on the English language make no efforts to analyze it.[67] Their depreciation of it partakes of the haziness of their conception of eloquence, and the terms they use to describe it express for the most part a rather vague dissatisfaction with its literary inadequacy. Probably many intangible factors—social, intellectual, artistic—played their part in determining this unfavorable attitude.

There was, however, one factor which must considerably modify our interpretation of the unfavorable opinion of the English language characteristic of this age. The adjectives frequently applied to the vernacular, though now they strike us as unusually harsh, meant little more than "uneloquent." And

---

[67] A partial exception to this statement is furnished by the author of *The boke callyd the Myrroure of Oure Lady*, 1530, who says in the second prologue that he encountered difficulties in using the vernacular because of dialectical variations, inconsistencies in the meanings given words, and the multiplicity of meanings given a single word.

the figurative expressions used to describe it—homespun cloth, coarse bread, wooden casket—do not always suggest entire displeasure with its character. In fact, condemnation of the mother tongue varies according to the value placed upon eloquence, or rhetoric. It is true that in the eyes of the Humanists this value stood exceedingly high, but out of the Reformation there developed a spirit which came to inhabit a large number of the English, whom we generally term Puritans. In them, and sometimes in others, we discover an ascetic distrust of beauty of expression, somewhat akin to their later dislike of poetry. They frequently inveigh against the immorality of a deceitful and vainglorious style, and as a consequence insist upon plainness and simplicity as the natural vesture of truth, especially in religious matters. Furthermore, there developed in this class an emphasis upon utility, which was beginning to attach, as later it succeeded only too well in doing, a somewhat immoral nature to that which seemed to them vain, empty, and useless. Perhaps a more important factor, which will soon be considered, was the conviction that learned men were faced with the solemn duty of educating by means of the vernacular their less fortunate brothers. Thus anything which interfered with the fulfillment of this obligation, such as the obscurity arising from neologisms and rhetorical figures,[68] could not but be considered immoral. In short, this antirhetorical spirit, so much in evidence during the second and third quarters of the century, made no demands which the mother tongue could not meet, and thus did not deny it virtue, even though it was denied eloquence.[69]

[68] Elyot says that he sought to translate a work in idiomatic English, "desiringe more to make it playne to all readers, than to flourishe it with ouermoch eloquence." (*The Image of Governance,* 1541, preface.) There is evidence to show, however, that Elyot's view of eloquence differed significantly from the prevailing attitude, inasmuch as the latter had its roots in the moral spirit of the times, whereas Sir Thomas distinguishes between sophistic and true rhetoric in a manner characteristic of the anti-Ciceronian movement. He approves highly of true rhetoric. Cf. *The boke named the Gouernour,* Book I, fol. 47^v.

[69] See an article by the present writer entitled "The Moral Sense of Simplicity," in *Studies in Honor of Frederck W. Shipley* ("Washington University Studies," New Series, Language and Literature, No. 14, 1942). This article, which was originally composed as part of the present work, is the basis for many statements made in the latter.

CHAPTER II

THE LANGUAGE OF POPULAR INSTRUCTION

SINCE, for the greater part of the sixteenth century, English was with few exceptions considered an uneloquent, or unliterary, language, the demands of pure literature could hardly have exerted any appreciable influence upon opinions concerning its use. But since, in many quarters at any rate, the rhetorical deficiency was considered more of a virtue than a defect, it did not prevent widespread advocacy of its use for more general purposes. Of all the factors making for the use of the vernacular during this period, the invention of printing seems to have been the most important.[1] The value of the printing

[1] The inventions of printing, gunpowder, and the compass won high praise in the Renaissance and were considered the strongest argument for the superiority of modern over ancient times. "There be not yet two hundred yeares past since the admirable art of Printing was found out, an inuention so excellent and so vsefull, so much tending to the honour of God, the manifestation of the truth, propagation of the Gospell, restoration of learning, diffusion of knowledge, and consequently the discouerie and destruction of Poperie, that the Pope and Popish Politicians wish it had neuer beene, and haue bestowed many a secret curse vpon him that first reueiled it; and no meruaile, for it hastens and helps forward his confusion more then all the Mechanicke mysteries in the World." (Silvester Jourdan, *A Plaine Description of the Barmudas, now called Sommer Ilands,* 1613 [1610], dedication.) Evidence for this opinion could have been secured from the preface to the Catholic translation of the New Testament, published at Rheims in 1582, which states that inasmuch as in the past every schoolmaster and scholar with a little Latin and Greek did not translate the Bible, it was not found in the hands of every farmer, mechanic, girl, and boy: "No in those better times men were neither so ill, nor so curious of them selues, so to abuse the blessed booke of Christ: neither was there any such easy means before printing was inuented, to disperse the copies into the hands of euery man, as now is." John Foxe in his *Acts and Monuments* (7th ed., 1632, I, 926–27) attributes the success of the Reformation to printing, and praises the latter in the highest terms. Walton Haddon maintains that Catholicism kept the world in darkness "vntill of late by the incomprehensible prouidence of Almightie God, the worthy Arte of Emprintyng was erected, by meanes whereof good Letters and Bookes came to the Marte: and Printers shoppes discouered the soggy and darkened cloudes of this olde motheaten barbarousnes.

press lay in the multiplication of copies of books made possible by it, but this value in turn depended upon an increased reading public, for had the latter remained restricted to those familiar with the classical languages, the opportunities offered by the invention would have been seriously narrowed. Another important factor was the Reformation. When religious authority was transferred from the Church to the Bible, not only was a translation of the Scriptures rendered imperative,[2] but also English expository works on them were considered highly desirable if not necessary.[3] Furthermore, the importance attached to the indi-

Hereby it came to passe, that the tedious and deepe doungeons of lothesome ignoraunce beyng surprised with a certein new and cleare dawnyng day of purer doctrine, as also of all other liberall Sciences beganne to shyne abroade . . ." (*Against Ierome Osorius*, tr. James Bell, 1581, dedication.) Foxe says that if Luther, Bucer, and Calvin had never lived, the Reformation would have come about through "that inestimable benefit of Gods blessing, prepared for the behoofe of his Church, I meane the singuler and most excellent Art of Emprinting." *Against Ierome Osorius*, fols. 480ᵛ–481ᵛ.

　[2] See, for example, the preface to John Shute's translation of Pierre Viret's *The first parte of the Christian Instruction*, 1565, in which Shute defends the translation of the Bible into English on the ground that the Word of God is the only authority, that the layman in the battles of life needs it more than the sequestered monk, and that the plowman's opinion, when nearer to the Bible than the Pope's, is to be preferred to the latter.

　[3] In the preface to *A Commentary in Englyshe vpon Sayncte Paules Epystle to the Ephesyans*, 1540, Lancelot Ridley says that he was moved to write because he perceived "fewe or none to go about to open by commentaries or exposicions in Englysh to the vnlearned to declare the holy Scriptures nowe suffered to all people of this realme to rede and to study at their pleasure." Such commentaries, he insists, are necessary to their understanding the Bible. Richard Whitforde said he wrote *The Pomander of prayer*, composed in 1527 though not published until 1568, not "for the learned/(for they vnderstand scrypture . . .) but for the vnlerned that lack knowledge of holy scrypture/to instruct them in the ordre of prayer." (See also a work headed *Here begynneth a new Treatyse deuyded in thre parties* (1550?), sig. Biv; the preface to a translation of Antonius Corvinus entitled *A Postill or Collection of Moste Godly Doctrine vpon every gospell through the yeare*, 1550; John Walker's preface to Robert Norton's translation of Rudolph Walther's *Certaine godlie Homilies . . . vpon the Prophets Abdias and Ionas*, 1573; and the preface of Anthony Gilby's translation of Beza's exposition of the *Psalms*, 1581.) By the end of the century the situation of which the author complains had been completely changed, if we may believe the preface of an anonymous translator of Pierre Merlin's *A Most Plaine and profitable Exposition of the Booke of Ester*, 1599: "Thou [the reader] hast (the Lordes name be euer blessed therefore) the holie Bible, the most necessary, the most profitable booke, euen the booke of lyfe, and that dispearsed in infinit

vidual and the desire to gain as many adherents as possible recommended that much of the controversial literature of the Reformation, both Catholic and Protestant, be written in or translated into the mother tongue.[4] Finally, geographical explorations, the vitalized interest in classical literature, and the generally quickened intellectual spirit in the Renaissance had resulted in the composition of so many books, written for the most part in ancient or foreign languages, that the desire to spread this learning through vernacular translations as widely as possible naturally followed.[5]

One characteristic of the sixteenth century worthy of considerable emphasis was the unceasing, if not universal, desire to educate those people, high and low, who did not possess the linguistic keys to learning. The Renaissance Englishman, looking around him, saw, on the one hand, the richest stores of knowledge in constant process of being increased but confined within the strict limits of the learned tongues, and, on the other, a vernacular which, as regards learning, offered for the most part only a vacuum. To fill this vacuum became his earnest desire and deep-felt duty.[6] Again and again during this century we hear

---

numbers easie to be gotten. Thou hast also euen in thy mother tongue, Expositios, Readings, Comments, Sermons, Catechismes innumerable, which all tend to the opening of that booke, and to make the vnderstanding therof easie vnto thee."

[4] In justifying the publication of a work in English entitled *A Dialogue betweene a Papist and a Protestant, applied to the capacitie of the vnlearned*, 1582, George Gifford says that "wheras sundry men of fame haue shewed deep skil, in setting forth their books to confute the Papists, ful of learning out of the auncient Doctors, Counsels, Hystoriographers and others: it doth not so wel serue the turne of the simple vnlearned man, neyther can hee defende himself there with, because it is beyonde his reach. This is the thing whiche hath mooued mee to write somewhat of these matters." See also the translator's dedication of *The Rekening and declaracion of the faith and beleif of Huldrik Zwingly*, 1543.

[5] In *A Compendious or briefe examination of certayne ordinary complaints, of diuers of our country men in these our dayes*, 1581, fol. 8ᵛ, an interesting and important book throwing much light on the economic ideas and condition of England at this time, the author, William Stafford, has one of the characters, the Knight, ask if they might not have the works of Vigetius and Columella "in our English tongue, and read them ouer though we neuer wente to schoole."

[6] In the prologue to *The vertuose boke of the Distyllacyon of the waters of all maner of herbs*, 1527, written by Hieronymous von Braunschweig, Law-

voices denouncing the selfishness of those of the learned who, content with their own knowledge, would do nothing to extend it to the educationally underprivileged. Declaring that man should not live for himself alone, the typical writer in English insisted upon an uncompromising altruism, and claimed such as his motive for using the native language. Having found Cicero's *De Officiis* to his liking, Nicholas Grimald says, "I wisshed, many mo to be parteners of such sweetnesse, as I had partly felt myself: and to declare, that I ment nolesse, than I wisshed: I laid to, my helping hand."[7] In the translation of an astrological work, Fabian Wither denounces roundly those who "as though they were borne only for themselves and to their own uses, haue altogether neglected to publish or set forth any thing for the common commoditie of their countrey," and he goes to some length to show how unchristianlike such an attitude is.[8] To the same effect Sir Thomas Hoby complains that Englishmen, unlike other Europeans, "weene it sufficient to haue a perfecte knowledge, to no other ende, but to profite themselues, and (as it were) after muche paynes in breaking vp a gap, bestow no lesse to close it vp againe, that others maye with like trauaile folowe after."[9]

rence Andrew maintains that no profitable book in any other language should lack a translator in English. That the unlearned world would respond to this effort to educate it seems to have been considered a foregone conclusion. "And yet I thincke," says William Ward, "there is no man so bestiall, so rude, or so blunte of wyt, but that he is (by a certaine instinct of natural inclination) desirous to know things not before knowen, to heare newes not before heard, and to vnderstand bokes in his maternall tongue, written first in a foreign langage, to thende not to seeme altogether ignoraunte in matters both of the liberall sciences, and also of histories, set forth for his rudiment and instruction. (See the dedication of *The Secretes of the Reverende Maister Alexis of Piemount*, 1558.) Thomas Hill offers no other explanation for one of his translations than the fact that there was no other such work in English. Bartholomeus Cocles, *A brief and most pleasaunt . . . Phisiognomye*, 1556, preface.

instinct for knowledge

[7] *Marcus Tullius Ciceroes thre bokes of duties*, 1556 (1553), "The Epistle."

[8] *A Briefe and most easie Introduction to the Astrologicall Iudgement of the Starres—Written by Claudius Dariot* (1583?), dedication. See also the preface of George Baker's translation of one of Gesner's works, entitled *The newe Iewell of Health*, 1576.

[9] See "The Epistle of the translatour" prefixed to *The Courtier*, 1561. Richard Rowlands, having read a Dutch treatise, "thought it a thing very vncourteous, and worthy of reproofe, to witholde so needefull a commoditie

The cleavage between the learned and unlearned, in the minds of those employing the vernacular, was pronounced,[10] and the latter make it plain that their efforts were directed to the unlatined. The consistency with which they designated the unlearned as the object of their writing suggests that such announcements were an apology for writing in English and also a precaution against a possible reprimand from the learned. Sometimes an author attempted to write for both kinds of readers, or else was conscious of the fact that the learned as well as the unlearned might peruse his work, in which case he generally made an apologetic bow to the former. In explaining why the quotations from the Bible and the Church Fathers were translated in his book, Edward Cradocke says,

> I considered I had to doe with two sorts of men: with some, that perchaunce are ignorant, and know neither the Greeke nor Latine speache, and contrariwise with other that haue good skill, and be profoundly learned in them bothe. Therefore, althoughe the inculcating of muche Greeke and Latine, might peraduenture haue made a good showe, and very well haue serued for the enlarging and amplifying of my discourse: yet the vnskilfull, I knewe well inoughe, coulde haue slender forderance by suche meanes.[11]

In general, vernacular writers during the first three quarters of the century pursue an undeviating course toward an educational goal. Thomas Paynell finds it advisable to translate a work by

any longer from our voulgare spech." (Dedication of *The Post for diuers partes of the world*, 1576.) Some idea of the importance of rendering ancient and modern works into English may be gained from William Painter's words: "I follow the tracte and practise of other, by whose meanes, so manifold sciences in our knowne tongue, and translation of Histories bee frequent and rife amongst vs. All which be done for our commoditie, pleasure, solace, preseruation and comfort, and without the which we cannot be long sustained in this miserable life, but shall become not much vnlike the barbarous, ne discrepant from the sauage sort." *The second Tome of the Palace of Pleasure*, 1567, dedication.

[10] The division between the two audiences for the most part does not follow a social but rather an educational line of demarcation. The prevailing use of such epithets as "unlatined" and "unlettered" is proof of this fact. Of course, many were conscious of the various social elements which constituted the larger group, and references to a specific element as humble, simple, rude, etc., are not surprising.

[11] *Shippe of Assured Safetie*, 1572, preface.

Constantius Felicius to teach the "unlearned" that rebellion against kings does not pay.[12] In the poetical preface to a translation of an Italian poem, the translator says that his muse commanded him to turn

> my poettes stately style,
> To vulgar speche in natiue tounge:
> that all may vnderstande.[13]

Philip Moore more carefully explains that his simple medical treatise is not intended "to instruct the learned and skilful," but to enable the common man to preserve his health.[14] Especially did writers in English deem it necessary to educate people in religious matters. "I haue translated," says Hugh Goughe, "into our vulgar speche, this little booke, that herein, the vnacquainted with the latine tounge, may learne reade and see the sume of their belefe."[15] William Gace expresses the same solicitude for those ignorant of Latin,[16] and an unnamed translator answers a possible objection to his work in these words: "If (happelie) it be said, that it is therefore fruitles, because it is a doing of a thing that is alreadie done, by a worthy workeman of the Lord Maister *Dudley Fenner*, it were sufficient answere, that the same is made English, which before was Latin, and brought into the artificer's shop, which was before in the studies and closets of the learned alone."[17] John Dolman translated Cicero, "although not elegantly, yet playnely," for the unlearned, so that "our country, might at length flowe with the workes of philosophye," and James Bell Englished a Latin work by Walter Haddon and John Foxe "to profit the unlettered English."[18] The demands of the

[12] *The Conspiracie of Lucius Catiline*, 1541, preface.

[13] Somewhere in the wide field of sixteenth-century writings these lines occur, but where I do not know.

[14] *The hope of health*, 1565, Dedication.

[15] Bartholomeus Georgievits, *The Ofspring of the house of Ottomano* (1570?), dedication.

[16] See the dedication of his translation of Nicolas Hemminge's *A Learned And fruitefull Commentarie vpon the Epistle of Iames the Apostle*, 1577.

[17] See the preface, dated January 1, 1589, of *The Sacred Doctrine of Diuinitie*, 1599.

[18] See *Those fyue Questions, which Marke Tullye Cicero disputed in his Manor of Tusculanum*, 1561, dedication; and the dedication of *Against Ierome Osorius*, 1581. Cf. the dedication of John Field's translation of a treatise

two audiences were different: one required Latin and eloquence; the other needed to be educated. And so great was the urge,[19] nay duty, to educate the ignorant that preference was shown to them, and the use of the mother tongue, no matter how uneloquent, was assured.[20]

In the face of possible criticism for not using Latin, writers employed the vernacular in the interest of the uneducated. George Gifford, in the dedication of *A Discourse of the subtill Practises of Deuilles*, 1587, proclaims that he intends no large discourse stuffed with Latin and Greek quotations, and so the learned may think his treatise slender because lacking ancient authorities, but he writes not for them, nor does he seek their commendation. He is writing for the unlearned, who stand in great need of instruction. Especially did the authors of scientific and semiscientific works and translations realize that practical and useful knowledge should be disseminated among the masses. Writers on medical topics in particular, though subject, as we shall see, to the most violent opposition, noted this pressing need of knowledge. Christopher Langton announces that he does not write for the educated, who can read Galen in the original, but for those unacquainted with the ancient languages, and he expresses the belief that if Galen's works "were englysshed, I woulde then thynke that we shoulde haue al thynges in Phisicke a greate deale the playner, to the great profit and welth of the realm dyuers wayes."[21] John Caius, however, appealed to both

---

by Jean de L'Espine entitled *An Excellent Treatise of Christian Righteousnes*, 1580.

[19] Early in the century Alexander Barclay perceived this educational urge, and also the various kinds of literary activity unified by it: "Many and dyuers lettred men experte in sondry scyences haue done theyr devoyr to inclere the dulnesse and wylfull ignoraunce of theyr countrees natyfe: And to brynge this theyr enterpryse to effect/some haue wryten in solute langage maternall of our englyshe tonge: some in the same langage hath coarted theyr style in meter/and balades of dyuers kynde: some hath compyled/some translated/and some deuysed of dyuers maters to dyuers purposes." *Here begynneth the introductory to wryte and to pronounce Frenche*, 1521, prologue.

[20] "I haue here made a rude, and a symple litle boke, euen for the rude and simple people." William Salesbury, *The baterie of the Popes Botereulx, commonlye called the high Altare*, 1550, preface.

[21] *A uery brefe treatise, ordrely declaryng the principal partes of phisick*, 1547, dedication.

audiences, and in the manner proper to each, saying that he wrote "one boke in Englishe, onely for Englishemen not learned, one other in latine for men of learninge more at large."[22] It would seem that a gownsman could not be instructed by an English treatise, or that he was insulted by being offered one.

In both translations and original works one is struck with the seeming unawareness of any obstacle other than language standing in the way of the education of the people, and also with the general assumption of the adequacy of the English language to express the thought contained in other languages. As we shall see in the next chapter, this assumption, which represented wishful thinking rather than experience, was contradicted on every hand, but in most of the translations of this period, no hint is given of any inability to render the meaning of an original in English, though much is said of the inadequacy of the vernacular to reproduce the eloquence of other languages. Nicholas Udall is one of the few exceptions to this rule, for in a translation of one of Vermigli's theological treatises, he says,

althoughe in treatynge of suche hygh matiers it can not bee auoided that by reason of some schoole termes or argumentes there must nedes bee many thynges, that maye seme to passe the capacitee and vnderstanding of the vnlettred sorte: yet is not suche a notable good worke as this discourse of Peter Martyr . . . to bee suppressed or kepte (as it wer) hidden vnder a bushel. For yf no booke should bee sette foorth but suche as euery bodye yea euen of the vnlearned and grosse multitude mighte bee hable to vnderstande whan they heare it or reade it: than what should Chauncer [*sic*], Goore [*sic*], Lidgate and others doe abrode, whom some euen of the learned sorte doe in some places scarcely take? than were it vayne to set foorthe Chronicles or statutes in whiche is bothe a great noumbre of wordes, and also much matier not easie to be perceyued of euery body: than wer it laboure loste to sette foorthe in Englyshe bookes of seruice and homilies vnto the grosse and rusticall

---

[22] *A boke, or counseill against the disease commonly called the sweate*, 1552, dedication. See also Robert Recorde, *The Whetstone of Witte*, 1557, dedication; and Thomas Hill, *The Profitable Arte of Gardeninge*, 1572 (1563), dedication. There seems to have been a disposition to think that knowledge when expressed in the vernacular ceased to be knowledge, or at least lost most of its value. John Jones speaks of those who "suppose knowledge nothinge worth vttered in their own language," and a correspondent of Hoby's had to insist that learning expressed in English was learning. See *infra*, note 43.

multitude, whose capacite is not hable to conceiue that is in them conteined than wer vayn to haue translated and sette foorth the bible in
Englyshe to the vulgare people, and most vain to reade it in the
Churches, forasmuche as a greate noumbre of thynges which the symple
ignoraunt people rede and heare thereout, are ferre aboue the reache of
theyr grosse vnderstandynge. But all such good and godly bookes as well
as of holy wryte as of other profane argumentes, are to this entente
sette foorth and published, that euerye bodye maye be edifyed as ferre
foorth as hys capacyte wyll serue. And lyke as wythout any reading or
hearynge at all, they shoulde continue euermore blynde and ignoraunt: so
by continuall readynge and hearing the vnlearned and simple maie take
enstructions and from dai to day procede and growe in knowledge till at
laste they shall by due vse and exercise, be hable to vnderstande as much
as shall bee necessarye or expedient for them. Now this boke I haue laboured to make as plain as I could do, and therfore in som places I haue
either altered or leaft the scoole termes whych otherwise would haue
made the thing more derke, and brought it as nere I could to the familiar
phrase of English speakyng, or else haue added suche circumstaunce of
other woordes, as might declare it and make it plain. Wherfore thoughe
for the cause abouesaide I maie seme in some places to haue somewhat
swerued from the precise woordes of the latin booke: yet I trust it shall to
the fauorable and indifferent reader appere that I haue not any thynge
degressed from the autours mynde.[23]

So great seemed the linguistic bar to learning that the process
of education was thought to consist largely in putting into the
vernacular any book whatsoever, and all other impediments
to the securing of knowledge were ignored. Udall is almost
unique in recognizing these latter, and even he optimistically
views them as quite superable. Yet certainly, not only a simplified vocabulary but also simplicity of thought is essential for the
understanding of uneducated people, and this fact gave rise to
a problem which assumed much more importance in biblical
translations, for it furnished one of the main arguments against
them. But for the most part the publishing of books in English

[23] *A discourse or traictise . . . concernynge the Sacrament of the Lordes
supper* (1550?), preface. It should be noted, however, that frequently those
who uphold the adequacy of the vernacular to express the ideas of an original
do not necessarily maintain that the English vocabulary contains equivalents for
all Greek or Latin terms, but that the meaning may be expressed by circumlocutions, explanatory additions, and the like.

was considered the most effective educational means of the times.

Though possessed of a firm faith in the educational value of English books, translators and other vernacular writers are so much on the defensive as to indicate a steady opposition to the use of English. A consistently apologetic note attends the inevitable defenses of their use of the native tongue. They offer various arguments. To begin with, the author of a letter to Hoby, prefixed to the latter's *Courtier* (1561), maintains "that knowledge may be obtained in studying only a mans owne natiue tongue. So that to be skilfull and exercised in authours translated is no lesse to be called learning, then is the very same in the Latin and Greeke tongue."[24] For proof of his statement he cites Italy as a country renowned for learning contained in the vernacular, many of the writers of which possessed little or no Latin. Palsgrave goes farther, and insists that the English language can express more accurately the meaning of a Latin work than other modern languages, since the latter, owing to the corruption of languages brought about by the Germanic invasions, depart much more widely from the nature of Latin than his own mother tongue.[25] Thomas Wilson acknowledges that English cannot approximate the excellence (i.e., eloquence) of Demosthenes' Greek, but he maintains that since men in their discourses express in English Demosthenes' thought, or ideas of equal value, "may I not or any other sette downe those reasons by penne, the which are vttered daily in our common speach, by men of vnderstanding." Wilson's position is simply that since the vernacular may be employed in speech, it should likewise be allowed in printed books. "And therefore in my simple reason, there is no harm done I saye to anye body by this my English translation."[26] From a practical point of view, the mother tongue was considered ade-

[24] He goes on to say that "the translation of Latin and Greeke authours doeth not onely not hinder learning, but it furthereth it, yea it is learning it self." The necessity of the latter statement suggests the very real obstacles which the English language had to overcome in its rise to dignity and importance.

[25] Gulielmus Fullonius, *The Comedye of Acolastus*, tr. William Palsgrave, 1540, dedication to Henry VIII.

[26] *The three Orations of Demosthenes*, 1570, "The Epistle." St. Thomas More, forty years earlier, had argued for the adequacy of the English language for the same reason. See *infra*, p. 56.

quate to express the substance of any work, and such a position
circumvented the usual objection of its barbarousness.[27]

One of the most popular and telling arguments of the users
of English was drawn from the fact that Latin and Greek themselves were once vernaculars and universally employed for all
purposes. If Cicero and Demosthenes wrote in their mother
tongues, why might not English authors? "Did Aristotle and
Plato, Greke philosophers," asks a Scotch translator of Pierre de
la Ramée's sensational logic,

Hipocrates and Galen Greke Phisitions, leue the Greke tongue, because
it was their natiue language, to seek some Hebrewe or Latin? Did Cicero
who was a Latinist borne write his Philosophie and Rethorike in the
Greke tongue? or was he content with his mother tongue? and surely as
he testifiethe hym self, he had the perfecte knowledg of the Greke
toonge, yet he wrote nothing therin which we haue extant at this day.[28]

In the preface to a translation of a medical treatise by Conrad
Gesner, George Baker upholds the privilege of a translator by
declaring that

if . . . I did not feare to be too long in this Preface, I would prooue
howe all Artes and sciences may be published in that tongue which is
best vnderstanded: as for example, *Hippocrates, Galen, Paulus Ægineta,*
Aetius, were Grecians, and wrote all in the Greeke, to the perfect vnderstanding of their countrey men. Also *Cornelius Celsus* being a Latinist,
wrote in the Latine. *Auicen* and *Albucrasis,* Arabians wrote in the
Arabicke tongue. The eternal fame of which worthy men shall neuer
bee extinguished or drowned in obliuion, nor their noble workes for euer
bee out of remembrance . . . [and] our English is as meet and necessary for vs, as is the Greeke for the Grecians.[29]

[27] In the first chapter I called attention to Wilson's comparing the classical
languages to "fine Manchet" and velvet, and his native tongue to "cheate
breade" and "home-spun cloth," the difference lying in eloquence.

[28] *The Logike of the moste excellent philosopher P. Ramus Martyr,
newly translated, and in diuers places corrected after the mynde of the Author.
Per. M. Roll. Makylmenæum Scotum,* 1574, p. 15.

[29] *The practice of the new and old phisicke,* 1599. This had appeared in
1576 under the title *The newe Iewell of Health.* The preface is dated February
21, 1576. In arguing only from classical precedent for the possibility of translating all arts and sciences, Baker overlooks what most of his predecessors and
contemporaries noted—namely, the great dearth of "terms of art" in the English language.

J. Mosan likewise cites ancient precedents for his translation, pointing out that he is only "imitating therein the most famous Authors of auncient and moderne age: namely such as Hippocrates, Galen, Auicen, Paracelsus, and others, that haue in their natiue toongs opened and reuealed to posteritie the very depths and secrets of that excellent arte of Physicke."[30] In fact, translators seem never to tire of pointing out that when Plato, Aristotle, Plutarch, and other ancient worthies wrote, they "made choise of their owne mother languages."[31] The same argument extends into the next century, when the need to defend the use of English had all but vanished. In the preface to a translation of Pliny under the title *The Historie of the World* (1601), Philemon Holland solemnly asks,

As for our speech, was not Latine as common and naturall in Italie, as English here with us. And if *Plinie* faulted not but deserued well of the Romane name, in laying abroad the riches and hidden treasures of Nature, in that Dialect or Idiome which was familiar to the basest clowne: why should any man be blamed for enterprising the semblable, to the commoditie of that countrey in which and for which he was borne. Are we the onely nation under heaven unworthie to taste of such knowledge? or is our language so barbarous, that it will not admit in proper tearms a forrein phrase?

There are not many aspects of the English Renaissance in which the nationalistic spirit is not revealed. And this spirit justifies and urges translations into the vernacular by pointing out the greater number of translations found in other languages, and

[30] See the preface of his translation of Christoph Wirsung's *Praxis Medicinæ vniver salis*, 1598.

[31] Annibale Romei, *The Courtiers Academie*, tr. I. K[epers], 1598, preface. Cf. Nicholas Udall, *Floures For Latine Spekynge . . . gathered oute of Terence*, 1533, preface; Lanfrancus, *A most excellent and Learned Woorke of Chirurgerie*, tr. John Hall, 1565, Thomas Gale's letter to Hall; and *Certaine Workes of Galens*, tr. Thomas Gale, 1586, dedication dated November 7, 1566. In a section entitled "Ane exclamatioun to the Redar, Twycheyng the wryttyng of Vulgare, and Maternall Language" and inserted in his *Ane Dialog betuix Experience and ane Courteour*, 1554, Sir David Lindsay points out that God gave Moses the Ten Commandments, not in Greek or Latin but in Hebrew; that Aristotle and Plato wrote their philosophy in their native tongue; that Virgil, the prince of poets, and Cicero, the flower of oratory, employed the vernacular; and that St. Jerome translated the Scriptures into his mother tongue.

by asserting that it is an Englishman's patriotic duty to even the balance. Nicholas Grimald claims as his motive for Englishing Cicero the desire "to do likewise for my countriemen: as Italians, Frenchmen, Spaniardes, Dutchmen, and other foreins haue liberally done for theyrs," and John Brende as his, the wish that the English might be found as forward as other nations that have all worthy histories in their natural languages.[32] In order to give the argument as much force as possible, the enviable situation in other countries, especially France and Italy, was considerably exaggerated. Henry Parker, Lord Morley, asserts that in those two countries every Latin work of any importance is immediately translated into the vernacular, and he laments that the same is not true of England.[33] William Painter gives an even brighter picture of conditions in other countries. English translators, he says, have no other end in view than

> that our faces be not tainted with the blushing color, to see the passing diligence of other Countreys, by curious imbelishing of their states, with the troublous trauaile of their brain, and laborsome course of penne, Who altogether imploye those paines, that no Science lurke in corner, that no knowledge be shut vp in cloisters, that no Historie remain vnder the maske and vnknowne attire of other tongues.[34]

Henry Billingsley, the translator of Euclid, sees in the translations rife in other countries the reason for their mechanical superiority to England, and he expresses the hope that his work may incite others to bring it about that

> our Englishe tounge shall no lesse be enriched with good Authors, then are other straunge tounges: as the Dutch, French, Italian, and Spanishe: in which are red all good authors in a maner, founde amongest the

---

[32] *Marcus Tullius Ciceroes thre bokes of duties,* 1556, preface; and *The Historie of Quintus Curcius,* 1553, preface.

[33] *The trymphes of Fraunces Petrarcke, translated out of Italian into English* (1565?), dedication. George Baker hopes to inspire more English translations by asking, "For what kinde of science or knowledge euer was inuented by man, which is not now in the Italian or French? And what more prerogatiue haue they then we English men (of which many learned men haue made sufficient proofe within these few yeeres, fully to furnish and satisfie our nation with many goodly workes)." Preface, dated 1576, of his translation of Gesner's *The practice of the new and old phisicke,* 1599.

[34] *The second Tome of the Palace of Pleasure,* 1567, dedication.

Grekes or Latines. Which is the chiefest cause that amongest them do florishe so many cunning and skilfull men, in the inuention of straunge and wonderfull thinges, as in these our daies we see there do.[35]

Fabian Wither goes to even greater lengths in his exaggeration of the riches contained in other languages:

When I doe often times reuolue with my selfe . . . the great laboures, continuall paynes, and incessant diligence whiche the forraine Nations vse for the aduancement of their countrey and people, to bring them vnto the vnderstanding and knowledge of all, and all maner of Artes and science: in so much there is not anye Authour that hath written in any tongue, or of any Art or Science which they haue not translated into their owne proper and vulgar tongue, for the common commoditie of their countrey: as dayly experience without further proofe doth sufficiently approue and testifie, I cannot a little maruell at the slacknesse, or rather contemptuous negligence of our countrey men in these our dayes.[36]

The duty of educating the masses greatly enhanced the importance of translation, and thus in a way made translations a gauge of the culture of a country. So it is not surprising that nationalistic souls, urged by the example of foreign nations, advocated as much activity as possible in that direction. And this is one of several reasons why the "barbarousness" of the vernacular did little to diminish estimates of its practical value and interfered to no great extent with its general use.

These seemingly unprovoked apologies for the employment of the mother tongue not only argue the reality of the hostility to it but also indicate that a sense of this hostility was foremost in the minds of those who wrote in English. The latter themselves give more than an indication of the grounds of the opposition. There is, however, little evidence that the English language was considered inadequate to express original ideas or ideas contained in other languages, even though the English vocabu-

[35] *The Elements of Geometrie of the most auncient Philosopher Euclide of Megara*, 1570, translator's preface.

[36] Dedication of Claude Dariot's *A breefe . . . Introduction to the Astrological iudgement of the Starres* (1583?). In the dedication of *The Courtier*, Sir Thomas Hoby holds that the English are inferior to most other nations in translations. Cf. Dudley Fenner, *Artes of Logike and Rethorike*, 1584.

lary might not be able to match, word for word, the classical. Circumlocutions and loan words could always be employed.[37] One important objection, however, made to the use of English was based, as we should expect, upon its supposedly uneloquent character. One translator asks, "shall we . . . be more vnkinde to our natiue tongue and countrey then was thiese men [Cicero and Aristotle] to theirs? But thou wilt say, our tongue is barbarous, and theirs is eloquent," to which he replies, "euery mans tongue is eloquent ynough for hym self, and that of others in respect of it is had as barbarous."[38] But for the most part, translators admitted the accusation of rudeness, and emphasized the importance of substance rather than style. Thomas Wilson finds it impossible to translate Demosthenes "according to the excellencie [i.e., eloquence] of his tongue," and "as the excellencie of this Orator deserueth in Greek," but he insists that the philosopher's ideas and arguments can be adequately represented in English.[39] On the other hand, the prevalent idea of the grossness of the native language created among the learned and their apes a supercilious attitude which considered the vernacular hardly worthy of containing any important matter. The tendency of many of the learned to turn up their noses at the vernacular is too obvious to be overlooked. Early in the century Alexander Barclay tried to placate those who "shal dysdane to rede my translation in Englysshe."[40] Thomas Gale finds it necessary to defend himself against those who "shall saie it [his translation] is not good because it is in the English tongue."[41] George Baker calls attention to "some, more curious than wyse, [who] esteeme of nothing but that which is most rare, or in harde and vnknowne languages."[42]

---

[37] The translator of Ramus' logic admits that some hold that there are not enough words in English and Scotch to translate the Latin of the original, but he answers that words can always be borrowed from it. *The Logike of the moste excellent philosopher P. Ramus Martyr*, 1574, p. 15.

[38] *Loc. cit.* To answer the charge of barbarousness this translator was compelled, as were others, to fall back on the classical meaning of the term in place of the much more widely accepted meaning of "lack of eloquence."

[39] *The three Orations of Demosthenes . . . in fauour of the Olynthians*, tr. Thomas Wilson, 1570, dedication.

[40] See the dedicatory preface of his translation of Sallust's *Jugurtha*, 1557.

[41] *Certaine Workes of Galens*, 1586, dedication dated 1566.

[42] Conrad Gesner, *The newe Iewell of Health*, tr. George Baker, 1576.

The strongest and most serious opposition to the employment of the mother tongue in printed books was one in which
the nature of the language was in no way involved. So closely
was knowledge associated with the classics that any separation
of the two was viewed by the educated as a distinct injury to
learning. When Sir Thomas Hoby makes a plea for more English translations, he is constrained to admit that "our learned
menne for the moste part hold opinion, to haue the sciences in
the mother tunge, hurteth memorie and hindreth lerning."[43]
John Dee thinks it expedient to show that a translation of Euclid
will not injure the honor and estimation of the universities and
their graduates.[44] The classicists sincerely believed that the publication of books in English would impair the particular prestige
due the universities and educated men, and that learning would
suffer through the removal of the incentive to attend the universities. In other words, the vested interests of learning frowned
upon any activity likely to disturb their privileges and honors.
Thomas Rogers must have this idea in mind when he says that
there are "among the learned some (as among all sortes there
bee, whiche, so themselues doe gaine, care not howe many bee
vndone) bothe think and speake muche against the divulgatyng
of good thinges into a common tongue."[45] Ralph Lever likewise
speaks of those who "judge it hurtfull, to haue thys arte [logic]
written and setfoorth in englishe because . . . they suppose,
that it should bee a greate decaye and hynderaunce vnto learnynge."[46] Some thought that the evil of translations would assume even wider proportions.

[43] See Hoby's Epistle, dated 1556, prefixed to *The Courtier*. Hoby contradicts this view with the statement that translations "open a gap for others to
folow their steppes, and a vertuous exercise for the vnlatined to come by
learning, and to fill their minde with the morall vertues, and their body with
ciuyll condicions, that they may bothe talke freely in all company, liue vp-
rightly though there were no lawes, and be in readinesse against all kinde of
worldlye chaunces that happen, whiche is the profite that cometh of philosophy." In a letter addressed to Hoby and prefixed to *The Courtier*, the writer
insists that translation "furthereth it [learning]), nay it is learning itself."

[44] *Elements of Geometrie*, 1570, preface, sig. Aiiiᵛ.

[45] Philip Caesar, *A General Discovrse Against the damnable sect of Usu-
rers*, tr. Thomas Rogers, 1578, dedication.

[46] *The Arte of Reason, rightly termed, Witcraft*, 1573, "The Forespeache."

Translations therefore in generall by some vaine pretendants, in tongues, and languages, hath bin thought altogether a thing, not only vnnecessary, but further preiudicial, the chiefest reason leading them thereunto, being this as I suppose, that knowledge being an ornament, most befitting those noble or honorable, who command, ignorance agreeing best with the vulgar sort, who be subject and obey: it is therfore requisit (say they) that high wisedome, and excellent workes, should be concealed from common sight, lest they through equall experience, and knowledge in things (according to the ordinary condition therof) puffed vp, shake off likewise that humility of spirit, which shuld comprehend them vnder the obedience of laws and magistrates.

The author of this quotation, while not altogether unsympathetic with the idea expressed, suspects the motive for advancing it, which, he says, is "a vaine ostentation in themselues wherby they would willingly retaine, some colour of excellencie, by reseruing vnto themselues in a restrained tongue, that which . . . by publication may be an . . . instruction to al men."[47]

But the vested interest more likely than any to suffer from the use of English was medicine. Inasmuch as the science was learned largely from ancient books or books based upon antiquity and written in Latin, a linguistic equipment was the main requisite for a physician, and any innovation which removed this bar to medical knowledge could literally make every man his own physician, or at least increase the number of practitioners many fold. So reasoned the classical doctors, with few exceptions, in their violent opposition to medical treatises published in English.[48] In 1541 Sir Thomas Elyot expressed concern that doctors would be angry because "I haue wryten phisike in englyshe," to whom he replies that if the Greeks and Romans, who wrote in their native languages, had been as much affected "with enuy and couatise as some nowe seeme to be, they wolde haue deuysed

[47] Annibale Romei, *The Courtiers Academie*, tr. I. K[epers], 1598, preface.

[48] In a postscript to a medical work, John Read tells of an incident in which "being . . . in companie, by chaunce it was tolde me vnto my face, that there were too many bookes set foorth in the English toung, . . . and that the Arte therby is made common. For that quoth he, euerie Gentleman is as wel able to reason therin, as our selues." See his translation of a work by Arcæus Franciscus entitled *A most excellent and compendious method of curing wounds*, 1588.

somme particuler language with a strange syphre or fourme of lettres, wherein they wold have writen their science, which language or lettres no man shoulde haue knowen that hadde not professyd and practised phisycke."[49] The same charge is brought against the established physicians and the same defense of the use of the vernacular is advanced in the preface of another medical work, which is worthy of being quoted at length since it reveals many aspects of the general attitude toward translations, pro and con. The purpose of this work, the author says, is

to distrybute in Englysshe to them that are vnlerned part of the treasure that is in other languages, to prouoke them that are of better lernyng, to vtter theyr knowlege in such lyke attemptes: finallye to declare that to the vse of many, which ought not to be secrete for Lucre of a fewe: and to comunicat the frute of my labours, to them that wyl gently and thankfully receyue them, which yf any be so proud or supercilious, that they immediately wil despise, I shal frendly desire them, wyth the words of Horace: . . . If they knowe better, let vs haue parte: yf they do not, why repyne they at me? why condempne they the thing that they cannot amend? or if they can, why dissimule they theyr connyng? how longe would they haue the people ignoraunt? why grutche they phisik to come forth in Englysshe? wolde they haue no man to knowe but onely they? Or what make they them selues? Marchauntes of our luyes and deathes, that we shulde bye our health only of them, and at theyr pryces? no good phisicion is of that mynde. For yf Galene the prynce of thys art beinge a Grecian wrote in the Greke, kyng Auicenne of Arabie in the speche of his Arabyans: yf Plinius, Celsus, Serenus, and other of the Latynes wrote to the people in the Latyne tonge, Marsilius Ficinus (whome all men assente to be singulerly learned) disdayned not to wryte in the language of Italy: generally, yf the entent of all that euer set forth any noble studye, haue ben to be redde, of as many as wolde: What reason is it that we shuld huther muther here amonge a fewe, the thynge that was made to be common to all. Chryst sayeth, no man lyghteth a candle to couer it with a bushell, but setteth it to serue euery mans nede, and these go about, not only to couer it when it is lyghted, but to quench it afore it be kendled (yf they myght by malyce) whych as it is a detestable thyng in any godlye science: so me thynketh in thys so necessarye an arte, it is exceedynge dampnable and deuylyshe, to debarre the fruycion of so inestimable benefytes, which our heauenlye father hath prepared for oure

---

[49] *Castel of Helth*, 1541, preface. The first edition, 1539, contains a different preface.

comfort and innumerable vses, wherwyth he hath armed oure impotent nature agaynst the assaultes of so manye sicknesses.

The translator expresses the hope that others will bring it about that "all commodyties that are here amongst vs, shall be earnestly and trulye declared, in oure owne natyue speche, by the grace of God," and he vows "to bestowe my laboure" toward that end.[50] The passion to educate the people would brook no interference on the part of proud, selfish, and mercenary physicians. This opposition to the use of English in medical works must have been strong. In defending his translation of Gesner, George Baker says that some "cannot abyde that good and laudable Artes shoulde be common to many, fearing that their name and practise shoulde decay, or at the least shoulde diminishe."[51] One who may be Leonard Mascall prefaces his translation with due notice that "Some peraduenture will obiect that it is preiudiciall vnto phisitions, Apothecaries, and such other, that such manner bookes as this should be diuulged in the English tongue."[52] It is hardly necessary to lengthen a list which has already perhaps become tedious, and much of which may be superfluous. The instances given above leave little doubt that those who employed English in medical works were constantly under impending rebuke from physicians who thought their interests would suffer by such a practice. They are, however, not deterred, but seek to answer their critics by insisting that the public good transcends private gain, and by pointing out that the ancients used their mother tongue in medical writings.[53]

[50] Jehan Goeurot, *The Regiment of Lyfe, wherunto is added a treatise of the pestilence,* tr. Thomas Phaer, 1544, preface.

[51] *The newe Iewell of Health,* 1576, preface.

[52] Nicolaus Miropsius, *Prepositas his Practise,* tr. L. M., 1588, preface.

[53] The only altruistic element in the doctors' opposition to English treatises was the fear that through them ignorant men might be encouraged to practice, and the lives of patients be endangered. William Turner, medical botanist and active Puritan, combats this idea with the deadly parallel from the ancients. "Dioscorides wrote hys great herball in greke, in whose tyme all the Grekes and many Romanes vnderstode it that Dioscorides wrote, Galene wrote also in greke: not only his boke of simples, as of herbes, stones, earthes, beastes, and metalles, but all the rest of his bokes where in he taught the hole and perfyt course of Phisick, and in his tyme coulde all the grekes vnderstand greke and a great nombre of Romanes also. Dyd Dioscorides and Galene gyue occasion for

It was against such opposition as this that the English language had to struggle in its transition from a spoken to a printed tongue. Though this opposition involved no consideration of the nature of the language, it had everything to do with its use. The upholders of the vernacular, however, bring forth one argument that has a direct bearing on opinions of its value. The idea that the worth of a language is in direct proportion to the amount of knowledge to which it furnishes the key finds frequent expression, both as a motive for, and an argument in behalf of, translations and original works, for the more works published in English, the more valuable it becomes. In the dedication of *The Courtier* (1561), Sir Thomas Hoby says, "so could I wishe with al my hart, profounde learned men in the Greeke and Latin shoulde make the lyke proofe, and euerye man store the tunge accordinge to hys knowledge and delite aboue other men, in some piece of learnynge, that wee alone of the worlde maye not bee styll counted barbarous in our tunge, as in time out of minde we haue bene in our maners." Here the lack of recorded knowledge and not the lack of eloquence makes for barbarousness. Arthur Golding, after apologizing for his uneloquent style, expresses the hope

. . . . that all such students as
Doo trauell to enrich our toong with knowledge heretofore
Not common to our vulgar speech . . .[54]

may through Leicester's encouragement continue to do so. The translator of Euclid hopes to incite learned men to an activity, "By means wherof, our Englishe tounge shall no lesse be en-

euery old wyfe to take in hand the practise of Phisick? Dyd they gyue any iust occasyon of murther? Were they hynderers of the study of liberall sciences in Greke because they wrote their workes of Phisick in the Greke tong? If they gaue no occasyon vnto euery old wyfe to practyse physike, then gyue I none, if they gave no occasion of murther: then gyue I none, if they were no hynderers from the study of lyberall sciences, then am I no hynderer wryting vnto the English my countremen, an English herball." *A new Herball, wherin are conteyned the names of Herbes in Greke, Latin, Englysh, Dutch, French, and in the Poticaris and Herbaries Latin,* 1551, prologue. Cf. Thomas Gale's letter to John Hall, dated May 14, 1565, prefixed to the latter's translation of a work of Lanfrancus entitled *A most excellent and Learned Woorke of Chirurgerie,* 1565.

[54] See the dedication of his translation of Ovid's *Metamorphoses,* 1565.

riched with good Authors, then are other straunge tounges: as
the Dutch, French, Italian, and Spanishe."[55]   Thomas Digges,
the son of Leonard Digges, after completing a treatise left un-
finished by his father, assures the reader that if it should be favorably received,

> I shall be prouoked not onelye to publishe the demonstrations of these
> and many moe strange and rare *Mathematicall Theoremes*, hytherto
> hidden and not knowen to the worlde, but also to imprinte sundry other
> volumes of my fathers, which hee long sithence compiled in the Englishe
> tong, desiring rather with playne and profitable conclusions to store his
> natiue language and benefite his Countrey men, then by publishing in
> the Latin rare and Curiouse demonstrations, to purchase fame among
> straungers.

The same nationalistic pride in and love for his country's language make him vow "to imploy no small portion of this my
shorte and transitorie time in storing our natiue tongue with
Mathematical demonstrations, and some suche other rare experiments and practicall conclusions, as no forrayne Realme hath
hytherto been, I suppose, partaker of."[56]

John Florio the Resolute, in the preface to his translation
of Montaigne's essays (1603), cites and answers most of the arguments against translation discussed above, so that his words
furnish us with a fitting summary. To the charge that the use
of English tended to the subversion of the universities, he re-
plied that in the past all learning came from translations, the
Greeks translating Egyptian works, and the Egyptians, Chal-
dean. Against the argument that learning should not be made
common, and that scholars should possess "some priviledge of
preeminence," he declares that the more common learning is, the
better, and that scholars may find their prestige in the honor of
translating, which they alone are qualified to do. To the opinion
that the common people should not possess knowledge of everything, he makes the obvious reply that such omniscience is impossible for them as well as for scholars. Though it may be true

---

[55] *The Elements of Geometrie*, tr. H. Billingsley, 1570, translator's preface.

[56] *A Geometrical Practise, named Pantometria*, 1571, dedication and
preface.

that pearls should not be cast before swine, yet even swine should know what is good for them. One of the reasons advanced for not translating the Scriptures was that "it is not wel Divinitie should be a childes or olde wives, a coblers, or clothiers tale or table-talk," which Florio answers with an idea frequently adduced in behalf of poetry, namely, that there are both a proper and an improper use of the vernacular. In the eyes of the classicists, propriety demanded that learning be wrapped in an erudite mantle, but Florio holds that it is more fitting for the learned to unwrap knowledge, since if the best is good for some, it should be good for all. Although the ancients wrote in a tongue now known only to a few, their language was their own native tongue and intelligible to those for whom they wrote. Florio boldly states that if more honor is paid to one using the learned languages than to one employing English, the reason is that the former is not understood. Moreover, one should write not for his own honor but for the benefit of others. And how can a writer be honored if not understood? He concludes by saying, with illustrative examples, that since there is nothing new under the sun, all men in the past have been translators in that they have secured their learning from others, Virgil from Homer, and Petrarch from both.

Of course, the problem of the use of English was most acute in connection with the translation of the Bible. A vital element of the Reformation and the storm center of the early conflict between the Protestants and Catholics, the question of biblical translations assumes an importance that can hardly be overemphasized. Yet it is well to consider it in the light of translations in general. For after all, the former were only one manifestation, though the most important, of the widespread urge to educate those who were ignorant of the learned languages. The spirit that prompted Tyndale to declare that he would bring it about that the boy who followed the plow would know more of the Scriptures than learned bishops is just as clearly revealed in prefatory comments on innumerable other translations. In both cases we recognize the altruistic obsession that it was one's duty to raise the uneducated to a higher plane of knowledge and understanding, a democracy of learning. In the light of Protestant theology and of the religious intensity of the day, a knowledge of the Scriptures was of much greater importance than any other learning. Sir David Lindsay would allow scholars to write "curious" treatises on logic, astronomy, medicine, and philosophy in Greek and Latin,

> Bot lat vs haif the bukis necessare
> To commoun weill and our Saluatioun
> Iustlye translatit, in our toung Vulgare.[57]

Edward Dering accuses the Catholics of being willing that the people should read in English tales of Robinhood, Bevis of Hampton, Guy of Warwick, Launcelot du Lac, Lamorak de Galis, Sir Tristram de Lyones, and Merlin, but of wishing to bring it about that "of Paule, of Peter, Iames or John besides the bare names, not one among a hundred could tell a lyne, notwithstanding the continual crying of wysoome in the streetes, the callyng of our Sauiour for the sielie lyttleones."[58]

The problem of biblical translations was not new. Part of the new Scriptures had been translated in both prose and poetry in Anglo-Saxon times, and the Wycliffite versions in the fourteenth century had created more than a stir, after which it is probable that the question never disappeared. When it was being

[margin note: Romance & Bible]

----

[57] *Ane Dialog betuix Experience and ane Courteour,* 1558 (1554), sig. Dii[r]. The deep joy felt at possessing the Bible in English, as well as a kind of wonderment that the high truth enshrined in the learned languages has found expression in the lowly vernacular, is apparent in the printer's (Anthony Scholoker) preface to the sermons of Bernadino Ochino translated by R. Argentine (1548): ". . . also the very prophets and Patriarkes and also the whole company that haue been euen from the beginning of the worlde/are now familiar vnto vs/and are become Inglishmen. Yea/god him selfe of his great infinite mercie in our owne tongue speaketh vnto vs/oute of his moost sacred worde/to our great ioye and spirituall comforte. And Paul being an hebrue borne/hath chaunged his tonge/and is become oures/as though he had been bredde and brought vp all the dayes of his lyfe amongst vs." (Cf. "The Conclusion" of Thomas Cogan's *Well of Wisedome,* 1577.) The English Prayer Book inspired the same feelings. See Henry VIII's injunction "for autorising and establyshyng the vse of this Primer" found in *The Primer,* 1545; and the English translation of Bishop Jewel's *Apologie, or aunswer in defence of the Church of England,* 1562, fol. 17[r].

[58] *A Sparing Restraint, of many lauishe Vntruthes, which M. Doctor Harding dothe chalenge, in the first Article of my Lorde of Sarisburies Replie,* 1568, p. 6.

violently debated after the appearance of Tyndale's translation, there was published in defense of the latter a work, to which the date 1400 was assigned, entitled *A compendious olde treatyse/shewynge/howe that we ought to haue the scripture in Englysshe* (1530). In 1482 Caxton prefixed a dialogue to his edition of Trevisa's translation of Higden's *Polycronicon,* in which a nobleman argues for English translations with a scholar, much of which argument looks directly toward a translation of the Bible. But it was Tyndale's version that precipitated the controversy. The most important charge brought against the translation concerned the heresies supposed to be contained in it; next in importance was criticism of the vernacular, which was not considered a worthy medium. As we noticed in the first chapter, the mother tongue was all but universally viewed as barbarous, rude, gross, base, or, in short, uneloquent. This opinion Tyndale thought necessary to answer at some length.

Thei wil saye it [the Bible] can not be translated into our tonge/it is so rude. It is not so rude as thei are false lyers. For the Greke tonge agreeth moare with the englysh then with the latyne. And the properties of the Hebrue tonge agreeth a thousande tymes moare with the englysh then with the latyne. The maner of speaking is both one/so that in a thousande places thou neadest not but to translat it in to the englysh worde for worde/when thou must seke a compasse in the latyne/and yet shalt haue moch worke to translate it welfaueredly/so that it haue the same grace and sweetnesse/sence and pure vnderstandinge with it in the latyne/as it hath in the Hebrue. A thousand partes better maye it be translated in to the english/then into the latyne, yea and except my memory fayle me/and that I haue forgotten what I redde when I was a child though shall finde in the englesh croncycle how that kynge Adelstone caused the holy scripture to be translated into the tongue that then was in Englonde/and how the prelates exhorted him therto.[59]

Tyndale

N.B.

rhythms & syntax

It is possible that this confidence in the vernacular was inspired by the necessity of defending his own achievement, but such was not the case with St. Thomas More, who shows the charge as short shrift as Tyndale.

More

Nor I never yet heard any reason laid [out] why it were not convenient to have the bible translated into the English tongue, but all those reasons,

[59] *The Obedience of a Christen man,* 1528, fol. xv.

seemed they never so gay and glorious at the first sight, yet when they were well examined they might in effect, for aught that I can see, as well be laid against the holy writers that wrote the scripture in the Hebrew tongue, and against the blessed Evangelists that wrote the Scriptures in Greek, and against all those in likewise that translated it out of every of those tongues into Latin, as to their charge that would well and faithfully translate it out of Latin into our English tongue. For as for that our tongue is called barbarous, is but a fantasy; for so is, as every learned man knoweth, every strange language to other. And if they would call it barren of words, there is no doubt but it is plenteous enough to express our minds in anything whereof one man hath used to speak with another. Now as touching the difficulty which a translator findeth in expressing well and lively the sentence of his author (which is hard alway to do so surely but that he shall sometime minish either of the sentence or of the grace that it beareth in the former tongue) that point hath lien in their light that have translated the scripture already either out of Greek into Latin, or out of Hebrew into any of them both, as by many translations which we read already, to them that be learned, appeareth.[60]

Tyndale does not directly answer the charge concerning the rudeness of the vernacular by showing it is eloquent, though he may imply that it can reproduce the "grace and sweetnesse" of the original. He contents himself by pointing out, as Sir Thomas Elyot did a few years later,[61] that the analogy between the ways of expressing thought was closer between English, on the one hand, and Greek and Hebrew, on the other, than between the latter two and Latin. More answers the common charge of the inadequacy of the English vocabulary for written compositions by pointing to its practical adequacy for conversation, a position which, as we have seen, was maintained by Ascham.[62] The charge of "barbarousness" he answers by giving the word its classical,

---

[60] *Dialogue Concerning Tyndale*, ed. and modernized by W. E. Campbell, 1927, p. 247. Cf. *ibid.*, p. 244, where clergymen are reported to "say . . . that it is hard to translate the scripture out of one tongue into another, and especially, they say, into ours which they call a tongue vulgar and barbarous." More was unreservedly in favor of translating the Bible into English.

[61] See *supra*, chapter i, p. 13, note 25.

[62] See *supra*, chapter i, p. 15. Though for the most part during the first three quarters of the century, the English vocabulary was considered insufficient, particularly in terms of art, there was at the time More was writing an appreciable body of opinion that held the opposite view because of words borrowed from other languages. See *infra*, pp. 83–90.

but less frequently used, meaning of "strangeness" or "unfamiliarity," rather than "lack of eloquence," the signification usually accorded it and certainly uppermost in the minds of the critics of the biblical translation. In this way he avoided the necessity of maintaining that the vernacular was eloquent.[63] Both the Protestant and the Catholic writer indicate how firmly fixed was the opinion that the mother tongue was barbarous, and how important a part the idea played in the controversy.

Thomas Harding, one of the most violent enemies to the *T. Harding* English version of the Bible, more than once introduces the "barbarous" charge. He strenuously denies that lay people had ever been commanded

> to read the woorde of God in their owne tongue, being vulgare and barbarous. By vulgare and barbarous tongues, I vnderstande, as before, al other, beside the three learned and principal tongues, Hebrew, Greke, and Latine. Which, as they were once natiue, and vulgare to those three people, so nowe to none be they natiue, and vulgare, but common to be obteigned by learninge, for meditation of the Scriptures, and other knowledge.[64]

Five years later John Foxe bears witness that the barbarousness of the language was a mighty argument in the hands of the Catholics. "Some againe," he says, "haue iudged our natiue

[63] Cf. *supra*, chapter i, pp. 7–9. This method of combating the charge of barbarousness was perhaps the most effective, and certainly the most popular and persistent. Jewel employs it against his adversary (*A Replie vnto M. Hardinges Answeare*, 1565, p. 155), and more than a century later his words are echoed in *A Discourse Concerning the Celebration of Divine Service in an Unknown Tongue*, 1685, p. 39, attributed to John Williams. The preface to the King James version of the Bible quotes and comments upon I Corinthians 14, as follows: "*Except I know the power of the voyce, I shall be to him that speaketh, a Barbarian, and he that speaketh, shalbe a Barbarian to me.* The Apostle excepteth no tongue; not Hebrewe the ancientest, not Greeke the most copious, not Latine the finest . . . The *Scythian* counted the *Athenian*, whom he did not vnderstand, barbarous: so the *Romane* did the *Syrian*, and the Iew (euen Saint *Hierome* himselfe calleth the Hebrew tongue barbarous, belike because it was strange to so many) so the Emperour of *Constantinople* called the *Latine* tongue, barbarous, though Pope *Nicolas* do storme at it." Nearly three quarters of a century earlier the biblical passage quoted above had been noted as bearing directly on the use of English for religious purposes; an annotation on it, in the Matthew's Bible, reads, "The vulgar tong is preferred."

[64] John Jewel, *A Replie vnto M. Hardinges Answeare*, 1565, p. 518. Cf. p. 541.

Foxe

tounge vnmet to expresse Gods high secret mysteries, being so barbarous and imperfecte a language as they say it is. As though the holy spirite of truth mente by his appearing in clouen tounges, to debarre any nation, or any tounge, from vttering forth the magnificent maiestie of God's miraculous workes." He points to Anglo-Saxon versions of the Scriptures and to the favorable attitude in past centuries toward scriptural translations as precedents for his own age; "so that neither the difficulties of the Scriptures, as is alleaged, nor yet the profunditie of the mysteries in the same, nor the baseness of our language (as it is commonly slaundered) was any sufficient cause to hinder these good fathers of thys their diligent labours."[65] "Commonly" speaks volumes as regards the attitude toward the language at this time.

Becon

It is in Thomas Becon, however, that we find the most extensive and interesting reply to the charge of barbarousness that had been advanced against the English translation. For he does not side-step the issue by advancing the definition of the term found useful by St. Thomas More and others, but he seemingly accepts the charge and then invalidates it by the antirhetorical ideas mentioned at the end of the preceding chapter. In his treatise, entitled "The glorious triumph of gods most blessed word," he represents the English version of the Bible as speaking in the first person, a fact which must not be forgotten in considering the quotations given below.[66] In true Puritan fashion he envis-

---

[65] See the dedication to Queen Elizabeth of *The Gospels of the fower Euangelistes translated in the olde Saxons tyme out of Latin into the vulgare toung of the Saxons, newly collected out of Aucient Monumentes of the sayd Saxons, and now published for testimonie of the same,* 1571. Even in the middle of the next century the Catholic attitude is still taken to task: "The next thing faulted (as you [Catholics] say) in the Reformation, is the committing so much heavenly treasure to such rotten vessels, the trusting so much excellent Wine to such musty bottles: I mean the versions of the Scriptures and the publick Liturgies into the usual Languages of the common people." Peter Heylyn, *The Way and Manner of the Reformation of the Church of England Declared and Justified,* 1657, p. 70.

[66] The treatise was first published in *The Thyrd parte of the Bookes whiche Thomas Becon, hath hytherto made: nowe first of all published and set forth in printe this present yeare of our Lord,* 1562, which, in turn, is contained in the second volume of *The worckes of Thomas Becon,* 1564. That the English translation is intended by "gods most blessed word" is made clear by the last section, "A confutation of certayne blasphemys wherewith the wicked world-

ages two enemies of the English version—the Catholics, who deface it with charges of heresies, and the Humanists, who prefer classical learning and eloquence to it. At one time he seems to have in mind the Catholics, at another, the Humanists, but more frequently the two merge, so that Humanism and Catholicism are considered one in their hostility to the "barbarousness" of the translation. Becon does not deny the validity of the accusation of rudeness, but he meets it with an earnest depreciation of eloquence. In fact, the dedication (also called the preface) begins by saying that in all ages men "with a pleasaunt vayne of witty and sugred eloquence" have praised unworthy things, "only for the vayne ostentation of their witte, knowledge, and eloquence: and so in matter haue brought small and slender profyt to the readers, or rather none at all." In opposition to this attitude, the author expresses the wish to emphasize substance and wisdom rather than to "glyster with vayn eloquence of words." He speaks of his "Oration" in praise of God's word as homely, simple, base, and rude, and his style is indeed simple, clear, direct, and mostly free from rhetorical ornaments.

That he is satisfied to have the English Bible characterized in the same way as his oration is apparent from the words he puts in its mouth. "Yet min enemies thinck verly to bring me into confusion. Therefore some deface mine honor by calling me heresy, new learning, blasphemous doctrine, sedicious teaching, and what not? Other despise me as barbarous and rude doctrin, vnworthy to be red of them, that desire to haue eloquence and ornate erudicioun."[67] It contrasts the "barbarous" wisdom of the Bible with eloquent vanity:

I can not maruel ynough at the madnesse of some men, which for a lytyll vayn eloquence and paynted manner [of] speakyng forsake me thalone fountayne of all wysedome, and the treasure house of all Godlye and necessary knowledge, as a thing that is rude, barbarous, and vnpleasaunt to the eare, and run with handes and fete vnto profane and ungodlye Authors, whiche as they teache a lyttle vayne and triflyng eloquence, so

lynges laboure to deface and obscure the glorye of Gods worde." See also fols. 478ᵛ, 499ᵛ, 500ᵛ.

[67] Fol. 471ᵛ. Becon says that "The baser" the language of the English translation "seemeth, the higher doth it excel other, not with windiness and vayne bablyng, but with solidite and graue doctrine." Fol. 475ᵛ.

do they bryng forth to the Readers or hearers many wicked and pernicious opinions . . . But they object, that I am rude, gross, barbarous, impolite, vntrimmed, vnpleasante, vneloquent.[68]

To the same effect, it asks,

what do many of you meane to forsake me, and to flye vnto other, which teach not so much as the shadow of true learning in comparison of me, being only entised therunto with the vayn perswasion of worldly and fleshly eloquence, or as I maie speake playnly, worldly babling? For what doth eloquence profite without a good mind? Al humanyn doctrine in the world can not make the mind good and godly without me . . . my doctrine doth beyonde al measure excell all humayne teaching, seme it neuer so ornate, venuste, eloquent and paynted with all the colours of Rhetoryke.[69]

After citing those men in the past who had preferred the Scriptures to all other writings, the English Bible exclaims, "How gretly doth this make vnto the condemnation of them, which forsake me and my doctrin as barbarous, rough, grosse, and rude things, and with tooth and nayle, as they saye, pursue and continually follow the vayn sciences of men, bycause they glytter with a little smokye beautye of vayne eloquence."[70] The charges brought against the English version by the Catholics are quite apparent in these passages. It was heretical because of the way the thought was rendered; it was barbarous because the English language was barbarous. It is important to note that Becon meets this latter charge, not by showing that his native tongue was eloquent, but by depreciating eloquence and associating wisdom and truth with rudeness of expression, an attitude which has already been noticed.[71] Instead of meeting the charge of barbar-

---

[68] *The worckes of Thomas Becon*, fol. 475ᵛ.

[69] Fol. 477ᵛ.

[70] Fol. 478ᵛ.

[71] See the present writer's "The Moral Sense of Simplicity," in *Studies in Honor of Frederick W. Shipley*.

In a passage which expresses the very essence of the Puritan spirit, the English Bible says, "Man againe selected and choseth out for the publishing of his learned fantasy them that are galante, sumptuously apparelled, greatly enriched, highly esteemed, worldly wise, prudent, politike, craftye, suttle wytted, eloquent, etc. But God choseth them that are simple, lytyll ones, poore, fooles, idiotes, beggars, and very abiectes of the world to set forth his most holy will . . . God chose to confounde the wise, and . . . the mighty. And vile thinges

ousness as St. Thomas More and others did, by giving the term the meaning of strangeness, which was quite different from that in the minds of the detractors of the vernacular who use the word, he adopts the procedure followed by many of the defenders of the tongue—he attacks rhetoric and exalts uneloquent simplicity.[72]

Though Becon turns his attention primarily to the Catholic adversaries of the English Bible, he pays more than casual attention to the Humanists and their high regard for classical literature and philosophy. In fact, in him Puritanism squarely faces Humanism. The Revival of Learning, if we may speak of it as such, and the Reformation become contradictory elements in the Renaissance. Becon contrasts strongly the religious wisdom of the Bible and the great inferiority and even vanity of classical learning.

Moreover the reading of God's word shal teach the in aduersitie, patience, in prosperity, modesty and temperance. It shal also teach the to haue a godly affection toward God, charitie towarde thy neighboures, and in doubtfull thinges it shall giue thee councel, in perelles help. in the strife of tentations victory, what *Tullius,* what *Demosthenes,* what *Socrates,* what *Aristotle,* or if thou hast a respect vnto the poetes what *Homere* or *Virgil* is able to give the this thinge? For they could nothing profite them selues, seyng they wer vtterly ignorant of the truth, whiche is shewed vnto vs euen from God.[73]

It is also with the classical writers in mind that Becon represents the English Bible as saying,

And here may you see disclosed the malicious blyndnesse of certeine bablers, whiche shame not to say, that there come no lesse profyte to the readers of the doctrine of prophane Authours, than of me, and that I

of the world and thinges whiche are despised hath God chosen"—such as a simple style and the English language. Fol. 493[v].

[72] In a translation of Johannes Boemus' *Omnium gentium mores* entitled *The Fardle of facions,* 1555, William Watreman says that in translating "holy writinges deliuered vs fro God," the translator should seek "not so muche to flourishe in painted penning, as sobrely, and sensibly to giue the meaninge of those infinite threasoures, with suche wordes as falle moste felinglie for them, ronne thei neuer so simple and harde framing with our phrase." See the preface to "The Treatise of Josephus" contained in the volume. Fol. 448[r].

[73] Fol. 488[r].

am the cause of heresy, sectes, diuision, commocion, carnall libertye, etc.
O blasphemous mouthes. Whether any mannes doctrine vnder heauen,
yea or man hym selfe can shewed [*sic*] you so many commodities . . .
But why do I once name them, seyng that none of them all, be they neuer
so famous and eloquente, dare once approche vnto my presence for to
enter disputacion with me.[74]

In this passage Humanism, Catholicism, and eloquence form a
triad. The identification of Catholicism with classical learning,
which signifies more than the fusion of Aristotelianism and theology, is revealed in the following passage:

So long as mans doctrine was only serched, and al things tryde by that,
no man perceaued the falsehode and hipocrisye of the Romish secte, bicause that outwardly it glystered with a certayn kynde of Pope holynesse,
and semed very pleasaunt and godly to the eyes of carnal iudgement, but
whan men began to loke in the glasse of my truth, hys iugling was perceaued strayghtwaies, and all his hipocrisie disclosed.[75]

Though there are some interesting implications in the association
of Catholicism with Humanism, there is only one that is directly
pertinent to our theme. In denouncing the vernacular as barbarous, and in decrying its use in the translation of the Bible,
the Catholics were subscribing to the humanistic creed of eloquence, and in considering the learned tongues the only worthy
medium for the expression of holy truths, they were placing the
same high value upon these languages which the Humanists
accorded them. That the two should have been linked together
in Becon's mind is not strange. But since there were humanistic
Anglicans, it must have been the puritanic element in Becon and
others which found in Humanism a suggestion of Catholicism,
with which the more conservative Protestants were thought to
be contaminated. In this complex relationship the uneloquent
English vernacular played no small part, since it stood in sharp
contrast to the learned languages, its honesty being frequently
advanced against the vanity and deceitfulness of the eloquent

[74] *The worckes of Thomas Becon*, fol. 488ᵛ. Walton Haddon and John
Foxe follow Becon in opposing the simplicity of the Bible to worldly eloquence,
especially Cicero's, and in associating Humanism with Catholicism. See *Against
Ierome Osorius*, tr. James Bell, 1581, Book II, fols. 258ᵛ–265ʳ. (The Latin
original appeared in 1577.)

[75] Fol. 486ʳ, misnumbered 485.

tongues. Resentment of the charge of barbarousness may have had something to do with the hostility to the classics, since it partly inspired the attack on rhetoric which for the most part was associated only with the classical languages until the last quarter of the century.[76]

Besides the charge that the "barbarous" English language was an unworthy medium for the translation of the Scriptures, the Catholics advanced other arguments against the use of the vernacular. Harding, for instance, asserted that some of the mysteries of the Bible should not be divulged to nor understood by some of the people,[77] and another maintained that the publication of these mysteries in English had brought them into contempt and hatred, and that the Bible "is not a mystery . . . that is open to euery man, or that is blowen in to euery mans eare." The latter also asserts that Christ does not wish the herd to handle his mysteries, that translating the Scriptures is like casting pearls before swine—a sentiment echoed in the preface to the Catholic translation of the New Testament—and that the rude and unlearned, not being able to understand the mysteries, stick to the letter which killeth.[78] Harding goes to greater lengths in his scorn of the people: "Yee [Protestants] prostitute the Scriptures . . . as baudes doo theire Harlottes, to the Vngodly, Vnlearned, Rascal people . . . Prentises, Light Personnes, and the rifferaffe of the people"; and he expresses the unqualified opinion that "The Vnlearned people were keapte from the Readinge of the Scriptures by the special prouidence of God, that pretious stoanes should not be throwen before

[76] Becon would not deny "all becoming eloquence" to the English version. He exalts David above the ethnic poets, and Isaiah and Jeremiah above Cicero, Demosthenes, and Isocrates. (Fol. 476^r. Cf. the dedication of Edward Topsell's *The Reward of Religion*, 1596.) Becon contrasts favorably the uneloquent vernacular with the learned tongues in *An humble supplicacion vnto God, for the restoringe of hys holye woorde, vnto the churche of Englande*, 1544, which earnestly upholds the value of prayers, homilies, litany, and catechism in English rather than in Latin, and continues to attack the eloquence of both the Catholics and the Humanists.

[77] John Jewel, *A Replie vnto M. Hardinges Answeare*, 1565, p. 552.

[78] John Standish, *A Discourse wherin is debated whether it be expedient that the Scripture be in English for al men to reade that wyll*, 1554, sig. Diii^v, Fv^v, Giiii^r. This is a clear, restrained, and succinct exposition of the arguments advanced against the English Bible.

Swine."[79] These quotations throw into high relief the democratic spirit manifested in the Reformation, and the essentially
undemocratic spirit of Catholicism at this time.[80] Certainly the
emphasis placed by Protestant theology upon the individual soul
paved the way for the later development of political democracy,
and the vernacular was an indispensable instrumentality for the
purpose. This emphasis may have been partly responsible for the
manifestation of the democratic spirit in the wide desire to educate people generally. In this argument against the use of the
vernacular there is manifested at times a spirit closely akin to that
which inspired the cult of significant darkness. The belief that
the function of literature was to express truth darkly so that it
would be revealed only to the elite and not be desecrated by
being gazed upon by profane eyes[81] is pretty much the same as
the attitude which would restrict an understanding of the Scriptures to those worthy of it, and so prevent the throwing of pearls
before swine.[82] And finally, the idea that what is easy of acqui-
sition soon loses its value, played its part in the opposition to the
use of the vernacular.[83]

[79] John Jewel, *A Defence of the Apologie of the Churche of Englande,*
1567, "To the Christian Reader."

[80] For an unusually clear example of the democratic spirit revealed in the
controversy over the translation of the Bible see the section entitled "An Addy-
cyon to the Reader" at the end of William Turner's *The huntyng and fyndyng
out of the Romish foxe,* 1543.

[81] John Dolman says that there will be objected to his translation of Cicero
"the prophaning of the secretes of Philosophy, whiche are esteemed onely of
the learned, and neglected of the multitude. And therefore, vnmeete to be
made commen for euerye man." *Those fyue Questions, which Marke Tullye
Cicero disputed in his Manor of Tusculanum,* 1561, preface.

[82] In answering objections which he thought would be made to his work,
John Dolman says: "as touching the second objection, which containeth the
vnprofitable disclosing of the misteries of lady Philosophye (as mayster Gry-
moalde termeth her) I thynke that suffycientlye satysfied, yf they consyder, that
besydes the raskall multitude, and the learned sages, there is a meane sort of men:
which although they be not learned, yet by the quicknes of their wits, can conceiue all such poynts of arte, as nature could giue. To those, I saye, there is
nothing in this book to darke . . . and thus in my opinion, I am discharged
of vnprofitable reuealing of the secretes of philosophye." *Ibid.,* preface.

[83] This last attitude is clearly revealed in the preface to Robert Norton's
translation of Rudolph Walther's *Certaine godlie Homilies . . . vpon the
Prophets Abdias and Ionas,* 1573. Its author, John Walker, though no Catholic,
speaks of the difficulty of understanding the Bible because of its figurative style

Catholic arguments:

One may detect a difference in spirit between the genuine objections which the Catholics offered to vernacular translations of the Bible and those which they hit upon to justify a position maintained for other reasons. They certainly did fear the heretical opinions which the English translation seemed to favor. They may very well have shared the view held by the admirers of antiquity, that the worth of any matter was diminished by being expressed through a barbarous medium. But the suggestion of sincerity lessens as we follow their other arguments: that the Bible cannot be translated into English; that if it could be, it would not be understood by the people, who would misinterpret it to their own hurt; and that if its true meaning were recognized, it would suffer from being profaned by vulgar eyes, and its worth would not be perceived. Even the statement that, if all men were Catholics and not evil Protestants, a faithful translation of the Scriptures might be permissible sounds more like a compromise than an uncoerced opinion. One motive that may aid in accounting for the Catholic hostility to biblical translations was that which we have noticed in connection with the opposition of learned men, and physicians in particular, to other English translations, namely, self-interest.[84] As long as the Church stood as the only purveyor of the Word of God to men, the prestige and importance of its officers and learned men were greatly enhanced. It is not strange that the latter battled stoutly to defend their privileged position.[85]

and the languages in which it was written, but from this situation he derives the comfort that "if the vnderstanding of the scriptures in all things were plaine, it woulde waxe vile and of no estimation, but when the sense is founde in certaine obscure places, it so much delighteth more with a greater sweetnesse, as the seeking therof did wearye the mynde with paynefull labour." This idea is attributed to St. Gregory by Thomas Heskyns in *The Parliament of Chryste*, 1566, fol. ix[v].

[84] The translator of Ramus' logic says, "I will speake nothing of the enuious, that thinketh it not decent to wryte any liberall arte in the vulgar tongue, but would haue all things kept close eyther in the Hebrewe, Greke, or Latyn tongues. I knowe what greate hurte hathe come to the Churche of God by the defence of this mischeuous opinion." *The Logike of the moste excellent philosopher P. Ramus Martyr*, 1574, preface. Cf. Barnabe Riche, *The true report of a late practise enterprised by a Papist, with a yong Maiden in Wales*, 1582, sig. Eiii.

[85] A somewhat unusual and interesting argument against translations of

The opposition to the use of English, in translations particularly, was formidable. The learned world, fortunately not without exception, both because of a supercilious pride in the classical tongues and because of a desire to retain unto themselves the prestige and prerogatives of learning, frowned upon the use of their native language. In some of the professions such as medicine the financial interests of the learned motivated an even stronger hostility to the employment of English in printed books. It is also quite possible that the undue emphasis upon eloquence created a genuine distrust of the vernacular, which, even by its supporters, was conceded little of that quality. All of the motives suggested above, together with others, worked strongly to prevent the use of English in religious translations and compositions. The fear of heresy and the natural dislike of innovation in sacred matters greatly strengthened the opposition. Also the fact that unlearned men could and did employ the vernacular in printed books, whereas the learned less frequently did, prejudiced some against it, and the results of such writings in some cases must have confirmed the prejudice. But the opposition, strong as it was, failed in its purpose, and largely for three reasons. One was the invention of printing, which required for its justification a larger reading public, and which promoted the desire of publishers for profit. Another was the deeply felt and

---

the Bible is advanced by Nicholas Sanders, a Catholic recusant and Professor of Theology at Louvain, who maintains that the universality of Latin makes it possible for the Vulgate to establish bonds and promote harmony and unity in the Church all over the world, and that the immutability of Latin renders it more suitable for the preservation of biblical truth than unstable modern languages. (*Sacræ . . . Tres Orationes in scholis Publicis Louanii, 14 Cal. Ianuari. An. Domini 1565.* Antwerp, 1566. fols. 44–67. Nearly a score of years before, Bishop Gardiner, in a letter to Somerset dated June 6, 1547, had contrasted the changing nature of English with the immutability of Latin as a vehicle for religious truths. *The Letters of Stephen Gardiner*, ed. J. A. Muller, 1933, p. 289.) For attacks on the English translation see, among others, the dedication of George Marshall's *Compendious treatise in metre declaring the firste originall of the Sacrifice,* 1554 (found in *Fugitive Poetical Tracts,* 1875); and Gregory Martin's *Discouerie of the Manifold Corruptions of the Holy Scriptures by the Heretikes of our daies, specially the English Sectaries,* Rhemes, 1582, answered by William Fulke in *A Defense of the sincere and true Translations of the holie Scriptures into the English tong,* 1583. The preface of John Bridges' translation of Rudolph Walther's *Homilies,* 1572, contains an earnest defense of the English translation.

loudly proclaimed duty of educating the people, an obsession which breaks through all conventional statements. The third, closely allied to the preceding, was the Reformation, the main tenets of which required a knowledge of religious truth on the part of the people. In translations of the Scriptures, in commentaries upon them, and in controversial treatises against the Catholics, writers sought to educate the people to the new responsibilities and demands of religion which had been placed upon them, and necessarily the mother tongue was used.

In all these considerations no provision was made for the artistic use of the language. In the first three quarters of the century no pressing need in that direction seems to have been felt, and if it had been, it is quite possible that the deeply rooted distrust of the literary, or eloquential, possibilities of the tongue would have acted against it. When, near the end of the century, the age itself was impressed by the number of books which had been published in English, and when a large bibliography of such books was printed,[86] it contained only theological, scientific, historical, and general expository volumes. Plays, poetry, romances, and the like had been entirely ignored. Printing for knowledge had triumphed.

[86] Andrew Maunsell, *The First Part of the Catalogue of English printed Bookes; Which concerneth . . . Diuinitie. The second parte . . . which concerneth the Sciences Mathematicall . . . And also of phisick, and Surgerie.* Two parts, 1595. See also Louis B. Wright's *Middle-Class Culture in Elizabethan England,* 1935.

Chapter III

THE INADEQUATE LANGUAGE, PART I

As we have seen in the preceding chapters, it was almost unanimously agreed, during the greater part of the sixteenth century, that the English language in itself could not reproduce the eloquence or elegance of other languages, ancient and modern; and also that attempts to render an English style eloquent through the introduction of neologisms and rhetorical devices defeated the purposes for which the vernacular was used—the instruction and edification of the unlearned—by the obscurity and difficulty of understanding thus created. But on the other hand, it was tacitly assumed, and indeed frequently stated, by translators that the English vocabulary was adequate to express the thought or "sentence" of an original. In short, the mother tongue was inadequate for eloquence but adequate for the expression of ideas. The first part of this assumption, even though widely accepted, was, of course, fallacious, and was destined in the last quarter of the century to be vigorously combated and refuted. The second part was necessary as a justification of a translator's work and as an assurance of its efficiency. It was equally fallacious, and was constantly refuted by experience itself. Translators, as well as original writers in English, found themselves in an unfortunate dilemma. The English vocabulary was not sufficient to express all the ideas found in the rapidly increasing knowledge of the Renaissance, whether new or borrowed from antiquity, and yet the fact that the vernacular was used primarily, if not entirely, for the uneducated, argued against the introduction of borrowed words. Again, many antirhetorical souls resented neologisms as a rhetorical vanity and did not always distinguish between a word introduced from necessity and one introduced for eloquence. Furthermore, the nationalistic spirit, with its pride in things native, resented the imputation of verbal deficiency and the appearance of foreigners among good native citizens. The result of all these factors was that the most vehement linguistic discussions of the period were concerned with the proper means of remedying the inadequacy of the English vocabulary in general, and with neologisms in particular.

The situation during the English Renaissance is clear enough. There had been in the world a great increase in knowledge of and interest in ancient art and learning. There had also been a tremendous expansion of geographical knowledge. And third, the stimulating influence of the spirit of the age worked busily in men's minds for the development of new ideas and conceptions of all kinds. All this might have resulted merely in the widened use of Latin for the benefit of the relatively few learned people, had it not been for the invention of printing. Whether the obvious possibilities of the invention inspired the strong urge to educate the unlatined, or this urge, arising elsewhere, seized upon the invention as means of achieving its end, one cannot say, but it seems certain that printing and the English language became the chief instrumentalities by which the public was to be enlightened in every kind of knowledge, but more particularly in religious matters from a first-hand acquaintance with the Scriptures to familiarity with the ideas upon which the Protestant revolt was founded. The problem, then, was both to transfer the learning contained in the ancient and modern languages to the English tongue, and to enable original writers to disseminate their own ideas. In the attempt to solve this problem writers soon discovered that the English vocabulary was not sufficient to express even the traditional learning, much less the rapidly expanding knowledge, experience, and generally increased intellectual activity of the age. As one Elizabethan remarks, there were "moe things, then there are words to expresse things by."[1]

[1] Ralph Lever, *The Arte of Reason*, 1573, "The Forespeache." Richard Mulcaster, who will be discussed in later chapters, affords us the clearest contemporary picture of the situation: "While the inhabitants of our cuntrie neither encumbred their braines with much studie, neither bissied their heds with great trafik, neither pleased their fantsies with far trauell, theie vsed no other terms, then such as their own nede enforced them vnto, which being allwaie fed with home occasions desired no help of foren tungs, to vtter those things with their words which were deuised without their wits. But after that the desire of learning enflamed studie, the longing for gain brought in great traffik, the delight to range, did cause men trauell, new occasions brought furth new

W.
Hilton
(1494)
d. 1396

It is not strange, then, to find numerous complaints regarding the barrenness of the mother tongue.¹ As early as 1494 Walter Hilton, at the end of the first part of his *Scala perfectionis*, explains possible inadequacies or omissions in his treatise on the ground of "lackynge of englysshe," and some years later another translator finds the difficulty of his task to lie in the fact that "there ys many wordes in Latyn that we haue no propre englyssh accordynge therto."² A translator of Xenophon excuses his defects both in eloquence and in meaning on the ground that "our grosse tongue is a rude and a barren tong, when it is compared with so florishinge and plentifull a tongue" as Greek. In the preface to his translation of the *Aeneid* (1553), Gawin Douglas states that he could find no English equivalent to many of the Latin words, such as "animal," "homo," and the like. One translator acknowledges that the scarcity of good terms in the vernacular has driven him to borrowing,³ and William Hergest complains of the "barrenness of the tongue in some parts."⁴

words, as either more cunning made waie to more terms, or as strange deuises did seke strange deliueries. For when the minde is fraught with matter to deliuer, it is still in pain vntill it haue deliuered, and therefor to haue the deliuerie such, as maie discharge the thing well, and content all parties, both by whom and to whom the matter is deliuered, it seketh both home helps, where theie be sufficient, and significant, and where the own home yeildeth nothing at all, or not pithie enough, it craueth help of that tung, from whence it receiued the matter of deliuerie. Hence commeth it that we haue our tung commonlie both stored and enlarged with our neighbours speches, and the old learned tungs." *The First Part of the Elementarie*, ed. E. T. Compagnac, 1925, pp. 172–73.

² *Hereafter Folowith the boke callyd the Myrroure of Oure Lady*, 1530, the second prologue. The passage reads in full as follows: "Yt is not lyght for euery man to drawe eny longe thyng from latyn in to oure Englyshe tongue. For there ys many wordes in Latyn that we haue no propre englyssh accordynge therto. And then such wordes must be turnyd as the sentence may beste be vnderstondyd. And therfore though I laboure to kepe bothe the wordes and the sentence in this boke as farre as our language wyll well assente: yet some tyme I folowe the sentence and not the wordes as the matter asketh." About the same time Sir Thomas Wyatt excuses the tediousness of his translation of one of Plutarch's works on the ground that his mother tongue lacked "the plentuousnesse and fair diuersyte of language" characteristic of the Greek. *Tho. wyatis translatyon of Plutarckes boke/of the Quyete mynde* [n.d.], dedication.

³ See the first preface of William Barkar's *The VIII Bookes of Xenophon*, 1567 (1560?); and the preface to I. Kepers' translation of *The Courtiers Academie* by Annibale Romei, 1598.

⁴ See the dedication of *The Right Rule of Christian Chastitie*, 1580.

Even Sir Thomas Elyot, who used his native language so effectively as to be considered by Elizabethans a master of it, recognized "the insufficiencie of our owne langage" in regard to vocabulary, and was genuinely interested in augmenting it, even though some might object to his "strange termes."[5]

In no field was the lack of English words more clearly revealed than in what the sixteenth century called terms of art.[6] These had reference to the more or less standardized terminology of all kinds of organized learning, such as logic, rhetoric, mathematics, and the like. Since, in the past, learning had to all intents and purposes been confined to the ancient languages, it is not strange that no proper terminology developed in the vernacular. So the zealous translator or original writer immediately ran upon a snag in his efforts to educate the people. In almost every branch of knowledge we find recognition of this situation. In his book on logic Ralph Lever admits that "a number of men doe suppose, that our language hath no words fitte to expresse the rules of this Arte: and . . . some men do argue, that it must needes be so, bycause they that speake or write thereof at large, vse termes and wordes, that no mere English man can vnderstande";[7] that is, writers are forced to borrow foreign terms. Richard Sherry defends himself against those who, he admits, will condemn and laugh at his work on rhetoric because it is written in English.[8] Grammatical terms offered the same difficulty as rhetorical. In introducing his translation of Andreas Guarna's *Bellum Grammaticale* (1569), William Hayward explains that

albeit that there be not the same sweetnesse in our phrase that it hath in

---

[5] *The boke named the Gouernour*, 1531, fol. 1ᵛ; and *Of the Knowledg whiche maketh a wise man*, 1533, "The proheme."

[6] "For, vnlesse it were in such thinges as the Lodgicians [*sic*] terme names of arte, for the whych, we haue no proper Englyse words: I haue vsed none but the playne and accustomed termes." See the preface to John Dolman's translation of Cicero's *Those fyue Questions . . . Tusculanum*, 1561.

[7] *The Arte of Reason*, 1573, "The Forespeache." See Cicero (*De Finibus*, 3,3 and 3,5) for evidence of a similar situation as regards terms of art in Latin. For this reference I am indebted to Professor P. W. Harsh.

[8] See the dedication to his *Treatise of the Figures of Grammer and Rhetorike*, 1555. Sherry seems not to recognize any impropriety in defending the use of English in a dedication written in Latin.

his owne tongue, yet I doubt not but it shall seeme that I digresse but easilie from mine Aucthor: For as the learned knowe, it is an absurde and harde matter in this treatise properlie to english the greatest part of those words that touch the argument in apt phrase correspondent to the Latin . . . Wherfore in my translation I thought it requisit (yea, and also no lesse necessarie) to leave the most parte of the wordes of this argument in their owne tongue, especiallye for that this discourse of Grammer warre was made upon the Grammer of the latine tongue . . ."[9]

These terms we still have with us, to the disgust of some critics of grammar. The same difficulty appears in mathematics, as may be seen in a treatise on the compass by William Borough, who, after stating that he was writing for the unlearned and the learned, says, "yet because some of the rules are deducted from the fountaines of the Mathematicall Sciences, and wrought by the doctrine of Sines and Triangles, whiche maie seeme strange in our Englishe tonge, and wherwith fewe Sea-men are yet acquainted, I maie seem to haue missed of my first good meanyng."[10] It is not strange that botany, the technical terminology of which is far from popular today, should have caused the herbalists considerable difficulty.[11] The same was true of medicine, the vocabulary of which in modern times has furnished the substance of many an ancient joke. Robert Recorde finds it neces-

---

[9] In *Certaine grammar questions for the exercise of young Schollers in the learning of the Accidence* (1602?), sig. A2ʳ, the use of "Orthographia," "Etymologia," "Syntaxis," and "Prosodia" is explained on the ground that "there is no fitte termes vsed for them in Englishe," and that they were retained in Latin, "Because the Romanes . . . had the knowledge of the learned artes from the Greekes, and for that at the first they had not deuised in the Latin tongue fit words to expresse the meaning of these Greeke termes, therefore they kept still the greeke woordes, not onely in Grammar but also in all the other liberall Sciences."

[10] See the preface to "A Discours of the Variation of the Cumpass," appended to Robert Norman's *The newe Attractiue*, 1581. Thomas Digges holds that there is a lack of fit English equivalents for classical mathematical terms. (*A Geometrical Practical Treatize Named Pantometria*, 1591, p. 97.) The first edition, called *A geometrical practise called Pantometria*, appeared in 1571. See Francis R. Johnson, *Astronomical Thought in Renaissance England*, 1937, p. 295.

[11] John Gerard noted that there were more Latin botanical terms "than our vulgar toong can well expresse." *The Herball or Generall Historie of Plantes*, 1597, p. 1.

sary not only to explain why he is writing a medical treatise in English but also to point out the difficulty of the task.

But now as touchyng myne entent in writyng this treatise in the english. Though this cause might seme sufficient to satisfy many men that I am an englysh man, and therefore may more easely and plainly write in my natyue tonge, rather then in any other: yet vnto them that know the hardnes of the mater, this answer shuld seme vnlykely: considering that it is more harder to translate into such a tonge, wherein the arte hath not ben written before, then to write in those tongues that are accustomed, and (as I might say) acquainted with the termes of the science.[12]

William Cuningham found difficulty with some geographical proper names "whiche names also the latinest vse, Amphiscii, Heteroscii, Periscii, and we want apt English termes for them, yet I will make it plain thoughe I vse the more wordes."[13] Thomas Bedingfield looked in vain in his native language for proper words with which to translate a treatise on horseback riding.[14]

The same difficulty was encountered in works dealing with religious matters, only here the problem was much more pressing, as the subject was much more necessary and important than other subjects. One translator indicates his inability "to expresse

[12] See the preface to *The Vrinal of Physick*, 1547. At the end the work is dated 1548, but the dedication to the Wardens and Company of Surgeons in London is dated November 8, 1547.

[13] *The Cosmographical Glasse*, 1559, p. 58.

[14] "For although some men," he says, "suppose it an easie thing, to reduce the conceipt of anie author into another language; yet am I assured it behooueth him not onelie to haue an exact vnderstanding in that toong, wherein the author writeth, but also apt words, and fit phrases in his owne, to expresse the same. Which is also the more hard, if the matter be demonstratiue and artificiall (as this is) conteining diuers particular termes in our English not to be expressed." See the dedication to his translation of Claudio Corte's *The Art of Riding*, 1584. Legal terminolgy offered the same obstacle to English treatises: "For those [statutes] that were first written in latin or in frenche, dare I not presume to translate into Englishe, for feare of misse interpretacion. For many wordes and termes be there in diuers statutes, both in latyn and in frenche, which bee very hard to translate aptly into English." William Rastell, *A collection of all the Statutes (from the begynning of Magna Carta vnto the yere of our Lorde, 1557) which were before that yere imprinted*, 1557, preface. Thirty years previously his father had maintained the opposite point of view. See *infra*, p. 89.

in Englishe, the sentences of so manye Poets and auncient famous doctors of the church, as are comprehended and cited in this little booke."[15] At the request of Sir Philip Sidney, Arthur Golding finished the former's translation of a theological work, "Wherein if any words or phrases shall seeme straunge, (as in some places perchaunce they may) I doubt not but your good Lordship will impute it to the rarenesse and profoundnesse of the matters there handled, not accustomed heretofore to bee treated of in our language."[16] One of the clearest illustrations of the very formidable obstacles confronting those who wished to make common the learning locked up in the classical languages is disclosed in the preface to John Horsfal's translation of a Latin treatise on preaching, for the translator specifies particular terms which gave him trouble, and which, in some part, later generations have taken over unchanged from the Latin. This method of solving the problem Horsfal was evidently loth to adopt, for the need of the audience addressed for simple words was perhaps more vividly realized in the Renaissance than in any other period. He pays tribute, however, to his predecessors in the work of imparting learning to the people, and by their example he is encouraged to persevere with his difficult task. The work to be translated, he says, may

be termed Christiana Rhetorica, that is to say, an arte out of the whiche the true and faithfull Ministers of Christ, may learne playnely, and orderly, to breake and distribute the worde of God vnto the people, and flocke committed to their charge. Nowe it is not vnknowen howe harde a thing it is to translate any arte written, either in the Latyne, or in the Greeke tongue, especially into our Englishe and vulgare tongue, in the which we haue wordes, neither sufficient, nor yet apte enough to declare and expresse the same: that is to saye, the termes and proper names of arte: as *Genus, differentia, species, adiuncta, exordium, enarratio, genus didascalcium, parœneticum*, etc. notwithstanding this greate difficultie whiche might altogether seeme to haue bene sufficient to disswade, hinder, and

---

[15] *The tranquillitie of the minde. A very excellent and most comfortable Oration . . . Compyled in Latine by Iohn Bernarde . . . now lately translated by Anthony Marten,* 1570, dedication.

[16] *A Woorke concerning the trewenesse of the Christian Religion, written in French . . . By Philip of Mornay,* 1587, dedication to Leicester. Golding's effort to surmount the difficulty will be discussed in the next chapter.

discourage mee, to haue taken this little harde, and profitable woorke in hande: yet the example of other wyse and learned men (who before me haue brought into our tongue the artes of Grammer, Logike, Rhetoricke, Arithmeticke, Astronomie, Geographie, etc.) did not a little encourage and bolden mee hereunto: so that I thought if other graue, wyse, and learned men, before me, both Romaynes, Italians, Germaines, Frenchemen, and Englishmen, haue thought good for the aduauncement of Philosophie, and humaine knowledge, to bring into their mother tongue those and other like artes firste written in the Greeke tongue, though they could not always finde out proper wordes euery one in their owne tongue to declare the proper termes of arte. I with much more bouldnes might take in hande to interprete this little arte of Christian Rhetoricke, especially seing that the same doth so farre passe the arte of Rhetoricke, as the holy worde of God doth exceede the knowledge of all manner of humaine philosophie.[17]

The inadequacy of the vernacular being encountered and recognized, especially in matters of learning, the only recourse left to those composing or translating in English lay through the introduction of more words into the standard vocabulary. The methods of securing these words were various, but the most popular, natural, and important was through borrowing from ancient and modern languages, particularly the former. This was a conscious process, frequently attended by due notice and, sometimes, apology, for, as we shall see, there was some opposition to it. One word that was the center of a good deal of controversy in the Reformation was "charity," and it was with distinct self-consciousness that Thomas Lupset, in *A Treatise of Charitie* (1533, fol. 33ᵛ), employed it, for after stating that it was no English word, he adds,

how be it whan we be driuen to speake of thynges that lacke the names in oure tonge, we be also driuen to borowe the wordes, that we haue not, sometyme out of latin, sometyme out of greke, euen as the latin tonge doth in like necessitie borowe and take of other. And though now at fyrst heryng, this word stondethe straungelye with you, yet by vse it shall waxe familiar, specially when you haue it in this maner expressed vnto you.

[17] *The Preacher, or Methode of preachinge, written in Latine by Nicolas Heminge,* 1574, "Epistle to the Reader."

The attitude revealed in this passage finds many years later a more complete statement in a mathematical treatise by Thomas Digges:

. . . let no man muse that writing in the English toung, I haue retained the Latin or Greeke names of sundry lines and figures, as cordes Pentagonall, lines Diagonall, Icosaedron, Dodecaedron or such like, for as the Romanes and other Latin writers, notwithstandinge the copiouse and abundant eloquence of their tongue, haue not shamed to borrow of the Grecians these and many other terms of arte: so surely do I thinke it no reproche, either to the English tongue, or any English writer, where fit words faile to borowe of them both, but rather should we seeme thereby to do them great iniurie, these beeing in deede certaine testimonies and memorials where such sciences first tooke their originall, and in what languages and countries they chieflie florished, which names or wordes how straunge soeuer they seeme at the firste acquaintaunce, by vse wyll growe as familiar as these, a Triangle, a circle, or such like, which by custome and continuance seeme meere English, yet to auoide all obscuritie that maie growe by the noueltie of them, I haue adioined euery of their diffinitions . . .[18]

There are several ideas in these two quotations which we shall frequently meet in relation to the neologizing movement. One is the encouragement and justification furnished by the precedent which the Latin language afforded in its borrowings from the Greek; another is the need of explaining the loan word when it is first introduced; a third is the assurance given readers likely to be surprised by its strangeness that use will produce familiarity and satisfaction with the term. And last, there is the definite suggestion that in some quarters, at least, borrowing was considered a reproach to the language.

Sometimes a word is borrowed with only a casual statement of the need of it in the language. In the dedication to *The Right Rule of Christian Chastitie* (1580), William Hergest describes "an excellent vertue, especially beseming all Gentlefolkes, in Latine commonly called (*Candor*) a proper name in English, for the which vertue (such is the barrennesse of the tongue in

'Candor'

---

[18] *A Geometrical Practical Treatize Named Pantometria*, 1591 (1571), pp. 97–98, quoted in F. R. Johnson, *Astronomical Thought in Renaissance England*, p. 295. The idea that a loan word should be employed out of justice to the language from which the learning was first derived was peculiar to Digges.

some parts) we lack." Thus not only a word but also a virtue, or, what is pretty much the same thing, the realization of a virtue, was gained. "Candor" was taken over intact, and has remained so, but more thought was frequently paid to adapting a word to the demands of the vernacular than this instance indicates. In the process of adaptation a good deal of attention was paid to analogy. A passage from a work on geography furnishes a simple but clear illustration.

In my translation, I trust I haue obserued all requisite conditions, expressing (so well as I coulde) the intent of the Authour. And for thy commoditie Adioyning to the names of countreys and other places, in olde tyme frequented, the vsuall names also wherby they are knowne by all trauailers at this day, not omitting of certaine woordes, whiche were alwayes Latine, and so vsed, to make them Englishe for orders sake, not knowing any cause to the contraye. As bycause out of *Europa*, wee terme commonly *Europe*: so lykewyse to say for *Asia*, *Asie*, and for *Africa*, *Afrike*, with such lyke what euer.[19]

A more remarkable example of the thought given to the form which a word based upon the Latin should assume is found in a book devoted to describing and illustrating by anecdotes the habits and practices of the gangsters of the period. The author, Thomas Harman, for some reason wanting a new word for them, derived one from a Latin verb and inserted it in his title. Since the purists, or "curyous heds," however, objected to the unfamiliar "cursetor" as a "greate faulte," the author in the preface to the second edition of his work found it necessary to explain at some length the process whereby he arrived at the term, in order to justify his

[handwritten margin note: T. Harman]

[handwritten margin note: 'Cursetors']

callinge these Vagabonds Cursetors in the intytelynge of my booke as runneres or rangers aboute the countrey, deriued of this Laten word (cvrro). Neither do I wryght it Cooresetores with a duble oo or Cowresetors with a w, which hath an other singnification. Is there no deuersite betwen a gardein and a garden, maynteynaunce and maintenance, Streytes and stretes? Those that haue vnderstanding knowe there is a great dyfference. Who is so ignorant by these dayes as knoweth not the meaning of a vaga-

---

[19] Periegetes Dionysius, *The Surueye of the World, or Situation of the Earth*, tr. Thomas Twine, 1572, preface. Unfortunately the English language has not proved so logical as Twine.

bone, and yf an ydell leuterar should so be called of eny man, would
not he think it bothe odyous and reproachefull, wyll he not shonne the
name? Ye and where as he maye and dare, with bent browes [he] wyll
reueng that name of Ingnomy. Yet this playne name vagabone is de-
ryued as others be of Laten wordes, and now vse makes it commen to
al men, but let vs loke back four .C. yeres sithens, and let vs se whether
this playn word vagabon was vsed or no. I beleue not, and why? because
I rede of no such name in the old estatutes of this realme, vnles it be in
the margente of the booke, or in the Table, which in the collection and
pryntinge was set in. But these were then the commen names of these
leud leuterares: Faytores, Robardesmen, Drawlatches, and valyant beg-
gares. Yf I should haue vsed such wordes or the same order of wryting
as this realme vsed in kynge Henry the thyrd or Edward the fyrstes time,
Oh what a grose, barberous fellow haue we here. His wryting is both
homely and darke that wee had nede to haue an interpretar. Yet then it
was verye well and in short season a great change toe see. Well, this
delycat age shall haue his tyme on the other syde. Eloquence haue I
none; I neuer was acquaynted with the muses; I neuer tasted of Helycon.
But accordinge to my playne order, I haue set forth this worke symplye
and truelye, with such vsual words and termes as is among vs wel known
and frequented.[20]

It would certainly seem to be inconsistent to conclude a passage
which seeks to establish a new word in the language with the
statement that only usual words have been used, but the inconsistency is more apparent than real. In disclaiming eloquence,
he is in effect saying that he is introducing no strange word for
rhetorical effect. Harman, as well as other of his contemporaries,
is aware of the changing nature of the language, by virtue of
which old words drop out and new come in, and this gives him
confidence that new terms may be consciously introduced and by
use established in the mother tongue.

Elyot

The most deliberate and conscientious neologizer of the
period was undoubtedly Sir Thomas Elyot, whose undeniable
learning and excellent English works must have had considerable
influence in furthering the movement. Seeing clearly the in-

[20] *A Caueat . . . For Commen Cursetors Vulgarely Called Vagabones, set
forth by Thomas Harman, Esquier, for the vtilite and proffyt of hys naturall
Countrey. Newly agmented and Imprinted,* 1567. I have been unable to
locate the first edition. I have tinkered with the punctuation of this passage
because in the original it is so confused that the meaning is obscured.

Elyot

adequacy of his mother tongue and the consequent necessity of augmenting it, he determined upon borrowing as the only method for remedying the situation. "The wordes publike and commune," he says, are "borowed of the latin tonge for the insufficiencie of our owne langage."[21] One of the declared purposes of his most famous book was to repair this defect.

His highnesse [Henry VIII] benignely receyuynge my boke/whiche I named the Gouernour, in the redynge therof sone perceyued that I intended to augment our Englyshe tongue, wherby men shulde as well expresse more abundantly the thynge that they conceyued in theyr hartis (wherfore language was ordeyned) hauynge wordes apte for the pourpose: as also interprete out of greke, latyn/or any other tonge into Englysshe, as sufficiently/as out of any one of the said tongues into an other. His grace also perceyued/that through out the boke there was no terme new made by me of a latine or frenche worde, but it is there declared so playnly by one mene or other to a diligent reder that no sentence is therby made derke or harde to vnderstande.[22]

Elyot laid great emphasis upon the necessity of clear definitions of borrowed words, so that their proper meaning would not be mistaken. In speaking of celerity and slowness in dancing, he says,

of them two springeth an excellent vertue: where vnto we lacke a name in englisshe. Wherefore I am constrained to vsurpe a latine worde callyng it *Maturitie*: which worde though it be strange and darke/yet by declaring the vertue in a fewe mo wordes/the name ones brought in custom/shall be as facile to vnderstande as other wordes late commen out of Italy and Fraunce/and made deinizins amonge vs.

'maturity'

After an extended explanation of the meaning of the term, he concludes with "And this do I nowe remembre for the necessary augmentation of our langage."[23] He goes to considerable length

---

[21] *The boke named the Gouernour*, 1531, fol. 1ᵛ.

[22] *Of the Knowledg whiche maketh a wise man*, 1533, "The proheme."

[23] *The Gouernour*, 1531, fol. 85. About the time that Elyot was insisting upon clear definitions for borrowed words, another writer, who was interested in the vernacular, illustrated this view: "I haue drawen youre legende and all youre seruyce in to Englyshe/that ye shulde se by the vnderstonding therof/how worthy and holy praysynge of oure gloryous Lady is contente therein/and the more deuoutely and knowyngly synge yt and rede yt/and say yt to her worshyp. And in many places where the nakyd letter is thoughe

to show that "discretion," borrowed from "discretio," meaning separation, is commonly used to express a conception for which the term "modesty" should be employed.

> In euery of these thinges and their sembable/is Modestie: whiche worde nat beinge knowen in the englisshe tonge . . . they improprely named this vertue discretion. And nowe some men do as moche abuse the worde modestie/as the other dyd discretion. For if a man haue a sadde countenance at al times/and yet not beinge meued with wrathe/but pacient/and of moche gentilnesse: they/whiche wold be sene to be lerned/wil say that the man is of a great modestie. Where they shulde rather saye that he were of a great mansuetude: whiche terme beinge semblably before this time vnknowen in our tonge/may be by the sufferaunce of wise men nowe receiued by custome: wherby the terme shall be made familiare. That lyke as the Romanes translated the wisedom of Grecia into their citie: we maye/if we liste/bringe the lernynges and wisedomes of them both in to this realme of England/by the translation of their warkes: sens lyke entreprise hath ben taken by frenche men/Italions/and Germanes/to our no litle reproche for our negligence and slouth.[24]

Elyot was definitely committed to the idea of increasing the vocabulary by borrowing, which practice would make possible the transfer of learning contained in other languages to English. When a word for any conception was lacking in the vernacular, the right term was to be taken from Latin or Greek. But its meaning must be clearly defined so that its proper use might be established in the language. After explaining the meaning of "providence," he says, "Industrie hath nat ben so longe tyme

---

yt be set in englyshe/ys not easy for some symple soulles to vnderstonde: I expounde yt and declare yt more openly/other before the letter/or after or else fourthe wyth together. And farthermore/that ye shulde haue the more spyrytuall loue/and inwarde delyte and deuocyon in thys holy seruyce I tell the causes and the meanynges of eche parte therof that is to say/whan I come to the fyrste Inuitory: I tell what an Inuitory ys to say/and why yt ys namyd so and set in suche a place. And so I do of Psalmes/and Hympnes/and Antempnes/and responses and versicles/and all suche other. For I declare why they ar callyd so . . . and why they ar set and sayde in suche wyse/as ye may se more playnely in the story of the Sonday/eche thynge in hys place." *Hereafter Folowith the boke callyd the Myrroure of Oure Lady*, 1530, the first prologue.

[24] *The Gouernour*, fol. 94.

vsed in the englisshe tonge as Prouidence: wherefore it is the
more straunge and requireth the more plaine exposition." He
then defines the meaning of the word as "a qualitie procedyng
of witte and experience/by the whiche a man perceyueth quick-
ly/inuenteth fresshly/and counsayleth spedily." He elaborates
upon this definition and gives an account of Alcibiades and a
longer one of Julius Caesar as examples of industry. Referring
to the latter, he says, "Here is the perfecte paterne of Indus-
trie/whiche I trust shal suffice to make the propre signification
therof to be vnderstande of the reders. And consequently to incende them to approche to the true practising therof."[25] He was
as much interested in putting into circulation words of true signification as he was in introducing them for his own needs. The
other demands of his book, however, must have prevented him
from explaining all his neologisms, such as "incende," "illece-
brous," "coarted," and the like. Sometimes he bows to the widespread distrust of strange words and tries to find satisfactory
substitutes in the accepted vocabulary, though he can scarcely
conceal his preference for neologisms.[26]

Elyot was a Humanist, and the glamour of the classics attracted him, but it did not rob him of a genuine interest in, and
concern for, his native tongue. He was interested both in improving the tongue and in trying it out to see what its good points
were. In fact, he was a linguistic experimenter testing and observing the vernacular, pointing out its strength, and remedying
its weakness. He translated a Greek treatise, "Not presumynge
to contende with them, whiche haue doone the same in latine:

[25] *Ibid.*, fols. 87ʳ–88ᵛ.

[26] After praising the virtue of magnanimity, he pulls up short with "But
nowe I remember me/this worde Magnanimitie/beinge yet straunge as late
borowed out of the latyne/shall nat content all men/and specially them/whome
nothing contenteth out of their accustomed Mumpsimus: I will aduenture to
put for Magnanimitie/a worde more familiar/callynge it good courage/whiche
hauynge respecte to the sayd definition/shall nat seme moche inconuenient."
(*Ibid.*, fol. 208ᵛ.) He does not, however, give up the new word, but continues
to use it more frequently than the English expression. In attacking the dislike
of innovation current in his day, he alludes to the story of the monk, who,
owning to a mistake in his text, in the church service kept saying "mumpsimus"
for "sumpsimus," and when his attention was called to the error, refused to
rectify it.

[handwritten margin note: magnanimity cf. Spenser]

but to thintent onely that I wolde assaie, if our Englisshe tunge mought receiue the quicke and propre sentences pronounced by the greekes." The meaning of "sentences" is thoughts or ideas, and it is interesting to note that he does not even consider the possibility of the eloquence of the original being reproduced. The result of his experiment convinced him that the analogy of the two languages was sufficient for the reproduction of the substance of the original, even though his native vocabulary might not in all respects equal the Greek.

And in this experience I haue founde (if I be not muche deceiued) that the forme of speakyng, vsed of the Greekes, called in greeke and also in latine, *Phrasis*, muche nere approcheth to that whiche at this daie we vse: than the order of the latine tunge: I meane in the sentences, and not in the wordes: whiche I doubte not shall be affirmed by them, who sufficiently instructed in all the saide three tunges, shall with a good iudgement read this worke.[27]

His experiment affirmed the assumption of most of the translators of this period, that the learning contained in other tongues could be expressed in English, even though the eloquence could not be, and though the native vocabulary might be imperfect.[28]

In realizing the necessity of foreign words in matters of learning, and also the necessity of explaining them, Elyot is followed by Nicholas Udall. In a preface to a translation of Vermigli's *A discourse or traictise . . . concernynge the Sacrement of the Lordes supper* (1550?) Udall says that "in treactynge of suche hygh matiers it can not bee auoided but that by reason of some schoole termes or argumentes there must nedes bee many thynges, that maye seme to passe the capacitee and

----

[27] *The Doctrinal of Princes made by the noble oratour Isocrates and translated out of Greke into English*, 1534, preface. See *supra*, p. 55.

[28] Elyot's belief that the thoughts or "sentences" of an original might be expressed in the vernacular even though there were not sufficient English words to match all the Latin or Greek terms, had been anticipated by a translator, who, after stating that there were many Latin words for which there were no English equivalents, says, "And then suche wordes muste be turnyd as the sentence may beste be vnderstondyd. And therefor though I laboure to kepe bothe the wordes and the sentence in this boke as farre as oure language wyll well assente: yet some tyme I folowe the sentence and not the wordes as the mater asketh." *Hereafter Folowith the boke callyd the Myrroure of Oure Lady*, 1530, the second prologue.

vnderstanding of the vnlettered sorte." But, he insists, that is no reason for withholding a good work from the public, for otherwise the publication of the works of Chaucer, Gower, and Lydgate, of the chronicles and statutes of the realm, of religious treatises, and even of the English Bible itself would have been in vain, for in all of them are many words and matters above the ordinary comprehension. He gives the assurance that "by continuall readynge and hearing the vnlearned and simple maie take enstructions and from dai to day procede and growe in knowelage till at laste they shall by due vse and exercise, be hable to vnderstande as muche as shall bee necessarye or expedient for them." He states, however, that he has done his best to make his translation clear, altering the strange words where possible, and in other cases explaining their meaning.

Now this boke I haue laboured to make as plainas I could do, and therfore in som places I haue either altered or leaft the scoole termes whych otherwise would haue made the thing more derke, and brought it as nere [as] I could to the familiar phrase of English speakyng, or els haue added suche circumstaunce of other woordes, as might declare it and make it plain. Wherfore thoughe for the cause abouesaide I mai seme in some places to haue somewhat swerued from the precise woordes of the latin booke: Yet I trust it shall to the fauourable and indifferent reader appere that I haue not any thynge degressed from the autours mynde.

Of course, the process of borrowing words from other languages, Latin and Greek in particular, had been going on for a long time. There were indeed those who, about the third decade of the century, considered the English language adequate for many purposes because of previous borrowing. A translation of Terence's *Andria*[29] is prefaced with a prologue and concluded

---

[29] *Terens in englysh* (1520?). The Latin of the original is given in the wide margins. Professor A. W. Reed would place the date of publication about ten years later, and would also give to Nicholas Udall a hand in the translation, apparently because some years later Udall published *Floures for Latine spekynge*, 1534, consisting of translations from Terence. (*The Year's Work in English Studies*, VIII [1927], 137.) Though no printer is indicated in the volume, the *Short Title Catalogue* ascribes its printing without question to John Rastell, an ascription which, if correct, raises some interesting suggestions, for the next passage which we consider is taken from *A new interlude and a mery of the*

with an epilogue, both of which are called "The Poet," and which
are important enough to be quoted at length.

> The famous renown through the worlde is sprong
> Of poetys ornate that vsyd to indyte
> Of dyuers matters in theyr moder tong
> Some toke vppon them translacions to wryte
> Some to compile bokys for theyr delyte
> But in our english tong for to speke playn
> I rede but of few haue take any gret payn
>
> Except master Gowre which furst began
> And of moralite wrote ryght craftely
> Than master Chaucer that excellent man
> Which wrote as compendious and elygantly
> As in any other tong euer dyd any
> Ludgate also which adournyd our tong
> Whose nobe famys through the world be sprong.

The lament over the scarcity of English writers, and the tribute
to Chaucer, Gower, and Lydgate are no original ideas, but the
influence the latter exerted upon the language, as revealed in
the next stanza, would seem to be, for most of those who praise
these poets for adorning the tongue speak as if they had left no
permanent impression upon it. The poet continues:

> By these men our tong is amplyfyed so
> That we therin now translate as well may
> As in eny other tongis other can do
> yet the greke tong and laten dyuers men say

---

nature of the .iiij. elements, of which Rastell was both author and printer, and
the opening lines of which, together with a passage from Rastell's *Abridgment
of the Statutes,* 1527, to be discussed later, reveal the same attitude toward the
vernacular found in *Terens in englysh.* In fact, one line is practically the same
in both: "Consyderyng that our tonge is now suffycyent" (*.iiij. elements*), and
"And sith our english tong is now sufficient" (*Terens*). It would seem possible,
then, that Rastell bore the same relationship, that of author and printer, to the
Terens that he bore to the other. Since the prologue and epilogue of the latter
speak as if there were more than one translator, Rastell may only have had a
hand in it, or else may have been the author of only the prologue and epilogue,
there being nothing in them to exclude such a conjecture. If this theory is
correct, then Rastell within a comparatively short compass of time in three distinct works expressed unshaken confidence in the adequacy of his mother tongue.

> Haue many wordys can not be englyshid this day
> So lyke wyse in englysh many wordys do habound
> That no greke nor laten for them can be found.

This early confidence in the sufficiency of the mother tongue refuses to be impressed by the argument that the superiority of the classical languages rests on the fact that many of their words have no equivalent in English. For the converse is also true. That the three poets mentioned above amplified the language by borrowing is indicated by the next stanza.

> And the cause that our tong is so plenteouse now
> For we kepe our englysh contynually
> And of other tongis many wordis we borow
> Which now for englysh we vse and occupy
> These thingis haue gyuen corage gretly
> To dyuers and specyally now of late
> To them that this comedy haue translate.

The author's idea is that the words introduced by earlier poets are retained in the language, while more words are constantly being borrowed from other languages, and thus the enriched vocabulary encourages Englishmen to translate. He recognizes the fact that there is still need of neologizing. Like most of the users of English he is aware that the learned will frown upon the employment of the vernacular by the translators of the comedy.

> Which all discrete men now do besech
> And specyally lernyd men to take no dysdayn
> Though this be compyled in our vulgare spech
> yet lernyng therby some men may attayn
> For they that in this comedy haue take payn
> Pray your to correct where faut shalbe found
> And of our matter lo here is the ground.

For the shortcomings of the version he pleads the difficulty offered by rhyme and the necessity of clearly expressing the meaning within the same short compass found in the Latin original, for had periphrases, or "a long expocysyon," been admitted, "Then were it a comment and no translacion." He again makes his bow to the learned, introduces the usual classical precedent, and reaffirms his confidence in his native language.

> And for this thing is broughte into thenglish tong
> we pray you all not to be discontent
> For the laten boke which hath be vsyd so long
> was translate out of greke this is euydent
> And sith our english tong is now sufficient
> The matter to expresse we think it best alway
> Before english men in english it to play.

In conclusion he says that the translators hope more capable men will translate this or some other comedy for the "erudicion" of those willing to learn.

It is worth while noting that he insists on the adequacy of the vernacular to express the meaning, or "matter," and not to reproduce the eloquence of the original. The same is true of John Rastell who, lamenting that the vernacular has been employed for only trifling compositions, insists that it is quite adequate for the expression of such philosophical truths as the interlude, which his words introduce, attempts to set forth.[30] He informs us that he

J. Rastell

> . . . in his mynde hath oft tymes ponderyd
> What nombre of bokes in our tonge maternall
> Of toyes and tryfellys be made and impryntyd
> And few of them of matter substancyall
> For though many make bokes yet vnneth ye shall
> In our englyse tonge fynde any warkes
> Of connynge that is regardyd by clerkes.

He next introduces the inevitable classical precedent in order to justify the translation of books into English, for which, he de-

[30] *A new interlude and a mery of the nature of the .iiij. elements.* The date is uncertain, but probably it falls somewhere near the end of the first quarter of the century. The lines quoted are those spoken by the Messenger at the opening of the play. They have been previously discussed by C. R. Baskerville, "John Rastell's Dramatic Activities," *Modern Philology*, XIII (1915–16), 557–60, and by F. R. Johnson, *Astronomical Thought in Renaissance England*, p. 86. The interlude has been edited for the Percy Society by Halliwell-Phillipps, who in his preface says that it furnishes the only example of an attempt to popularize scientific ideas in dramatic form. The play has also been reproduced in *Old English Drama* (Students' Facsimile Edition), 1908.

clares, the native tongue is quite sufficient, and which will make it possible for the unlearned of high and low estate to secure knowledge.

> The grekes the romayns with many other mo
> In their moder tonge wrot warkes excellent
> Than yf clerkes in this realme wolde take payn so
> Consyderyng that our tonge is now suffycyent
> To expoun any hard sentence euydent
> They myght yf they wolde in our englyshe tonge
> write workys of grauyte sometyme amonge
> For dyuers prengnaunt wyttes be in this lande
> As well of noble men as of meane estate
> which nothynge but englyshe can vnderstande
> Than yf connynge laten bokys were translate
> In to englyshe/wel correct and approbate
> All subtell sciens in englyshe myght be lernyd
> As well as other people in their owne tonges dyd
> But now so it is that in our englyshe tonge
> Many one there is that can but rede and wryte
> For his pleasure wyll oft presume amonge
> New bokys to compyle and balats to indyte
> Some of loue or other matter not worth a myte
> Some to opteyn fauour wyll flatter and glose
> Some wryte curyous termes nothyng to purpose
> Thus euery man after his fantasye
> wyll wryte his conseyte be it neuer so rude
> Be it virtuous vycyous wysdome or foly.

He concludes by saying that he writes without elegance, which is not appropriate to the subject and would distort the meaning. His direct assertion that the language is sufficient to render the "sentence," or idea, without mention of eloquence, and his evident dislike of "curyous termes," which certainly mean words borrowed for eloquence, show that he is not contending for the eloquential properties of his mother tongue.

Though he says nothing of borrowing in this work, in his next he makes clear enough his idea of the way in which the English language has become sufficient. Unlike his son, William Rastell, who a generation later was afraid to translate the statutes written in French or Latin into English because many terms contained therein could hardly be rendered by English words,[31] John issued a translation and abridgment of the laws of England in 1527, the preface to which goes into the historical reasons for the laws and decrees of England having in the past been expressed in French, and also into the reasons for his translation. Beginning with the statement that all laws should be in the language of the people who must obey them, he says that after the coming of William the Conqueror, a great number of his followers did not understand Anglo-Saxon, and

the seyd kyng and other grete wyse men of hys counsel perseyuyd and suposeyd that the vulgar tong which was then vsed in thys realme was in a manere but homely and rude nor had not so grete copy and haboundaunce of wordys as the Frenche tong than had nor that [the] vulgare thong [*sic*] was not of yt selff suffycyent to expoun and to declare the matter of such lawys and ordinauncis as they had determinid to be made for the good gouernaunce of the people so effectually and so substancyally as they cowd indyte them in the French tong.

After pointing out that Edward III in the thirty-sixth year of his reign decreed that all legal cases should be tried in English, he bestows great praise upon Henry VII, who

concyderynge and well parceyvyng that our vulgare Englysh tong maruellously amended and augmentyd by reason that dyuers famous clerkis and lerned men had translate and made many noble workis into our Englysh tong wherby there was mych more plenty and haboundance off Englysh vsed than there was in tymys past and by reason therof our vulgar tong so amplyfyed and suffycyent of hyt self to expoun any lawys or ordynancys which was nedeful to be made for the order of this realm/and also the same wyse prince consideryng that the vniuersal people of this realme had gret plesur and gaue themself greatly to the redynge of the vulgare Englysh tonge: ordeynyd and causyd that all the statutys and ordynauncys which were made for the commyn welth of this realm in hys days shuld be endytyd and wrytyn in the vulgare Englysh tonge.

After remarking that Henry VIII likewise ordered all laws made in his reign to be composed in English, he concludes: "All

[31] See *supra*, note 14.

whych goodly purposys and intentys in my mynde ofte tymys reuoluyde: hath causyd me to take thys lytyll payne to translate out of Frenche into Englisshe the abbreuiacyon of the statutys made before the fyrst yere of the reyn of our late souerin lorde kyng Henry the vii."[32] Rastell traces the amplification of the English vocabulary directly to translations made by learned men, and the only way in which this activity could contribute words to the vernacular was through borrowing. So he believes that by virtue of neologisms the English language is adequate for legal purposes, and also philosophical, since it is reasonable to suppose that his belief in the sufficiency of his native tongue, maintained in the interlude, rested on the same basis.

Rastell was a brother-in-law of St. Thomas More, who a few years later, as we have seen, denied the charge of barrenness advanced as a reason for not translating the Scriptures into the vernacular, and insisted upon the adequacy of the latter to meet all demands. However, he says nothing about borrowing but rests his case on the fact that in spoken discourse the mother tongue is quite sufficient to express all ideas. It is well worth noting that the earliest expressions of confidence in the mother tongue originated in More's circle.

But expressions of confidence in the adequacy of the English vocabulary are not confined to the group discussed above. Examples, though very infrequent, may be discovered much later, and in the last quarter of the century are fairly numerous. About the middle of the century Richard Sherry, probably influenced by Sir Thomas Elyot, boldly introduced what he considered neologisms into the title of *A treatise of Schemes and Tropes*, and then in the Epistle proceded to justify them on the ground that many familiar words had begun their careers as strange expressions.

I Doubt not but that the title of this treatise all straunge vnto our Englyshe eares, wil cause some men at the fyrst syghte to maruayle what the matter of it should meane: . . . These words, *Scheme* and *Trope*, are

---

[32] *An Abridgment of the Statutes*, 1527, "Prohemium." At the end of the book, 1520 is given as the date of publication. See *Typographical Antiquities*, begun by Joseph Ames and augmented by William Herbert, 3 vols., 1785, I, 328–29.

R. Sherry

not vsed in our Englishe tongue, neither bene they Englyshe wordes. No more be manye whiche nowe in oure tyme be made by continual vse, very familier to most men, and come so often in speakyng, that aswel is knowen amongest vs the meanyng of them, as if they had bene of oure owne natiue bloode. Who hath not in hys mouthe nowe thys worde Paraphrasis, homelies, vsurped, abolyshed, wyth manye other lyke?

Fully conscious of the extent to which the language had through neologizing been enriched and rendered adequate for wide use, his heart goes out in gratitude to those men who in the past had engaged in the practice.

Good cause haue we therefore to gyue thankes vnto certayne godlye and well learned men, which by their greate studye enrychynge our tongue both wyth matter and wordes, have endeuoured to make it so copyous and plentyfull that therein it maye compare wyth anye other whiche so euer is the best.

He realizes, however, that his attitude is not representative of the age, and he hastens to point out that the common conception of the poverty of the vernacular arises from the fact that men have seldom explored its potentialities, which are clearly revealed in the work of Chaucer and others in the past, and in the modern efforts of men like Sir Thomas Elyot.

It is not vnknowen that oure language for the barbarousnes and lacke of eloquence hathe bene complayned of, and yet not trewely, for anye defaut in the toungue it selfe, but rather for slackenes of our countrimen, whiche haue alwayes set lyght by searchyng out the elegance and proper speaches that be ful many in it: as plainly doth appere not only by the most excellent monumentes of our auncient forewriters, Gower, Chawcer and Lydgate, but also by the famous workes of many other later: inespeciall of the ryght worshipful knyght syr Thomas Eliot, which first in hys dictionarye as it were generallye searchinge oute the copye of oure language in all kynde of wordes and phrases, after that setting abrode goodlye monumentes of hys wytte, lernynge and industrye, aswell in historycall knowledge, as of eyther the Philosophies, hathe herebi declared the plentyfulnes of our mother tounge, loue toward hys country, hys tyme not spent in vanitye and tryfles.

Whereas Rastell was content to proclaim the sufficiency of English to express ideas and learning only, Sherry goes further and

would completely refute the universal charge of barbarousness
brought against his mother tongue, by firmly asserting the power
of eloquence inherent in it. For proof he refers specifically to
Wyatt, whose verse he must have read in manuscript.

What shuld I speake of that ornamente Syr Thomas Wyat? which beside
most excellente gyftes bothe of fortune and bodye, so flouryshed in the
eloquence of hys natiue tongue, that as he passed therin those wyth
whome he lyued, so was he lykelye to haue bene equal wyth anye other
before hym, had not enuious death to hastely beriued vs of thys iewel:
. . . Manye other there be yet lyuyng whose excellente wrytynges do
testifye wyth vs to be wordes apte and mete elogantly to declare oure
myndes in al kinds of Sciences.

As has been shown in previous chapters, the vernacular was
almost invariably considered barbarous, or uneloquent, so that
the view which Sherry reveals was most unusual; it was, indeed,
prophetic of the attitude which appeared in the last two decades
of the century. But a few years later, Thomas Phaer, in a postscript to his translation of the *Aeneid* (1558) affirmed his confidence in the poetic, or eloquential, properties of his native
tongue. Yet at the same time he recognizes the fact that his opinion is by no means characteristic of the period. It was, in fact,
to refute the disparagers of their own tongue that he undertook
his work "for defence of my countrye language which I haue
heard discommended of many, and estemyed of some to be more
than barbarous." As evidence of the poetic possibilities in the
language he offers his translation as "a gate," which, if

now the young writers will vouch saue to enter: they may finde in this
language, both large and abundant Campes of varietie, wherein they
maie gather innumberable sortes of all kinds of most beautifull floures,
figures, and phrases, not onely to supplie the imperfection of me: but also
to garnishe their owne verses with a more cleane and compendious order
of meter, than heretofore commonly hath ben accustomed.

One other expression of belief in the adequacy of the English language to meet intellectual needs is afforded by Richard
Eden. This adequacy, however, he ascribes to neologizing, and
he undoubtedly believed that the practice had by no means out-
lived its usefulness. It seems that Sir William Cecil had ex-

pressed doubt that a geographical treatise could be translated into the vernacular because of the inadequacy of its vocabulary, and in an open letter to him (1562), Richard Eden firmly dissents from this view:

And wheras the Master of Savoye tolde that your Honour sumwhat Doubted that the booke coulde not be translated into the Englysshe toonge, I assure you Honour that this I Dare saye without arrogancie, that to translate the variable historie of Plinie into our toonge, I wolde be ashamed to borowe so muche of the Latine as he Doth of the Greke, althowgh the Latine toonge be accompted ryche, and the Englysshe indigent and barbarous, as it hathe byn in tyme past, muche more then it nowe is, before it was enriched and amplyfied by sundry bookes in manner of all artes translated owt of Latine and other toonges into Englysshe . . . Agen, it is not vnknowen vnto your Honour that ons all toonges were barbarous and needie, before the knowleadge of thinges browght in plentie of woordes and names. Wherby it maye well appeare that men in the first age of the worlde, had a shorte language, consistinge of fewe woordes: which euer after increased by the knowleage and inuention of thinges.[33]

Eden perceived that the great increase of knowledge in his own day necessitated the expansion of the vocabulary, which he, like Rastell, believed was achieved by translators, who, in transferring the learning contained in other tongues to their native language, borrowed words from the originals. While most neologizers were content merely to cite the classical precedent, he goes further, and ascribes to English an even greater sufficiency than Latin possessed, though he suggests that this superiority was of recent origin, and though he recognizes the fact that in general the tongue was considered barren.

Although in the passages discussed above we find contrasting views regarding the sufficiency of the native language, one viewing it as inadequate and in need of borrowing, the other as adequate because of past borrowing, there is not such a great difference between them. Both recognize the need of the expansion of the language, in the past or in the present, and both approve of neologizing as the proper method of augmentation. We may confidently conclude, therefore, that there was a large

[33] *First Three books on America*, ed. Edward Arber, 1885, p. xliii.

body of opinion strongly supporting the importation of words, and thus may seriously question the usual opinion that the first three quarters of the century were opposed to neologizing,[34] an attitude directly opposed to the logic of the situation. Inasmuch as learning had in the past been confined to the learned languages, how was it possible for English to develop a proper terminology for all the branches of knowledge? When the strong educational urge of the century incited translators to transfer this learning to the vernacular, they could not but notice the cause of the difficulty encountered, and they could not but hit upon the remedy that most naturally suggested itself. Yet there was strong opposition to the method, an opposition that has not been thoroughly analyzed, so that the so-called puristic movement of the century has not been clearly understood.

[34] See the late Sir Walter Raleigh's introduction to an edition of Hoby's translation of Castiglione's *Courtier*, 1900, in the Tudor Translations. Raleigh includes Elyot among those opposed to neologizing!

CHAPTER IV

THE INADEQUATE LANGUAGE, PART II

W E have seen in the preceding chapter that many Renaissance Englishmen not only perceived the necessity of supplementing the vocabulary of their native tongue but also exerted themselves strenuously in that direction. The method most frequently advocated and adopted was that of borrowing from other tongues in general and the classical languages in particular. But unfortunately this method presented problems and complications. One of the most dominant attitudes of the century insisted upon the education of the people by means of books printed in the vernacular, and another, somewhat less dominant but still very conspicuous, sustained a definite hostility to eloquence, or rhetoric. Neologizing fell foul of both. The unlatined readers were not likely to be much edified by words introduced with little or no change from unfamiliar languages.[1] Some neologizers, especially Elyot, realized the difficulty and attempted to overcome it by explanations of borrowed words when first introduced, but others were not careful to follow this principle. As a result, the very end for which the mother tongue was employed was in danger of being defeated. Furthermore, the most widely recognized way of securing eloquence, and of showing learning, which was much the same thing, was through

---

[1] Speaking of neologisms William Fulwood says, "most part of our English termes, are very farre different from our vulgare and maternall speache, in such sort, that who so fully vnderstandeth not the Latin tongue, yea and also the Greek, can scarse vnderstand them." (*The Enimie of Idlenesse*, 1568, sig. K2ᵛ.) Ten years later Thomas Churchyard explains that, his learning being insufficient to treat "high" matters, "I haue chosen familier thinges too write vpon. And so presenting to the people that whiche they are beste acquainted withall. I shall not weery them with a straunge and statelie style, nor ouercharge their iudgements with farre fetched wordes or weightie deuises." (*A Prayse, and Reporte of Maister Martyne Forboishers Voyage to Meta Incognita*, dedication.) John Hart declares that in his writing he will eschew "manye an Inckhorne terme (which I could vse) bicause I regarde for whose sake I doe it." *An Orthographie*, 1569, fol. 21ʳ.

the introduction of Greek and Latin words. This fact caused the antirhetorical spirits of the age to look with disfavor upon what they considered an affectation of fine or eloquent writing. The antagonism thus engendered overshadowed all other elements in the opposition to loan words.

The frequency with which we come across weird-looking words in much of the vernacular literature of the day suggests the difficulty which the unlearned must have encountered in trying to understand what they read. The age itself pointed out glaring examples of obscure diction, to which others can easily be added. In his *Arte of Rhetorique*[2] (1553) Thomas Wilson has printed a letter too well known to be quoted here, which is so bad that "Some will thinke and sweare it too, that there was neuer any such thing written . . . but I will say thus much, and abide by it too, the like haue been made heretofore, and praised aboue the Moone." In Henry Huth's *Fugitive Poetical Tracts* (First Series, 1875) there may be found a poem (*c.* 1540) which is introduced in this incredible fashion:

An artificiall Apologie, articulerlye answerynge to the obstreperous Obgannynges of one W. S. Euometyd to the vituperacion of the tryumphant trollynge Thomas smyth. Repercussed by the ryght redolent and rotunde rethorician R. Smyth P. with annotacions of the mellifluous and misticall Master Mynterne, marked in the mergent for the enucliacion of certen obscure obelisques, to thende that the imprudent lector shulde not tytubate or hallucinate in the labyrinthes of this lucubratiuncle.

It is hardly possible to take this title with entire seriousness, and it may be that Wilson himself composed the letter which he offered as a horrible example. But there is certainly no reason to doubt the seriousness of the doctor who begins his "Prologue" in this manner: "Egregious doctours and maysters of the Eximiouse and Archane Science of physicke, of your Urbanitie Exasperate not your selfe agaynste me for makynge of this lytle volume of Phisycke."[3]

---

[2] Ed. G. H. Mair, 1909, p. 163. During this period reading must have been an exciting occupation, for there was no telling what verbal fauna one might come upon.

[3] Andrew Borde, *The Breuiary of Healthe*, 1552. As we shall soon see, many years later Angel Day quoted and discussed this passage. In view of

Since the purpose of those writing in English was to make clear their ideas, translated or original, to the uneducated public, a plain comprehensible diction was a desideratum of the highest value. For this reason borrowed words are frequently criticized for their obscurity, but it must be noticed that in almost every case where the charge is preferred, the neologisms attacked are looked upon as manifestations of affected eloquence. The obscurity of borrowed terms justifies criticism when the motive behind them is vanity. It is an argument against affected, not necessary neologisms. The inadequacy of the English vocabulary was too clearly realized to permit an indiscriminate attack on inkhorn terms. It is true that in the case of those who offer substitutes for neologisms, the difficulty of understanding the latter is frequently advanced as an argument in favor of their own devices, but for the most part the attack on borrowing was directed against the vanity of the practice. The necessity of neologizing to express ideas is either ignored or, more frequently,

---

present-day examples, it is not strange that medical terminology should have presented some extreme examples of hard words. In an English version of a German collection of medical prescriptions (Oswald Gaebelkhover, *The Boock of Physicke*, Dort, 1599, p. 42), we find such directions as: "contund together the rootes with the herbes in a Morter, then impose it in a nue Pot, infuse theron 3 pintes of water, and being closelye occludede let it seeth and ebulliat . . . and when it is sufficientlye decoctede . . . let it frigefy." Though the translator, A. M., says he is a German a long time removed from England, he gives complete evidence that he was familiar with the simple terms available in the English language, for he appends to his work a glossary of all the strange terms used therein, as for example, *frigifye* is defined as "cool," *ebulliated* as "boiled," *occluding* as "shutting," *impose* as "put," and *contunde* as "beat." Why he did not use the simpler words in the first place passeth understanding. Some of his hard words are no longer hard: *immature* (unripe), *humid* (wet), *agitate* (stir up), *altitude* (height), *excavate* (make hollow); but others, though in most cases logically formed, are posers: *amaritude* (bitterness), *foraminated* (holed), *effodicated* (digged), *floscles* (flowers), *cenation* (supper), *pluviutile* (rain), *periclitatione* (danger), *pistated* (baked), *gibbositie* (crookedness), *supranominated* (aforesaid). It is to be noted that most of his difficult terms occur in directions and not as names of the elements of his medicines. In another pharmacopoeia Thomas Gale assures the reader that "though my speach for want of vse, semth somewhat straunge to thee," yet in time it will become familiar. *An Antidotarie*, 1563, prefatory poem by W. Cuningham. This is found in *Certaine Workes of Chirurgerie, newly compiled and published by Thomas Gale, Maister in Chirurgerie*, 1563. Cf. Thomas Bastard, *Chrestoleros*, 1598, epigram 15.

conceded.[4] In the prologue to the *Eneydos* (1490) Caxton says, in respect to the French version of the *Aeneid* which he had determined to translate,

I . . . toke a penne and ynke and wrote a leef or tweyne/whyche I ouersawe agayn to corecte it/And whan I saw the fayr and straunge terms therin/I doubted that it sholde not please some gentylmen whiche late blamed me sayeng that in my translacyons I had ouer curyous termes which coude not be vnderstande of comyn peple.

At this early date objection to "curious" terms was raised on the basis of obscurity, but the use of the adjective strongly suggests that words introduced for rhetorical effect are meant. The suggestion is strengthened by Caxton's further statement that "some honest and grete clerkes haue ben with me and desired me to wryte the most curyous termes that I could fynde," for eloquence was closely associated with learning. Caxton concludes the discussion with the assurance, though rather shaky, that he had employed "the comyn termes that be dayli vsed [and] ben lighter to be vnderstonde."

Ascham, who has frequently been cited as a foe to neologizing, lays down a clear principle regarding the plain diction to be used in English compositions, but his words require careful analysis.

Ascham

He that wyll wryte well in any tongue, muste folowe thys councel of Aristotle, to speake as the common people do, to thinke as wise men do: and so shoulde euery man vnderstande hym, and the iudgement of wyse men alowe hym. Many English writers haue not done so, but vsinge straunge wordes as latin, french, and Italian, do make all thinges darke and harde. Ones I communed with a man whiche reasoned the englyshe tongue to be enryched and encreased therby, sayinge: Who wyll not prayse that feaste, where a man shall drinke at a diner, bothe wyne, ale and beere.[5]

---

[4] In the preface to his translation of Pierre de la Primaudaye's *The French Academie*, 1586, Thomas Bowes stresses soundness of substance as opposed to "the swelling froth of curious phrases," and so finds it necessary to explain why "many words vsed by the Author, and retained by me, are almost the same with the originall toongs from whence they were deriued." They are, he says, terms of art, and thus, having no English equivalents, must be borrowed. He furnishes a clear example of hostility to eloquence joined with approval of necessary borrowing.

[5] *Toxophilus*, 1545, dedication. Ascham thought that the "strange and

Ascham

That the copiousness of the English tongue was due to loan words was a view much more widely expressed near the end of the century. Ascham turns the inappropriate figure to his own purposes by saying that each of the drinks mentioned is good by itself, but that a mixture of all three would be quite unpalatable. He then expresses an important, and perhaps necessary, idea to the effect that Cicero "in folowynge Isocrates, Plato, and Demosthenes increased the latine tounge after another sorte. This waye, bycause dyuers men that write, do not know they can neyther folowe it, bycause of theyr ignorancie, nor yet will prayse it, for verye arrogancie." In spite of the incisive words which express the principle of a plain style, Ascham takes no unqualified stand against neologisms. What he objects to is ignorant, and perhaps, affected borrowing. Since Cicero justified (*De Finibus*, 3,3) his use of terms borrowed from the Greek on the grounds of necessity, the English writer evidently approved necessary neologizing.

Obscurity continues to be recognized as an evil inherent in borrowed terms, which, however, are generally represented as being introduced for eloquence rather than from necessity. Peter Ashton requests the dedicatee of one of his translations[6]

not so muche to regarde and loke for picked termes and straunge englishe wordes, (whiche in deed be not here) as for the playne settinge forthe of the sentence and right declaration of the history. For truly, throwghe out al this simple and rude translation, I studyed rather to vse the most playn and famylier english speche, then . . . inkhorne termes, (as they call them) whiche the common people, for lacke of latin, do not vnderstand. And . . . in this poynt I dyffer sumwhat from the most parte of writers now a dayes.

The translator indicates that in his day the prevailing view was favorable to neologizing, and his opposition to it is motivated by his dislike of affectation, for the expression "picked termes"

inkhorne termes of Hall's *Chronicle*" should be changed into "proper and commonlie vsed wordes." (*Ibid.*, fol. 43ʳ.) The quotation from Aristotle continued to figure in linguistic views for a long time. Cf. *The Brutish Thunderbolt*, by Pope Sixtus V, tr. Christopher Fetherstone, 1586, preface.

 [6] *A shorte treatise vpon the Turkes Chronicles, written in Italian by Paulus Jouius, bishop of Lucern*, 1546. Ashton translated a Latin version of the Italian original of Paolo Giovio.

is used over and over again to describe affected eloquence. Whereas he expresses a strong preference for plain diction over borrowed words, he has in mind neologisms of a rhetorical nature. The same attitude is revealed by a well-known Puritan, William Turner, who in commenting upon a religious treatise published two years after Aston's work, says,

It hath not so many newe french englishe blossomes as many bokes haue: but better fruite then thys hath, I thinke ye shal finde either none that writteth of this argument or else very few. This translatour hath applied him selfe as much as he can to find out the most plain and vsed wordes that be in england that men of all shyres of England maye the more easly percieue the meaneing of the boke. Summe nowe adayes more sekyng their owne glorye then the profite of the readers: writ so french Englishe and so latine that no man except he be both a latin man, a french man and also an englishe man shalbe able to vnderstande their writinge whose example I would disswade all men to folowe. For the people if they should haue any profite by such mennes laboures had nede of two dictionaries euer by them, one in french and an other in englise. Which thing because it is to tedious, it would pluck back all men from the redynge of suche good and christen bokes as they do translate.[7]

The use of such expressions as "french englishe blossomes" and "sekyng their owne glorye" clearly show that Turner is not thinking of necessary but of affected neologisms. He seems to be either blind or indifferent to the need of loan words frequently recognized by others, and he sees in them evidence only of the affected vanity of fine writing. Ulpian Fulwell views them in the same light, and holds that they serve but to obscure and discredit a work.

I confesse I haue not the gifte of flowing eloquence, neyther can I enterlace my phrase with Italian termes, nor powder my style with frenche Englishe or Inkhorne Rhetoricke, neyther cowche my matter vnder a cloake of curious inuentions, to feede the daintie eares of delicate yonkers. Also as I cannot: So if I could, I woulde not. For I see that manye men are so affected with these premisses, that manye good matters are

[7] *The sum of diuinitie drawen out of the holy scripture very necessarye, not onlye for Curates and yong studentes in diuinitie: but also for al christen men and women what so euer age thei be of. Drawen out of Latine into Englishe by Roberte Hutten*, 1548, "William Turner to the Reader." The original was by Johann Spangenberg.

obscured, the Aucthors encombred, the woorkes but meanely commended, and the Reader deceaued. For while he coueteth to come to the purpose, he is lead amasked in the wylde Desert of circumstance and digression, seeking farre and finding little, feeding his humor on pleasant woordes of slender wayght, guyded (or rather giddyed) with plaucible eloquence.[8]

This clear and sweeping indictment of exotic words requires little comment. Its phraseology makes it clear that they are envisaged only as evidence of affected eloquence, as unnecessary adornments that defeat the purpose for which the vernacular should be used.

The passages considered in the previous chapter, and to a less degree those discussed in this, make it evident that neologizing was both frequently approved and widely practiced. The opposition to it sprang from antipathy to affectation, and from a realization of the need of simplicity and clearness to meet the demands of the audience addressed. With the exception of Ascham, the purists so far mentioned are strangely silent regarding words borrowed from necessity. They constantly contrast the clear, plain style required of their reading public with the obscurity of affected terms without reference to the need of words to express ideas. There were, however, critics of the vernacular who did not ignore the problem. In fact, some of the authors who in the past have been most frequently cited as foes to neologizing have expressed themselves in words which when duly noticed point in a somewhat different direction.[9] Ascham is one; Thomas Wilson and Sir John Cheke, however, offer even

---

[8] *The Flower of Fame*, 1575, preface. Sometimes, though rarely, technical terms are discarded, as today, for the sake of the laymen to whom the work is addressed, with no reference to eloquence. The author of a treatise on bookkeeping says, "Neither haue I had so muche respecte, to please suche as haue perfect knowledge in this order of accomptes (with subtle tearmes of other languages) but rather vsed as plain and familier speache, in our owne language, as I could deuise, whereby the learners, the soner might be instructed." James Peele, *The maner and fourme how to kepe a perfecte reconyng, after the order of the moste worthie and notable accompte of Debitour and Creditour*, 1553, preface.

[9] The puristic movement has been treated by Wilhelm Prein in *Puristische Strömungen im 16. Jahrhundert. Ein Beitrag zur englischen Sprachgeschichte.* Eikel i.w., 1909.

clearer examples. The former at first seems to express himself in unequivocal language.

Qualified opposition

T. Wilson

Among all other lessons this should first be learned, that wee neuer affect any straunge ynkehorne termes, but to speake as is commonly receiued: neither seeking to be ouer fine, nor yet liuing ouer-carelesse vsing our speeche as most men doe, and ordering our wittes as the fewest haue done. Some seeke so far for outlandish English, that they forget altogether their mothers language. And I dare sweare this, if some of their mothers were aliue, thei were not able to tell what they say: and yet these fine English clerkes will say, they speake in their mother tongue, if a man should charge them for counterfeiting the Kings English. Some farre iourneyed gentleman at their returne home, like as they loue to goe in forraine apparell, so thei wil pouder their talke with ouersea language. He that commeth lately out of Fraunce, will talke French English and neuer blush at the matter. An other chops in with English Italienated, and applieth the Italian phrase to our English speaking, the which is, as if an Oratour that professeth to vtter his mind in plaine Latine, would needs speake Poetrie, and farre fetched colours of straunge antiquitie . . . The vnlearned or foolish phantasticall, that smelles but of learning (such fellowes as haue seen learned men in their daies) wil so Latin their tongues, that the simple can not but wonder at their talke, and thinke surely they speake by some reuelation. I know them that thinke *Rhetorique* to stande wholie vpon darke wordes, and hee that can catche an ynke horne terme by the taile, him they coumpt to be a fine Englishman, and a good *Rhetorician*.

Wilson's determined opposition to borrowed words obviously has reference only to those employed for the purpose of vain eloquence. In sharp contrast to this attitude is his opinion of words borrowed from necessity, for of these he heartily approves.

Now whereas wordes be receiued, aswell Greeke as Latine, to set forth our meaning in the English tongue, either for lacke of store, or els because we would enrich the language: it is well doen to vse them, and no man therein can be charged for any affectation, when all other are agreed to followe the same waie. There is no man agreeued when he heareth (Letters Patents) and yet Patentes is Latine, and signifieth open to all men. The Communion is a fellowship, or a comming together, rather Latin then English: the kings prerogatiue declareth his power roiall aboue all other, and yet I know no man greeued for these termes, being vsed in their place, nor yet any one suspected of affectation when such generall wordes are spoken. The folie is espied, when either we will vse such wordes as fewe men do vse, or vse them out of place, when an other might serue much better.[10]

Like Ascham, he closes his discussion with a reference to Cicero as a guide in the use of words. Wilson recognizes the necessity of neologisms, and he sanctions those which have been received into the language and appear familiar and natural. He does not, however, reveal how a new term can become familiar without passing through a period of strangeness. As may be noted in the quotations given in this chapter, the strangeness of loan words is so frequently remarked as to suggest that it operated strongly against their adoption. Again and again neologizers insist that use will render familiar and acceptable the words which they are introducing into the language.

Cheke

Perhaps even more than Wilson, Sir John Cheke has been represented as an enemy to inkhorn terms, but his position is essentially that of his predecessor. Evidently Sir Thomas Hoby had sent the manuscript of his translation of Castiglione's *Courtier* to Cheke for comment, for in a letter dated July 16, 1557, and later appended to the printed volume (1561), Sir John praises the translation and preface in general, but remarks that he has taken pains to change some of the words, "which might verie well be let aloan, but that I am verie curious in mi freendes matters, not to determijn, but to debaat what is best." In justification of his action he says,

I am of this opinion that our own tung shold be written cleane and pure, vnmixt and vnmangled with borowing of other tunges, wherein if we take not heed bi tijm, euer borowing and neuer payeng, she shall be fain to keep her house as bankrupt. For then doth our tung naturallie and praisablie vtter her meaning, whan she bouroweth no conterfeitness of other tunges to attire her self withall, but vseth plainlie her own with such shift, as nature, craft, experiens and folowing of other excellent doth lead her vnto.

Had Cheke stopped here, he would necessarily be considered a determined foe to loan words, but he continues in a different vein:

[10] *The Arte of Rhetorique*, ed. G. H. Mair, 1909, pp. 162–65. The rhetoric was published in 1553.

. . . if she [the language] want at ani tijm (as being vnperfight she must) yet let her borow with suche bashfulnes that it mai appeer, that if either the mould of our own tung could serue vs to fascion a woord of our own, or if the old denisoned wordes could content and ease this neede we wold not boldly venture of vnknowen wordes. This I say not for reproof of you, who haue scarslie and necessarily vsed whear occasion serueth a strange word so, as it seemeth to grow out of the matter and not to be sought for: but for mijn own defens, who might be counted ouer-straight a deemer of thinges, if I gaue not thys account to you . . . of mi marring this your handiwork.

Cheke

Cheke's position is clear. He recognizes the insufficiency of the vernacular, and he approves of borrowing to overcome the defect. But he insists that the practice be adopted only when strictly necessary, and when all other means have been exhausted, and that no words be "sought for," evidently for rhetorical effect. Ascham, Wilson, and Cheke are opposed to neologizing only so far as the practice made for affected eloquence, and they may legitimately be classed with Elyot, Udall, Rastell, and others considered in the preceding chapter, who upheld the necessary augmentation of their native tongue.

N.B.

Although the sentiment in favor of necessary borrowing was far in the preponderance, the opposition to unnecessary or "eloquent" neologizing was all but unanimous. Many examples could be added to those already cited, but only a few need be given. The honest Grafton seriously objected to the bombastic neologisms used in a petition to Richard II.[11] John Charlton[12] assures us that "The studious sercher of wisdom will more seriouslie pursue the holsom and necessarie instructions for life, then the exquisite situation of wordes, and will rather couet fruit-full lessons, and good admonicions, than sugred sentences, ora-

---

[11] "Sir John Bushe in all his prepositions to the king, did not onely attribute to him worldly honours, but diuyne names, inuentyng flatteryng wordes, and vnused termes, and to a mortall man not conuenient, for as oft as he spake vnto the king in his Throne he cast his handes abrode, as he had adoured and worshipped God, besechyng his excelse, high, and adorant Maisetie, that he woulde witsafe to graunt him this or that." *A Chronicle at large and meere History of the affayres of Englande*, 1569, II, 390.

[12] Cornelius Valerius, *The Casket of Iewels: Contaynynge a playne description of Morall Philosophie*, tr. I. C., 1571, translator's preface.

torical trickes, and outlandish termes." Richard Robinson is comforted with the thought that though his *Rewarde of Wickednesse* (1574) "bee a Drousie Dreaming peece of worke, neither garnished with *Rhetoricke, Eloquence, Curious* tearmes, nor pleasaunt matter, to purchase prayse of daintie Dames, and fantastical Knights of *Cupid's Court:* (As it is not painted with these properties) so I am assured that your worship doth not mislike the want thereof."[13] It is not strange that ambitious preachers in their desire to be eloquent should have employed one widely recognized means of being so, and in view of the strong antirhetorical spirit frequently manifested in matters pertaining to religion, it appears equally natural that strong objection to such a practice should have been offered. Lawrence Chaderton, first master of Emanuel College, Cambridge, a college with which Puritanism was associated, complains that "many doe stuffe their sermons with new deuised words, and affected speaches of vanitie, not being content with the words which the holy Ghost teacheth [probably in the English translation]."[14] The impropriety of rhetoric, as well as the desirability of familiar language insisted upon by most of those using the vernacular, was all the more

[13] See the "Epistle Dedicatorie." William Bourne tells the reader not to "looke for fyne or eloquent schole termes" in his simple treatise. (*A booke called the Treasure for traueilers,* 1578, preface.) Nicholas Grimald attacks translations "uttered with ynkhorne termes, and not with vsuall words: or . . . phrased with wrasted, or farrefetched fourmes of speche." (*Marcus Tullius Ciceroes thre bokes of duties,* 1556, preface.) William Fulwood follows the golden mean in his linguistic views, holding that "the fayrest language that may bee, is the common and familiar speache, and not that of rare and diffused phrases, or inckhorne termes skummed from the Latin, nor of to base termes and barbarous, or termes vnknowne except in certain places . . ." *The Enimie of Idlenesse,* 1568, sig. B4ᵛ.

[14] *An excellent and godly sermon preached at Paules Crosse the xxvi daye of October 1578* (1580), sig. F6ᵛ. Paul's Cross seems to have been a favorite place for the delivery of antirhetorical sermons. In one preached there on August 24, 1578, John Stockwood eschews "all rhetorical flourishes," "curious and picked out words and termes," and "painted, labored, and of purpose sought for eloquence . . . knowing that the worde of the Lorde simply and plainly handled, is able without the help of the persuading speeche of mans wisdome, to pierce even to the hart." In another delivered on January 3, 1580, William Fisher warns his congregation not to look for "any wanton Eloquence too make you too wonder at: neither come I in any brauery of wordes to amase you withall."

apparent in the imparting of religious truth to the uneducated.[15]

Various factors were responsible for the dissatisfaction with linguistic borrowing. Foremost among them was concern over the obscurity produced by the practice, which ran counter to the end sought by users of the vernacular. The affectation of the borrowers disgusted even those who were not unsympathetic with eloquence, and the fact that loan words were considered, and were employed as, an important rhetorical device repelled the antirhetorical spirits of the age. Still another factor is revealed in the antagonism generated by the misuse of borrowed words. In the desire to be "fine," neologizers were not always careful in regard to the meaning of their rhetorical importations. A Puritan participant in the vestiarian controversy says to his opponent:

As yow deligiht in ynkehorne terms, and borowed spechis, as exagerat, diuulged, dispensed, comprehension, expend, concorde, infarce, expect, intimate, etc. so somtime yow vse them as one not well acquainted with them. Whan yow say publickly diuulged, *Non loqueris vulgo.* yow speke not to the common people, yow can speke twise as much, as yow doe.[16]

We have one extended contemporary criticism of the misuse of borrowed terms. Angel Day, the author of a book on rhetoric, had his attention called to the preface of Andrew Borde's *Breuiary of Healthe* (1552), cited earlier in this chapter, and he introduced it as a horrible example into his discussion of the improper use of words. "This errour," he says,

is not onely common to the vnlearned, for as well this one, who in his profession (as I was enformed by him that shewed me the letter) was well reputed of, but also some of the forwarder sort, only by affectation of words, which they haue vsed, haue bene misliked, and yet learned ynough. Among which a Doctor of Physicke long since, intending to be very eloquent in words, and such as euery Carter should not conceiue of, began an Epistle to a booke by him published in this sort: wherein secondly appeareth this errour of old improper or new coyned tearmes, and this was the forme.

[15] See William Haller, *The Rise of Puritanism*, 1938, chap. iv, "The Rhetoric of the Spirit."

[16] *An answere For The Tyme, To The Examination put in print, with out the authours name, pretending to mayntayne the apparrell prescribed against the declaration of the mynisters of London* (Geneva?), 1566, sig. A6ʳ.

Egregious Doctors and masters of the eximious and Archane Science of Physicke, of your Urbanitie exasperate not your selues against mee, for making of this little volume of Physick. Considering that my pretense is for an vtilitie and a common wealth. And this is not only, but also I doe it for no detriment but for a preferment of your laudable science, that euery man shuld esteeme, repute and regard the excellent faculty. And also you to be extolled and highly preferred, that hath and doth studie, practise and labor this said Archane Science, to the which none inartious persons, can nor shal attaine to the knowledge: yet notwithstanding fooles and insipient persons, yea and many the which doth think themselues wise (the which in this faculty be fools indeed) wil enterprise to smatter, etc. Was there euer seene from a learned man a more preposterous and confused kind of writing, farced with so many and such odde coyned tearmes in so litle vttering? . . . Neuerthelesse howe wise so euer stood his imaginatione: this one thing do I knowe, that diuers to whome I haue showed the booke haue very hartily laughed in perusing the parts of his writing. For these *egregious, eximious, vrbanitie,* and *exasperate,* although the wordes be in some sort tollerable, yet because any of them are amongst vs very rarely vsed, and in this writing two of them especially very vnproperly placed, the maner thereof soundeth (in mine opinion) nothing pleasant. In so much as *exasperate* is properly to set him in a farther rage, that is alreadie furiously bent in a thing, and besides, by the action of another man then himself, who as it were of a resolute wil and meaning, would goe about to procure it, so that it may be wel saide, *hee did exasperate his furies the more, by inducing such a speach or such an acte.* . . . *Urbanitie* likewise . . . [is a] word not common amongst vs, nor so apt to the sence as if he had said, *your curtesie, your modestie* . . . Then his comming in with *arcane science, inartious fooles* and *insipient persons,* had it not bene lesse improper, if he had said *profound science,* and *vnskilfull* or *vnlearned,* for *inartious,* and to haue contented himselfe with his fools, without adding to the same *insipient persons* . . . *And many the which* . . . Here is *the which and the which,* a phrase neuer with vs accustomed, nor with any good writer in his time (which was not many yeares since) the sence whereof might in this sort more plainely bee deliuered.[17]

Day concludes with the principle that in the use of diction congruity and meaning must be carefully observed, "whereby he [the learner] shall avoid the like errour, and absurditie in con-

[17] *The English Secretorie,* 1595 (1586), pp. 5–7.

ueyance hereby expressed and already so much reprehended."
Since Elyot had anticipated Day in criticism of misused neologisms by more than a half-century, the fault was indeed of long
standing. Only too frequently the borrower of eloquent terms
must have been so blinded by their glory as not to scrutinize their
meaning, so that the inaccuracy of such words must often have
been as conspicuous to the learned as their strangeness was to the
unlearned.

If the educated were likely to misuse inkhorn terms in this
fashion, what could be expected of the unlearned who aped
them? Since the latter furnished few authors, much less evidence of their linguistic efforts has survived, but references to
them afford indubitable proof that they did exist. At the beginning of the quotation given above, Angel Day indicates that
the misuse of unfamiliar terms was common to the unlatined.
John Hart, one of the advocates of the simplified-spelling re-   *J. Hart*
form of the day, is very explicit in what he has to say about this
misuse. In expressing the usual antagonism to affected neologizing, he says,

it must needes be, that either blind affectation in some, and nice curiositie,
or vaine imitation in others, haue caused our predecessors to consent to
certaine straunge termes, when their owne mother speach might much
better expresse the qualitie of the thing (from the mother and nurse)
to their succession.

But the fault he finds lies not so much in the eloquence secured
in this fashion, of which he seems to approve where the learned
are concerned, as in the resulting obscurity and in the mistakes
which the unlearned are led to make.

Howbeit, I must confesse it [borrowing] beautifieth an Orators tale,
which knoweth what he speaketh, and to whom: but it hindereth the
vnlerned from vnderstanding of the matter, and causeth many of the
Countrie men to speake chalke for cheese, and so nickname such straunge
tearmes as it pleaseth many well to heare them: as to say for temperate,
temporall: for surrender, sullender: for stature, statute: for abiect,   *abiect:*
obiect: for heare, heier: certisfied, for both certified, and satisfied: dis-   *obiect*
pence, for suspence: defende, for offende: surgiant, for surgian: which
the French term *chirurgian*, which is flesh clenser.

After giving a list of words taken over in the past from the French language,[18] he says,

> And yet were our Predecessours contented for infinit other wordes, as *Arbalestrier*, for Crossebowmaker: and such like (as easie in French, as those aboue) to kepe them in their mother tongue, as good reason was, except they would haue chaunged the whole Englishe Saxon language, to the French tongue, or nere vnto it. These and such like hinderances to the rude, haue so long continued, as they are hard to be reformed. And though the rude doe endeuour to immitate the learned, though it be to a contrarye sense: yet I meruaile howe by any meanes the lyke shoulde come in print, seeing it doth passe so many handes, as for this word *Mestier* in French, signifying handie craft, I finde imprinted by the worde misterie, signifying a worde or ceremonie, sounding or shewing one thing, and meaning another.[19]

Hart is willing to concede to the learned the right to be eloquent, but he stresses the injurious effects of the practice both in closing the doors of knowledge to the uneducated and in the corruption of the language through ignorant misuse and distortion of words, which in their deformed state and misunderstood

[18] "In like maner the French and we doe vse Biscuyte, which signifieth twise baekt: and for Ouenheader, furner, deriued from *Four* an Ouen: *Barbier* of *Barbe*, we saye Barber, which deriued from the Englishe Primitiue Bearde, should by like reason be in English bearder: the like for *Rasoer* a shaver, or euen maker: . . . a *garde*, or warde, a keepe or defence: a *Gardebras*, or wardebras, an arme keeper: a *Portier* a gate wayter, or gater: a *Porteur*, a bearer, or burdener: a *Pantier* or Pantler, a Breadseruer: a *Bottelier*, a Bottelseruer: a *Cordoanier*, a Shoonmaker: a *Marenier*, a Seaman, or sayler: a *Scribe*, or Scriuener, a Plumber, of *Plumb*, for Lead: a *Tailour*, a cutter, or shaper, as we say for a woman Shapester: a *Marchaunt* a Monger, a *Lauadier* and *Lauandiere*, a washer, and many others."

[19] *A Methode or comfortable beginning for all vnlearned, whereby they may bee taught to read English, in a very short time, with pleasure: So profitable as straunge, put in light by,* I. H. Chester Heralt, 1570, preface. Cf. Thomas Wilson's *Arte of Rhetorique*, 1560 (1553), fol. 84ʳ; and Henry Peacham's *Garden of Eloquence*, 1577, sig. G2ᵛ. Peacham describes this fault as "Cacozelon, an ill imitation or affection, that is, when words be vsed ouerthwartly, or contrarily for want of iudgement, vsed of foolish folk, who coueting to tell an eloquent tale, doe deface that which they would fainest beautifie, men not being content to speake plaine english, doe desire to vs wordes borowed of the latine tongue, imitatyng learned men, when they knowe no more their signification, then a Goose, and therefore many tymes they apply them so contrarily, that wyse men are enforced to laugh at their folly, and absurditie."

meaning sometimes reach print and become established in the language.

Since the attack on imported words was based on their obscurity and vain eloquence, it was inevitable that the translation of the Bible should have become involved in the problem. Repugnance to eloquence was stronger and the need for clearness greater in religious matters than in any other field. Before the middle of the century Sir John Cheke objected so strenuously to the number of foreign terms which translators of the Scriptures had found necessary to retain in their versions that he began a translation of his own, which was to contain only words traditionally English. This attitude may have been induced in him by Bishop Gardiner, his opponent in the controversy over the proper pronunciation of Greek, who, in a convocation of February 16, 1542, called to revise the translation of the New Testament, proposed ninety-nine words which he held to be sacred and therefore not to be translated by English terms. This action Cheke considered an obvious attempt on the part of the Bishop and his associates to render the English version useless to the common people through the obscurity of its diction.[20] On the other hand, Gardiner impugned Cheke's motive in demanding simplicity and plainness, and attempted to show that some Latin words cannot be rendered by familiar English terms. Cyprian, he says,

vseth the worde *Panis*, and calleth the blessed sacramente *sacramentalem panem*, whiche wordes be not perfitely expressed in englysh, if in translation it were termed sacramental bread (as malicious fayned simplicitie pretendeth) but rather sacramental fode, for *Panis* in latyn is a general word, and signifieth not only bread wherwith men be fed, but also all other nourriture wherwith man is susteined, which the word (bread) doth not in englysh . . . Now if any man shall vnder pretence of symple playne speache cal always that breade in English which he findeth

<hr>

[20] *The Gospel according to Saint Matthew and Part of the First Chapter of the Gospel according to Saint Mark translated into English from the Greek, with Original Notes, By Sir John Cheke, Knight, formerly Regius Professor of Greek and Public Orator in the University of Cambridge afterwards Tutor, Privy Counsellor and Secretary of State to King Edward VI*, ed. James Goodwin, 1843, pp. 11–12.

in laten called *panis*, he myghte as well . . . call it [sella] in englysh a saddell.[21]

It was, however, the Catholic translation of the Bible that made the problem of neologizing in this field acute. The Protestant version coerced the Catholics to issue one of their own to compete with it among the masses.[22] In order to avoid heretical mistakes, of which they had accused the Protestant Bible, and since, perhaps, they were not very much concerned over the clearness of their rendering, the papists retained a large number of the words of the original texts, and thus laid themselves open to the charge of neologizing. Indeed, the preface to their translation of the New Testament[23] anticipated the accusation of ink-

---

[21] *A Detection of the Deuils Sophistrie, wherwith he robbeth the vnlearned people, of the true byleef, in the most blessed Sacrament of the aulter,* 1546, fol. 79[v]. Elsewhere he speaks of "sophistrie, cloked vnder pretence of plaines." *Ibid.,* fol. 81[r].

[22] In view of their censure of the Protestants for translating the Bible, the Catholics found it necessary to explain the reasons for their own version. This they did in the preface to their translation of the New Testament, 1582, which in part reads as follow: "Which translation we doe not for all that publish, vpon erroneous opinion of necessitie, that the holy Scriptures should alwaies be in our mother tonge, or that they ought or were ordained by God, to be read indifferently of all, or could be easily vnderstood of euery one that readeth or heareth them in a knowen language: or that they were not often through mans malice or infirmitie, pernicious and much hurtful to many: or that we generally and absolutely deemed it more conuenient in it self, and more agreeable to Gods word and honour or edification of the faithful, to haue them turned into vulgar tonges, then to be kept and studied only in the Ecclesiastical learned languages: Not for these nor any such like causes doe we translate this sacred booke, but vpon special consideration of the present time, state and condition of our countrie, vnto which, diuers things are either necessarie, or profitable and medicinable now, that otherwise in the peace of the Church were neither much requisite, nor perchance wholy tolerable."

[23] *The New Testament of Iesvs Christ, Translated Faithfvlly into English, out of the authentical Latin, according to the best corrected copies of the same, diligently conferred with the Greeke and other editions in diuers languages: With Arguments of bookes and chapters, Annotations, and other necessarie helpes, for the better vnderstanding of the text, and specially for the discouerie of the Corruptions of diuers late translations, and for cleering the Controversies in religion of these daies: In the English College of Rhemes . . . Printed at Rhemes by Iohn Fogny,* 1582. More than a quarter of a century later appeared their translation of the Old Testament only, but with the title: *The Holie Bible Faithfully translated into English, out of the Authentical Latin . . . By the English College of Doway,* 1609.

horn terms, and defended them on the ground that

In this our Translation, because we wish it to be most sincere, as becometh a Catholike translation, and haue endeuoured so to make it: we are very precise and religious in folowin our copie the old vulgar approued Latin: not onely in sense, which we hope we alwaies doe, but sometime in very wordes also and phrases, which may seeme to the vulgar Reader and to common English eares not yet acquainted therewith, rudeness or ignorance: but to the discrete Reader that deepely weigheth and considereth the importance of sacred wordes and speaches, and how easily the voluntarie Translatour may misse the true sense of the Holy Ghost, we doubt not but our consideration and doing therein, shal seeme reasonable and necessarie: yea and that al sortes of Catholike Readers wil in short time thinke that familiar, which at the first may seeme strange, and wil esteeme it more, when they shal otherwise be taught to vnderstand it, then if it were the common knowen English.

Since the Catholics had to be on guard not to make such mistakes as those with which they charged the Protestants, they were compelled to employ and to defend words retained from the original in the same way in which secular writers had upheld borrowing—namely, that necessity justified the practice, and that strange words would in the course of time become familiar. The preface also calls attention to the fact that although the Protestants had in some cases retained the original expressions, in others they had inconsistently attempted to translate words that could not with any more reason be rendered by English terms, with the result that heretical corruptions had been introduced.[24] And finally the preface seeks cover under the example of secular neologizing: "And why should we be squeamish at new words or phrases in the Scripture, which are necessarie: when we do easily admit and folow new words coyned in court and in courtly or other secular writings." In short, words borrowed from necessity in biblical translations are certainly as permissible as words introduced for eloquence in worldly writings.

This explanation, however, did not forestall Protestant at-

---

[24] For instance, "Pentecost" was retained, but "Azymes" was, presumably, falsely translated by "the feast of sweete bread." Among the neologisms which the preface defends are "Alleluia," "Pasche," "neophyte," "prepuce," "paraclete," and "euangelize."

tacks, for in the next year, Anthony Marten, in the preface to his translation of Pietro Vermigli's *Common Places* (1583), utilized some of the traditional arguments against the practice.

We confesse that we in our translations are not so precise, but that when the words of the Greeke, or Hebrue, or Latine be so difficult, as they cannot be liuelie expressed word for word, especiallie in the English toong, we haue sometimes added a necessarie word by the sense of the place to be vnderstood; which you haue not doone in your translation of the new testament: and therefore haue you left such vnperfect sentences, and haue giuen such absurd terms as euerie good man dooth pitie and lament your great fruitlesse labour . . . [in] your phantasticall and new deuised termes.

As examples of "your new inkpot termes" he mentions "Chalice," "penance," "superstantial," "impudicitie," "longanimitie," "præcursor," "euangelize," "scandalize," "contristate," "propiciate,"

and infinite other such obscure and new inuented words; which might easilie enough with some small Periphrasis, without hinderance of the sense, haue been put in plaine English . . . What need the common people be now set to schoole to their dieng daie, before they can learne that out of Latin, by strange and difficult words, which alreadie they know as perfectlie as their Pater noster in plaine English, with a long acquainted custome? Was this Christs and his Apostles maner of teaching? Did they not speake in the plainest termes they could possible deuise, to make those whom they spake vnto vnderstand them?

Though there is an occasional glance at the vanity and fantastical nature of the Catholic neologisms, the Protestant objectors are generally concerned with the obscurity which foreign terms introduced into vernacular versions of the Bible, and which thus defeated the very important end of such versions. In fact, we perceive in some of their arguments the suggestion that the Catholics were deliberately trying to nullify the value of their translation and to withhold from the unlearned that which they were ostensibly seeking to impart. William Fulke maintains that the Catholic Bible is "obscured without anie necessarie or iust cause, with suche a multitude of so strange and vnusuall termes, as to the ignorant are no lesse difficult to vnderstande, than the Latine or Greeke it self."[25] A few years later George Wither declared that the Catholics by their expressions sought to convince men that the Scriptures were more obscure and dark than they really were, and for this reason they deliberately avoided perspicuity and plainness: "For they haue both hunted for words of purpose, which the people do not vnderstand, as superstantiall, didrachmes, cense, stater, scandall . . . and such like."[26]

In the preface to their translation of the Old Testament, which repeats much that is contained in the preface to their version of the New, the Catholics attempted to answer the charge of intentional obscurity by pleading, as other advocates of neologizing had done, the inadequacy of the English language.

Again, for necessitie, English not hauing a name, or sufficient terme, we either kepe the word, as we find it, or only turne it to our English termination, because it would otherwise require manie wordes in English, to signifie one word of an other tongue. In which cases, we commonly put the explication in the margent. Briefly our Apologie is easie against Protestants; because they also reserue some words in the original tongues, not translated into English: as *Sabbath, Ephod, Pentecost, Proselyte,* and some others. The sense wherof is in dede as soone lerned, as if they were turned so nere as is possible into English. And why then may we not say *Prepuce, Phase,* or *Pasch, Azimes, Breades of Proposition, Holo-*

---

[25] *A Defense of the sincere and true Translations of the holie Scriptures into the English tong, against the manifolde cauils, friuolous quarels, and impudent slaunders of Gregorie Martin, one of the readers of Popish diuinitie in the trayterous Seminarie of Rhemes,* 1583, dedication. Elsewhere he gives a definite example of the obscurity caused by neologisms: "S. Paule in deede speaketh plainely in Greeke, but if you speake English and say schismes, fortie thousand of the people in England will sweare they vnderstande you not." (*Ibid.,* p. 135.) The accusation of intended obscurity continues as late as the second half of the next century. See Peter Heylyn, *Observations on the Historie of the Reign of King Charles,* 1656, pp. 1–7.

[26] See *A View of the Marginal Notes of the Popish Testament, translated into English by the English fugitiue Papists resiant at Rhemes in France,* 1588, dedication. Even in the next century, on the eve of the Puritan triumph, the Protestants are still condemning the neologisms of the Catholic translation of the Bible. Edward Leigh declares that "The *Rhemists* Translation of the New Testament, is so full of affected phrases and ink-horne termes, obscure and strange words, that it is easie to perceive they desired rather to be admired than vnderstood by the common people." *Critica Sacra,* 1639, preface.

caust, and the like? rather then as the Protestantes translate them: *For-skinne, Passeouer, The feast of sweete breades, Burnt Offerings.* etc."[27]

As we have already seen, there had been little objection in secular literature to terms borrowed from necessity, though in such cases, immediate explanation of the word in simple terms had been urged. Fulke would extend that privilege even to biblical translations, laying down the rule

that if any Greeke termes, or words of other language, haue of long time bene vsurped in our English language, the true vnderstanding of which is vnknownen at this day, to the common people: . . . the same termes may be either in translation, or exposition, set out plainly, to enforme the simplicitie of the ignorant, by such wordes, as of them are better vnderstoode.[28]

The two quotations just given show that at some points Catholic and Protestant attitudes almost converged, and it is quite possible that the Protestants would have been more lenient in their criticism of the practice of their adversaries had they not felt that the latter had in their version retained words from the original, not because there were possibly no English equivalents, but in order to render the text obscure. The earlier attacks on the Protestant translations made them suspect that the papists, even in their vernacular renderings of the Bible, were attempting to withhold the Gospel from the common people.[29]

Though, in general, the affected eloquence and the obscurity of neologisms were responsible for the repugnance felt toward them, a third factor, the nationalistic spirit, is discernible. Its

[27] A list of these untranslated terms may be found in Thomas Cartwright's *A Confutation of the Rhemists Translation, Glosses and Annotations on The New Testament,* 1618, which gives some sixty words and their definitions under the heading, "The Explication of certain Words in the Rhemists Translation, not familiar to the vulgar Reader, which (if we may beleeve them) might not conveniently bee vttered otherwise."

[28] *A Defense of the sincere and true Translations of the holie Scriptures,* 1583, p. 132.

[29] The Catholics also maintained that some original words should be retained because of their religious connotations and because of the low and worldly connotations of their humble English equivalents. From this position Fulke heartily dissents: "Is there more profanenesse and secularitie in the Englishe worde Elders, than in the Latine worde *Maiores natu,* or in your Frenchenglishe terme, Auncients?" *Ibid,* p. 167.

importance has perhaps been exaggerated, but it can by no means be ignored.[30] George Gascoigne's view of the vernacular is inspired entirely by this spirit. "I have," he says, "rather regarde to make our native language commendable in it selfe, than gay with the feathers of straunge birdes."[31] In his instructions to poets (1575) his patriotism incites him to recommend the use of monosyllables, though they were in general considered rather intractable in poetry.

> Here by the way I thinke it not amisse to forewarne you that you thrust as few wordes of many sillables into your verse as may be: and hereunto I might alledge many reasons: first that the most aunctient English wordes are of one sillable, so that the more monasyllables that you use, the truer Englishman you shall seeme, and the lesse you shall smell of the Inkehorne.[32]

Gascoigne staunchly maintains that an Englishman should write in the English language uncontaminated by foreign elements. His scorn of borrowed terms seems to have no other source but his nationalism. Yet in another passage he hints that the vernacular of his day is not entirely adequate, but rather than borrow from other tongues he seeks a remedy elsewhere.

> Next unto this, I have always been of opinion, that it is not unpossible eyther in Poemes or in Prose too write both compendiously, and perfectly in our Englishe tongue. And therefore although I challenge not vnto my selfe the name of an English Poet, yet may the Reader finde oute in my wrytings, that I have more faulted in keeping the olde English wordes (*quamvis iam obsoleta*) than in borrowing of other languages, such Epithetes and Adjectiues as smell of the Inkhorne.[33]

Realizing that the English vocabulary was inadequate, but feeling a nationalistic aversion to taking words from other tongues, he seeks to supply the need by calling back into use

[30] See *Elizabethan Critical Essays*, ed. G. G. Smith, I, lv. When we note that the period which witnessed the most favorable attitude toward borrowing also entertained the strongest nationalistic feelings, we are warned from attributing to nationalism any great part of the opposition to neologizing.

[31] *Complete Works*, ed. J. W. Cunliffe, 1907, I, 6.

[32] *Ibid.*, I, 468. Gascoigne, however, also looked upon monosyllables as poetically effective as well as patriotic, for three years earlier he had ranked them among the poetic virtues of the language.

[33] *Ibid.*, I, 5.

words which had dropped out of the language. Nor was he alone in adopting this method of augmenting the vernacular.

Archaism   The idea of substituting old words for neologisms can be traced back to the preceding century. In that remarkable prologue to the *Eneydos* (1490), to which reference has already been made, Caxton speaks of some gentlemen who

> blamed me sayeng that in my translacyons I had ouer curyous termes whiche coude not be vnderstande of comyn peple/and desired me to vse olde and homely termes in my translacyons. and fayn wolde I satysfye euery man/and so to doo toke an olde boke and redde therin/and certaynly the englysshe was so rude and brood that I coude not wele vnderstande it.

The nationalistic spirit in Caxton was not so strong as to blind him to the rudeness of his mother tongue nor to the fact that obsolete words, through their strangeness and obscurity, created as much difficulty as neologisms, which some of his learned friends wished him to employ. For this reason he reached the conclusion that the "comyn termes that be dayli vsed ben lyghter to be vnderstonde then the olde and auncyent englysshe." But his sensible attitude toward archaisms was not shared by others. Thomas Berthelette, the printer of Gower's *Confessio Amantis* (1532), in the dedication to Henry VIII, justifies the edition on the ground that it will furnish a great supply of old words to writers, and thus remove the necessity of appropriating foreign terms.

> There is to my dome/no man/but that he may bi reding of this warke get right great knowledge/as wel for the vnderstandyng of many and diuers autors/whose resons/sayenges/and histories are translated in to this warke/as for the plenty of englysshe wordes and vulgars/besyde the furtheraunce of the lyfe to vertue, whiche olde englysshe wordes and vulgars no wyse man/bycause of theyr antiquite/wyll throwe asyde. For the wryters of later dayes/the whiche beganne to loth and hate these olde vulgars/when they them selfe wolde wryte in our englysshe tonge/were constrayned to brynge in/in their writynges, newe termes (as some calle them) whiche they borowed out of latyne/frenche/and other langages/whiche caused/that they that vnderstode not those langages/from whens these newe vulgars are fette/coude not perceyue theyr wrytynges. And though our most allowed olde autors dydde otherwhyle vse to

borowe of other langages/eyther bycause of theyr metre/or elles for lacke of a feete englysshe worde/yet that ought not to be a president to vs/to heape them in/where as nedeth not/and where as we haue all redy wordes approued and receyued of the same effecte and strength. The whiche if any man wante/let hym resorte to this worthy olde wryter John Gower/that shall as a lanterne gyue hym lyghte to wryte counnyngly/and to garnysshe his sentences in our vulgar tonge.

Berthelette is quite aware of the past history of neologizing, which he divides into an early and a later period. In the age of Chaucer and Gower borrowing was employed because of metrical necessity and the insufficiency of the English vocabulary, a practice he fully approved of. In his own time, however, he believed that writers scorned the vernacular and imported inkhorn terms because of rhetorical vanity and affectation. This procedure he condemned, at the same time denying that the early neologizers furnished any precedent for modern practice, since their works furnished an ample supply of words to meet all needs.

Sir John Cheke, who respected his native tongue, and whose view of neologizing has already been discussed, was of the opinion that when the vernacular proved inadequate an attempt should be made to find appropriate obsolete terms before any recourse was taken to borrowing; ". . . if the old denisoned words," he says, "could content and ease this need we wold not boldly venture of unknown wordes."[34] The preface to *The Shepheardes Calender* (1579) goes further. Spenser's annotator reveals a nationalistic love of his mother tongue which incenses him against foreign expressions and against those who acted as if borrowing were necessary.

. . . in my opinion it is one special prayse, of many whych are dew to this Poete, that he hath laboured to restore, as to theyr rightfull heritage such good and naturall words as haue ben long time out of vse and almost cleare disherited. Which is the onely cause, that our Mother tonge, which truely of it self is both ful enough for prose and stately enough for verse, hath long time ben counted most bare and barrein of both.

[34] See his letter appended to Hoby's translation of *The Courtier*, 1561. It is possible, of course, that by "old denisoned words" Cheke means only current terms of long standing.

F. K.   The inadequacy of the mother tongue is to be remedied by restoring lost words to good standing, and not by patching up "the
holes with peces and rags of other languages, borrowing here of
French, there of the Italian, euery where of the Latine, not
weighing how il, those tongues accorde with themselues, but
much worse with ours: So now they have made our English
tongue a gallimaufray or hodgepodge of al other speches."
Those who, he says, cry out against old words, no matter how
natural and significant, should feel shame at not knowing their
own language. Condemning what they do not understand, they
think so poorly of English that they not only fail to embellish it
but even resent others doing so.[35]

There is little doubt that the currency and popularity of
Chaucer, and, to a less degree, of Gower and Lydgate, did much
during this period to keep obsolete words alive. Berthelette's
conception of his edition of Gower as a storehouse of words
which could be revived points in this direction. E. K. praises
Spenser because through his imitation of Chaucer he restored
many words to their former standing. Furthermore, these
earlier poets furnished a standard for determining what words
should be called back into use. One writer justifies his practice
on the ground that "If I haue vsed any rare and obsolete words,
they are eyther such as the Coryphees of our English writers,
Chaucer and *Lidgate,* haued vsed before me, and now are decayed for want of practise; or else such as by an apt translation
out of the *Greekes* and *Latins* which *Crasius* in *Tullies* bookes
de Oratore allowes for lawfull) are fitly contriued into our English language."[36] Of course the procedure ran the same danger

---

[35] It should be noted that the nationalistic spirit was for the most part
restricted to the revivalists, for the simple reason, as we shall soon see, that the
same charge of obscurity, and even of affectation, that was brought against
neologisms could be brought against archaisms. Thus the chief argument in
behalf of the latter had to rest on a nationalistic appeal for the preservation of
the mother tongue. This attitude continued into the next century. In the
preface to his translation of Livy (1600), Philemon Holland asserts that he
has avoided borrowed words, but he implies that this procedure forced him to
revive some old expressions, though he ostensibly attributes them to patriotic
love of the vernacular: "I framed my pen, not to any affected phrase, but to a
meane and popular stile. Wherein, if I have called againe into use some old
words, let it be attributed to the love of my countrey language."

[36] Brian Melbancke, *Philotimus. The Warre betwixt Nature and Fortune,*

of affectation and obscurity as neologizing. As we have seen, Caxton rejected the importunities of friends to use old words because he himself could hardly understand them.[37] Early in the next century St. Thomas More noted that if anyone "hath a lytell smacke of learnynge, he reiecteth as homely and commen ware whatsoeuer is not stuffed full of olde moughteaten wordes, and that be worne out of vse. Some there be that haue pleasure onely in olde rustie antiquities."[38] Thomas Wilson probably bears witness to the same affectation, when he says that "The fine courtier wil talke nothing but *Chaucer.*"[39] That the use of archaisms was by no means infrequent is revealed by another writer who goes out of his way to assure us that "I studyed rather to vse the most playn and famylier englishe speche, then ether Chaucers wordes (which by reason of antiquitie be almost out of vse) or else inkhorne termes, (as they call them) which the common people, for lacke of latin, do not vnderstand." He remarks, however, that his position is different from the usual attitude of his day.[40]

So far our discussion of the "revival" movement has viewed it as based upon a recognition of the inadequacy of the native vocabulary and upon a nationalistic dislike of inkhorn terms as

1583, "To the Gentlemen Students in the Innes of Court and Cambridge." John Baret, however, maintains that no good writer will stuff his book with old obsolete terms.

[37] Nicholas Udall remarks that "some euen of the learned sorte doe in some places scarcely take [understand]" Chaucer, Gower, and Lydgate. See the preface to his translation entitled *A discourse or traictise of Petur Martyr Vermill . . . concernynge the Sacrament of the Lordes supper* (1550?).

[38] See the Epistle to Giles, prefixed to the *Eutopia*, tr. Richard Robinson, 1551.

[39] *The Arte of Rhetorique*, ed. G. H. Mair, 1909, p. 162.

[40] William Bullokar, though favorably inclined toward well-established loan words, prefers old to borrowed expressions for the unique reason that they are more easily ruled by grammar and cause less trouble with spelling. But the nationalistic spirit is also strong in him: "where a meere Inglish word appeleth to my memorie, (though he haue bene kept out of possession many yeeres) the stranger (for deriuations sake only) shall neuer prescribe against him, by my judgement." Apropos of his use of the verb "deem" he exclaims: "I am not ashamed of our olde wordes . . . more perfect and plaine in speech and signification, than a great many of vs can rightly vnderstande the reason thereof." *Bullokars Booke at large* (1580), ed. Max Plessow in *Palaestra*, LII (1906), 284.

a means of supplying words. In addition, there was an element of affectation in the use of old words, especially in court circles. But the field in which archaisms were chiefly employed was poetry, and the motive of the practice was not concerned with increasing the number of words in the language, but with utilizing the poetic force and imaginative suggestiveness of old expressions. So revival came to have more to do with poetic diction and style than with the language per se, though it might be considered a means of adding eloquence to the language by increasing its poetic vocabulary. Subsequent discussions of archaisms, with fluctuating attitudes of approval and disapproval, for the most part view them as pertinent to poetry only.[41] The antiquarians furnish the only exception.

The proposal to increase the number of words in the language by reviving those that had dropped out was hardly feasible. Besides the almost inevitable obscurity of archaisms, another difficulty appears in the fact that the plan envisaged a much richer supply of words in the past than existed. It could do nothing to meet one of the chief linguistic needs of the period, namely, that of terms of art, since little learning had been recorded in the English language. The relatively narrow intellectual limits of preceding centuries could hardly afford terms to satisfy the demands of the greatly increased intellectual interests of the Renaissance. Archaisms did undoubtedly contribute to poetic diction, as they have done at various times since, but they could add little to the language in other respects.

Another method of augmenting the language proposed by some opponents of neologizing had more to recommend it, though it was not much more successful. It was devised to satisfy national pride by obviating the necessity of borrowed terms, and at the same time to avoid the obscurity of old words. This plan called for the formation of terms, in a manner analogical

---

[41] See, e.g., a poem entitled "The Authors farewell to his Booke" prefixed to John Norden's *The Labyrinth of Mans Life, or Vertues Delight and Enuies opposite,* 1614. Spenser was praised for adorning "his owne stile with that beauty and grauitie, which *Tully* speaks of: and his much frequenting of *Chaucers* antient speeches causeth many to allow farre better of him, then otherwise they would." See F. B.'s letter to Thomas Speght, prefixed to the latter's edition of Chaucer (1598).

to the nature and composition of the word for which a translation or an equivalent was being sought, by compounding, by the addition of prefixes or suffixes, or by using a word in a different sense or as a different part of speech from its usual meaning or accepted nature.[42] It is in the light of this proposal that we should interpret Sir John Cheke's words when he prohibits neologizing "if . . . the mould of our own tung could serue vs to fascion a word of our own." Cheke himself attempted to do just that. Reference has already been made to his controversy with Bishop Gardiner over biblical neologisms, and to his effort to translate part of the New Testament into simple English terms unmixed with any borrowed words. He did not achieve his ideal in its entirety, but that he sincerely tried to is revealed by the word formations which he introduced into his version in order to translate expressions for which there were no native equivalents. For instance, where the authorized version now reads "lunatic," Cheke's translation reads "moond"; where "founded," "ground-wrought"; where "centurion," "hunderder"; where "publicans," "tollers"; where "parables," "biwordes"; and where "crucified," "crossed."[43] Cheke, however, is not always consistent in the use of these words.

[42] As we have seen earlier in this chapter, John Hart found fault with his ancestors for using French terms rather than constructing, in a manner analogous to the French, words out of native materials; e.g., "bearder" for "barber," "gater" for "porter," "breadserver" for "pantler," etc.

[43] For a longer list of the more peculiar of Cheke's renderings, see James Goodwin's edition of his translation, 1843, p. 15.

"What he [Cheke] did further for the English language was, that he brought in a short and expressive way of writing, without long and intricate periods. And moreover, in writing any discourse, he would allow no words but such as were true English, or of Saxon original; suffering no adoption of any foreign word into the *English* speech, which he thought was copious enough of itself, without borrowing words from other countries. Thus in his own translations into *English* he would not use any but pure English phrase and expression: which indeed made his style here and there a little affected and hard; and forced him to use some times odd and uncouth words, as *desürful, ungrevous,* tollers for *publicans,* etc. . . . But to return where we were, that indeed was Cheke's conceit, that in writing English none but English words should be used, thinking it a dishonour to our mother tongue, to be beholden to other nations for their words and phrases to express our minds.

"Upon this account Cheke seemed to dislike the English translation of the

Even after opposition to neologizing had grown much weaker in the last quarter of the century, the effort to enrich the language by words formed from materials furnished by the vernacular continues. In the dedication to Leicester of a translation of one of Philip de Mornay's treatises, which had been begun by Sir Philip Sidney and completed by Arthur Golding, the latter says,

In his [Sidney's] name therefore and as executor of his will in that behalf, I humbly offer this excellent worke vnto your good Lordship, as his and not myne. Wherein if any words or phrases shall seeme straunge, (as in some places perchaunce they may) I doubt not but your good Lordship will impute it to the rareness and profoundnesse of the matters there handled, not accustomed heretofore to bee treated in our language. For the auoyding of which inconuenience as much as might be, great care hath been taken, by forming and deryuing of fit names and termes, out of the fountaynes of our own tongue, though not altogether most vsuall, yet alwaies conceyuable and easie to be vnderstood; rather than by vsurping the Latin termes, or by borrowing the words of any forreine language, least the matters which in some cases are misticall enough of themselues by reason of their owne profoundnesse, might haue bene made more obscure to the vnlearned, by setting them downe in terms vtterly vnknowne vnto them.[44]

Bible, because in it were so many foreign words: which made him once attempt a new translation of the New Testament, and he completed the Gospel of *St. Matthew*, and made an entrance into St. Mark; wherein all along he laboured to use only true English Saxon words." John Strype, *Life of the Learned Sir John Cheke*, Oxford, 1821, pp. 162–63.

The most thorough investigation of Cheke's vocabulary is to be found in Professor Herbert Meritt's article, "The Vocabulary of Sir John Cheke's Partial Version of the Gospels," *Journal of English and Germanic Philology*, XXXIX (1940), 450–55.

[44] *A Woorke concerning the trewnesse of the Christian Religion*, 1587, dedication. Golding's opposition to neologisms was of long standing. In a poem prefixed to Baret's *Alvearie*, 1573, he inveighs against them as the chief defect of English, which prevents it from approximating the excellence of the classical languages. But then it was the affectation revealed in them rather than their obscurity that was reprehensible.

And were wee giuen as well to like our owne,
And for too clense it from the noisome weede
Of affectation which hath ouergrowne
Ungraciously the good and natiue seede,
As for to borrowe where wee haue no neede:

Golding's "fountaynes of our owne tongue" is the same as Cheke's "mould of our own tung." Realizing the inadequacy of the English vocabulary to translate ideas not hitherto expressed by the vernacular, and desiring to avoid the obscurity of loan words, the translators adopt the method of forming new terms, either by compounding native words or by using them in a way not employed before, with the hope that, since the constituent elements of the new expression are familiar to readers, the whole will be easily understood. Though his coinages at first sight may appear strange, Golding thinks that their self-explanatory nature will soon wear off their newness. Examples found in the translation bear him out. Obviously compounds like "comediewryter," "tragediewryter," and "commonwealemen"[45] could cause no one any trouble, and substantives like "leachcraft," "aspworm," "nurcechild," "fleshstrings" (muscles), and "primetyme"[46] offer little difficulty. Adjectives like "bacemynded," "hartbyting," and "grossewitted"[47] are self-explanatory. Sometimes intransitive verbs are used transitively, and nouns are changed into verbs as in the expression "to turmoyle the earth."[48] Though the translators use an abundance of terms originally borrowed from other languages, they do not seem to have borrowed many themselves. Golding is motivated not only by a nationalistic love of his native tongue but also by a desire to be clear and by an antipathy to eloquence.[49]

Since the need of new words was felt more keenly with reference to terms of art than in any other connection, it is not strange that the most important efforts of the compounders, as they may

---

It would pricke neere the learned tungs in strength,
Perchaunce and match mee some of them at length.

He goes on to emphasize the facility with which words may be compounded in English.

[45] *Ibid.*, pp. 197, 290, 468.

[46] *Ibid.*, pp. 170, 205, 210, 223, 459.

[47] *Ibid.*, pp. 190, 290, 468.

[48] *Ibid.*, pp. 183, 185.

[49] The wording of Golding's dedication implies that Sidney was animated by the same motive that inspired Golding. We know from his *Apologie for Poetrie*, written near this time, that Sir Philip was opposed to both archaisms and neologisms, a consistent attitude of the compounders.

be called, are revealed in compositions in which such terms had to be employed. In a mathematical treatise Robert Recorde vacillated between compounding and borrowing in his effort to express current geometrical conceptions. "In his text he may, for some terms," says Professor Francis R. Johnson, "consistently employ his new-minted English word; for others, he generally reverts to the Latin or Greek word." Professor Johnson calls attention to such coinages as "gemowe lines" for parallel lines, "likejamme" for parallelogram, "tweylike" and "threlike" triangles for isosceles and equilateral triangles.[50] Just how hard Recorde struggled to draw only upon his own language for the terms requisite for his study, it is impossible to say, but we get the impression that he is the most fainthearted of the compounders. It is also quite possible that the field in which he was working resisted the process more than other subjects.

A much braver and more ambitious attempt to construct words with native materials is found in a treatise on logic.[51] As was the case with mathematics, the terminology of logic presented a problem to any writer averse to borrowing. In the title itself, the author, Ralph Lever, informs us that the right word for the art of reasoning is not logic but witcraft, and in a preface termed, in a manner consistent with his theory, "The Forespeache," he upholds at considerable length the thesis that an Englishman is capable of composing a logic and of expressing it in his native tongue without any neologisms, even though the current vocabulary may be deficient. He begins in brave fashion:

To proue that the arte of Reasoning may be taught in englishe, I reason thus: First, we Englishmen haue wits, as wel as men of other nations

---

[50] *Astronomical Thought in Renaissance England*, pp. 292–94. See also his "Latin versus English," *Studies in Philology*, XLI (1944), 109–35. In Recorde's *Castle of Knowledge* (1556, sig. H3ʳ) constructed in the form of a dialogue between a schoolmaster and his pupil, the former remarks that there are no English equivalents of the scientific terms which he wishes to use, to which remark the latter replies that though words formed in imitation of the classical terms may seem strange, it "is better to make new english names, then to lacke words." The possibility of borrowing is not mentioned.

[51] Ralph Lever, *The Arte of Reason, rightly termed, Witcraft, teaching a perfect way to argue and dispute*, 1573. In the middle of the next century Lever finds a dishonorable mention in the preface to Bishop Bramhall's *Castigations of Mr. Hobbes*, 1657.

haue: Whereby we conceyue what standeth with reason, and is well doone, and what seemeth to be so, and is not. Wee haue also framed vnto our selues a language, wherby we do expresse by voyce or writing, all deuises that wee conceyue in our mynde: and do by this means let men looke into our heartes, and see what wee thinke. Then, as Englishe men can compasse this Arte by wit: so can they also declare and sette it foorth by speache.

In view of the unanimous acknowledgment that terms of art were lacking in the vernacular, the conclusion reached by Lever was indeed audacious, and he himself recognizes it to be so, for he pauses to answer an objection:

Nowe whereas a number of men doe suppose, that our language hath no words fitte to expresse the rules of this Arte: and where as some men do argue, that it must needes be so, bycause they that speake or write thereof at large, vse termes and wordes, that no mere English man can vnderstande:[52] It is playn, that neyther their supposition is true: nor yet their reason good. For as time doth inuent a newe forme of building, a straunge fashion of apparell, and a newe kinde of artillerie, and munitions: so doe men by consent of speache, frame and deuise new names, fit to make knowen their strange deuises.

The fact that men employ borrowed terms does not necessarily mean that they do so from necessity; they may be borrowing for eloquence only.

As for straunge and inckhorne termes, (vsed of many without cause) they argue a misuse to be in the speaker: but they proue not directly, that there is anye lacke in our language: no more then the rudenes of Lawyers latine, proueth that there is a want of good wordes in the Latine tonnge.

Yet though he refutes the argument, he finds it necessary to admit the situation which the argument supports—namely, the

[52] Though elsewhere Lever implies that his was the first logic to be printed in English, this passage might have been inspired by Thomas Wilson's *Logique*, 1552 (1551), in the dedication of which the author says: "This fruit [his book] being of a straunge kinde (such as no Englishe grounde hath before this time, and in this sorte by any tillage brought forth,) maye perhaps at the first tasting seme somewhat rough and harsh in the mouth, because of the straungenesse."

inadequacy of the standard English vocabulary to express all of the rapidly expanding knowledge of the Renaissance.

I see and confesse, that there be *Plura rerum, quam verborum genera,* (that is, moe things, then there are words to expresse things by) and do know withall, that Aristotle founde that want in the Greeke tongue, whiche for finenesse of speache, and store of woordes, farre excelleth all other languages.

He next proceeds to describe the shifts, as Cheke calls them, to which one might resort in order to obviate this verbal deficiency, and in doing so he apparently but not actually contradicts what he has said about inkhorn terms.

Yet is there this help in speach, that we ofte vse manye wordes to expresse one thing: yea and sometimes one word is vsed to signifie sundry matters. Moreouer, one language borroweth from another, and where there is want, men sometimes deuise newe names and compounded termes. So that after a man hath conceyued anye newe deuise in hys heade, and is desirous to haue the same published, and made common to manye, he findeth euer some shifte, by one meane or other, to make the same knowen. And bycause there is none so good a waye to do it by, as speache, man maketh that hys chiefe meane. Thus ye may see the originall groundworke, and beginning of artes.

Lever does not mention revival as a means of meeting the situation, but after all, that method was more germane to poetry than to prose, with which he is chiefly concerned. It now becomes necessary for him to express his own preference among the "shifts" that he has described, and to demonstrate its superiority to neologizing.

As for deuising of newe termes, and compounding of wordes, our tongue hath a speciall grace, wherein it excelleth many other, and is comparable with the best. The cause is, for that the moste parte of Englyshe wordes are shorte, and stande on one sillable a peece. So that two or three of them are ofte times fitly ioyned in one. Of these kinde of wordes, I haue deuysed many, and am now to giue a reason of my dooing.

At this point he finds it necessary to answer the charge of strangeness, which had also been directed very frequently at neologizing, in the course of which answer he says, and says truly, that the objection is pertinent only when a satisfactory familiar word could have been found in the language.

But first I desire thee (gentle Reader) not to scoffe at them afore thou knowe what they meane: or that thou hast founde out thy selfe, or learned of others, more apte and fit termes then they are. And if any man do cast out a reason, and say, *Loquendum vt vulgus,* that is to say, he that speaketh, must vse such termes as the common people is in vse withall: and therfore that we may not deuise newe names, but reteyne and vse the olde. I answer, this common saying taketh place, where there are words already extant, and in vse, fit to make the minde of the speaker, knowne to his audience: but the matter stands not so with vs.

He makes crystal clear the genuine need which the Elizabethans felt in transferring the learning locked up in Latin and Greek into the vernacular. He also recognizes the method usually employed in meeting this need, and he carefully demonstrates its inferiority to that which he advocates.

Therefore consider the case as it is: An arte is to be taughte in that toung, in whiche it was neuer written afore. [If he is referring to his own work, he either did not know or had forgotten Wilson.] Nowe the question lyeth, whether it were better to borrowe termes of some other toung, in which this sayde Arte hath bene written: and by a little chaunge of pronouncing, to seeke to make them Englishe wordes, which are none in deede: or else of simple vsual wordes, to make compounded termes, whose seuerall partes considered alone, are familiar and knowne to all english men. For trial hereof, I wish you to aske of an english man, who understandeth neither Greek nor Latin, what he conceiueth in his mind, when he heareth this word a backset, and what he doth conceiue when he heareth this terme a Predicate. And doubtlesse he must confesse, if he consider the matter aright or haue any sharpnesse of wit at al, that by a backset, he conceiueth a thing that muste be set after, and by a predicate, that he doth understande nothing at all. The like shall fall foorth when comparison is made, betwixt any of our new termes compounded of true english words, and the inkhorne termes deriued of straunge and forain languages: For he that is an englishman born, and understandeth no toung but his owne, shal at the first, eyther conceiue the meaning of oure words by himself, or else soon learne them vpon an other mans instruction and teaching: but for these inkhorne termes, it is certaine, that he shall neither vnderstande them by himselfe: nor keepe them in remembraunce when he is taught theyr signification of others, bicause the worde can make him no helpe.

Lever clearly recognized the dilemma in which vernacular writers found themselves, in that the very means they employed to render the English language adequate for the conveying of knowledge to the uneducated defeated the purpose for which the language was used. The fact that his plan appeared to solve that dilemma and to render his discourse clear to the unlearned furnished in his eyes the strongest argument in its favor. But he wished to strengthen his case by introducing all the current charges brought against neologizing, and having already introduced the accusations of affectation and obscurity, he assumes the nationalistic attitude.

We therefore, that deuise vnderstandable termes, compounded of true and auncient english woords, do rather maintain and continue the antiquitie of our mother tongue: then they, that with inckhorne termes doe chaunge and corrupt the same, making a mingle mangle of their natiue speache, and not obseruing the propertie thereof.

The same argument had been used by the revivalists. Cheke had advocated keeping the vernacular "unmangled with borrowing of other tongues," and E. K. was to declaim against making English a hodgepodge of other languages. Indeed, most of the revivalists had invoked the nationalistic spirit against neologizing. But Lever does not rest his case upon nationalistic pride only. He invokes the law of linguistic growth which calls for new terms when the vocabulary proves inadequate, though he condemns them when unnecessary, and he declares that a tongue is not subject to arbitrary or individualistic innovations. He justifies his method on the grounds of need and the fact that his words are understandable because they are composed of indigenous material.

They that will haue no newe wordes deuised where there is want, seme not well to consider how speache groweth, or wherefore it was deuised by man: For names are not giuen vnto things afore the things themselues are inuented. Therefore olde names will not serue to make newe deuises knowen. It is a fondnesse (I graunt) to deuise newe names, when there are olde in vse, which agreeing to the propertie of the speach, may serue the turne well enoughe. For no man is of power to change or make a language when he will: but when fit names are deuised and spoken, they force the hearers to like of them and to vse them: and so do they by consent of manye, growe to a speache. Therfore (gentle reader) if thou doubt, what is ment, by any of our strange and new deuised termes, consider their partes, as they are taken by themselues alone: and the consideration of the partes, shall leade thee to the knowledge of the whole.

Lever optimistically believed that the fitness of new terms was sufficient of itself to secure a favorable reception for them, and that, as many had previously said in respect to neologisms, use would wear away their strangeness. He stresses the one factor which determines the superiority of his method over neologizing, namely, the self-explanatory nature of his terms, the constituent elements of which were familiar to everyone. Yet he was realistic enough to perceive that this claim might not be universally true, for he says:

But if thys shall not serue thy turne, thou maist looke in the table placed in the end of our booke, and it shall shewe thee in order their meanyng, eyther by numbers referring thee to the places, where they are plainely taughte: or making some shorte exposition of them, if there be none in the booke afore. There shalbe added also (for some mens better contentation) the Latine termes. And thus much, for proufe, that this arte may be taught in oure mother tongue, and for defence of the termes that we haue deuised to teache and set forth the same.[53]

Another compounder almost as interesting as Lever was the author of *The Arte of English Poesie* (1589), probably George Puttenham.[54] The general purpose of the treatise, like that of

Geo. Puttenham

[53] For most of his terms the reader must be referred to the "table," but a sample may be given, in which the Latin equivalents as given by Lever are enclosed in parentheses: bounder (terminus), endsay (conclusio), foresayes (premissae), gaynsets (opposita), inholder (subiectum), inbeer (accidens), ifsaye (propositio conditionalis), naysay (negatio), shewsay (propositio), yokefellows (relata, relativa ad aliquid), saywhat (definitio), storehouse (praedicamentum), yeasay (affirmatio).

[54] This work is now available in a modern edition by Gladys D. Willcock and Alice Walker, Cambridge, 1936. The editors make out a very good case in behalf of Puttenham's authorship. Their attempt, however, to explain the contradictions and omissions in the treatise by the theory that it was begun in

Puttenham

Lever's book, is to show that there may be an art of English poetry as there is of Latin and Greek, but its specific purpose is to instruct the ladies and courtiers in the gentle art of rhyming. It is aristocratic in tone, and clearly reveals an antipathy to the pedantry of the schools. This fact helps to explain some of the inconsistencies with which it abounds. It was distinctly the unlearned nature of the audience to which it is addressed that inspired Puttenham to devise his terms, and it was the association of neologisms with scholastic pedantry which in part determined his criticism of them. But at best his attitude toward borrowed terms is complex. He would rule them entirely out of poetry. Among the "vices or deformities of speach" he discusses "Cacozelia" and "Soraismus," which he defines as "fonde affectation" and "mingle mangle." The first, he says,

> is when we affect new words and phrases other then the good speakers and writers in any language, or then custome hath allowed, and is the common fault of young schollers not halfe well studied before they come from the Vniversitie or schooles, and when they come to their friends, or happen to get some benefice or other promotion in their countreys, will seeme to coigne fine wordes out of the Latin, and to vse new fangled speaches, thereby to shew themselues among the ignorant the better learned.

"Mingle mangle" comes into being "when we make our speach or writinges of sundry languages vsing some Italian word, or French, or Spanish, or Dutch, or Scottish, not for the nonce or for any purpose (which were in part excusable) but ignorantly and affectedly." And he goes on to say that the popularity of Ronsard with English poets had resulted in their robbing him of many expressions, such as *freddon, egar, superbous, filanding, celest,* etc.[55] The only difference between these two vices is that in the first case words are borrowed from the classical languages, and in the second, from the modern. Both are condemned be-

---

the early days of Elizabeth's reign, and revised and completed in the 'eighties, while ingenious, is hardly convincing. It raises almost as many problems as it attempts to solve.

[55] *The Arte of English Poesie,* ed. Willcock and Walker, 1936, pp. 251–52.

cause of the element of affectation. His words seem to imply approval of necessary neologisms.

The section in which diction is treated discusses borrowed words more at length, in which discussion the same distinction between inkhorn terms and words borrowed from modern languages is made. The first are associated with the schools, and the second with the court, but the author objects both to the affectation of learned terms and to the obscurity and cacophony of the others.

Albeit peraduenture some small admonition be not impertinent, for we finde in our English writers many wordes and speaches amendable, and ye shall see in some inkhorne termes so ill affected brought in by men of learning as preachers and schoolemasters: and many straunge termes of other languages by Secretaries and Marchaunts and trauailours, and many darke wordes and not vsuall nor well sounding, though they be dayly spoken in Court. Wherefore great heed must be taken by our maker in this point and his choice be good.[56]

Puttenham is not against all neologisms, but, somewhat like Gabriel Harvey, who will be considered in a later chapter, he is applying a standard to them, by which the good may be separated from the bad. This standard is the same that he proposed for the language of poetry, which, he maintains, must be natural, pure, and the most current, current not in the country or out-of-way places, nor in the ports, which strangers haunt, nor in the universities "where Schollers vse much peeuish affectation of words out of the primitiue languages," but in the court or in the most cultured circles of the most civilized cities.[57] The standard is an aristocratic standard, opposed alike to the pedantry of the universities and to the vulgarity of the lower classes. Usage in the court puts the stamp of approval upon borrowed terms. This standard, however, is not consistently applied, nor is it his only standard, for in the quotation above he objects to strange, affected, dark, or cacophonous neologisms even though current in the court. In fact, his own practice, as we shall see, forced him to apply other criteria.

[56] *Ibid.*, p. 145.
[57] *Ibid.*, pp. 144–45.

After his criticism of borrowed words, Puttenham feels called upon to defend his own practice.

And peraduenture the writer hereof be in that behalfe no lesse faultie then any other, vsing many straunge and vnaccustomed wordes and borrowed from other languages: and in that respect him selfe no meete Magistrate to reforme the same errours in any other person, but since he is not vnwilling to acknowledge his owne fault, and can the better tell how to amend it, he may seeme a more excusable correctour of other mens: he intendeth therefore for an indifferent way and vniuersall benefite to taxe him selfe first and before any others.

List:

He then proceeds to explain his reasons for using borrowed terms: *scientificke,* because no other word furnishes such an exact antithesis to *mechanicall*; *Major-domo,* because it is accepted among courtiers "for whom this [treatise] is specially written"; *Politien,* because it is current in the court and there is no other word to express the idea; *Conduict,* because it is well allowed and long since usual; and *Idiome,* because more than one word would be required to express the idea in English. He defends *significatiue,* borrowed, he states, from Latin and French and brought in by some secretary, on the ground that it expresses the meaning so well it cannot be spared, and he says that the same is true of other words taken from the two languages, such as *Methode, methodicall, placation, function, assubtiling, refining, compendious, prolixe, figuratiue,* and *inueigle.* He approves of *impression,* "a new word," because it expresses the idea better than any native term. "*Numerous, numerositee, metricall, harmonicall* . . . cannot be refused, specially in this place for description of the arte." *Penetrate, penetrable, indignitie,* cannot be spared, "whatsoeuer fault wee finde with Ink-horne termes: for our speach wanteth wordes to . . . such sence so well to be vsed," for *peerce* is not so "well sounding." Even though *declination, delineation, dimention* are scholastical terms, yet they are very proper. By this time he has become so enmeshed in the exceptions to his general condemnation that he can only express disapproval of *audacious* (bold), *facunditie* (eloquence), *egregious* (notable), *implete* (replenished), *attemptat* (attempt), and *compatible* (agreeable in nature) without, unfortunately, giving any reasons for his antipathy, and then seek cover under Horace's *Multa renascentur quæ iam cecidere cadentque,* etc.[58]

Though the exceptions he makes in the case of certain words are so numerous as to create confusion regarding his criteria for judging borrowed terms, yet a few principles do emerge, somewhat wobbly, from the extreme liberality with which his standards are applied. Use, especially that found at court, or in the best circles, is one. This test, of course, makes no provision for the first appearance of a word.[59] Verbal economy, by which one loan word may do the work of several native terms, is another. Euphony, as a standard for judging loan words, is perhaps more in order in a treatise on poetry than a more general view would permit. But the criterion most widely applied and with the fewest exceptions is, as in the past, necessity. The inadequacy of the vocabulary sanctions the introduction of those loan words which express conceptions unrepresented by native

[58] *The Arte of English Poesie,* pp. 145–46. He may object to the five terms given above because they do not have a pleasant sound or do not move in the best society. Thomas Nash defended his practice of compounding on the basis of eloquence. To him, monosyllables were trivial and ineffective, but they could be combined to produce forceful and persuasive polysyllables. *Christs Teares Over Ierusalem,* 1594 (1593), "To the Reader."

[59] Puttenham, as well as others, seems to imply that, though a borrowed word when first introduced is to be condemned, yet if it stands the test of time and through use wears off its strangeness and clarifies its meaning, it is to be accepted as a legitimate term. He is indeed familiar enough with the development of the vernacular to know that many of the most acceptable words of his own day came into the language as reprehensible neologisms. In ascribing the polysyllables in the vernacular to "our Normane English which hath growen since *William* the Conqueror," he explains that the "corruption hath bene occasioned chiefly by the peeuish affectation not of the Normans them selues, but of clerks and scholers or secretaries long since, who not content with the vsual Normane or Saxon word, would conuert the very Latine and Greeke word into vulgar French, as to say innumerable for innombrable, reuocable, irreuocable, irradiation, depopulation and such like, which are not naturall Normans nor yet French, but altered Latines, and without any imitation at all: which therefore were long time despised for inkehorne termes, and now be reputed the best and most delicat of any other. Of which and many other causes of corruption of our speach we haue in another place more amply discoursed." (*The Arte of English Poesie,* pp. 117, 144.) This last reference is to his undiscovered "bookes of the originals and pedigree of the English tong." See also p. 160, where he objects to learned neologisms "vnlesse they be qualified or by much vse and custome allowed and our eares made acquainted with them."

terms, or which express them more accurately and aptly than English words can. Puttenham was possessed of an aristocratic temperament; his personal prejudices against the schools and the mob confused his linguistic attitudes and introduced many apparent contradictions, but from this confusion emerges the strongest traditional defense of borrowing—necessity.

Puttenham, however, found himself face to face with the inevitable problem presented by even necessary borrowed terms, namely, their obscurity to an unlearned audience. For it is to such an audience that his work is addressed. This is the reason that he is finally found among the compounders rather than with the neologizers.[60] Book III of his volume, entitled "Of Ornament," is really a rhetorical treatise confined to "elocutio," in which a considerable number of figures are defined and discussed.[61] Naturally rhetoric, like mathematics and logic, presented a large number of terms of art for which there were few traditional English equivalents. Puttenham attempts to solve the problem in the same manner as Recorde and Lever. But he can best tell his own story.

"The Greekes," he says, "were a happy people for the freedome and liberty of their language." They could invent any new word they wished, and where a single word was not available, they could combine two or more words to form a significant compound. In this way they constructed names of figures of speech, which the Romans at first took over. Then later Cicero, Varro, and Quintilian devised Latin names, but not so good as the Greek.

The same course are we driuen to follow in this description, since we are enforced to cull out for the vse of our Poet or maker all the most commendable figures. Now to make them knowen (as behoueth) either we

[60] Though he is concerned only with poetry, like Sidney he is definitely opposed to the revival of old words, and thus to the whole Spenserian school of archaists. Unlike Gascoigne he seems to have been devoid of nationalistic pride in the antiquity and survival of his mother tongue. He is an aristocratic modern with firm confidence in the customs and values of the court.

[61] Unless otherwise indicated, the passages which are to be quoted or discussed are found in chapter ix, "How the Greeks first, and afterward the Latines, inuented new names for euery figure, which this Author is also enforced to doo in his vulgar."

must do it by th' originall Greeke name or by the Latine, or by our owne. But when I consider to what sort of Readers I write, and how ill faring the Greeke terme would sound in the English eare, then also how short the Latines come to expresse manie of the Greeke originals. Finally, how well our language serueth to supplie the full signification of them both, I haue thought it no lesse lawfull, yea peraduenture vnder license of the learned, more laudable to vse our own naturall, if they be well chosen, and of proper signification, than to borrow theirs. So shall not our English Poets, though they be to seeke of the Greeke and Latin languages, lament for lack of knowledge sufficient to the purpose of this arte.

He wishes to devise terms out of the "fountains" or "mould" of the English language, which possesses abundance of material for the work, terms that will be self-explanatory for the un-latined, and thus avoid the darkness of neologisms. He cites, as many did in the sixteenth century, ancient practice as a justi-fication and a model for his procedure. But I think we should be wrong in supposing that classical practice alone inspired him. He probably received a hint from his own countrymen. In show-ing how the Greeks fashioned a name for one of their figures of speech, he insists that he has as much right as the Greeks to devise a name for it "without scorne of a new inuented terme." Not content, however, with a classical precedent, he cites Sir Thomas Smith, who gave "spitewed" or "wedspite" as an equivalent of ἄγαμος, and "Master Secretary *Wilson*," who called his logic "Witcraft." But it was Lever, not Wilson, who so designated his treatise, and we may be sure that Puttenham's memory, though faulty as regards names, carried more of Lever's book than the mere title. He follows these citations with "me thinke I may be bolde with like liberty to call the figure *Etiologia* [Tell cause], much better answering the Greeke original" than "spitewed" or "witcraft."[62]

Like most of the neologizers and compounders, Puttenham is haunted by fears of the "strangeness" or "novelty" with which his new terms may strike the ears of his readers.[63] This had in-

[62] *The Arte of English Poesie*, p. 228. Smith presented his "wedspite" in an *Oration* on the Queen's proposed marriage, now found in John Strype's *Life of the Learned Sir Thomas Smith*, 1698, Appendix III, p. 24.

[63] Here is a sample of his terms, placed in parentheses following the

deed been the chief stumbling block in the way of all those who desired to augment their native tongue. He not only seeks the usual refuge from this difficulty in the assurance which he gives the learned that time and use will solve the problem, but he also demands that

such others as are not learned in the primitiue languages, if they happen to hit vpon any new name of myne (so ridiculous in their opinion) as may moue them to laughter . . . assure themselues that such names go as neare as may be to their originals, or els serue better to the purpose of the figure then the very originall, reseruing alwayes, that such new name should not be vnpleasant in our vulgar nor harsh vpon the tong: and where it shall happen otherwise, that it may please the reader to thinke that hardly any other name in our English could be found to serue the turne better. Againe if to auoid the hazard of this blame I should haue kept the Greek or Latin still it would haue appeared a little too scholasticall for our makers, and a peece of worke more fit for clerkes then for Courtiers for whose instruction this trauaile is taken: and if I should haue left out both the Greeke and Latine name, and put in none of our owne neither: well perchance might the rule of the figure haue bene set downe, but no conuenient name to hold him in memory. It is therfore expedient we deuised for euery figure of importance his vulgar name, and to ioyne the Greeke or Latine originall with them; after that sort much better satisfying aswel the vulgar as the learned learner, and also the authors owne purpose, which is to make of a rude rimer, a learned and a Courtly Poet.

He still clings to the euphonic test for new words and emphasizes the need of intelligible terms which exactly express the conception. Though here, as frequently elsewhere, his strong antischolastic spirit appears, with its abhorrence of the suggestion of pedantry, he makes a bow to the learned in his concluding words.[64]

---

classical names: zeugma (single supply), prozeugma (ringleader), hypozeugma (rerewarder), metonimia (misnamer), allegoria (false semblant), ironia (dry mock), hiperbole (ouer-reacher), synesiosis (crossecouple), apostrophe (turn tale), periergia (ouerlabour), anadiplosis (redouble), epizeuxis (cooko-spel).

[64] The reader frequently has difficulty in picking his way between the apparent as well as real inconsistencies in the treatise. The above quotation reveals Puttenham's fear that the strangeness of his coinages may offend the learned and amuse the unlatined, but in another passage he indicates that the latter are pleased with novelties. In choosing as names for two kinds of figures of speech

The problem with which the neologizers, compounders, and, to a certain extent, the revivalists struggled was essentially a linguistic one. It was the inadequacy of the mother tongue which inspired their efforts, and the remedying of which was their chief concern. But it was capable of becoming a stylistic, or rhetorical, problem. The question of obtaining necessary words could easily, and sometimes did, change into that of selecting proper words. When this change took place, there were ample classical authorities to follow—Horace, Quintilian, and Cicero[65]—and on several occasions we have noted references to them. Furthermore, it was sometimes possible to defend a practice adopted from necessity by authorized principles of style. Thus neologisms and archaisms advocated for the mere expression of meaning find justification in the rhetorical canons of Cicero and Quintilian. But, on the other hand, the *norma loquendi* could be adduced as an argument against both. This stylistic principle presented a standard for diction, so that the question of proper English could become as important as that of adequate English. And sometimes the two demands clashed. John Hart speaks of the difficulty of keeping the vernacular pure from neologisms and local terms. The standard for "that best and most per-

aricular and *sensable* instead of *orthographical* and *syntactical*, "which the learned Grammarians left ready made to our hands," he bows to the censure of the learned, whose "laudable endeuour to allow antiquitie and flie innouation" he seems to approve of, but he adds the hope that "they will beare with me writing in the vulgar speach and seeking by my nouelties to satisfie not the schoole but the Court: whereas they know very well all old things soone waxe stale and lothsome, and the new deuises are euer dainty and delicate, the vulgar instruction requiring also vulgar and communicable termes, not clerkly or vncouthe as are all these of the Greeke and Latine languages . . . primitiuely receiued," unless allowed by custom. (*The Arte of English Poesie*, p. 160.) In another passage, however, which discusses Greek accents, he speaks of the dislike of novel terms: "if new termes were not odious, we might very properly call him [the circumflex] the (windabout) for so is the Greek word." *Ibid.*, p. 78.

[65] *Ars Poetica*, 45–72; *De Oratore*, III, 38, and *Orator* 24; *Institutio Oratoria* XI, 1, 6. In the next century, Richard Flecknoe considers our problem a stylistic rather than linguistic one. After tracing the history of the language down to the sixteenth century, he says: "Since which time the change and alteration it [the language] hath sustayned, hath rather been in the *Accessory*, then the *Principall* of the *Tongue*, the style rather varying then the *Language*." *Miscellania*, 1653, p. 77.

fite English: which by Gods grace I will the neerest I can follow," though it leaves small room for borrowed terms, is to be found, he thinks, in the language used by the "learned sort in the ruled Latin." This language, which excludes dialect words from the West and North, is spoken in the court and in London, where "the flower" of the English tongue is used. Hart notes the difficulty of determining and of preserving correct English. Only learned and experienced men, he says, can distinguish good expressions from bad, and even they at times use a Western or a Northern term in print, and thus bestow authority upon a rude word.[66] Puttenham, either influenced by Hart or expressing what had become a current view, lays down a standard for poetic diction very similar to his predecessor's. We have already noted that he positively forbids poets the use of neologisms, and he is just as determined in his opposition both to archaisms, which had by now become largely a poetic problem, and to Northern terms, though he sees in the latter the most correct English from the historical point of view.

> Our maker therefore at these dayes shall not follow *Piers plowman* nor *Gower* nor *Lydgate* nor yet *Chaucer*, for their language is now out of vse with vs: neither shall he take termes of Northernmen, such as they vse in dayly talke, whether they be noble men or gentlemen, or of their best clarkes all is a matter: nor in effect any speach vsed beyond the riuer of Trent, though no man can deny but that theirs is the purer English Saxon at this day, yet it is not so Courtly nor so currant as our Southerne English is, no more is the far Westerne mans speach: ye shall therfore take the vsuall speach of the Court, and that of London and the shires lying about London within lx myles, and not much aboue.[67]

Both Hart and Puttenham see in the court and in London and its environs the home of the most proper English,[68] but Puttenham, in full keeping with his aristocratic antipathy to scholastic pedantry, does not share the other's belief that learned men

---

[66] See *An Orthographie*, fol. 21ʳ, and *A Methode*, sig. Bi.

[67] *The Arte of English Poesie*, p. 144.

[68] In the next century Edmund Bolton (*Hypercritica*, 1618) also holds that the best English is that spoken at the court and by the nobility and upper class in London. See *Critical Essays of the Seventeenth Century*, ed. J. E. Spingarn, I, 110.

should be made the arbiters of diction. It is necessary to distinguish the stylistic attitude revealed in these two men from the linguistic views which we have been discussing. To confuse them is to ascribe to the sixteenth century a more widespread artistic feeling than actually existed.[69]

Three important factors determined the attitude toward neologizing in the first three quarters of the sixteenth century: the inadequacy of the English vocabulary; the audience for whom the vernacular was employed; and the antirhetorical spirit, or dislike of vain eloquence. The nationalistic spirit, the importance of which in respect to borrowing has been overemphasized, is so limited in its influence as not to merit much attention. It is largely revealed in the revivalists and sometimes in the compounders, for both of whom it furnished an argument as much as it did a motive. The fact that neologizing was most highly valued when the nationalistic spirit was the strongest, and that the Elizabethans were more interested in the benefit derived by the mother tongue from borrowed words than resentful at any supposed confession of linguistic inferiority, discounts the influence which may be attributed to pride in the traditional language. The central fact is that those who employed English wished to educate the unlatined public. In attempting to do so, they discovered that the mother tongue was inadequate for the purpose, since little learning had been expressed in it and no terminology, or "terms of art," for the various fields of knowledge had developed. The most obvious solution of the problem

[69] The belief that words of native composition could and should supplant the foreign element in the vernacular occasionally crops out during the next century. In 1674 Dr. Nathaneal Fairfax published a book the title of which suggests his linguistic views: *A Treatise of the Bulk and Selvedge of the World. Wherein the Greatness, Littleness and Lastingness of Bodies are freely Handled.* The preface reveals the author as an ardent admirer of the new philosophy in general and of the Royal Society in particular, while the text shows his desire to find, in his scientific writings, substitutes for words of classical origin. For instance, "everlastingness" is used for "eternity," "all-fillingness" for "immensity," etc. He sometimes gives the classical term for which the native expression is used, probably for an explanation of the latter: "successive or jogging on and on"; "a cleaveless or indivisible *now*"; "reality or thingsomeness"; "vice versa or heads and heels." See Joseph Glanvill's *Essay Concerning Preaching,* 1678, p. 13, and also Peter Motteux in *The Gentlemans Journal; or the Monthly Miscellany* (May 1693), p. 156.

was to borrow words from those languages which possessed the proper terms, and this was the method which triumphed, and which, the subsequent development of the language has shown, yielded the best results. At the time, however, two serious obstacles stood in the way of this remedy. The antirhetorical bias, produced in part by the antipathy of the democratic spirit of the Reformation to aristocratic learning, and also in part, perhaps, by the need to make a virtue out of a necessity by placing a high value upon the homespun qualities of the mother tongue, furnished a keenly felt opposition to loan words when viewed as manifestations of affectation and rhetorical vanity. The other obstacle was the inevitable obscurity of neologisms, whether affected or necessary, which militated against the very purpose for which the vernacular was used. Recognition of their necessity mollified hostility to them and limited criticism to those which were the product of vanity.

There were several opinions concerning the way in which the darkness of borrowed terms might be lessened. Elyot proposed, though he did not always put his own proposal into practice, that the meaning of a word be explained when it was first introduced into the language. Some writers thought that time and frequent use would render familiar and intelligible words which were strange and obscure when first employed. A new loan word was to be reprehended, an old one accepted. One may infer that the law of the survival of the fittest operated in the matter. Others proposed compounding and revival as substitutes for neologizing. The second was the more quixotic proposal because it rested upon the fallacy that in the past the mother tongue had contained terms capable of expressing the greatly expanded knowledge of the Renaissance. Its proponents were few, but they could at least make a patriotic appeal, and fortunately they did discover an authentic use for archaisms in poetry independent of learning. The compounders could make out a much better case for their proposal, since it involved a procedure which had already produced results in the English language, and which in cognate Germanic dialects had been developed to a high degree. Had it been adopted, and it might have, our language today would be quite different from what it is. Its advocates had a distinct advantage in argument over the neologizers and revivalists, in that the words proposed by them were self-explanatory and thus free from the obscurity of borrowed terms and archaisms, and, being formed from native material, they could appeal to the nationalistic spirit of the English, an advantage denied neologisms. But whatever the relative merits of the three methods of augmenting the English vocabulary, they represented no idle or academic thinking, for they were necessitated by a pressing problem, and were sincerely proposed as its solution.[70]

[70] Mr. W. L. Renwick maintains that, in their ideas regarding borrowing, reviving, and coining, the English were indebted to the Pléiade group, especially Du Bellay and Ronsard (*Edmund Spenser—An Essay on Renaissance Poetry*, 1925, pp. 65–96), but Elyot's neologizing, Berthelette's reviving, and Cheke's compounding come so early as to render his thesis unnecessary.

Chapter V

THE MISSPELLED LANGUAGE

THE necessity of expanding the vocabulary to support the new uses to which the English language was being put, uses made possible and perhaps partly suggested by the invention of printing, created the most pressing problem that faced vernacular writers. Their awareness of the problem, the various ways in which they tried to solve it, and the difficulties encountered have been described in the preceding chapters. The success that finally rewarded their efforts in the many words brought into the vernacular from other languages represents the most significant improvement made upon the mother tongue in the sixteenth century. The necessity of rendering the language an adequate medium, first for the transmission of ideas, and later for the expression of artistic conceptions, rightly took precedence over all other demands for linguistic reformation. Had sufficient words not been available for the needs of the mind, other improvements in the vernacular would have lost much of their value. Nevertheless, the neologizing movement represented by no means the only approach to the improvement of the mother tongue which appealed to the sixteenth century.

It is not surprising that the next step taken to produce a better language should have been concerned with words, traditional and borrowed. This was a movement for a simplified and standardized spelling based upon phonetic principles. The age could hardly fail to see the need for such a reform. In its transition from the Middle English of the fourteenth century to the Modern English of the sixteenth, the language passed through a stage of confusion worse confounded, with no great writers to furnish a standard. Caxton bears witness to the rapid linguistic changes which were taking place and to the wide dialectical differences which developed. When the invention of printing brought words from manuscript obscurity to the sunlight of books, their orthographic instability and waywardness became all the more apparent. Though there was a slow progress toward a more homogeneous and respectable spelling, at the beginning of the century orthography was fluid and at the end it was far from fixed. This situation could not but attract the awakened intellectual attention of men who were familiar with the often heated discussions over the pronunciation of Greek, and who saw in France efforts being made to improve the orthography of that country. At any rate, shortly before the middle of the century an orthographic movement began which for a generation enjoyed a vigorous growth, and repercussions of which continued to be heard much longer. The extent to which this movement influenced the actual practice of the age has never been determined, but that it had something to do with the improved spelling of the last decades seems plausible. In fact, we sometimes come across books in which the authors or printers seem to be consciously following some of the principles laid down by the linguistic reformers.

Early in the fifth decade of the century attention began to be paid to orthography. It is probable that critics of the language took their cue from the orthographic reformers in France who had been active since the beginning of the preceding decade.[1] Another probable source of this interest may be found in the controversy over the pronunciation of Greek between Bishop Gardiner, who upheld the traditional practice, and Sir John Cheke and Sir Thomas Smith, who insisted upon what they considered the ancient pronunciation.[2] But whatever the source of the movement in England, we can be fairly certain of the time of its beginning. Strype assigns Smith's and Cheke's interest in

c. 1550 [handwritten marginal note]

---

[1] See A. J. Ellis, *Early English Pronunciation*, Part III (E.E.T.S., E.S., No. 14), p. 33. Cf. Otto Jespersen, *John Hart's Pronunciation of English*, 1907, p. 9.

[2] Gardiner, who was at this time Chancellor of Cambridge University, finally closed the controversy with the decree that "none should philosophize at all in sounds, but all use the present," attended by threats of various penalties. The results of the epistolary quarrel are now to be found in Cheke's *Disputationes de Pronunciatione Linguæ Græcæ*, Basil, 1555. (Ellis, *op. cit.*, p. 34.) Possible evidence of a relationship between the interest in Greek pronunciation and that in English orthography may be discovered in the fact that in the same volume in which Smith published his *De recta et emendata Linguæ Græcæ Pronunciatione*, 1568, he also included his treatise on English spelling. See John Strype, *The Life of the Learned Sir Thomas Smith*, 1698, pp. 33–34.

the matter to 1542, when the Greek controversy was at its height. In a dictionary published in 1547, William Salesbury points out numerous instances in which the English "do not read and pronounce every word literally and fully as it is written."[3] In the preface to a treatise entitled *An Orthographie* (1569), John Hart says that he was first impressed by the confusion in the spelling of his native tongue, and was first inspired to do something about it twenty years earlier.[4] Though not apparent in print, the movement grew rapidly enough to reach a keenly controversial stage by 1576, in which year Claude Holyband (Claude Desainliens) speaks of "the great strife betwene them that woulde haue our tongue written after the auncient orthographie, and those that do take away many letters as superfluous in writing," and he tries to mediate between conservatives and reformers by retaining "all the letters according to the olde custome," and by designating with "a speciall marke" all superfluous letters.[5]

Cheke and Smith were in large part responsible for the movement, but unlike the latter, Cheke left no treatise on spelling, and therefore his views can be learned only from his practice, which Strype has described clearly and comprehensively:

And whereas the Writing and Spelling of our *English* Tongue was in those Times very bad, even Scholars themselves taking little heed how they spelt (as appears both by the MSS. and Books then Printed) he endeavoured the correcting and regulating thereof, in these Respects following. 1. He would have none of the Letter E put to the end of Words, as needless and unexpressive of any Sounds, as in these Words, *Excus, giv, deceiv, prais, commun*: Vnless where it is sounded, and then to be writ with a double E. as in *Necessitee*. 2. Where the Letter A was

[margin note: Cheke's system]

---

[3] *A Dictionary in Englyshe and Welsh . . . wherevnto is prefixed a litle treatyse of the englyshe pronunciacion of the letters.* Cf. his *A playne and a familiar Introduction, teaching how to pronounce the letters in . . . Welshe,* 1567 (1550), sig. C2[r]. The quoted sentence is from a translation of an account of English pronunciation written in Welsh and prefixed to the dictionary. See A. J. Ellis, *op. cit.,* p. 773.

[4] In *Tudor Studies,* p. 158, E. R. Adair mentions a manuscript treatise (Royal MS. 17.C.VII) of Hart's entitled *The opening of the unreasonable writing of our Inglish Tongue,* and dated 1551.

[5] See the dedication of *The Frenche Littelton: A Most Easie Perfect And Absolvte way to learne the frenche tongue.*

sounded long, he would have it writ with a double A in distinction from A short: as in *maad, Straat, Daar.* 3. Where the Letter I was sounded long, to be writ with double I, as in *Desiir, Liif.* 4. He wholy threw out the Letter Y out of the Alphabet, as useless, and supplied it euer with I, as *mi, sai, awai.* 5. U long he wrote with a long stroke over it, as in *Presūm.* 6. The rest of the long vowels he would have to be written with double Letters, as *Weer, theer* (and sometimes *thear*) *noo, noon, adoo, thoos, loov,* to avoid an E at the end. 7. Letters without sound he threw out; as in these Words, *Frutes, Wold, Faut, Dout, Again* for *Against, hole, meen* for *mean.* And 8. changed the spelling in some Words to make them the better expressive of the sounds: as in *Gud, Britil, Praisabil, Sufferabil.*[6]

Cheke was much more conservative than subsequent reformers. He seems to have been concerned chiefly if not entirely with removing all unsounded letters from words, and with devising means other than silent letters to indicate length. He was unaware of or indifferent to the fact that the same letter was frequently employed to represent a variety of sounds, for he made no proposal to devise characters to represent the various sounds given to a single letter.

His companion in arms, Sir Thomas Smith, was much more ambitious in the attempt to establish English spelling upon a phonetic basis. His ideas found complete expression in a Latin treatise published at Paris, *De recta et emendata Linguæ Anglicæ Scriptione, Dialogus,* 1568.[7] Smith indicates that he had taken the problem in hand at a much earlier date, probably while at Cambridge with Sir John Cheke in 1542, and that he had finished it while on a diplomatic mission in France. His first embassy to that country occurred in 1562. He begins by maintaining that writing is as much a picture of speech, or sound, as painting is a picture of the body or features—*ut pictura, orthographia*—a confusion which led the reformers into as deceitful

---

[6] *The Life of the Learned Sir John Cheke,* 1705, p. 211. He tried to use his system of simplified spelling in his translations from the New Testament, in which also, as we have seen, he employed for the most part traditional English words only. See *The Gospel according to Saint Matthew and Part of the First Chapter of the Gospel according to Saint Mark,* ed. James Goodwin, 1843.

[7] This is now accessible in Dr. Otto Deibel's editon.

T. Smith

paths as a similar confusion in criticism led the critics. For this reason, he thought, the first two should correspond as closely as the second two. In his eyes the "nature" of letters was established by common agreement and general consent, and so when a letter is made to represent no sound, or to express a sound other than that which properly belongs to it, its nature is abused. And great must have been the abuses in the current spelling, for Smith calls it inept, maimed, detestable, uncertain, inconsistent, unstable, and stupid. He places the blame for such a deplorable condition upon custom and the barbarians. The Elizabethans attributed other real or fancied ills, such as rhyme, to the "Hunnes and Gothians." In this case their invasions were supposed to have brought about the corruption of Latin into the romance languages, and after the Norman Conquest the English, who in Anglo-Saxon had enjoyed a much more rational orthography, copied the confusion of the French. Then long use and blind custom fastened monstrous errors upon the English people, so that not only were learned and unlearned alike under the yoke, but some even went so far as to defend the current orthography on the ground that if the received mode could be understood, no change was necessary.[8] This position, Smith avers, would undermine all arts and prevent all progress. He believed that the trouble lay in the English alphabet, which, though containing both Latin and Greek letters, did not possess a sufficient number of characters to express all sounds, there being some sounds not known to Greeks or Romans. Moreover, the English preferred to "abuse" letters, that is, make single letters represent several sounds rather than introduce any character different from the Latin, a position directly contradicted by the manner in which language developed, namely, by successive additions of letters. Smith seems to think that at one time in the dawn of writing a definite sound was assigned a definite character, which became its nature "by hypothesis," and that to assign any other sound to it was to distort nature. He also found fault with the silent letters which were used to denote quantity, such as the doubling

---

[8] This was essentially Bishop Gardiner's attitude in the controversy over the pronunciation of Greek.

of the consonant to indicate shortness in words like *denne*, and the adding of *e* to indicate length as in *meane*.

The purpose of his book was to bring order into all this confusion by a scheme that would make spelling correspond exactly to sound. He discusses at length the various letters and diphthongs, explaining their values and especially showing the difference in sounds represented by single letters or combinations, in which discussion he certainly shows a disposition to play fast and loose with the English alphabet. Two letters, *c*, "a monster of a letter," and *q*, an utterly superfluous one, he would gladly expel forever, had he the authority, and he would just as gladly admit the Greek *psi* to supplant *ps* wherever the combination appears in English words. He did advocate the use of a sufficient number of new characters, partly taken from Greek and Anglo-Saxon and partly of his own contrivance, to make him declare at the end of his work, "Ex harum literarum coagmentatione inter se, omnes Anglicae linguae soni poterunt in scripturam redigi, nihil ut deficiat, nihilque fit aut redundans aut supervacaneum." He introduced the thorn from Anglo-Saxon to express the sound of *th* in "pith," theta from Greek to indicate the sound of the same two letters in "thin," and he invented a kind of deflected *z* to represent the sound of *sh*. Nor were these all the innovations advocated. Length he would express by a circumflex, dash, or two dots over the vowel. He did his best to remove the "abuse" of letters by making orthography the imitation of speech, which he said it should be, just as painting is an imitation of the body.[9]

The movement thus openly brought before the public by Sir Thomas was continued by John Hart, to whom his contemporaries and successors generally referred as Mr. Chester.[10] His

[9] In one passage he says that his purpose is rather to show the nature and diversity of sounds than to establish a new alphabet: "Et characteres hi, si quidem rudiores videantur, poterunt excogitari faciliores. Satis est factum nostro labori si differentiam sonorum et naturas ac vires harum literarum explicuerimus, vt internosci possint." (Fol. 38 in Deibel's edition.) But throughout his book he writes as one whose hope is better.

[10] The mistake arose from the manner in which Hart indicated his authorship on the title page of his first treatise: *An Orthographie, conteyning the due order and reason, howe to write or paint thimage of mannes voice, most like to the life or nature. Composed by I. H. Chester Heralt* . . . 1569. His full

interest in phonetic spelling antedates the middle of the century, and his first treatise, which remained unpublished, was composed in 1551.[11] Ellis thinks that this work was not intended for publication, and it is quite possible that his later work would not have appeared had Smith's volume not stimulated him or given him sufficient courage to publish it.[12] That his attitude and purpose were the same as his predecessor's is clearly seen in the preface of the *Orthographie*:

. . . the liuing doe knowe themselues no further bounde to this our instant maner, than our predecessors were to the Saxon letters and writing, which hath bene altered as the speach hath chaunged, much differing from that which was vsed with in these fiue hundreth, I maye say within these two hundreth yeares: which I considered of about .XX. yeares passed, and thought it worth my labour, if I coulde finde the meane of remedie, of our present abuse. And so framed a treatise therevpon, and would then it had bene published, but I am the gladder it hath bene stayed vntill this time, wherein so well a learned gentilman, in the Greeke and Latine tongues, and traualied in certain vulgares sir *Thomas Smith* knight, hath written his minde, touching this matter, in hys booke of late set forth in Latin entituled, *De recta et emendata linguæ Anglicæ scriptione*. Whereof and of this my treatise, the summe, effect, and ende is one. Which is, to vse as many letters in our writing, as we doe voyces or breathes in speaking, and no more; and neuer to abuse one for another, and to write as we speake: which we must needes doe if we will euer haue our writing perfite . . .

Hart makes a great deal of Smith's comparison of writing with painting, and he follows the latter's discussion very closely when he points out the four ways in which writing may be corrupted: by diminution, when one letter is used to represent two or more sounds; by superfluity, when letters are not sounded

---

name appears in the dedication to his second treatise: *A Methode or comfortable beginning for all vnlearned, whereby they may bee taught to read English, in a very short time, with pleasure: So profitable as straunge, put in light by, I. H. Chester Herald*, 1570. The first title was evidently influenced by Smith's comparison of spelling and painting.

[11] Unlike Smith, he seems to have been inspired by the orthographic movement in France. In his *Orthographie* he definitely refers to *Traité touchant le commun usage de l'escriture*, 1545, by Loys Meigret, "whose reasons and arguments I do here before partly use, as he did Quintilians, whom it appeared he had well studied." See Jespersen, *op. cit.*, p. 9.

[12] Ellis, *op. cit.*, p. 794.

but are employed merely to denote quantity as in double vowels and consonants; by usurpation, when one character takes the place of another, as *g* for *j* in "gentle"; and by misplacing, when the proper order of letters is violated. He devotes some time to answering the arguments of those who advocated the employment of unsounded letters to denote derivation, to distinguish between words of the same sounds, to denote quantity, or to follow established custom. Against this last argument he is especially severe, claiming that use should be followed no farther than reason permits, and that ignorant custom is generally wrong and is always a foe to progress. Moreover, "the law of Reason which is in us," he says, ought to dictate the reformation of English writing on a purely phonetic basis. Toward this end Hart would omit *y*, *w*, and *c* from the alphabet and silent *e* from all words containing it, and he invents five or six new characters, one something like a written *z* to represent consonantal *i*, a *c* with a loop in it for *ch*, and a character something like a written delta for vocalic *l*. To express length he places a dot under a vowel. There is no better example of the absurd degree to which the peculiar idea of a letter's "nature" was carried than Hart's refusal to use capital letters on the ground that, though different in form from small letters, they represent the same sounds. In place of such he advocated putting a slanting line before the word. Ellis considers Hart's work disappointing for purposes of determining early pronunciation, but Jespersen places much value upon it, saying that his is the only purely phonetic system of the period.[13] At least, he published the first bit of connected discourse written phonetically.[14]

His procrastination in publishing his ideas may very well have been due to the opposition which he encountered and which he explains on the ground that men hate the idea of learning a second alphabet, and that many believe that, had there been any defect in English spelling, it would have been corrected long

[13] *John Hart's Pronunciation of English*, p. 19.
[14] Hart believed the court and London speech was the "flower" of English, "for that vnto these two places, do dayly resort from all townes and Countries, of the best of all professions, aswel of the own landsmen, as of aliens and straungers, and therefore they haue the best meanes to take the best and leaue the worst." *A Methode*, 1570, sig. Bi.

before. He laments the fact that though all progress depends upon change, many people resist every innovation and resent every attack made upon their customs however irrational the latter may be. He acknowledges one well-founded objection to his proposals, namely, that there were no books in his spelling. To remedy this situation he advocates editions of the Prayer Book, Psalter, and New Testament in his orthography. In his general ideas he follows Smith closely. He subscribes to the latter's view that through the passage of time the "nature" of letters had become corrupted because sounds other than those which they first expressed were represented by them. This process he, like Smith, calls an abuse of a letter's nature. The only remedy he could see for this bad condition was the invention of new characters to express these sounds.

Three years after the publication of Hart's second treatise there appeared what has been called "the most charming dictionary in our language."[15] Seven years later a second edition was published.[16] The nature of the work prevented the author, John Baret, from any extended discussion of orthography, but in paragraphs introducing some of the letters of the alphabet, he did manage to express some decided opinions on the subject of silent or useless characters, and of sounds for which there were no symbols. Upon reading his dictionary one soon realizes that he has little or nothing to add to what his predecessors had said. Indeed, in the preface he speaks of having been encouraged by Sir Thomas Smith, and elsewhere he refers to "Mr. Chester." He advocates the use of some of the same Saxon and Greek letters suggested by Smith; he follows Hart in maintaining that *y, w,* and *c* be dropped from the alphabet. He is especially severe with silent *e* at the end of words, the omission of which, he asserts, would do much to purify

our corrupt writing, and reduce it againe to true Orthography. The number of vowelles (Aristotle saith) nature has taught vs, and likewise the

---

[15] See the *North American Review* (April 1864), p. 346.

[16] The title of the first is *An Alvearie or Triple Dictionarie, in Englishe, Latin, and French,* 1573, and of the second, *An Alvearie or Quadruple Dictionarie, containing foure sundrie tongues: namelie, English, Latine, Greek, and French. Newlie enriched with varietie of Wordes, Phrases, Prouerbs, and diuers lightsome obseruations of Grammar,* 1580.

seuerall soundes or names thereof. But the proper characters must be aptly deuized by mans inuention. These therefore may be of diuers formes and facions in diuers countries, and also may be altered and changed as often as they will. But the other be immutable, and can neuer be changed, without the violation of nature's law, and peruerting of all reason.[17]

Though Baret makes some effort to distinguish between a sound and a conventional symbol, others associated symbol so closely with sound that the nature of the latter became the nature of the former, to vary from which was a grave abuse.

Other recommendations are discovered in the dictionary. New letters should be devised to represent the sounds of soft *g*, *ch* as in "cheese," *sh* as in "she," and voiceless *th*. He objects to the use of *i* and *v* as both vowel and consonant, advocates the use of *f* for *ph* in Greek words, and would banish *q* because it may easily be expressed by *ku*. He refuses to trouble himself with the various pronunciations of *e*,

For surely we may still woonder and finde fault with our Orthography (or rather Cacography in deede) but it is impossible (in mine opinion) for any priuate man to amend it, vntill the learned Vniuersities haue determined vpon the truth thereof, and after the Prince also with the noble Counsell, ratefied and confirmed the same, to be publickly taught and vsed in the Realme.

Pessimism, however, inspired by the futility of private endeavors, did not restrain him from saying that

as our forefathers in olde time haue by their diligent and daily serch, traced out the truth in letters, syllables and single woordes, and at length by their vigilant and painfull industry haue framed and builded vp the art of Grammar, and left it all ready polished to our handes to their commendation and immortall fame: So methinke to be ouer careless, not looking to amend faults betimes, but suffer it to fall in decay, as not being able to kepe it now in reparation, we shal be all worthy of perpetuall shame. And although theis heauy heads are loth to learne, and theis cunning clerks scorne to be taught: yet the poore young infant which learneth to spell I know suerly should finde much ease and readinesse by this meanes. . . .[18]

---

[17] See under "E."

[18] See under "K." In the "Epistola ad Comitem Penbroch," prefixed to

Among the numerous prefatory poems, expressing appreciation of Baret's labors, and incidentally revealing how widespread interest in orthography was, is one by Arthur Golding. After attacking the affectation of unnecessary neologisms and stressing the richness of his mother tongue in compound terms, the author praises the lexicographer for his desire to establish a sound orthography, the lack of which has in the eyes of all good writers corrupted the language and caused it to be

> Dismembred, hacked, maymed, rent, and torne,
> Defaced, patched, mar'd, and made a skorn.

On the other hand, the English language would manifest its full excellence,

> . . . were there once a sound Orthographye
> Set out by learning and aduysed skill,
> (Which certesse might be done full easilye)
> And then confirmed by the Souereines will,
> (For else woold blynd and cankred custome still
> His former errors wilfully maynteyne
> And bring vs to his *Chaos* backe ageyne:)

Like Hart, Golding sees in the government the only force strong enough to overcome inveterate custom, uncertain and irrational practice which prevents the laying down of sound rules especially for the spelling of derived and compound words, in the latter of which he was particularly interested. He goes so far as to say that through corrupt spelling the grammatical forms and relationship of words may become so obscure as to militate against grammar itself. How, he asks, can the difference between the Northern and Southern dialects be preserved except through proper spelling, and "How shall a man assure true quantitie Of time or tune?" To those who wished to introduce the principles of classical prosody into English verse orthographic reform meant much, since the quantity of syllables was frequently determined by spelling.[19]

---

his *Historiæ Brytannicæ Defensio,* 1573, Sir John Price comments upon the confused orthography of the French and English languages, to which he contrasts the correct spelling in the Welsh tongue.

[19] See *Elizabethan Critical Essays,* ed. G. G. Smith, I, 102.

In the same year in which the second edition of Baret's dictionary was published there appeared two treatises on orthography by William Bullokar, copies of the first of which are exceedingly rare.[20] Jespersen calls Bullokar "a muddle-headed spelling reformer," who did not keep *u* and *v* apart, who used a good many mute letters, who employed a sign for syllabic consonants where no new syllable is produced, and "whose system is nothing but the traditional spelling with a host of mystical and inconsistently employed dots and accents over and under the letters."[21] Yet he envisaged linguistic reformation in a more comprehensive manner than any of his predecessors. For not only did he wish to establish spelling upon a firm foundation, but he also advocated a dictionary to preserve the reformed orthography and a grammar to stabilize and dignify his native tongue. In fact Bullokar was one of the first to emphasize the importance of grammar in the improvement of the vernacular.[22] At the end of his *A short Introduction* there is a section called "The commodities of the amendment of ortographie for Inglish speech," in which he several times comments on the value of his grammar[23]

[20] The only copy I have found is in the Huntington Library, which considers it unique. The long title contains so much information concerning the author's plans that it merits quotation almost in full: *A short Introduction or guiding to print, write, and reade Inglish speech: conferred with the olde printing and writing: deuised by William Bullokar: And he that doubteth in any part thereof, shall be more fully satisfied by a booke deuised by the same Author at large, for the amendment of ortographie for Inglish speech, which shall be imprinted shortly, which booke at large answereth all obiections, and openeth all doubts in this amendment of ortographie. So that this pamphlet is printed for a short proofe of the same worke at large, both for the short shew of the vse of that amendment, and a briefe collection (out of the same booke at large) of the commodities like to growe by the vse of the same amendment: By the helpe whereof a ruled Grammar for Inglish is made (not yet in print): to the great helpe of a perfite Dictionarie in time to come, and alreadie purposed: To the perfite staie and easie vse of Inglish speech, as long as letters endure, to no small commoditie of this our nation, with great credit for Inglish speech among all other strange nations: herevnto also is added (at the end) the vse of the same ortographie in writing easie to be followed of all writers. . . .* 1580. In a prefatory poem the author explains that he did not have sufficient money to publish the larger work, but he promises that if his first venture succeeds, he will publish it together with the other works mentioned in the title.

[21] *John Hart's Pronunciation of English*, p. 19.

[22] Baret and Golding both mention grammar.

[23] *Bref Grammar for English*, 1586. This is a serious English grammar

as yet unpublished. When once his treatise is learned, and it can be learned by small children, he says, the mastery of Latin "and other ruled languages" will be comparatively easy, and much time will be saved in the educational process.[24] Furthermore, without such a grammar as his, it is difficult to translate other languages into English, because translators are "driven to know the parts of speech, declinings, derivations, compositions and phrases by learning first other ruled languages." In short, the vernacular can be learned much more easily and quickly when its syntax is learned directly than when it is approached through Latin grammar, the comprehension of which requires much time. He offers his grammar as evidence of the superiority of his linguistic endeavors over those of Sir Thomas Smith and "maister Chester," who ignored the need of one. After touching upon the dignity and respect which a ruled language possesses, he asserts that when grammatical principles are laid down for his native tongue, it will earn the gratitude and respect of foreigners, will be brought into agreement with other grammatical tongues, and will last as long as letters endure.

It is easy to discover in Bullokar's sentiments the high respect which the age maintained for a ruled language. In the preface to his grammar he boasts that by his labors the vernacular has become "a perfect ruled tongue," equal to any language in grammatical principles. The extensive and intensive study of the classical languages had emphasized the importance of grammar ("He settled *Hoti's* business"), upon which much of the excellence of those languages was thought to rest. It is not strange that the failure to see the grammatical potentialities in the mother tongue and to establish an English grammar should have

---

written throughout in his orthography. Its second title, "W. Bullokars abbreuiation of his Grammar for english extracted out of his Grammar at larg, for the spedi parcing of english spech, and the easier coming too the knowledge of Grammar for other languages," indicates that the published work was only part of a more extended treatise. His *Pamphlet for Grammar*, 1586, is a slight work of four or five pages devoted to an explanation of his orthography.

[24] He expresses the firm conviction that English "must be the foundation to such as desire farder learning, for that our owne language serueth euery mans turne in euery estate and dealing." (*Bullokars Booke at large*, 1580, p. 14.) This obvious truth almost missed expression in the sixteenth century, but was heavily stressed in the next.

made the vernacular seem a poor thing indeed. Much of the barbarousness attributed to it arose not only from a conviction of its uneloquent nature but also from the belief that it was not and, perhaps, could not be regulated by grammatical principles.[25]

Bullokar's orthographic ideas are more extensively and clearly revealed in his second treatise.[26] Though he frequently refers to Smith and Hart, he denies that his proposals were inspired by their treatises. He does, however, challenge comparison of his work with theirs, pointing out that the superiority of his proposals lies in the fact that his predecessors made no

[25] At the end of *A short Introduction* he mentions as first among the benefits of his spelling reform the improved reputation of the vernacular, "so long time vnperfect, and therfore accounted in time past barbarous: which we our selues can not denie, as touching the vnperfect writing thereof, not to be ruled by art of grammer." He repeats the idea in his *Booke at large* (p. 51) when he says that the confused spelling of the language has caused strangers to exclaim in disgust that English "was so rud and barbaros that it was not too be learned by wryting or printing." In his opinion an English grammar could not be constructed until the orthography was improved, and as long as the tongue remained in its confused and nongrammatical condition, it could not escape the charge of barbarousness.

[26] *Bullokars Booke at large, for the Amendment of Orthographie for English speech: wherein, a most perfect supplie is made, for the wantes and double sounde of letters in the olde Orthographie, with Examples for the same, with the easie conference and vse of both Orthographies, to saue expences in Bookes for a time, vntill this amendment grow to a generall vse, for the easie, speedie, and perfect reading and writing of English, (the speech not changed, as some vntruly and maliciously, or at the least ignorantlie blowe abroade) by the which amendement the same Authour hath also framed a ruled Grammar, to be imprinted heereafter, for the same speech, to no small commoditie of the English Nation, not only to come to easie, speedie, and perfect vse of our owne language, but also to their easie, speedie, and readie entrance into the secretes of other Languages, and easie and speedie pathway to all Straungers, to vse our Language, heeretofore very hard vnto them, to no small profite and credite to this our Nation, and stay therevnto in the weightiest causes. There is also imprinted with this Orthographie a short Pamphlet for all Learners, and a Primer agreeing to the same, and as learners shall go forward therein, other necessarie Bookes shall spedily be prouided with the same Orthographie. Heerevnto are also ioyned written Copies with the same Orthographie . . . 1580.* All that survives of the "other necessarie Bookes" are *The Fables of Æsop,* 1585; *Bref Grammar for English,* 1586; and *Pamphlet for Grammar,* 1586. These, together with the *Booke at large,* have been reprinted, with an introduction, by Max Plessow in *Palaestra,* Vol. LII, 1906. The last three chapters of the *Booke at large* and all the other works are in Bullokar's orthography. In the preface to his translation of *Æsop* he speaks of having translated the Psalter in 1585 in his orthography, but I have discovered no copy of it.

mention of a grammar or a dictionary, and that they tried to foist upon the language unfamiliar letters, whereas his characters represent little change from the traditional alphabet. He found it necessary, he says, to defend himself against the hostility which they had aroused in people to any change in orthography. Their radical innovations would eventually create a new language, and in time would render unintelligible all books written in the traditional tongue. He then proceeds to make much of the fact that he has preserved the old letters, in which he has made only a few relatively slight changes. Yet he is one with his predecessors in viewing the traditional spelling as chaotic and evil. Like Hart, he appropriates Smith's dictum that writing must be the image of speech, and like all the others he inveighs against custom because some letters are used to express more than one sound, or division of the voice, as he calls it; because for some sounds there are no letters; because some letters are not sounded at all; because more than one character is used to express the same sound; and because some letters are improperly named. This last calls to mind Hart's violent objection to calling *h* "ache." Bullokar received more from earlier writers than he is willing to admit; in fact, he adds little to their criticism of the vernacular.

After dogmatically asserting that there are only six perfect letters in the alphabet, *a, b, d, f, k, x,* he maintains that there are, excluding diphthongs, thirty-seven divisions of the voice to be represented, among which he includes long and short vowels. Length he would indicate by a "strike," or accent, over the vowel. He joined an apostrophe to the top of soft *c* and *g* to indicate their quality. He would express the sound of vocalic *l, m, n, r,* by a strike over the letter. He did invent symbols for *ph, sh,* voiced and voiceless *th,* and *wh,* but he tried to make them resemble at least one of the letters in the combinations. He used a character like the Greek zeta for both *s* and *z,* which he identified with *s.* These innovations, which he himself considered slight enough, are sufficient to give a passage written in his orthography about as weird a look as any from previous writers. In fact, there is not sufficient difference between his and their plans to justify the emphasis which he places upon it. His dots, hooks, accents, and hybrid characters possess no more virtue than the Greek and Saxon letters advocated by Smith.

His claim to superiority based upon the grammar and proposed dictionary merits more consideration. Though not very happy in his efforts to show that a sound and stabilized orthography is a necessary antecedent to a grammar, his insistence upon the need of grammatical regulation and upon the stabilizing influence which a dictionary would exert upon the vernacular is both original and sensible. He seems to have been the first to recommend an English dictionary, though a year or two later Mulcaster proposed one.[27] But Bullokar valued his grammar not so much for its intrinsic worth as for its conformity to the classical precedent. If English could be brought to resemble the "ruled" Latin in grammatical principles, it would *ipso facto* obtain the excellence of the learned languages. Latin presented a stabilized and more nearly phonetic orthography, a systematic and comprehensive grammar, and lexicons. Since English could offer none of these, it is not strange that their absence should have done much to undermine confidence in the mother tongue. Bullokar, at any rate, made an ambitious attempt to remedy the deficiency, and so in spirit if not in achievement takes his place in the forefront of those who wished to improve their native tongue.

It was, however, orthography that, next to neologizing,

[27] Sir James A. H. Murray (*Evolution of English Lexicography*, 1900, p. 26) remarks that, at first, Englishmen did not think they needed a dictionary to explain their own language, but by the end of the sixteenth century they felt the need of a dictionary to explain difficult or unusual words only. Practically all the dictionaries published in the century were concerned with other languages as well as with English. But Mulcaster, even more clearly and emphatically than Bullokar, expressed a desire for an exclusively English dictionary which would be both comprehensive and authoritative: "It were a thing verie praiseworthie in my opinion, and no lesse profitable then praise worthie, if som one well learned and as laborious a man, wold gather all the words which we vse in our English tung, whether naturall or incorporate, out of all professions, as well learned as not, into one dictionarie, and besides the right writing, which is incident to the Alphabete, wold open vnto vs therein, both their naturall force, and their proper vse: that by his honest trauell we might be as able to iudge of our own tung, which we haue by rote, as we ar of others, which we learn by rule. The want whereof, is the onelie cause why, that verie manie men, being excellentlie well learned in foren speche, can hardlie discern what theie haue at home, still shooting fair, but oft missing far, hard censors ouer other, ill executors themselues." *The First Part of the Elementarie*, 1582, p. 187.

chiefly interested Elizabethan critics of the vernacular. In their eyes confused spelling was the chief obstacle in the way of linguistic excellence. Since their efforts to reform orthography sprang from a sincere desire for strictly phonetic spelling, they were led to examine extensively the sounds of English speech and to borrow or contrive letters to express the sounds not cared for by the old alphabet. Imbued as they were with a firm faith in rationalistic principles as applied to orthography, they viewed with abhorrence the orthographic chaos of their times. They laid this chaos at the door of custom, blind and irrational. There were, however, some who resented attempted innovations, and who were ready to defend custom against the furious onslaughts made upon it. Anything which is as close to a people as language is sure to find upholders of tradition and haters of change. Nearly all the men mentioned above speak of the great resistance with which their designs met. In this as in other matters it would seem to be true that the progressive spirits were very vocal, while conservative resisters expressed their opposition through channels of speech rather than of books.

In Richard Mulcaster this opposition found its only voice audible today.[28] His position, however, did not rest on an obstinate conservatism, but on a clearer view of the nature of lan-

[28] *The First Part of the Elementarie which entreateth chefelie of the right writing of our English tung*, 1582. All references are to E. T. Campagnac's edition, Clarendon Press, 1925, Tudor and Stuart Library. Besides the biography in the *DNB*, an account of Mulcaster's life may be found in Theodor Klähr's *Leben und Werke Richard Mulcaster's, eines englischen Pädagogen des 16. Jahrhunderts*, Dresden, 1893, and in the Appendix to R. H. Quick's edition of his *Positions*, 1888. Scholars who have treated Mulcaster at any length have for the most part been chiefly interested in his educational theories: R. H. Quick in the Appendix to his edition of the *Positions* and in *Essays on Educational Reformers*, 1893, pp. 90–102; Cornelie Benndorf in *Die englische Pädagogik im 16. Jahrhundert*, Wien, 1905; Henry Barnard in *English Pedagogy*, Second Series, 1896, pp. 177–84; Foster Watson in *Mulcaster and Ascham*, 1899; James Oliphant in *The Educational Writings of Richard Mulcaster*, 1903, an abridgment and reduction to Modern English of Mulcaster's two works, to which is appended a critical estimate; E. T. Campagnac in his recent edition of the *Elementarie*; and various histories of education. I have not had the opportunity of examining Foster Watson's article, "Richard Mulcaster and his Elementaire," *Educational Times*, January 1893, which may treat Mulcaster's linguistic views. A short article on Mulcaster by Leo Wiener may be found in *Modern Language Notes*, XII (1897), 65–70.

guage and of its relationship to the people who speak it. That ^{Mulcaster}
he had pride and confidence in what the English had inherited
from their forefathers goes without saying, but his educational
views, as well as his sentiments on other things, reveal a most
liberal and independent mind. Besides the unique position that
he holds in the orthographic movement of his time, he interests
us today because his is the most significant pronouncement on the
English language in the Elizabethan period.

After some fifty-odd pages devoted to general educational
problems, Mulcaster embarks upon his chief design, to "rip vp
the hole certaintie of our English writing" that he "maie wipe
awaie that opinion of either vncertaintie for confusion, or impos-
sibilitie for direction, that both the naturall English maie haue
wherein to rest, and the desirous stranger maie haue whereby to
learn."[29] And at the outset he emphatically declares against
those who, dreaming of new devices, would remedy the supposed
deficiency of English orthography by altering old letters, devising new, or increasing the number of letters. In order to make
clear his attitude toward language in general, he develops an *argument by*
allegory, in which the characters are sound, reason, custom, art, *allegory:*
and prerogative, and the meaning of which may briefly be explained as follows. In the first period of linguistic development,
when sound held sway, the prerogative of inventing symbols to
express sounds belonged to everyone. But because of inevitable
differences in vocal organs, corresponding differences in sounds
arose, so that great uncertainty and confusion were introduced
into writing. Reason next appeared on the scene, and determined
what rules or principles might be observed, while custom by experience and proof confirmed what reason had devised, though
not without due reference to sound. Under this triumvirate rules
were established and exceptions made when reason and custom
perceived sufficient cause, but none were written down. Though
there was sufficient matter to furnish material for art, method
was lacking. Because there were no written principles nor authoritative standards, error began to creep in, and reason soon
saw the necessity of introducing a good "notary" as an authority
to prevent continual revolt. "For that is the difference, betwene

[29] *The First Part of the Elementarie*, p. 59.

Mulcaster

a reasonable *custom* and an artificiall method, that the first doth the thing for the second to assure, and the second assureth, by obseruing of the first."[30] This notary was art, who gathered into one body all random rules which custom had beaten out, so that reason should know his limits, custom his, and sound his. But since a language is in a state of constant change, sometimes for better, sometimes for worse, art should choose the period of highest linguistic development, as Greek in the time of Demosthenes, Latin in time of Cicero, and English in Mulcaster's own day.

Thus it appears that Mulcaster's attitude toward the current orthography is the antithesis of that of his predecessors. To them custom was the blind following of crooked paths, but to him it represented unwritten and unmethodized rational principles applied to writing. In fact, he has no patience with those who "rate at *custom* as a vile corrupter," and he devotes a number of pages to a defense of the much abused matter, besides frequent mentions elsewhere.[31] Since great writers have followed custom, he thinks that it must be sure and sound, a great and natural governor in matters of speech. Truth, he says, "pronounceth peremptorilie that *custom* doth, and must rule in all such cases, where manie ar to practis a thing, of their own procurement, but most of all there, where theie haue practised allredie, and ar most willing to continew in that, the which theie haue practised, as in this our writing."[32] He does, however, insist upon a distinction between "that right and reasonable *custom*" and "false error, which counterfeateth *custom*," the first being the practice of the learned and wise, and the second the abuse of the first by the ignorant multitude.

Mulcaster also attacks the prevalent view that sound alone should govern an alphabet and that spelling should be strictly phonetic. He perceived that sound furnished by no means a stable basis for letters, since there would always be variations due to differences in vocal organs and in the impressions produced upon the ear.[33] For this reason he opposed any increase or change

[30] *The First Part of the Elementarie*, p. 82.
[31] *Ibid.*, pp. 92–97.   [32] *Ibid.*, p. 114.
[33] "That no man hauing anie sense in the right of writing, which experience

in the alphabet. Against the peculiar idea that had come down from Sir Thomas Smith, that a letter had an inherent nature which made it appropriate to one sound only and that to apply it to another sound would be to abuse its nature, he proclaims that letters are "but elues and brats of the pens breding," and that they perform their function

> not by them selues or anie vertew in their form (for what likenesse or what affinitie hath the form of anie letter in his own natur, to answer the force or sound in mans voice?) but onelie by consent of those men, which first inuented them, and the pretie vse therof perceaued by those, which first did perceiue them.[34]

Since, therefore, they are but conventions, why may not reason use them in any way that may best accomplish its purpose? There is no more argument against permitting a letter to express more than one sound than against permitting a word to have more than one meaning, for "customarie acquaintance" will distinguish between the various uses of a letter, and thus prevent confusion. If any further distinction is necessary, then an accent may be used without introducing strangeness into writing. It is no abuse to use a letter in any way conformable to reason and not contrary to good custom. Furthermore, what is the necessity for more characters, when even a smaller number than the English alphabet possesses has sufficed for the best and bravest tongues, and since there is no reason why we may "not vse all our four and twentie letters, euen to four and twentie vses euerie of them, if occasion serue . . . ?"[35] What has sufficed for other nations and for our own learned men will certainly suffice for us, without encumbering the language with additional letters, strange to

had commended, wold yeild the direction to sound alone, which altereth still, and is neuer like to it self, as either the partie pronouncer is of ignorance or knowledg: or the parties that pronounce, be of clear or stop deliuerie: or as the ear it self is of iudgement to discern." (*Ibid.*, p. 75.) "But verie manie inconueniences did follow while that *sound* alone did command the pen, bycause of the difference in the instruments of our voice, wherewith we sound: bycause of the finenesse or grossenesse of the ear, wherewith we receiue sounds: bycause of the iudgement or ignorance in the partie, which is to pronounce, of the right or wrong expressing of the sound." *Ibid.*, p. 115.

[34] *Ibid.*, 72–73.
[35] *Ibid.*, p. 101.

behold and hard to write. Again, language resists arbitrary innovation, a fact that previous reformers of orthography had ignored,

For theie considered not, that whereas common reason, and common custom haue bene long dealers in seking out of their own currant, themselues wilbe councellers, and will neuer yeild to anie priuat conceit, which shall seme euidentlie either to force them or to crosse them, as theie themselues do, neuer giuing anie precept, how to write right, till theie have rated at custom, as a most pernicious enemie to truth and right, euen in that thing, where custom hath most right, if it haue right in anie.[36]

Finally, he touches upon the stoutest obstacle standing in the way of all violent attempts to change a language in any respect.

The vse and *custom* of our cuntrie, hath allredie chosen a kinde of penning, wherein she hath set down hir relligion, hir lawes, hir priuat and publik dealings: Euerie priuat man according to the allowance of his cuntrie in generall, hath so drawn his priuat writings, his euidence, his letters, as the thing semeth vnpossible to be remoued by anie so strange an alteration, tho it be most willing to receiue som reasonable proining, so that the substance maie remain, and the change take place in such points onelie, as maie please without noueltie, and profit without forcing . . . Naie were it not a wonderfull wish, euen but to wish that all our English scriptur and diuinitie, all our lawes and pollicie, all our euidence and writings, were pend anew . . . ?[37]

Mulcaster did not believe that English writing was in every particular what it should be, or that it could not be improved in some respects. He himself finds fault with those who think the customary orthography perfect, as well as with those who think it depraved. What he insists upon is that use must furnish the basis of any regulation and that all changes depart not too widely from custom. In the "Epistle" he says,

For I haue sounded the thing by the depth of our tung, and planted my rules vpon our ordinarie custom, the more my frind, bycause it is followed, nowhere my fo, bycause nowhere forced. Whereby I do perceiue, why we ought to write thus, as the common currant is, without

[36] *The First Part of the Elementarie*, p. 87.
[37] *Ibid.*, pp. 108–9.

the alteration of either custom, or charact, tho with som correction of *Mulcaster* certain wants, and generall direction for the hole pen.

In the rules which, he thinks, must be observed in any orthographic reformation, he states that every character or symbol is "creatur to deuise," and the use of it subject to consent; that reason, sound, and custom perform a joint function; that reformation lies in regulating the old, not in breeding new and strange devices; and that some inconsistencies must of necessity be left unreformed. He also emphasizes the rule "That the right in writing is a thing to be found out in our vse, as of acquaintance, and not to be forced in vpon our vse, as a stranger."[38] Elsewhere he calls daily custom "our beest and our commonest gide," and asserts that the English language will be improved, "not by rasing new characts, but by ruling old custom."

The principles which Mulcaster enunciates for the improvement of English writing are based firmly upon what he considers true custom; in good usage he seeks the proper rules for spelling, and when any words prove intractable he boldly defends them as exceptions. The chief orthographical faults which he lists are three: too many letters, as in monosyllables like "grubbe"; too few in words like "scrach"; and too diverse, that is, when two words spelled alike have different pronunciations, as "use," noun and verb. This last fault, he says, is chiefly responsible for the charge of confusion brought against the language, but he thinks it of little importance, and if an indication of difference need be given, an accent over the less usual sound will suffice. He then examines the native orthography under seven heads: general rule, proportion, composition, derivation, enfranchisement, distinction, and prerogative. Composition and derivation are introduced to show how it is possible to deduce the spelling of a word from the word from which it is derived, or from the words which combine to conform it. Distinction has reference only to punctuation and to accents and marks used to denote quantity and variations from the normal sound.[39]

[38] *Ibid.*, p. 120.

[39] Of proportion he says, "I call that *proportion*, when a number of words of like sound ar writen with like letters, or if the like sound haue not the like letters, the cause why is shewed, as in *hear*, *fear*, *dear*, *gear*, *wear*, the like

Under "General Rule" he describes and distinguishes between the various sounds of vowels and consonants, illustrating his comments with numerous words, besides explaining the customary spelling of words. Silent *e* he would drop, except when it "modifies," that is, shows the length of, the preceding vowel. He would omit the *u* in such words as "guide," and would use an accent to distinguish between hard and soft *ch* and to designate hard *g* before *e* and *i*. Doubling a consonant, he claimed, added a syllable, and since he did not consider *en*, *el*, or *le* full syllables, he always writes words ending in such combinations with one preceding consonant, though elsewhere he observes the shortening effect of a double consonant. In general, he suggests little for which he could not find authority in current use, though he does make some tentative and rather timid proposals. For instance, he sees no reason why *f* might not be written for *ph* in words derived from the Greek, *ou* be substituted for *oo* in "coop," etc., and "thumb" be written without the *b*. Yet he is everywhere amenable to custom, whether it can be explained or not. In short, Mulcaster tried to establish out of the common orthography a more rational way of writing, pointing out what consistency he could, suggesting changes where custom seemed to permit, but frankly accepting most exceptions as inconsistencies due to use and prerogative. In the text of his book he seldom follows his own suggestions with the exception of omitting *u* from words in which it is not pronounced. He realized that language could not be reduced to a strictly scientific basis, and at best was always subject to "general precept and priuat exception." It is to be noted, however, that he allows no double vowels, but indicates length by means of silent *e*, that he is generally consistent in omitting final *e*, when the preceding vowel is short as in "privat," and that he never ends a word in *y*.

---

proportion is kept: in *where*, *here*, *there* it faileth by *prerogatiue*, bycause our *custom*, hath won that writing in such aduerbs of place . . ." (*Ibid.*, p. 138.) Mr. C. C. Fries, in his article on Shakespearian pronunciation (*Studies in Shakespeare, Milton, and Donne*, "University of Michigan Publications," 1925), has missed Mulcaster's remarks on punctuation, which support his theory better than any of the authorities cited. (See *Elementarie*, pp. 166–67. Also see J. Hart, *An Orthographie*, 1569, fols. 40–43.) Mulcaster's ideas on enfranchisement will be discussed in the next chapter.

No one has ever perceived more clearly the necessary element of change in a speech, nor sensed more distinctly the essential nature of a living language, than Mulcaster. He saw an active force ceaselessly at work carrying a tongue from its primitive form to its highest development and then into degeneration. Such a linguistic height he perceived in the Greek of Demosthenes and the Latin of Cicero. This law of mutation, which he calls "prerogative," springs from what he describes in quaint terms as a "soulish substance," "a secret misterie," and a "quikning spirit." It is the lifeblood of a language, he says, and to deny it to a tongue is to remove that speech from use and to enshrine it in books where it will become immortal like the classics which "dream of no change." Prerogative "semeth to be a quiksiluer in *custom*, euer stirring, and neuer staied tho the generall *custom*, as a thing of good staie do still offer it self to be ordered by *rule*, as a nere frind to reason." Some people, he says, consider "This stirring quintessence, the leader to change in a thing that is naturallie changeable, and yet not blamed for the change," an error and tyrannical abuse, but without justification.

For in dede this *prerogatiue*, tho it chek generall conclusions, thorough priuat oppositions, yet that opposition came not of priuat men, but it is a priuat thing it self, and the verie life blood, which preserueth tungs in their naturall best from the first time that theie grew to account, till theie com to decaie, and a new period growen, different from the old, tho excellent in the altered kinde, and yet it self to depart, and make roum for another, when the circular turn shall haue ripened alteration.[40]

Mulcaster notes that the exceptions to the rules which he lays down for spelling spring from the "libertie in speche, to be hir own caruer," but he also is aware that it is responsible for progress in language, so that the writers of his own day surpassed those of previous centuries. He does not agree with those who

[40] *The First Part of the Elementarie*, p. 178. This idea of "circular progress" was later developed at great length by George Hakewill, who, in *An Apologie or Declaration of the Power and Providence of God in the Government of the World* . . . 1627, defended the moderns against the widespread idea of Nature's decay. See the present writer's "The Background of *The Battle of the Books*," *Washington University Studies*, VII, Humanistic Series II (1920), 97–162, and *Ancients and Moderns*, 1936, chap. ii.

Mulcaster

would seek to regulate these exceptions, since custom had established them, and since it is impossible to restrain this vital force in language from bursting through all bounds. In him alone do we find, clearly and directly stated, that fine faith in the tumultuous power of a free and vitalized language, that keen delight in the sheer means of expression which characterize Lyly, Marlowe, and their contemporaries. Indeed, he considered very foolish any attempt to put in a scientific strait jacket such a virile thing as the English tongue,

Bycause no banks can kepe it in so strait, bycause no strength can withstand such a stream, bycause no vessell can hold such a liquor, but onelie those banks which in flowing ar content to be sometimes ouerrun, onelie those staies which in furie of water will bend like a bulrush, onelie that vessell which in holding of the humor, will receiue som it self, as allowing of the relice.[41]

Mulcaster's views regarding language in general are saner than those of more ambitious philologists of his day. He was certainly right in recognizing the fact that every language has its peculiar characteristics and should not be subjected too severely to rules derived from other languages, that the principles introduced for the regulation of a tongue should be based squarely upon good usage in that tongue, no matter what exceptions may arise. His insistence that a language resists private laws and personal innovations is a truth some have been slow to learn, from John Wilkins' *Essay Towards A Real Character and a Philosophical Language*, 1668, down to the modern "simplified spellers" and Esperantists. Equally true is his belief that a language cannot be fixed, that change, though beneficially retarded, is essential to a living tongue. His idea of the conventional nature of letters is certainly much nearer the truth than the peculiar idea of an inviolable nature in letters themselves held by some of his contemporaries. And finally, his conception of the relation of letters to sound, of the part that reason may very well play in establishing custom, and of the function of "art," while naïvely expressed, is not far wrong.[42]

[41] *The First Part of the Elementarie*, p. 181.

[42] Although the matter remains to be worked out in detail, I believe that Mulcaster's influence is to be seen in the increasing respect for custom, in a

Whatever the beneficial effect the efforts at orthographic reformation may have had upon Elizabethan spelling, they certainly manifest great interest in the vernacular. It was not necessity, as in the case of neologizing, that incited men to strive for a phonetic spelling, but an authentic desire to improve the status of the mother tongue. If it could not be eloquent, it could at least be better spelled. This motive is especially apparent in Bullokar, who wished to extend the limits of the reform to include a dictionary and a grammar so that English might gain the dignity and respect which a "ruled" language like Latin possessed. It is significant of the change which was coming over linguistic opinions that the most conservative reformer because of his pride in the vernacular defended it against the vehement charges of earlier reformers, and, taking his stand firmly upon the language as it was at the time, proclaimed it the equal of Latin and Greek themselves. The tongue was rushing on past the demands of spelling, grammar, and lexicography to a rendezvous with the greatest literature England ever produced. For as one grammarian ruefully remarked near the end of the century, the English became eloquent before they were grammatical.[43]

more confident note in opinions of the vernacular, and in a more favorable attitude toward neologizing. Ellis bears witness to his influence on orthographic treatises: "Mulcaster's object in short was to teach, not the spelling of sounds, but what he considered the neatest style of spelling as derived from custom, in order to avoid the great confusion which then prevailed. He succeeded to the extent of largely influencing subsequent authorities. In Ben Jonson's *Grammar*, the chapters on orthography are little more than abridgements of Mulcaster's. Sometimes the same examples are used, and the very faults of description followed." (*Early English Pronunciation*, p. 910.) Alexander Gil, in *Logonomia Anglica*, 1619, shows the influence of the *Elementarie* in the respect paid custom and in expressed sympathy with Mulcaster's opinion of Sir Thomas Smith's new characters. (See Jespersen, *John Hart's Pronunciation of English*, pp. 59–60.) Much of what Mulcaster says is germane to linguistic discussions of the present.

[43] Paul Greaves, *Grammatica Anglicana*, 1594.

Chapter VI

THE ELOQUENT LANGUAGE

THE key to an understanding of the dominant attitude toward the vernacular during the first three quarters of the sixteenth century is found in the unhappy comparison with Latin and Greek and in the strong desire and earnest effort to educate the unlearned by translations and by original works written in English. The fact that the native language was associated with the rude multitude, in contrast to the learned few, that it was the medium through which the former were to be enlightened, that it could be employed in books by those unblessed by a classical education, that it had to be used in a simple, plain, "uneloquent" manner to achieve its end, and that it was an "unruled" tongue with an irrational orthography—all these facts led inexorably to the conclusion that the language itself was rude, or barbarous. The conception of it, for the most part, as a mere instrumentality by which knowledge was to be conveyed dominated the period, and tended to prevent its being considered a possible medium of artistic expression. Though Chaucer, sometimes together with Gower and Lydgate, is frequently cited as an eloquent poet, who made his rude mother tongue eloquent, the backward-looking Englishman, with few exceptions, seems to view that era as a closed chapter in the development of the vernacular. Sometimes contemporary writers are accorded the gift of eloquence, but such a grant is made more in the spirit of graceful compliment than of serious criticism, and gives testimony more to the desirability of the quality than to a belief in its existence. Had "pure" literature made more demands upon the vernacular, and thus widened its scope, the latter would certainly have revealed an eloquent character.

Such an event came to pass in the last quarter of the century. One might surmise that a changed attitude toward the vernacular, brought about in other ways, antedated and made possible the great literary outburst. But, as will be seen, this view is contradicted by numerous references to English poets as the refiners of the language. Whatever may have been the original cause of the outburst, the important moment arose when writers, most of whom were familiar with classical rhetoric, ceased to view their audience as an unlearned crowd, and were moved not by the desire to instruct the uneducated but to express their own concepts and inspirations. No longer was the vernacular only a practical instrument, the efficacy of which depended upon simple clarity and humble plainness; it was, instead, a free medium of expression, in which brave new words and elaborate figures could puzzle or displease whom they would.[1] Though past values and attitudes linger on, eloquence in English compositions becomes an accomplished fact, and the rhetorical potentialities of the mother tongue are revealed once and for all. The rude, gross, base, and barbarous mother tongue recedes into the

when? See p. 211

---

[1] The words which George Chapman addressed to Mathew Royden manifest the new spirit unequivocally. "The prophane multitude I hate, and onelie consecrate my strange Poems to these serching spirits, whom learning hath made noble, and nobilitie sacred; endeouuring that materiall Oration, which you call *Schema*; varying in some rare ficton, from popular custome, euen for the pure sakes of ornament and vtilitie . . .

"But that Poesie should be as peruiall as Oratorie, and plainnes her speciall ornament, were the plaine way to barbarisme: and to make the Asse runne proude of his eares; to take away strength from Lyons, and giue Cammels hornes.

"That, *Enargia*, or cleerenes of representation, requird in absolute Poems is not the perspicuous deliuery of a lowe inuention; but high, and harty inuention exprest in most significant, and vnaffected phrase; it serues not a skilfull Painters turne, to draw the figure of a face onely to make knowne who it represents; but hee must lymn, giue luster, shaddow, and heightning; which though ignorants will esteeme spic'd, and too curious, yet such as haue the iudiciall perspectiue, will see it hath motion, spirit, and life.

"There is no confection made to last, but it is admitted more cost and skill then presently to be vsed [as] simples; and in my opinion, that which being with a little endeuour serched, ads a kinde of maiestie to Poesie; is better then that which euery Cobler may sing to his patch.

"Obscuritie in affection of words, and indigested concets, is pedanticall and childish; but where it shroudeth it selfe in the hart of his subiect, vttered with fitnes of figure, and expressiue Epethites; with that darknes wil I still labour to be shaddowed; rich Minerals are digd out of the bowels of the earth, not found in the superficies and dust of it; . . . acquainted long since with the true habit of Poesie, and now since your labouring wits endeuour heauenhigh thoughts of Nature, you have actual meanes to sound the philosophical conceits, that my new pen so seriously courteth." *Ouids Banquet of Sence. A Coronet for his Mistresse Philosophie, and his amorous Jodiacke*, 1595, preface.

past, and its place is taken by an eloquent language, confidence
in which mounts higher and higher until it yields nothing even
to Latin and Greek.

Before this rich period of literary activity a few writers had
ventured to express their belief in the literary qualities of the
vernacular, generally in connection with an attempted artistic
use of English. John Rastell is hardly a case in point, for his
confidence was in the adequacy of the English vocabulary to
express meaning and not to achieve eloquence. In the grim controversy over the right to translate the Bible, Tyndale felt compelled to answer the serious charge of barbarism by asserting
that the mother tongue possessed grace. More, though no dis-
parager of his native tongue, avoided the central point in this
charge. Thomas Phaer, however, tells us that he deliberately
undertook to translate the *Aeneid* to defend his native tongue
against the charge of barbarism, and to encourage young writers
to engage in the composition of poetry by showing them the
potentialities of their native language.[2] Though Phaer seems to
have been thinking largely of metrical possibilities, the preface
to *Songes and Sonettes, written by the right honorable Lorde
Henry Haward late Earle of Surrey, and other* (1557) seeks to
recommend the poems contained in the volume by asserting that
the fact that

Tottel

our tong is able in that kinde [poetry] to do as praise worthelye as the
rest [Latins, Italians, and others], the honorable stile of the noble earle
of Surrey, and the weightinesse of the depewitted sir Thomas Wiat the

> [2] See the postscript at the end of *The seuen first bookes of the Eneidos,*
> 1558. It is possible that Phaer means that his translation will furnish a poetic
> vocabulary from which unlatined poets may "gather innumerable sortes, of the
> most beautifull floures, figures, and phrases." Certainly Stanyhurst placed this
> interpretation upon Phaer's words. See the preface to his translation of Virgil,
> *Thee First Foure Bookes of Virgil His Aeneis,* 1852.
>   Among the Baker MSS (xxxvii, 400–413 in the Cambridge University
> Library) there is a MS of Sir Thomas Smith's, pertaining to his second inaugural
> as Professor of Civil Law at Cambridge, which asserts that when the use of
> English "was marked by precision and purity it might compare even with Latin
> for beauty and force of expression." (J. B. Mullinger, *The University of
> Cambridge,* 1884, II, 132.) In the dedication of his translation of Fullonius'
> *Comedye of Acolastus* (1540) to Henry VIII, John Palsgrave makes the astound-
> ing statement that his mother tongue at that time had reached the height of
> perfection.

elders verse, with seueral graces in sondry good Englishe writers, do show
abundantly. It resteth now (gentle reder) that thou thinke it not euil
don, to publishe, to the honor of the English tong, and for profit of the
studious of Englishe eloquence those workes which the vngentle horders
vp of such tresure haue heretofore enuied the.

Barnabe Googe is even more enthusiastic in his expression of
confidence in the artistic powers of the vernacular. He recommends his verse translation of a Latin poem of Marcellus Palin-
genius by assuring us that if Chaucer, Homer, Virgil, and Ovid
were alive,

> All these myght well be sure
> Theyr matches here to fynde.
> So muche doth England florishe now
> With men of Muses kynde.[8]

After castigating the "pernicious Hipocrites," who object to the
Psalms being translated into English verse on the ground that
they would be sung in every cobler's shop, he says,

I know a number to be that can not abyde to reade anye thing written
in Englishe verse, which nowe is so plenteously enriched wyth a number
of eloquent writers, that in my fansy it is lyttle inferiour to the pleasaunt
verses of the auncient Romaines. For since the time of our excellente
countrey-man sir Geffray Chaucer who liueth in like estimation with
vs as did olde *Ennius* wyth the Latines. There hath flourished in England so fine and filed phrases, and so good and pleasant Poets as may
counteruayle the doings of *Virgill, Ouid, Horace, Iuuenall, Martiall,
Lucan, Perseus, Tibullus, Catullus, Seneca,* and *Propertius.*

And finally as we near the period of overwhelming confidence,
we find George Gascoigne, in an anthology[4] composed of poetic

---

[8] See the poem, "The Translatour to the Reader," appended to *The Firste
thre Bokes of . . . the Zodyake of lyfe,* 1560, and the preface to *The Zodiake
of Life,* 1565.

[4] *A Hundreth sundrie Flowres bounde vp in one small Poesie. Gathered
partely (by translation) in the fyne outlandish Gardins of Euripides, Ouid,
Petrarke, Ariosto, and others: and partly by inuention, out of our owne fruitefull Orchardes in Englande: Yelding sundrie sweete sauours of Tragical, Comi-
cal and Morall Discourses, bothe pleasaunt and profitable to the well smellyng
noses of learned Readers,* 1573, p. 204. The inclusion of monosyllables among
the virtues of the native tongue may be explained by the fact that Gascoigne
was an admirer of those ancient English words.

Gascoigne

translations and original verses, urging native poets to give over writing trifling love poems for subjects of more weight and profit, "For if quicknes of inuencion, proper vocables, apt Epythetes, and store of monasillables may help a pleasant brayne to be crowned with Lawrell. I doubt not but both our countrymen and countrie language might be entronised amonge the olde foreleaders vnto the mount *Helicon*." It should be noted that most of these very few expressions of confidence in the literary qualities of the mother tongue, scattered over nearly a half-century, have to do with the poetic use of the language, and show that when artistic demands were made upon the vernacular, realization of its powers was possible.

"In times past they did not care how plaine a thing were, so it were profitable, and now we force [care] not how bad it be, so it be pleasant," says one Charles Gibbon,[5] and his words furnish a neat statement of the change that had occurred. The goal of profitable instruction, with the plain humble style required by it,

---

[5] *A Work worth the Reading. Wherein is contayned, fiue profitable and pithy Questions, very expedient, aswell for Parents to perceiue howe to bestowe their Children in marriage* . . . . 1591, "To the Indifferent Reader." Gibbon's quotation continues: "it is this that maketh so many writers imploy their time more wantonly than wiselie, because they see a vaine trifle is more accepted than a diuine treatise. If it bee so, that those bookes which are most light are best liked, and those men that employ their learning to leuitie, are most laudable, then the tenor will but impaire the title of my booke: for it will not be worth the reading: but (good Reader) thou must obserue in writing, the manner of it according to the matter, wee must not paynt the Scriptures with superfluous speaches, as men doo their owne fictions after their fancies: for the maiestie of the word requireth modesty in the writer . . . this I am sure, there is none can afford so fruitefull a phrase as the Bible, though they practise neuer so fine tearmes in their bookes; I speake this not to that end I would glose to get credit by my words, or to disgrace those that deserue it by their workes, but to shew what difference there is betweene a pleasant story (which wee may handle according to our humour) and a graue discourse (which must be penned according to the platforme.)"

About the middle of the next century the same view is expressed by Richard Flecknoe, who says that "the change and alteration it [the English language] hath sustayned, hath rather been in the *Accessory*, then the *Principall* of the *Tongue*, the style rather varying then the *Language*, according to the severall Inclinations and Dispositions of *Princes* and of *Times*. That of our *Ancestors* having been plain and simple: That of Queen *Elizabeths* dayes, *flaunting* and *puffed* like her *Apparell*: That of King *Jame's Regis ad exemplum*, inclining much to the *Learned* and *Erudite* . . ." "*A Discourse of Languages, and particularly of the English Tongue*" in *Miscellania*, 1653, p. 77.

gave way to artistic creation, without any necessary instructive element, and to the eloquent mode of expression. The contrast between the natures and spirits of the two periods was quite noticeable to writers of the latter part of the century, who do not tire of contrasting the eloquence of their time with the barbarism of an earlier day. In 1586 Webbe says that the English tongue has been "purged from faultes, weeded of errours, and pollished from barbarousnes,"[6] and a few years later Nash also expresses the belief that it has been "cleansed . . . from barbarisme."[7] Harvey maintains that "It is not long since the goodliest graces of the most noble commonwealths vpon earth, eloquence in speech, and civility in manners, arrived in these remote parts of the world," and elsewhere he expresses the opinion that his native tongue was "never so furnished or embellished as of late."[8] William Covell thinks it very fortunate indeed that barbarism should have been expelled from the language in "the barren age of the worlde," when so little of good can be expected.[9] Edward Guilpin considers it a triumph of his age that "monstrous barbarismes" have been confounded,[10] and Samuel Rowlands asserts that "melfluvious sweete Rose-watred elloquence . . . hath hunted Barbarisme hence

> And taught the goodman *Cobbin*, at his plow,
> To be as elloquent as Tullie now.[11]

Awareness of the eloquent language of this period, especially as contrasted with the barbarous tongue of preceding generations, is discovered in the attitude maintained toward earlier compositions. In 1591 Robert Wilmot issued a modernized version of *Tancred and Gismund*,[12] to which was prefixed an address by

---

[6] *Elizabethan Critical Essays*, ed. G. G. Smith, I, 227.

[7] *Pierce Penilesse* (1592), in *Complete Works*, ed. A. B. Grosart, II, 61.

[8] *Pierces Supererogation*, 1593, p. 33; and *Four Letters*, 1592, p. 40, in *Archaica*, ed. Sir E. Brydges, 1815, Vol. II.

[9] *Polimanteia, or, the meanes lawfull and vnlawfull, to ivdge of the Fall of a Common-Wealth*, 1595, preface.

[10] *Skialetheia. Or, a shadowe of Truth*, 1598, sig. A3^r.

[11] *Letting of humours blood*, 1600, satire 4.

[12] *The Tragedie of Tancred and Gismund. Compiled By The Gentlemen of the Inner Temple, and by them presented before her Maiestie. Newly reuiued and polished according to the decorum of these daies*, 1591.

William Webbe, probably the author of *A Discourse of English Poetrie* (1586). Though Webbe, recognizing the relativity of stylistic standards, refuses to pass absolute judgment on the superiority of the modern over the older version, he says that Wilmot has clothed the play

in a new sute . . . in handsomenes and fashion more answerable to these times, wherein fashions are so often altered. Let one word suffice for your encouragement herein: namely, that your commendable pains in disrobing him of his antike curiositie, and adorning him with the approoued guise of our statliest Englishe termes (not diminishing, but more augmenting his artificiall colours of absolute poesie deriued from his first parents) cannot but bee grateful to most mens appetites, who vpon our experience we know highly to esteem such lofty measures of sententiously composed Tragedies.

In 1595 Gervase Markham saw fit to issue a new edition of an old and popular book on hunting,[13] in the preface to which he pays tribute to the refined language of his own day, but hardly conceals a worthy admiration for the "honest simplicitie" of bygone days, which, indeed, restrains his reforming hand.

Therfore I humbly craue pardon of the precise and iudicial Reader, if sometimes I vse the words of the Ancient authour, in such plaine and homely English, as that time affoorded, not being so regardful, nor tying myself so strictly to deliuer any thing in the proper and peculiar wordes and termes of arte, which for the loue I beare to antiquitie, and to the honest simplicitie of those former times, I obserue as wel beseming the subject, and no whit disgracefull to the worke, our tong being not of such puritie then, as at this day the Poets of our age haue raised it to: of whom and in whose behalf I wil say thus much, that our Nation may only thinke her selfe beholding for the glory and exact compendiousness of our longuage.

Markham's intelligent appreciation of the earlier spirit of his native language, however, is almost unique, and certainly was not shared by one, I. R., who simply says of an old agricultural work which he edited, "I haue . . . labored to purge the same

---

[13] *The Gentlemans Academie. Or, The Booke of S. Albans: Containing three most exact and excellent Bookes: the first of Hawking, the second of all the proper termes of Hunting, and the last of Armorie: all compiled by Iuliana Barnes, in the yere . . . 1486. and now reduced into a better method*, by G. M., 1595.

from the barbarisme of the former times";[14] nor to Abraham Fraunce, soon to publish a rhetoric of his own, who tells "the Learned Lawyers" of England that as for

the style of thease late Cyuilians, whiche is somewhat more laboured and less vnseemely then that of their forefathers, wee maye as iustly say that there is the lyke diuersitie to bee manifestly perceaued between the homely speach of oure auncient Lawyers, and the finer phrase of late wryters in our Common lawe.[15]

He is impressed, however, more by linguistic change than by the progress his mother tongue had made; and the "inconstancy [which] is in words," and for which he cites Horace as an authority, prompts him to advise writers to "vse that phrase which is most vsuall: and though in knowledge and conceipt wee contend to bee singular, yet in vttering our thoughts, let all bee made partakers."

Evidence of the change that had come over opinions of the vernacular is revealed even more strikingly in other ways than in definite statements regarding it. In 1563 Alexander Neville published a translation of Seneca's *Oedipus*, the dedication of which reads in part: "For I to no other ende remoued hym from his naturall and loftye Style to our corrupt and base, or as al men affyrme it: most barbarous Language." In a later edition

---

[14] *Fitzharberts Booke of Husbandrie: Devided into foure seuerall Bookes, very necessary and profitable for all sorts of people. And now newlie corrected amended, and reduced, into a more pleasing forme of English then before,* 1598. (The author was John Fitzherbert.)

[15] *The Lawiers Logike, exemplifying the præcepts of Logike by the practise of the common Lawe,* 1588. Sometimes the newly acquired confidence in the literary powers of the vernacular is perceptible in the changed tone with which translators speak of their work. In the dedication of a translation of a book by Francisco Sansovino, Robert Hitchcock says that the "golden booke beautified with a thousand graces, is translated out of the Italian tung, though not in such beauty as becomes the grauitie thereof, yet stripped gentlye out of his gaye garments, it is clothed and plainely apparelled in such comely weeds and cleane roabes, as euery parte and proportion of the booke may easily be seene and well perceiued, and albeit that a fine Italian in an English groce gaberdine is not fashioned in all formes to please euery strangers fancye, yet the personage may be passable when all comelines is vsed for the setting forth of the same . . . Sansouino is no whit disfigured to walke openly in such English habit as is found fitte for him." *The Quintesence of Wit,* 1590. Hitchcock goes as far as decent modesty will permit.

A. Neville :
change of
view from
1563 - 1581

of the translation Neville changed "al men" into "some men," and inserted "(but vntruly)" before "affyrme."[16] Here we have a clear picture of one man's opinion changing under the pressure of the times. But Neville was not the only man to oppose the old charge of barbarousness brought against the native tongue. Thomas Hudson translated into English verse a long French poem by the very popular poet Du Bartas to convince James VI of Scotland that his mother tongue was not barbarous. But let Hudson tell his own story.

As your Maiestie Sir, after your accustomed and vertuous maner was sometyme discoursing at Table with such your Domestiques, as chaunced to bee attendant. It pleased your Highnesse (not onely to esteeme the pereles stile of the Greke HOMER, and the Latin VIRGIL to be inimitable to vs, whose toung is barbarous and corrupted:) But also to alledge partly throw delite your Maiest. tooke in the Hautie stile of those most famous Writers, and partly to sounde the opinion of others, that also the loftie Phrase, the graue inditement, the facound termes of the French Salust (for the like resemblaunce) could not be followed, nor sufficiently expressed in our rude and impollished english language. Wherein, I more boldly then aduisedly [with your Maiest. lycence] declared my simple opinion. Not calling to mind that I was to giue my verdit in presens of so sharp and clear-eied a censure as your highnesse is: But rashly I alledged that it was nothing impossible euen to followe the footsteppes of the same great Poet Salust, and to translate his vearse (which neuerthelesse is of it selfe exquisite) succinctlie, and sensibly in our owne vulgar speech. Whereupon, it pleased your Maiestie . . . to assign me, *The Historie of Iudith*, as an agreable Subiect to your highnesse, to be turned by me into English verse: Not for any speciall gift or Science that was in mee, who am inferiour in knowledge and erudition to the least of your Maiesties Court: But by reason (peraduenture) of my bolde assertion your Maiestie, who will not haue the meanest of your house vnoccupied, would haue mee to beare the yoke, and driue forth the pennance, that I had rashly procured. . . . In the which I haue so behaued my self, that

[16] See *Seneca his tenne Tragedies*, 1581. In the preface to the early edition of the translation Neville speaks of the play being "far transformed" in style though not in sense by his version, but in the later edition the expression is softened to read "somewhat transformed." Though Neville retains his prayer to the reader "to beare with my rudenes, and consydre the grosnes of our owne Countrey language, which can by no means aspire to the hyghe lofty Latinists stile," his deliberate changes outweigh these words as evidence, and suggest that the latter are more conventional than significant.

through your Maiest. concurrence, I haue not exceeded the number of the lynes written by my author: In euerie one of the which, hee also hath two sillabes mo then my English beares. And this not withstanding, I suppose your Maies. shall find litle of my Authors meaning pretermitted. Wherefore if thus much be done by me, who am of an other profesion, and of so simple literature, I leaue it to be consired [*sic*] by your Maiest. what such as ar consummat in letters and knowes the weightie words, the pithie sentences, the pollished tearmes, and full efficacie of the English toung would haue done.[17]

When men reverse their position on the nature of the language, and when they firmly uphold its eloquence even against the King, certainly a decided change in opinion has taken place.

Just as we see Hudson breaking away from and contending against the traditional view of the vernacular, so we find others, naturally near the beginning of the new era, who recognize the opinions of the past and then combat them. Jacques Bellot calls ~~J. Bellot~~ attention to "the small account in the which the English tongue hath bene had hitherto, by reason that no mention thereof haue bene made for the beter education of those that are desirous of the same tongue." Against this attitude he declares that the language is so rich that it deserves to be placed among the most famous of the modern languages.[18] George Pettie is even more determined in the stand he takes against those who disparage their own country and nation as barbarous compared with France and Italy, and who prefer a mean work written in the languages of those countries to a fine English translation. (Pettie's attitude, of course, diverges widely from the traditional view of the relative merits of originals and translations.)

. . . they consider not the profite which commeth by reading thynges in theyr owne Tongue, whereby they shall be able to conceiue the matter much sooner, and beare it away farre better, then if they reade it in a strange Tongue, whereby also they shall be inabled to speake, to discourse, to write, to indite, properly, fitly, finely, and wysely, but the worst is, they thinke that impossible to be doone in our Tongue: for

[17] *The Historie of Iudith in Forme of a Poeme. Penned in French, by the Noble Poet, G. Salust. Lord of Bartas. Englished by Tho. Hudson.* Edinburgh, 1584, dedication. It was in this fashion that one had to discuss literary matters with his sovereign.

[18] *The English Scholemaister* (1580), ed. T. Spira, 1912, p. 4.

they count it barren, they count it barbarous, they count it unworthy to be accounted of.

After criticizing particularly the scornful opposition to neologizing maintained by the disparagers of their native language, he takes up the gauntlet in behalf of the English language, just as Hudson was to do in a less audacious manner.

But how hardly soeuer you deale with your tongue, how barbarous soeuer you count it, how little soeuer you esteeme it, I durst my selfe undertake (if I were furnished with learnyng otherwyse) to wryte in it as copiouslye for varietie, as compendiously for breuitie, as choycely for woordes, as pithily for sentences, as pleasauntly for figures, and euery way as eloquently, as any writer should do in any vulgar tongue whatsoeuer.[19]

How far we have come from Andrew Borde's assertion (1548) that "The speche of England is a base speche to other noble speches"!

The age itself entertained no doubts as to the causes of this change. In a passage quoted on a previous page, Markham asserts (1595) that the English nation owes the exact compendiousness, glory, and purity of their tongue to the poets alone, and Nash maintains (1592) that "the Poets of our time . . . haued cleansed our language from barbarisme, and made the vulgar sort, here in *London* . . . to aspire to a richer puritie of speach than is communicated with the Comminalty of any Nation vnder heauen."[20] Thomas Lodge believes (1593) that

[19] *The Civile Conuersation of M. Steeuen Guazzo, written first in Italian, and nowe translated out of French by George Pettie, deuided into foure bookes,* 1581, preface.

[20] *Complete Works,* ed. Grosart, II, 61. (See *supra,* p. 174.) Markham and others mentioned in this paragraph had been anticipated by Ralph Holinshed at the very beginning of this period of linguistic confidence. In 1577 he maintained that the vernacular had developed until "there is no one speache vnder the sonne spoken in our time, that hath or can haue more varietie of words, copie of phrases, or figures or floures of eloquence, then hath our Englishe tongue . . ." This condition he attributes in part to Chaucer, Gower, and others, "notwithstanding that it neuer came, vnto the type of perfection, vntill the time of Queene Elizabeth, wherein many excellent writers haue fully accomplished the ornature of the same, to their great prayse and immortall commendation." *The Firste volume of the Chronicles of England, Scotlande, and Irelande,* 1577, fol. 5ʳ.

Holinshed

it was the modern poets "Who brought the Chaos of our tongue
in frame," and Francis Meres (1598), that it is the eloquence of
"our English poets, which makes our language so gorgeous and
delectable among vs."[21] Nor do the poets who were thought
responsible for the eloquence of the vernacular receive only a
general reference; they frequently are specified. The author of
The Arte of English Poesie (1589) draws up a list of Elizabethan poets whom he affectionately thanks "for their studious
endeuours, commendably employed in enriching and polishing
their native Tongue, neuer so furnished or embellished as of
late," and he thinks that they have "so much beautified our
English tong as at this day it will be found our nation is nothing
inferior to the French or Italian." Meres likewise engages in a
roll call of Sidney, Spenser, Daniel, Drayton, Warner, Shakespeare, Marlowe, and Chapman, by whom "the English tongue
is mightily enriched, and gorgeouslie inuested in rare ornaments
and resplendent abiliments."[22] Harvey praises Stanyhurst,
Fraunce, Watson, Daniel, Nash, and especially Sidney and
Spenser, whose "lively springs of streaming eloquence" enriched
and polished their native tongue.[23] But it is Sidney and Spenser
to whom greatest praise is accorded for making the language
eloquent. The former, Nash says, was "the first (in our language) . . . that repurified Poetrie from Arts pedantisme, and
that instructed it to speake courtly,"[24] and Drayton pays a similar
compliment to Sidney's prose, which

> . . . throughly pac'd our language as to show
> That plenteous *English* hand in hand might goe
> With Greeke and Latine, and did first reduce
> Our tongue from Lillies writing then in use.[25]

[21] *Phillis*, 1593, "The Induction," and *Elizabethan Critical Essays*,
II, 310.

[22] *Elizabethan Critical Essays*, II, 62; and *Palladis Tamia*, 1598, fol. 280ʳ.
Meres says that if the Muses should speak English, they "would speak with
Shakespeares fine filed phrase." (*Ibid.*, fol. 282ʳ.) Puttenham looked upon
Wyatt and Surrey as "the first reformers" of the English tongue, and his opinion
was seconded by Harington. *Elizabethan Critical Essays*, II, 63, 219.

[23] *Archaica*, ed. Brydges, II, 39.

[24] *Complete Works*, ed. Grosart, III, 112.

[25] "To My Most Dearely-Loved Friend Henery Reynolds Esquire, of
Poets and Poesie" (1627), in *Works*, ed. J. W. Hebel, III, 228.

There was, however, a dissident voice raised amid the chorus of praise of poetry for refining the tongue, for as is frequently the case with the history of ideas, another thought movement cut across the one which we have been following. This was the attempt to introduce classical meters into English poetry, and its influence upon opinions of the vernacular is entirely intelligible. Underlying the change in the linguistic view of the age was the idea that the proper test of the eloquence of a language was its ability to make use of the principles (especially those pertaining to *elocutio*) of classical rhetoric, the mother of all eloquence. Though prosody was properly a function of grammar, rhetorical and metrical discussions are found together in English treatises on poetry, for eloquence was revealed in both poets and prose writers, and rhetorics were written for both. Thus the attempt to introduce classical prosody was only one aspect of the general effort to secure eloquence for the English language by following classical precepts. Webbe, who was an ardent supporter of the metrical principles of antiquity, and who recognized the part played by prose writers in the refinement of the mother tongue, remarks in sad tones that "onelie Poetrie hath founde fewest frends to amende it," and as a result "our English speeche, in some of the wysest mens iudgements, hath neuer attained to anie sufficient ripenes, nay not ful auoided the reproch of barbarousness in Poetry." If poets would but "consult one halfe houre with their heauenly Muse" they might win great credit to their native tongue, whether by classical principles or by rules "established by the naturall affectation of the speeche," that is, classical rules modified to suit the peculiar characteristics of English.[26]

Another critic of the traditional way of writing poetry praises, as praise he must, Golding, Harington, Phaer, Daniel, and especially Spenser, but he perceives a great lack in them. "I would to God," he exclaims, "they had done so well in trew hexameters, for they had then beautified our language. For the Greekes and

Webbe

---

[26] *Elizabethan Critical Essays*, I, 227. In the next century Alexander Gil flatly contradicted Webbe: "Nor, moreover, should you think that the brand of barbarism is placed upon the English language because we do not follow Latin numbers." *Logonomia Anglica*, 1619, p. 133.

Latines did in a manner abolish quite that kinde of rythme-prose; and why should not we doe the like in Englishe?" Though some might think the vernacular inadequate for classical meters, yet it would itself "be the more inriched, adorned, and more eloquent, if they [poets] would make trial thereof [classical principles], or could compose them [poems] artificially and eloquently to delight the Readers, to resound with a grace in their ears." He encourages those who think the task too diffi-cult by exclaiming "What language so hard, harsh, or barbarous, that time and art will not amend?" Among the benefits which "This trew kinde of hexametred and pentametred verse will bring" are: "First, it will enrich our speach with good and sig-nificant wordes," and "it will direct a trew Idioma, and will teach trew orthography, for as gould surpasseth leade, so the hex-ameters surpass rythme prose." This "artificial" way of writing verse gives poetry "a grace in our english tongue especially, above other tongues; so it be good rythme, though they be the harder to make." Disclaiming any desire to criticize any man's work, he maintains that "it is the enriching and beautifying of our language, and the credit and glory of the verse, that I regarde."[27] To understand the benefits which the author sees in the prosodical innovation, but upon which he fails to elaborate, it is necessary to turn to the neologizing, orthographic, and metrical move-ments of the century. Just as translators in order to render the meaning of their originals find it necessary to retain words and thus enrich the language, so those who write poetry according to classical principles will find it necessary to import terms for their quantitative feet. And since in the ancient metrical system quan-

---

[27] *The First Booke of the Preseruation of King Henry the vij* . . . *Compiled in english rythmicall Hexameters,* 1599, preface. (This work may be found in the second volume of J. P. Collier's *Illustrations of Old English Literature.*) In a prefatory poem addressed to Queen Elizabeth, which ex-presses the substance of the preface, the author gives his purpose in composing the work:

And to refyne our speach, to procure our natural English
Far to be more elegant; that verse may skilfully florish.
Which when it is re'difi'd, eloquent, and knowne to be perfit,
Unto thee, and to thy realme, (O puisant Prince) what a credit!
Hexameters will amend our speach (thou sacred Eliza)
Publish an orthography, and teach vs a trew idioma.

tity was in part determined by spelling, to introduce the system into English verse, it would be necessary to establish and standardize the spelling of the vernacular, a consummation dear to the hearts of the orthographic reformers. And finally, since nearly all the metrical innovators insisted that the propriety of the vernacular should always be observed in employing Latin and Greek feet, the latter process would necessarily bring to light and establish this propriety, or "idioma."

Though not of equal importance with the poets, prose writers are frequently cited as examples of the eloquence possible in the English tongue. The muddleheaded Webbe, who, as we have seen, thought that the refinement of the vernacular depended upon the employment of classical meters, makes a dubious distinction between the state of the language as employed by prose writers and by poets. The latter had left much to be desired in rendering the language eloquent, but the former, "who have aspyred to royall dignitie and statelie grace in our English tongue," have weeded it from errors, purged it from faults, and polished it from barbarism.[28] Harvey especially commends the prose of Sidney, as well as the poetry of Spenser, both of whom were his friends, and in addition looks back and praises the eloquence of Cheke and Ascham.[29] He also thinks that there are others, in London as well as at the universities, who are so capable of handling the vernacular that, were they encouraged to do so, "who can tell what comparison this tongue might wage with the most-floorishing Languages of Europe." Meres, who was willing to test the excellence of the vernacular by the touchstone of the classics, maintains that "eloquence hath found many preachers and oratours worthy fauourers of her in the English tongue."[30] Though recognizing in the style of the poets the clearest evidence of the ability of the language to express all kinds of rhetorical figures, which power constituted eloquence,

[28] *Elizabethan Critical Essays,* I, 227.

[29] *A New Letter of Notable Contents,* p. 8, in *Archaica,* Vol. II. In *Pierces Supererogation,* 1593 (*Archaica,* II, 188–89) Harvey gives an extended list of poets and prose writers who bear testimony to the excellence of the language, among them a number of preachers, each of whom is signalized by some stylistic virtue.

[30] *Elizabethan Critical Essays,* II, 310.

the Elizabethans could not fail to note the figurative language of Lyly, Sidney, and other prose writers,[31] and, with their eyes cleared by this experience, to look back to the time when for the most part eloquence was denied the language, and to perceive excellence in More, Smith, Ascham, Cheke, and others who had used the vernacular effectively.

Since, then, writers had revealed the literary possibilities of their native tongue, they were given due credit for having refined the language, which, in turn, lost its character of barbarousness and assumed that of eloquence. One other interesting element ↓ in this linguistic view should be emphasized. The refinement and adornment of the mother tongue were themselves considered the goal of literature. In other words, literature was considered instrumental to language, not language to literature. Writers are more frequently praised for what they have done for the medium of their expression than for the intrinsic value of their compositions; and in view of the humble opinion previously entertained of the vernacular, we can well understand the gratitude which was felt toward those who had raised it from its low estate. Holinshed attributes the "excellencie of the English tongue" to the "many excellent writers [who] haue fully accomplished the ornature of the [language] to their great prayse and immortall commendation."[32] The severest criticism that E. K. brings against these who objected to Spenser's revival of old words is that they not only do not know their own language but have such a low regard for it that they both refuse to embellish it, and regret that others do. The English poets whom Meres pits against the ancients derive their value from the "rare ornaments and resplendent abiliments" with which they have enriched the vernacular. The nameless advocate of English hexameters offers

---

[31] William Covell sees in Hooker's great work "the eloquence of a most pure stile," which he considers the best to be found among English writers. *A Iust and Temperate Defence of the Five Books of Ecclesiastical Policie,* 1603, Article 21, pp. 146–52.

[32] *The Firste volume of the Chronicles of England, Scotlande, and Irelande,* 1577, fol. 5ʳ. Holinshed believed that originally the English language was rough, "but now chaunged with vs into a farre more fine and easie kind of vtteraunce, and so polished and helped with new and milder wordes that it is" inferior to none.

as the only purpose of his proposal the beautifying of the English language, and Puttenham publishes a list of contemporary poets to secure for them due praise for adorning their mother tongue.[33] In the preface to his translation of Ariosto (1591) Harington "affectionately thanck[s] [Elizabethan poets] for their studious endeuours commendably employed in enriching and polishing their natiue Tongue, neuer so furnished or embellished of late." In fact, practically all the quotations relative to poetry given in this chapter bear testimony to this attitude. In order to remind writers of their proper subordination to the vernacular, William Warner asserts that, "whatsoeuer Writer is most famous, the same is therefore indebted to his natiue Language." The language was considered a prized possession; its improvement, an all-important goal and a notable achievement; and its revealed excellence, justification for pride and confidence. No finer expression of this pride has been uttered by any one than by Samuel Daniel, one of the rarest spirits in an age of rare spirits. Near the end of *Musophilus: Containing a generall defence of learning*,[34] he, as numerous others had done, elaborates upon the value and strength of "Powre aboue powres, O heavenly Eloquence," and exemplifies it by his native tongue:

> Should we this ornament of glorie then
> As th' immateriall fruits of shades, neglect?
> Or should we carelesse come behind the rest
> In powre of wordes, that go before in worth
> When as our accents equall to the best
> Is able greater wonders to bring forth:
> When all that euer hotter spirits exprest
> Comes bettered by the patience of the North?
> And who in time knowes whither we may vent
> The treasure of our tongue, to what strange shores
> This gaine of our best glorie shal be sent,
> T'enrich vnknowing Nations with our stores?
> What worlds in th' yet vnformed Occident
> May come refin'd with th' accents that are ours?

[33] *The Arte of English Poesie*, ed. Gladys D. Willcock and Alice Walker, p. 60.

[34] Found in *The Poeticall Essayes of Sam. Danyel. Newly corrected and augmented*, 1599.

Or who can tell for what great worke in hand
   The greatnes of our stile, is now ordain'd?
   What powres it shall bring in, what spirits command,
   What thoughts let out, what humors keep restrain'd
   What mischiefe it may powrefully withstand,
   And what faire ends may thereby be attain'd.
And as for Poesie (mother of this force)
   That breeds, brings forth, and nourishes this might,
   Teaching it in a loose, yet measured course,
   With comely motions how to go vpright:
   And fostring it with bountifull discourse
   Adorns it thus in fashions of delight.[35]

I have called the English language a prized possession of the Elizabethans, but in view of Daniel's "our best glorie," I see I have considerably underestimated it. Since the eloquential powers of the language had been fully revealed, and since eloquence was itself considered a quality of the highest value, equal even to wisdom,[36] this attitude is quite comprehensible.

But rhetoric was the mother of eloquence, and by the very nature of the case should have aroused great interest, especially with respect to its use in the vernacular. In surveying briefly the English rhetorics of the sixteenth century it is necessary to note that eloquence was for the most part associated only with that division of rhetoric called "elocutio," which in turn was considered largely a matter of figures of speech. There was little originality in the English treatises, but that is a matter of small importance for our purposes. As early as 1524 Leonard Cox partly translated and partly composed his *Arte or crafte of*

[35] In spirit Mulcaster is akin to Daniel. "If the spreading sea, and the spacious land could vse anie spech, theie would both show you, where, and in how manie strange places, theie haue sene our peple, and also giue you to wit, that theie deall in as much, and as great varietie of matters, as anie other peple do, whether at home or abrode. Which is the reason why our tung doth serue to so manie vses, bycause it is conuersant with so manie peple, and so well acquainted with so manie matters, in so sundrie kindes of dealing." *The First Part of the Elementarie*, 1582, p. 90.

[36] See the dedication of Henry Peacham's *Garden of Eloquence*, 1577. He calls "Wysedome, and Eloquence, the onelye Ornamentes, whereby mannes lyfe is bewtifyed."

L. Cox

Rhetoryke, which, though mentioning "elecutio" among the requisites of an orator, does not discuss it, but relying largely on Cicero, analyzes some orations, demonstrative and judicial, into their constituent parts. In the early years of the second half of the century there were several English rhetorics, the most famous being Thomas Wilson's *Arte of Rhetorique, for the vse of all suche as are studious of Eloquence* (1553), which reached a second edition in 1560. Wilson covers the field more ambitiously, comprehensively, and with more show of originality than any of the others, but less than a fifth of the book is devoted to elocution. His purpose was not so much to justify or promote the use of eloquence in the vernacular, but rather, as the title suggests, to teach the less educated something about the art so that they might understand and judge the works of the learned.[37] He does say that the purpose of rhetoric is "to dispose and order matters of our owne inuention," but it may be noted that he is silent regarding elocution, or eloquence.[38]   Richard Rainolde's *Booke called the Foundacion of Rhetorike* (1563) may be ignored since it does not deal with elocution, and since all its examples are from the classics. The case is different, however, with Richard Sherry, whose two treatises are concerned with nothing but elocution. In the dedication to the first, *A treatise of Schemes and Tropes* (1550), he earnestly upholds the thesis that eloquence is possible in the English language. Yet he asserts that the purpose of the book is "for the better vnderstandynge of such good authors as they [readers] reade," and "better to vnderstande and iudge of the goodlye gyftes and ornamentes in mooste famous and eloquente oratoures," evidently Latin and Greek. Though Sherry believes that writers have already demonstrated the eloquence of the vernacular, he seems not to have published his rhetorics to assist writers to be eloquent in English, but only for the pedagogical purpose of instructing students in the principles of the art. Certainly the title of his second treatise bears

Wilson

Sherry

---

[37] *The Arte of Rhetorique*, ed. G. H. Mair, p. 5. In some places, however, such as the famous section on style and borrowed terms, he directs his attention to English usage.

[38] Elsewhere he implies that little eloquence is to be found in English writings: "Many can tel their mind in English, but fewe can vse meete termes, and apt order." *Ibid.*, p. 161.

out this interpretation.[39] Furthermore, he follows his Latin original very closely. The book is composed of Latin sections devoted entirely to eloquence in that tongue, followed by English translations, in which all rhetorical principles are referred directly to the Latin language, except in one or two cases, such as in the definition of *barbaralexis*, where a sentence relative to the vernacular is inserted.[40]

In the last quarter of the century a quite different situation arose. Within a dozen years five rhetorical discussions were published in English, four within five years of each other, and all were concerned for the most part with elocution.[41] Though the title of Peacham's volume resembles those which we have discussed, yet the many illustrations introduced from the English

---

[39] *A Treatise of the Figures of Grammer and Rhetorike, profitable for al that be studious of Eloquence, and in especiall for suche as in Grammer scholes doe reade moste eloquente Poetes and Oratours: Whereunto is ioygned the oration which Cicero made to Cesar* . . . 1555.

[40] *Ibid.*, fol. 5ʳ. Cf. fol. 12.

[41] Henry Peacham, *The Garden of Eloquence conteyning the Figures of Grammer and Rhetorick, from whence maye bee gathered all manner of Flowers, Coulors, Ornaments, Exornations, Formes and Fashions of speech, very profitable for all those that be studious of Eloquence, and that reade most Eloquent Poets and Orators, and also helpeth much for the better vnderstanding of the holy Scriptures,* 1577 (1593); Dudley Fenner, *The Artes of Logike and Rhetorike, plainelie set foorth in the Englishe tounge, easie to be learned and practised: together with examples for the practise of the same, for Methode in the gouernment of the familie, prescribed in the word of God: And for the whole in the resolution or opening of certaine partes of Scripture, according to the same,* 1584 (1588); Angel Day, *The English Secretorie,* 1586 (1592, 1595, 1599); Abraham Fraunce, *The Arcadian Rhetorike: Or The Præcepts of Rhetorike made plaine by examples, Greeke, Latin, English, Italian, French, Spanish* . . . 1588; George Puttenham, *The Arte of English Poesie,* 1589. Including later editions published before the end of the century, the dates of which are inserted in the parentheses, five rhetorics were published in the ninth decade, and four in the tenth. Day's work, however, does not become an authentic rhetoric until the second edition, 1592. The title of the 1599 edition reads: *The English Secretary, Or Methode of writing Epistles and Letters; With A declaration of such Tropes, Figures, and Schemes, as either vsually or for ornament sake are therin required. Also the parts and office of a Secretarie, Deuided into two bookes. Now newly reuised and in many parts corrected and amended.* Another rhetoric composed near the end of the century but not published, and concerned only with elocution, was John Hoskins' *Directions for Speech and Style.* See the late Professor Hoyt Hudson's edition in *Princeton Studies in English,* 1935.

Bible clearly indicate that eloquence is possible in the vernacular.[42] The title of Fenner's treatise shows that he desires to teach his readers to employ eloquence in their own language. Nearly all his illustrations are also from the English Bible.[43] The title of Fraunce's little book reveals over what a wide range the author collected his examples, and, together with the text itself, proves his great indebtedness to Sidney. Though he has something to say about delivery, he is primarily interested in "Brauerie of speach," which in his mind consists only in rhetorical figures, and examples of which he abundantly discovered in the poetry and prose of Sidney, and occasionally in Spenser. Puttenham expressly wrote his book for English poets, with the firm conviction that eloquence was just as possible in English poetry as in Latin or Greek, "our language being no lesse copious pithie and significative" and "admitting no fewer rules and nice diuersities then theirs."[44] He states emphatically that the purpose of the English names given by him to the various figures of speech is to assist him in making "of a rude rimer, a learned and Courtly poet."[45] Book III of his work, which consists primarily of definitions and discussions of rhetorical figures, seeks to teach eloquence to "Ladies and young Gentlewomen, or idle Courtiers, desirous to become skilful in their owne mother tongue, and for their priuate recreation to make now and then ditties of pleasure."[46] Angel Day is, if anything, even more explicit in relating eloquence to the English language. In the second edition of his *English Secretorie* (1592) he not only marked in the margin of his many illustrative letters the names of the numerous figures of speech contained in them, but he also added

[In margin, handwritten:] Fraunce a Ramist. Jones sees no difference.

[42] Some additions, significant for the light they throw upon the changed attitude toward the study of rhetoric, appear in the second edition of 1593, in which most of the discussions of the various figures are followed by two sections, one explaining the use of the figure and the other giving cautions against its abuse. In short, Peacham's purpose now concentrates upon showing how eloquence may be achieved in the English language.

[43] Only thirteen pages of Fenner's small volume are devoted to "*The Arte of* Rhetorike, *plainely set foorth in* our English tounge, easie both to be vnderstoode and practised," and five of them are concerned with the "rules of Sophistrie." The others are concerned entirely with elocution.

[44] *The Arte of English Poesie*, ed. Willcock and Walker, p. 5.

[45] *Ibid.*, p. 158.

[46] *Loc. cit.*

a section in which these figures are defined and discussed "to the intent the learner maie aswell in his natiue tongue, know the right vse of figures and Tropes heretofore neuer by him vnderstoode, as also discerne and vse them, out of others and in his own writings," and to show "how much the phrase of our daylie speech by well ordering and deliurie is graced with Figures and other ornaments of Art."[47]

The difference between the early and later rhetorics is manifested in several ways. First, in the later period elocution much more nearly monopolizes rhetorical discussion. Again, the purpose of treatises on rhetoric changes from pedagogical instruction in the knowledge of the art of figures, largely relative to the classical languages, to instructions for its use in the vernacular. And third, the use of classical illustrations in large part gives way to the employment of English examples. The effect of all this was to emphasize the eloquential powers of the vernacular, in which all figures of speech necessary for eloquence could be employed.

The rhetoricians, then, assisted the poets and prose writers in convincing the age of the power of their language. And during the last quarter of the century this conviction is repeatedly expressed. As early as 1577, the year in which Peacham's rhetoric appeared, Holinshed gives a slight history of the English language from the time of the Anglo-Saxons to "the type of perfection" found in the Elizabethan period. The Saxon, he says, introduced

an hard and rough kinde of speach god wotte, when our nation was brought first into acquaintance withall, but now chaunged with vs into a farre more fine and easie kind of vtteraunce, and so polished and helped with new and milder wordes that it is to be aduouched howe there is no one speache vnder the sonne spoken in our time, that hath or can haue more varietie of words, copie of phrases, or figures or floures of eloquence, then hath our English tongue.[48]

Whereas in the past those associated with the universities and steeped in classical lore were the least likely to concede any

---

[47] *The English Secretary*, 1599, 1st Part, p. 9; 2d Part, p. 76.

[48] *The Firste volume of the Chronicles*, 1577, fol. 5ʳ. The account of the language, as we should expect, is considerably expanded by John Hooker in the edition of 1586.

literary qualities to the vernacular, the university wits of this period reveal a different attitude. Harvey holds that the vernacular is quite capable of imitating "the Greek or Latin, or other eloquent languages," and he urges English poets to "use heavenly eloquence," and "lively springs of streaming eloquence."[49] Nash speaks of the "sweet satietie of eloquence which the lauish of our copious Language maie procure."[50] In reply to the accusation that in one of his books "I shewed no eloquent phrases, nor fine figuratiue conueiance," Robert Greene replies that he was unwilling to "dishonor that high misterie of eloquence, and derogate from the dignitie of our English toonge, eyther to employ any figure or bestow one choyce English word vpon such disdained rakehels as those Conny-catchers."[51]

Even in translation, where comparison with the classics is frequently challenged, and where in the past the vernacular had suffered most by that comparison, a new tone is perceptible though the old lingers on. One translator is encouraged to undertake his task by the example of Arthur Golding, who made "*Ouid speake English in no worse Termes, than the Authors owne gifts gaue him grace to write in Latine,*" and another does not hesitate to consider a translation of Terence

> The perfect pattern of pure Latin speche
> In English phrase most fitly here exprest.[52]

These sentiments may have been determined only by the spirit of compliment, but certainly such was not always the case. The orthographic reformer, William Bullokar, in the preface to a translation of a Latin version of Aesop's *Fables* (1585), admits that his work is "not in the best phrase for english" since his purpose made him stick too close to his original, but he maintains that the language itself is "capable of the perfect sense thereof [Latin], and might be vsed in the best phrase," if more liberty

---

[49] *Four Letters*, 1592, pp. 16, 39, in *Archaica*, ed. Brydges, Vol. II.
[50] *Elizabethan Critical Essays*, I, 310.
[51] *The Second part of Conny-catching*, 1591, dedication.
[52] See the dedication of *Ten Books of Homers Iliades, translated out of French, By A. H*[all], 1581; and a poem by R. Cooke prefixed to *Andria. The first Comoedie of Terence, in English . . . Carefully translated out of Latin, by Maurice Kyffin*, 1588.

were permitted. Furthermore, he vows that in his future translations, "I wil bend my-self too follow the excellencie of English
in the best phrase thereof."[53] In the preface to his translation
of Homer (1598) Chapman speaks out against those who disparage his work because of the "defect of our language, not able
to expresse the coppie and elegancie of the originall," maintaining that no matter "how full of height and roundnesse soeuer
Greeke be aboue English, yet is there no depth of conceit triumphing in it, but . . . in a sufficient translator it may be
exprest." And if the Italians and French have not thought it
presumptuous to turn Homer into their own languages, "what
curious, proud, and poore shamefastnesse should let an English
muse to traduce [translate] him, when the language she workes
withall is more comfortable, fluent, and expressive; which I
would your Lordship would commaunde mee to proue against all
our whippers of their owne complement in their countries dialect."[54] No longer was it possible for a translator to advance the
inadequacy of the vernacular as an excuse for the defects of his
own work. Richard Haydocke echoes the past when he says that
for the sake of a common good, "I haue taught a good Italian to
speake a bad English phrase," but he expresses the spirit of his
contemporaries in explaining that "I indevoured nothing more,
than the true vse, benefit, and delight of the Reader, howsoever

---

[53] In a prefatory poem Bullokar insists that with its own phrase English
can keep the meaning of the original and yet produce "more comely grace,"
if not tied too strictly to the Latin. In a poem at the end of the translation,
entitled "William Bullokar to his chyld," he insists upon the dignity of English
and its equality with Latin.

[54] *Elizabethan Critical Essays*, II, 300. In a poem written before 1618
and prefixed to Holland's translation of Camden's *Britain*, 1637, John Davies
of Hereford asks:

> Shall English be so poore, and rudely-base
> As not be able (through meere penury)
> To tell what French hath said with gallant grace,
> And most tongues else of lesse facunditie?
> God shield it should; and Heav'n foresend that we
> Should so debase our owne deere mother-tongue,
> That shewes our thoughts (how ever high they be)
> With higher tearmes, and eloquence among,
> Then, let me muzzle those so dogged mouthes
> That byte and barke at what they should defend.

mine vnexercised stile shall come short of the sweetnesse of our much refined tongue."[55]

Mulcaster   It was Richard Mulcaster, however, who most loudly proclaimed the equality of the vernacular with the classical languages, most earnestly asserted its independence of them, and most confidently urged its widest use. English, he insists, when reduced to principles "is as artificiall, and of as sure note, as the best language is." He regrets the fact that Latin is more appreciated than English, simply because the first is studied and the second ignored.[56] No tongue, he continues, is by nature finer than another, but profits only by the industry of those who endeavor "to garnish it with eloquence, and to enrich it with learning." It was, he asserts, through such a nourishing of their native language that the Romans brought Latin to that excellence which made it the general depository of knowledge and the universal language even in his own day. We should honor Latin, but should we not also follow the practice of the Romans? "For did not those tungs vse euen the same means to braue themselves ear theie proued so beawtifull." Though not denying the value of Latin, he pleads with a prophetic voice for the right of English to supersede it, and he issues a declaration of linguistic independence, animated by fervent patriotism:

Which two considerations being fullie answered, that we seke them [learned languages] from *profit* and kepe them for that conference,

[55] *A Tracte Containing the Artes of curious Paintinge Caruinge and Buildinge written first in Italian by Jo. Paul Lomatius* [Paolo Giovanni Lomazzo] *painter of Milan and Englished by R. H. student in Physik,* 1598, preface. A few years later Philemon Holland says of his translation of Pliny, that a pen in an Englishman's hand "is able sufficiently to expresse Greeke, Latine, and Hebrew." *The Historie of the world . . . The first Tome,* 1601, preface.

Stanyhurst shows this pride and confidence in the vernacular in an interesting way. Interpreting Phaer's postscript to his translation of Virgil as meaning that the earlier translator offered his work as a source from which beginning poets might secure eloquent language, Stanyhurst declares that he would scorn to borrow widely from his rival's translation "in so copious and fluent a language, as oure English tongue is," and that he could easily have done without any of his words, "Which I speake not of vanitie, too enhaunce my coonning, but of meere veritie, too aduaunce thee riches of oure speeche." See the dedication to his translation of Virgil, 1582.

[56] *The First Part of the Elementarie,* 1582, pp. 56, 180.

whatsoeuer else maie be don in our tung, either to serue priuat vses, or
the beawtifying of our speche, I do not se, but it maie well be admitted,
euen tho in the end it displaced the *Latin*, as the *Latin* did others, and
furnished it self by the *Latin* learning. For is it not in dede a meruellous
bondage, to becom seruants to one tung for learning sake, the most of
our time, with losse of most time, whereas we maie haue the verie same
treasur in our own tung, with the gain of most time? our own bearing
the ioyfull title of our libertie and fredom, the *Latin* tung remembring
vs, of our thraldom and bondage? I loue *Rome*, but *London* better, I
fauor *Italie*, but England more, I honor the Latin, but I worship the
English.

He says that it is no dishonor to ancient languages to wish their
learning and grace in English, but that it is dishonor to the
mother tongue not to give it that which it is capable of receiving.
Again and again he expresses the idea that the learning contained
in the language and not any peculiar virtue of the language itself
accounts for the supposed superiority of the classics. "The diligent labor of learned cuntriemen did so enrich these tungs, and
not the tungs them selues, tho theie proued verie pliable, as our
tung will proue, I dare assure it of knowledge, if our learned
cuntriemen will put to their labor. And why not I praie you, as
well in *English*, as either in *Latin* or anie tung else?" In advocating the use of the native tongue, he emphasizes the great gain
in the time spent in learning Latin or in trying to understand it,
as well as in the clearer understanding afforded by English. If
the native language is uncouth, it is so merely because it is unused,
and "our *English* wits be verie wel able, thanks be to God, if
their wils were as good, to make those vncouth and vnknown
learnings verie familiar to our peple." The industry and ability
of the English people can, by using the tongue for translation and
other purposes, bring the English language to the highest degree
of development. Never has there been a more eloquent plea to
use the English language.

Though he argues for the use of English as a home necessity,
he thinks that if Englishmen would only bend their wills to the
matter and method of their tongue, foreigners might come to
England for knowledge as they came for trade. Nor need anyone doubt that English can be so refined that in eloquence an

Englishman may be comparable to Cicero and Demosthenes, "And why not in dede comparable vnto them in all points thorough out for his naturall tung?" Eloquence and ideas are limited to no tongue nor soil. He urges more than once that to write in English is no dishonor to Latin, but mere justice to the mother tongue, and that progress itself demands sometimes that antiquity be deserted. His enthusiasm for his native language reaches its climax in the following confident words:

Mulcaster

> But why not all in *English*, a tung of it self both depe in conceit, and frank in deliuerie? I do not think that anie language, be it whatsoeuer, is better able to vtter all arguments, either with more pith, or greater planesse, then our *English* tung is, if the *English* vtterer be as skilfull in the matter, which he is to vtter: as the foren vtterer is. Which methink I durst proue in anie most strange argument, euen mine own self, tho no great clark, but a great welwiller to my naturall cuntrie. And tho we vse and must vse manie foren terms, when we deal with such arguments, we do not anie more then the brauest tungs do and euen verie those, which crake of their cunning. . . . It is our accident which restrains our tung, and not the tung it self, which will strain with the strongest, and stretch to the furthest, for either gouernment if we were conquerors, or for cunning, if we were treasurers, not anie whit behind either the subtile *Greke* for couching close, or the statelie *Latin* for spreding fair. Our tung is capable, if our peple wold be painfull.[57]

The development of the language for artistic purposes was one of the goals of literary endeavors. Attention was focused upon the instrument of composition, the vernacular, which was viewed with confidence and pride. This regard is everywhere apparent, even in such unlikely places as in the attempts to foist the principles of classical prosody upon native verse. As we have already noticed, the effort to employ the metrical principles of the ancients was only one aspect of the general movement to secure classical eloquence. The new versifying in the eyes of several critics was capable of rendering the English language eloquent.[58] To us it seems that the obvious unadaptability of

---

[57] *The First Part of the Elementarie*, pp. 267–77.

[58] See *supra*, pp. 180–84. Puttenham considered the employment of classical feet a "maner of exornation" comparable with figurative language, and he expressed the opinion that such feet "adorne and commend" English poetry. (*The Arte of English Poesie*, 1589, ed. Willcock and Walker, p. 137.) In the

English to the prosodical principles of the classical languages
would have created distrust in the language itself when an attempt to apply them was made, but such was not the case. The
most ardent supporters of the innovation either express their
complete confidence in the ability of the vernacular to support
it, or when the classical principles conflict with the vernacular,
insist upon its inviolability and upon their own prerogative to
change these principles to suit the "propriety," or peculiar
nature, of their native tongue. This is quite apparent in the
correspondence between Harvey and Spenser. The poet asks,
"why a Gods name may not we, as else the Greeks, haue the
kingdome of our owne Language, and measure our Accents by
the sounde, reseruing the Quantitie to the Verse?"[59] Harvey,
who thought his native tongue capable of imitating the eloquence
of any ancient or modern language, and who wished to be re-
membered as the inventor of the English hexameter, resented
the taking of any liberties with the vernacular, and when Spenser
noted that according to the law of position the middle syllable
of "carpenter" would necessarily be long, he would not give his
consent "to make your *Carpēnter* our *Carpĕnter*, an inche longer,
or bigger than God and his Englishe people haue made him." He
insisted that the language, as molded by custom and established
by use, be free from disturbance or control, that no metrical innovators go farther "then we are licenced and authorized by the
ordinarie vse, and custome, and proprietie, and Idiome, and, as
it were, Maiestie of our speech: which I accounte the only infallible and souuerraine Rule of all Rules."[60] Stanyhurst, who

next century Alexander Gil stoutly denied "that the brand of barbarism is placed
upon the English language because we do not follow Latin numbers," and he
asks if all the languages which employ nonclassical principles of prosody can
be called barbarous. (*Logonomia Anglica*, 1619, pp. 133–34.) One reason
that English critics with few exceptions insisted that the English language was
capable of employing classical meter was the desire to free it from any imputation of barbarism. Ascham had traced the origin of rhyme to the German "barbarians," and his ascription was accepted by others.

[59] *Three Proper and wittie, familiar Letters*, 1580, in *Works of Gabriel
Harvey*, ed. Grosart, I, 35.

[60] *Ibid.*, pp. 100, 103. Nash, though his opinion of his mother tongue was
indeed high, thought that it was entirely unsuited for the classical hexameter.
Elizabethan Critical Essays, II, 240.

tried to practice what he preached, is of the same opinion. Those who stick too closely to the classical rules governing quantity, he says,

Stanyhurst

dooe attribute a greater prerogatiue too the Latine tongue, than reason wyl affurd, and lesse libertye too oure language, than nature may permit. For in as much as thee Latins haue not beene authors of theese verses, but traced in thee steps of thee Greekes, why should we with thee stringes of thee Latin rules cramp oure tongue, more than the Latins do fetter theyre speeche, as yt were, wyth thee chaynes of the greeke perceptes. Also that nature wyl not permit vs too fashion oure wordes in al poinctes correspondent too thee Latinistes, may easely appeere in suche termes as we borrow of them [e.g., briefly from breviter].[61]

Webbe also insists upon the inviolability of the vernacular, and upon the right to introduce into classical principles any modification demanded by its peculiar nature. "Cannot we," he asks, "as well as the Latines did, alter the cannon of the rule according to the quality of our worde, and where our wordes and theyrs . . . will not agree, there to establish a rule of our owne to be directed by?" Campion, whose practice, as Daniel pointed out, belied his theory, limits his ardent advocacy of ancient metrical principles by asserting that his native tongue need not be tied to rigid rules of quantity, and that "aboue all the accent of our words is diligently to be obseru'd, for chiefly by the accent in any language the true value of the sillables is to be measured. Neither can I remember any impediment except position that can alter the accent of any sillable in our English verse."[62] English critics in general did not consider that the nature of the English language was any bar to the employment of the most "artificial" meters. Spenser assures Harvey that "I like your late Englishe Hexameters so exceedingly well, that I also enure my Penne sometime in that kinde: whyche I fynd indeede, as I haue heard you often defende in worde, neither so harde, nor so harshe, that it will easily and fairely yeelde it selfe to our Moother tongue."[63] The confused Webbe, who thought that in

[61] *Thee First Foure Bookes of Virgil His Aeneis, Translated intoo English heroical verse,* 1582, preface.

[62] *Elizabethan Critical Essays,* I, 279; II, 351.

[63] *Three Proper and wittie, familiar Letters,* 1580, in *Works of Gabriel Harvey,* ed. Grosart, I, 35.

poetry the native language had not entirely lost its barbarous character owing to the failure to employ classical principles, held to the opinion that utilization of these principles in English verse would so develop the language as to make its possibilities equal to those of the learned tongues.

. . . and no doubt, if such regarde of our English speeche and curious handling of our verse had beene long since thought vppon, and from time to time been pollished and bettered by men of learning, iudgement, and authority, it would ere this haue matched them [Latin and Greek] in all respects.[64]

There were, of course, those who doubted the ability of the vernacular to sustain the old-new method of versification, and one of the objections was that the English vocabulary was not copious enough to furnish words suitable to classical feet. This objection an anonymous author of a poem in English hexameters emphatically denies: "But I say that it is."[65] The attitude toward the metrical proposal was similar to the fundamental attitude toward neologizing, namely, that use would wear off novelty, and that the language would be enriched. The metrical test was the severest to which the language was put, but, in the eyes of the later Elizabethans, the mother tongue came off with flying colors.

The last quarter of the century was not so vague as regards the actual elements that constituted eloquence as preceding generations had been. The writers of this period were not content only with proclaiming the vernacular eloquent; they also analyzed the language to discern some of the qualities which accounted for its excellence. The most important of these was copiousness. "There is," says Holinshed, "no one speache vnder the sonne spoken in our time, that hath or can haue more varietie of words and copie of phrases."[66] Webbe recognizes "the plenti-

---

[64] *Elizabethan Critical Essays*, I, 255–56.

[65] See the preface to *The First Booke of the Preseruation of King Henry the vij*, 1599, in J. P. Collier, *Illustrations of Old English Literature*, Vol. II.

[66] *The Firste volume of the Chronicles*, 1577, fol. 5ʳ. Richard Carew, in "The Excellencie of the English tongue," first printed in the second edition of Camden's *Remaines*, 1614, though believed by G. G. Smith (*Elizabethan Critical Essays*, II, 285) to have been composed a few years before the end of the century, finds four outstanding qualities in the vernacular: significancy, easiness, copiousness, and sweetness, but it was the third concerning which the Elizabethans and subsequent generations were most certain.

full fulness of our speeche," and Nash, "the lauish of our copious Language."[67] Puttenham thinks that his mother tongue is not inferior to French or Italian "for copie of language."[68] Robert Parry holds that English writers may challenge comparison with Cicero himself, though "writing in their owne mother tongue, which language is growne nowe to be so copious, that it may compare with most of the richest tongues in all *Europe,* such is the carefull industrie of our Countrimen (who in mine opinion deserue due praises,) to amplifie the same."[69] Parry believed, as undoubtedly the others did, that the richness of the English vocabulary was due to the methods of augmenting English which have been discussed in previous chapters, and his sentiment is echoed by John Florio. The latter emphasizes the "yeerely increase" of words in the vernacular, greater than in all other tongues, because "daily both new wordes are inuented; and books still found, that make a new supply of old." As a result of this borrowing and revival "it must needs be a pleasure to them [Englishmen] to see so rich a toong [Italian] out-vide by their mother-speech, as by the manie-fold Englishes of manie wordes in this is manifest."[70]

Although copiousness and variety are the linguistic virtues most frequently and justifiably emphasized, other qualities are claimed for the vernacular. Since, however, these were the product of enthusiasm as often as the object of perception, they may be cursorily treated. Sidney considered his mother tongue capable of any excellence such as the power to express thoughts sweetly and properly, freedom from the cramping rules of grammar, and felicity in compounding words, the last of which he considered the greatest of linguistic beauties. Puttenham viewed it as significative, that is, as able to express the subtleties of thought. Webbe and others found in it gallant grace, fluency, and rich possibilities for rhyme. Chapman stated that it was more fluent, expressive, and "conformable," that is, more adjustable to intellectual and artistic demands, than any

[67] *Elizabethan Critical Essays,* I, 274, 310.

[68] *Ibid.,* II, 62.

[69] *Moderatus, or the Adventures of the Black Knight,* 1595, preface.

[70] *A Worlde of Wordes, Or Most copious and exact Dictionarie in Italian and English,* 1598, "To the Reader."

modern language. Attention has already been called to Pettie's boast of his ability to write in it "as copiously for variety, as compendiously for breuity, as pithilie for sentences [thoughts]" as was possible in any other modern language. This insistence upon the eloquence of the vernacular had already appeared in Holinshed, who praised highly the ability of the tongue to employ rhetorical figures, the essence of an eloquent language. Mulcaster, who stated that the English language had reached the height of perfection in his own day, from which it would necessarily decline, and who bravely offered his own book as evidence of this perfection, praised the vernacular as strong, pithy, pliable, compact, suited to neologizing, and "redie to discharge a quick conceit." Besides meeting fully the practical needs of all men, it could furnish "beautie for the learned [and] braurie to ravish." The association of eloquence with classical learning lingers in unexpected quarters.

One authentic characteristic of the native tongue which the age noted, but concerning which opinion was divided, was the abundance of monosyllables usually ascribed to the Saxon element in the language. In some cases, as for example in Gascoigne, they were praised from a nationalistic rather than artistic motive. Lever valued them because the compounds for which his plan called could be easily made from them. Mulcaster thought that monosyllables, "which [are] the chefe ground and ordinarie pitch of both our pen and tung," gave strength and force to the vernacular. Holinshed, however, calls attention to the opinion that the use of monosyllables made the English bark like dogs. Nash, though recognizing their value in compounding, styled them the only scandal of the language, and asserted that "Books written in them and no other, seem like shop keepers boxes, that contain nothing else saue halfe-pence, three-farthings and two pence." They were frequently discussed in relation to versification. Puttenham thought that their heavy accents prevented English verse from attaining the fluency characteristic of classical feet. (Consider Pope's "And ten low words oft creep in one dull line.") Campion likewise opined that the stress which they demanded eliminated the use of the dactyl, anapest, and other feet in English poetry. Others, however, thought that monosyllables, being of common length, would facilitate the writing of poetry according to classical principles.

Early in the century John Rastell had attributed the abundance of the English vocabulary to neologizing, and since his time the process had been greatly accelerated, so that by the end of the century a very large number of words had been introduced.[71] It is not strange, therefore, that the later Elizabethans should have been impressed by the copiousness of their mother tongue. We should perhaps expect that the attitude toward the chief means of enriching the language would be universally favorable, and indeed it has been considered so. But such was not the case. The fact that the vernacular had grown so rich must have induced in some the belief that accepted terms were entirely sufficient for any purpose. Furthermore, the very definite element of affectation from which the neologizing movement was never entirely free could not fail to inspire in some an antipathy to borrowed terms. Also the desire to be clear still operated, though the consciousness of an untutored audience had considerably faded. As a result of these factors, and perhaps others, we do find a certain amount of opposition to the practice. For instance, Christopher Fetherstone, "Minister of Gods word," goes to considerable lengths to explain his rendering of the title of a work by Pope Sixtus V:

The title wherof being in the Latin copie, *Brutum Fulmen*, I was first of opinion that I might english it *The Brutish Thunderbolt*. But when I remembred with my selfe that words are no otherwise currant than as they are allowed by vse; and the philosopher giueth good aduise when he saith . . . Our speech must be such as is commonly vsed, howsoever our thoughts be the thoughts of the wiser sort; and it hath not bin lawfull for the emperors themselues to giue as it were freedome of citie to words in Rome, when they might enfranchise what persons they listed without controlement: I would not aduenture to be the first coiner of so strange a terme (strange indeed in respect of that sense to which it was

[71] Mulcaster states that "our *enfranchised* [borrowed] terms" constitute "one third part of our hole speche." That he somewhat underestimated the amount is suggested by what F. W. Bateson says: "An analysis of 40 pages of the *Shorter Oxford Dictionary* has shown that of every 100 words in use before 1600, 39 were introduced between 1500 and 1600." See *The First Parte of the Elementarie*, p. 246, and *English Poetry and the English Language*, 1934, p. 31 n.

to be applied) without better warrant, than I haue anie: and therefore I haue expressed the authors meaning in some other maner, thus, *The Feeble Fier-Flash* that is dull of force, vaine, and whereof no sufficient cause can be given in season.[72]

Though one of the terms he is concerned about is a Latin derivative, the other is a compound of perfectly good Anglo-Saxon words; but the quality of strangeness found in both induces him to bow to good use and to add the more familiar expressions. It is to be noted, however, that he retains the questionable terms.

Even Sidney, who rightly considered "elocutio" only the "outside" of poetry, but who in his own work followed the spirit of the times and made much of this outside, in his *Apologie for Poetry* (1586) criticized "that honny-flowing Matron Eloquence apparelled, or rather disguised, in a Curtizan-like painted affectation: one time with so farre fette words, they may seeme Monsters, but must seeme straungers to any poore English man"; and he goes on to criticize alliteration and scrawny figures of speech.[73] Lodge also finds fault with the predilection of his age for "coppy of new coined words" and yearns for the good old days of simplicity when "menne studied to illustrate matter with words" rather than "strive for words beside matter."[74] In his work on heraldry, William Wyrley answers those critics who insisted upon his using such French words as "d'azyer" and "d'argent" so as to be "more fine, skilfull, and Herauld like," with the expressed determination to "ioine in opinion with such as esteeme it to be more proper to speake and vse English termes and phrases in an English booke dedicated to Englishmen, than French or Latine, otherwise than cited authoritie leadeth."[75]

---

[72] *The Brvtish Thvnderbolt: or rather Feeble Fier-Flash of Pope Sixtvs the fift, against Henrie the most excellent King of Nauarre, and the most noble Henrie Borbon, Prince of Condie . . . Translated out of Latin into English,* 1586, preface.

[73] *Elizabethan Critical Essays,* I, 202. It is to be noted that Sidney considered affected rhetoric to consist of neologisms and figures of speech. In his *Arcadia,* he seems to ridicule strange borrowed terms. See the short prose section appended to the third issue of the *Arcadia,* 1598.

[74] *The Life and Death of William Long beard,* 1593, preface, found in the second volume of J. P. Collier's *Illustrations of Old English Literature.*

[75] *The True Vse of Armorie, Shewed by Historie, and plainly proued by example . . .* 1592, p. 27.

And finally, Robert Cawdrey, who published his dictionary in the following century, but who had been working on it for some time and thus had probably developed his opinions during the closing years of the sixteenth century, quotes, without acknowledgment, Wilson's attack on inkhorn terms, but not Wilson's modification or reservation. Wit, he maintains, "resteth [not] in strange words," but "in wholsome matter and apt declaring of a man's mind." Clarity, as well as the necessity of standardizing the vernacular, demands that

we must of necessitie banish all affected Rhetorique, and vse altogether one manner of language. Those therefore that will auoyde this follie, and acquaint themselues with the plainest and best kind of speech, must seek from time to time for such words as are commonlie receiued, and such as properly may expresse in plaine manner, the whole conceit of their mind. And looke what words wee best vnderstand, and know what they meane, the same should soonest be spoken, and first applied, to the vtterance of our purpose. Therfore for this end, foure things would chiefly be obserued in the choice of words. First, that such words as wee vse should be proper vnto the tongue wherein we speake. Againe, that they be plaine for all men to perceiue. Thirdly, that they be apt and meete, most properly to set out the matter. Fourthlie, that words translated, from one signification to another, (called of the Grecians *Tropes*) be vsed to beautifie the sentence, as precious stones are set in a ring, to commend the gold.[76]

Cawdrey is not opposed to eloquence, as the last words of the quotation show, but he would reconcile figurative language with clearness. He does attack that conception of rhetoric which considers eloquence to rest in hard words. The latter are in his mind only obscuring agents and evidences of affectation. This dislike of affectation, as well as an outraged nationalistic spirit, appears in the "well-languaged" Daniel, whose worshiping attitude toward the vernacular has already been cited. At the end of his *Defence of Ryme*, written against those who would impose classical meters upon English poetry, he expresses an equal antipathy to those who in poetry sought to introduce borrowed terms into their native tongue, and to the "compounders" of strange terms, and perhaps to the revivalists.

[76] *A Table Alphabeticall*, 1604, preface. It is interesting to note how long the idea lingers, that eloquence is embodied in borrowed terms.

Daniel

Next to this deformitie stands our affectation, wherein we alwayes be-
wray our selues to be both vnkinde and vnnaturall to our owne natiue
language, in disguising or forging strange or vnusuall wordes, as if it
were to make our verse seeme another kind of speach out of the course
of our vsuall practise, displacing our wordes, or inuenting new, onely
vpon a singularitie, when our owne accustomed phrase, set in the due
place, would expresse vs more familiarly and to better delight than all
this idle affectation of antiquitie or noueltie can euer doe. And I cannot
but wonder at the strange presumption of some men, that dare so auda-
ciously aduenture to introduce any whatsoeuer forraine wordes, be they
neuer so strange, and of themselues, as it were, without a Parliament,
without any consent or allowance, establish them as Free-denizens in our
language.

The above citations show that opposition to neologizing continued into the last quarter of the century. But, as was the case
in the earlier period, the practice was criticized largely on the
ground of affectation. In fact, condemnation of affected words
was almost universal and enabled controversialists to capitalize
upon it. This is especially true of the Nash-Harvey quarrel, in
the course of which charges and countercharges of inkhornism
were tossed about, but which is too well known to require much
comment. Yet even in this case, it is the extremes of the practice
rather than the practice itself which is reprehended.[77] The element of affectation (perennially the butt of satire) perceived in
borrowed terms, especially technical terms, furnished the satirist
and humorist with plenty of material.[78] This was especially true

[77] In *Pierces Supererogation* (*Works*, ed Grosart, p. 275; cf. p. 51) Harvey
compares the diction of his own letters with that of Nash's: "He is of no reading
in comparison, that doth not acknowledge euery terme in those Letters to be
autenticall English; and allow a thousand other ordinary Pragmaticall termes
more straunge then the straungest in those Letters, yet current at occasion." He
holds that Nash has no reason to object to these "artificiall wordes," but is very
much to blame when "in a phantasticall emulation [he] presumeth to forge a
mishapen rablement of absurde, and ridiculous wordes." Needless to say, both
used strange words at will. The effort to distinguish between desirable and
undesirable neologisms is, as we have seen (*supra*, p. 131), clearly revealed in
Puttenham, who would eliminate particularly words of pedantic and scholastic
connotations.

[78] See Joseph Hall, *Virgidemiarvm, Sixe Bookes*, 1597–98, I, 3, 6, 8;
Sir John Davies and Christopher Marlowe, *Epigrames and Elegies* (1590?),
nos. 15, 20; John Marston, *The Scovrge Of Villanie. Three Bookes of*

of those who despised the pedantic learning of the schools and, as Pettie says, "make a iest" at every borrowed word, "and terme it an Inkehorne terme."[79] Though there was undoubtedly some opposition to neologisms, one would hardly be justified in considering the satiric and humorous view of them an indication of it. It was quite possible for this attitude to exist side by side with serious approval of intelligent neologizing.

In fact, we find that during the last quarter of the century opinion is predominantly in favor of augmenting the language through borrowing, not only to express meaning but also, in sharp contrast to the preceding period, to secure eloquence. The best-known defender of neologizing was George Pettie, who, as we have seen, staunchly maintained the excellence of his native language against its shameless disparagers, especially those who assumed a scornful attitude toward borrowed terms. Pettie first expressed his approval of new words in *A Petite Pallace of Pettie his pleasure* (1576), where he justifies "some wordes and phrases, used contrary to their common custome" in "many pretie Histories by him set foorth in comely colours, and most delightfully discoursed," by the argument that since new fashions are permitted in clothes "it is as mutch reason wee should allow of new fashions in phrases and wordes."[80] Five years later he passed to a more serious apology for the practice of borrowing, on the ground that through it the language was enriched and rendered eloquent. He also took occasion to criticize the paradoxical attitude of those who approved of loan words when established by use but resented them when first introduced into the language. Though the passage is long and familiar, it merits extended quotation.

Satyres, 1598, *Prœmivm in librum secundum*; Samuel Rowlands, *Letting of humours blood,* 1600, satire 4, and *The Knave of Clubbes,* 1609, sig. E3, "*Signieur word-monger the* Ape *of* Eloquence." In a short prose selection appended to the third issue of the *Arcadia,* 1598, Sir Philip Sidney has much fun with a schoolmaster named Rombus, who, "fully perswaded of his owne learned wisedome," addresses the Queen with "a mishapen rabblement of absurde and ridiculous wordes," to use Harvey's words.

[79] *The Civile Conuersation of M. Steeuen Guazzo,* 1581, preface.

[80] See "The Letter of G. P. to R. B." prefixed to the work. He probably thought that his neologisms added to the excellence of the work so glowingly described in the title.

And though for my part I vse those [borrowed] words as litle as any, ~Pettie's~
yet I know no reason why I should not vse them, and I finde it a fault ~Guazzo~
in my selfe that I do not vse them: for it is in deed the ready way to
inrich our tongue, and make it copious, and it is the way which all tongues
haue taken to inrich them selues: For take the Latine woords from the
Spanish tongue, and it shall be as barren as most part of their Countrey;
take them from the *Italian*, and you take away in a manner the whole
tongue; take them from the *Frenche*, and you marre the grace of it:
yea take from the Latine it selfe the woordes deriued from the *Greeke*,
and it shall not be so flowing and flourishing as it is. Wherefore I
marueile how our english tongue hath cracke it[s] credite [Is this an
answer to Cheke's "bankrupt"?], that it may not borrow of the Latine
as well as other tongues: and if it haue broken, it is but of late, for it is
not vnknowen to all men how many woordes we haue fetcht from
thence within these few yeeres, which if they should be all counted inke-
pot termes, I know not how we should speake any thing without blacking
our mouthes with inke: for what woord can be more plaine then this
word *plaine* and yet what can come more neere to the Latine? what
more manifest then *manifest*? and yet in a manner Latine: What more
commune then *rare* or less rare then *commune*, and yet both of them
comming of the Latine? But you wyll say, long vse hath made these
woords curraunt: and why may not vse doo as much for these woords
which we shall now deriue? Why should not we doo as much for the
posteritie, as we haue receiued of the antiquitie? and yet if a thing be of
it selfe ill, I see not how the oldnesse of it can make it good, and if it be
of it selfe good, I see not how the newnesse of it can make it naught:
Wherevpon I infer, that those woords which your selues confesse, by
vse to be made good, are good the first time they are vttered, and therefore not to be iested at, nor to be misliked.[81]

Pettie's defense of borrowed terms is well known, but within
a year of its publication appeared a more enthusiastic and intelligent justification of them which has been noticed much less frequently. In fact, Mulcaster's words express the sanest and most
comprehensive view of the matter during the whole of Elizabeth's reign.[82] He sees in the expanding vocabulary of England
evidence of her development into a world power, and he defends

[81] *The Civile Conuersation of M. Steeuen Guazzo*, 1581, preface. Pettie's
argument seems to have made little impression upon Puttenham, who sanctioned
established neologisms but attacked others.
[82] *The First Part of the Elementarie*, 1582, pp. 172–76, and *passim*.

as a right the importation of any word which serves a need and which thus enriches the language. Furthermore, he justifies neologisms on rhetorical grounds as well as on the need of words to express the widening experiences and ideas of a rapidly developing people. The language, he says, "boroweth dailie from foren tungs, either of pure necessitie in new matters, or of mere brauerie, to garnish it self with all." His book furnishes convincing evidence that the Elizabethan was coming to regard his new words as the offspring of necessity, symbols of progress, purveyors of beauty, and instruments of power. He goes to great lengths to show how the increase of learning, travel, and commerce necessitated a larger vocabulary to match the greater knowledge of his countrymen. "The necessitie," he says, "of these foren words must nedes be verie great bycause the number of them is so verie manie."

Mulcaster insists that borrowed words, though they determine a rule of spelling of their own in English, must be naturalized, that is, they must conform to all linguistic principles peculiar to the native tongue, and be treated exactly as a native word. They are not to represent an alien element, but are to be assimilated by the language. He warns the reader against being displeased with a strange term, since it may be unusually appropriate and therefore worth the pains required to understand it. A little difficulty is not tedious to "a conquering mind," as his must be who desires to see his native tongue enlarged and made the instrument of his knowledge as it is of his daily needs. His own practice he defends in the following manner: "For mine own words and the terms, that I vse, theie be generallie *English*. And if anie be either an incorporate stranger, or otherwise translated, or quite coind a new, I haue shaped it as fit for the place, where I vse it, as my cunning will giue me."[83] Like Harman, Elyot, Puttenham, and others, Mulcaster believed that care should be taken in the introduction of foreign terms, and he lays down the principles which should be followed in the process:

And to be bold that waie for either enfranchising the foren, or translating our own, without to manifest insolence, and to wanton affecta-

[83] *The First Part of the Elementarie*, pp. 287–88. See also pp. 91, 161, 183, 246, 268, 270, 286, 289.

tion, or else to inuent new vpon euident note, which will bear witnesse, that it fitteth well, where it is to be vsed, the word following smoothlie, and the circumstances about bewraing, what it meneth, till oft vsing do make it well known, we ar sufficientlie warranted both by president and precept of them, that can iudge best.

The necessity of loan words and the enrichment of the vernacular through them are urged by another translator, who, perceiving the antipathy to the strangeness of newly borrowed words, assures his readers that use will make them familiar and acceptable. He likewise pleads the precedent of other nations in support of them.

True it is, that many words vsed by the Author, and retained by me, are almost the same with the originall toongs from whence they were deriued, and peraduenture will sound harsh at the first in their eares that neuer heard them before; but if they will haue patience a while, and let them passe to and fro vpon the file of their teeth, no doubt but in short time they will be as smooth as other Greeke and Latine words, which now are taken for meere English. I might heere alleadge reasons to prooue the necessitie of retaining such words in translating: namely, that many of them are proper names and wordes of Arte, that as all occupations and handicrafts haue their seuerall names of instruments belonging to their science, so is it with Philosophy, and with euery part thereof; but I make no doubt of finding the Reader fauourable in this point, considering that it tendeth to the enriching of our owne language, and hath beene practised by the learned of all nations that haue gone before vs, as is euident to such as are skilfull in the toongs.[84]

The age was preponderantly in favor of augmenting the language by borrowing, and the practice went merrily on. As Thomas Lodge says, "no conceits are held worthy commendations, but such as have coppy of new coined words."[85] John Florio noted the "yearely increase" of the native vocabulary,[86] *Florio* and in the preface to his translation of Montaigne's *Essayes* (1603) reveals a definite intent to add words to the language

[84] See the dedication of Thomas Bowes's translation of a treatise by Pierre da la Primaudaye entitled *The French Academie, wherin is discoursed the institution of maners, and whatsoeuer els concernth the good and happie life of all estates and callings*, 1586.

[85] See the preface to *The Life and Death of William Long beard*, 1593, in the second volume of J. P. Collier's *Illustrations of Old English Literature*.

[86] *A Worlde of Wordes*, 1598, "To the Reader."

even when not necessary. If, he says, his readers find fault with

some vncouth termes; as entraine, conscientious, endeare, tarnish, comporte, efface, facilitate, ammusing, debauching, regret, effort, emotion, and such like; if you like them not, take others most commonly set by them to expound them, since there they were set to make such likely French words familiar with our English, which well may beare them.

Some attention was also paid to the way in which words should be naturalized, a problem which had faced the neologizers throughout the century, and with which, as has been noted, a few like Harman, Elyot, and Mulcaster had struggled. Just as today those familiar with foreign languages may resent ignorant anglicizing of foreign terms, so in this period we find those who insist that such words should not be corrupted. In speaking of military expressions borrowed from other modern languages, Robert Barret holds that it is good

to vse such war termes and words, as we doe borrow from straungers (as most languages doe borrow some, more or lesse, one of another) neare after the same nature, orthographie and accent, as those nations do, from whom they are deriued: and not to pronounce and vse them ouer corruptly, as we commonly doe. As for example. The word *Caporall*, which is a meere Italian, and also vsed by the French, we corruptly do both write, and pronounce *Corporall*. . . . And againe, wee vse both to pronounce and write, *Core de guard*; which by the French is written *Corps de guard* . . .[87]

Literary history affords no more staunch defender of his native tongue than George Chapman, who seldom missed an opportunity to sing its praises, and who in his translation of Homer was in a position to test its efficacy to the full. Like Puttenham, he frowned upon cacophonous words and upon those furnished only by pedantry, but he fully realized that the English language was enriched by desirable terms. "For my varietie of new wordes," he says, "I haue none Inckepot I am sure you know, but such as I giue pasport with such authoritie, so significant and not ill sounding, that if my countrey language were an vsuerer, or a man of this age, speaking it, he would thanke mee for enriching him." He then turns his attention to the young

[87] *The Theorike And Practike of Moderne Warres*, 1598, p. 248.

blades who, in Pettie's words, jest at a borrowed word as an ink-horn term, and yet introduce all manner of slangy expressions:

> Why, alas, will my young mayster the reader affect nothing common, [Chapman] and yet like nothing extraordinarie? Swaggering is a new worde amongst them, and rounde headed custome giues it priueledge with much imitation, being created as it were by a naturall *Prosopopeia* without etimologie or deriuation; and why may not an elegancie authentically deriued, and as I may say of the vpper house, bee entertayned as well in their lower consultation with authoritie of Arte as their owne forgeries lickt up by nature?

Chapman would deny the right to introduce new words both to the pedantically learned and to the ignorant users of slang. But he defends the practice of neologizing, when subjected to proper standards, on the score both of the increased vocabulary and, what is more interesting in its contrast with an earlier attitude, of the increase in eloquence secured in this way. He introduces the usual precedents of other languages, and, in addition, that of Chaucer, who seems to have been closer to the second than to the first half of the century. And finally he sees in the increasing current of the vernacular, widened by continued additions of proper words, the chief defense against barbarism and the hope of future literature.

> All tongues haue inricht themselues from their originall (onely the Hebrew and Greeke which are not spoken amongst vs) with good neighbourly borrowing, and as with infusion of fresh ayre and nourishment of newe blood in their still growing bodies, and why may not ours? *Chaucer* (by whom we will needes authorise our true english) had more newe wordes for his time then any man needes to deuise now. And therefore for currant wits to crie from standing braines, like a broode of Frogs from a ditch, to haue the ceaselesse flowing riuer of our tongue turnde into their Frogpoole, is a song farre from their arrogation of sweetnes, and a sin wold soone bring the plague of barbarisme amongst vs; which in faith needes not bee hastned with defences of his ignorant furtherers, since it comes with mealemouth'd toleration too sauagely vpon vs.[88]

[88] *Elizabethan Critical Essays*, II, 305. The antiquarians, as will soon be seen, were very critical of Chaucer for introducing so many French words into the language.

"Good neighbourly borrowing" served the turn of eloquence as well as of necessity. One translator, in defending his neologisms, disclaimed any affectation, which he feared would be charged against him, but which he thought was revealed more in unnecessary rhetorical amplifications than in borrowing.

No lesse doubte I also of reprehension, for some words I haue vsed beyond common vse, propriety leading me therto, rather then any affectation which consisteth not in so tollerable and commendable liberty, but rather in a friuolous accumulation of words, vnnecessarily produced in dilating of any argument; yet if any may lay vp in this our common treasury of language, any choise ornaments, for the decorum and coppy of our tongue, I know not who may better then they, conuersant in forraine writers, seeing besides a laudable emulation of others aboundance, euen very necessity in explication, inuiteth them thereunto: and therefore for want of better tearmes I haue bin driuen to vse some forged words, as spiritally, vertually, armiger, and other, which otherwise I could not wel tel how to haue expressed.[89]

The plea of necessity would have been perfectly intelligible earlier in the century, but the removal of the stigma of rhetorical affectation from the practice and the approval of the latter on the grounds of eloquence would have aroused many critics. Another writer, who apparently looked upon the introduction of French words after the Conquest as a kind of neologizing process, attributed to the peaceful nature of Elizabeth's reign the fact that the language had in his own generation been much "enriched and beautified" by words borrowed to express "the learning that now flourisheth in this Kindome."[90] The discovery of a virtue in loan words other than that of ability to express meaning, though that, too, continues to be emphasized, is made by Thomas Nash. He defends his compound words and verbs borrowed from the Italian on the ground that "no winde that blowes strong, but is boystrous, no speech or wordes of any power or force to confute or perswade but must bee swelling and boystrous." His Italian verbs ending in *ize*, he says, "carrie farre

---

[89] Annibale Romei, *The Courtiers Academie*, tr. John Kepers, 1598, preface.

[90] G. Delamothe, *The French Alphabet*, 1615, p. 118. The work was entered in the Stationers' Register in 1592, and the two parts were first published in 1595 and 1596, respectively.

more state with them then any other, and are not halfe so harsh in their desinence as the old hobbling English verbs ending in R."[91] We have already noted in Puttenham and others the euphonic test for neologisms, which is itself an indication of the approval of loan words on the ground of eloquence. This standard would especially hold true in the case of poetry, in which borrowing is as conspicuous as in prose. George Peele praises "well letter'd" Harington

> That hath so purely naturalized
> Strange words, and made them all free-denyzons,

and also Campion who "richly cloth'st conceite with well made words."[92]

Seldom indeed has the spirit of an age changed so quickly as that which viewed the vernacular as inherently rude and uneloquent. The suddenness with which writers began to recognize the eloquent nature of the mother tongue enables us to date the turning point not earlier than 1575 nor later than 1580.[93] If we may believe contemporary witnesses, the poets were responsible for the transformation. We are not told how they "refined" or "adorned" the language; but undoubtedly their own compositions achieved the end by merely revealing the potentialities of their medium. Perhaps the influence of such works as *Tottel's Miscellany* (1557) and the early editions of *The Mirror for Magistrates* (1559, 1563, 1571, 1574), though slow in its operation, had been working quietly under the surface for a number of years. Contemporary references clearly indicate that Lyly's prose and Spenser's *Shepheardes Calender*, which appeared early in this period, were more responsible for opening the eyes of the Elizabethans to the artistic power of the vernacular than any other works. How vivid the realization of this power was is

---

[91] See the preface to the second issue of *Chrisis Teares Over Ierusalem,* 1594.

[92] *The Honour of the Garter* (1593?), "Ad Mæcænatum Prologue."

[93] F. W. Bateson, relying on J. L. Moore's *Tudor-Stuart Views of the English Language*, makes 1590 the turning point, but Moore's survey is entirely inadequate and his method of merely counting favorable and unfavorable opinions is not convincing. See *The English Language and English Poetry*, p. 34.

suggested by the repeated assertions of the eloquence of the mother tongue, frequently by way of contrast to the crudeness and barbarism of the earlier quarters of the century. The publication of numerous English rhetorics, with the chief purpose of teaching how to secure eloquence in the vernacular, and with examples entirely or in part from English writers, furnishes additional evidence of the strong confidence in the rhetorical power of the tongue. The age believed wholeheartedly in the literary value of its language.

So strong was this belief that writers came to view the native speech as the most valuable possession of the English people, and as an end itself rather than as a means to an end. It was not viewed merely as a medium of expression for literary conceptions; its refinement furnished an objective for literature, became, in fact, an important goal of literary activity. To serve the mother tongue was proposed as one motive in writing as early as Spenser and as late as Milton. Although there was a nationalistic element in this linguistic pride, and although the latter was found in more countries than England, an authentic source of it lay in the literal discovery by the Elizabethans that the vernacular could be used rhetorically, a discovery which raised the language to a higher plane than it has ever enjoyed and which gave it an identity independent of its use.

Confidence in the artistic capabilities of the mother tongue, and especially the sense of freedom from restricting limitations, whether verbal or grammatical, definitely influenced creative activity. Verbal abundance, or "copie," to use the contemporary expression, rendered possible by complete liberty of neologizing, especially borrowing for "bravery" or eloquence, which formerly had been severely reprehended,[94] offered a wide range to the

---

[94] The democratic humility of earlier vernacular writers gave way to the aristocratic spirit of the poets, a spirit influenced perhaps by the aristocratic criticism of the Continent. (Cf. Vernon Hall, Jr., *Renaissance Literary Criticism*, 1945.) The democratic implications in Protestantism and the invention of printing, both definitely associated with the vernacular, had something to do with the conception of English as honest and uneloquent, and with hostility to rhetoric. Elizabethan poets reverse both attitudes. They join with the Humanists in placing high value upon eloquence, but break with them in emphasizing the eloquent nature of the native tongue, and as a result, the

creative artist, while the relative laxness or absence of grammatical regulation, which Sidney and others considered a great asset, left him unencumbered. To quote Paul Greaves again, the Elizabethans became eloquent before they became grammatical.[95] The situation in which there were numerous rhetorics and only one or two elementary grammars is significant of the temper of the age.[96] The acute awareness of the literary power of English, especially as contrasted to the earlier opinion of it, is revealed in two ways. The literature of the period is overlaid with rhetorical devices; the conscious use of figures of speech is everywhere apparent. Fortunately the thought of the age was spacious enough and its emotions intense and sincere enough to support such expressions. Second, the literary spirit of the age was in part determined by the new-found confidence in the vernacular. The creative enthusiasm and the sheer delight in the use of language so characteristic of Elizabethan writers owed much to their discovery of the potentialities of the mother tongue and of the resultant confidence in their medium of expression. In fact, this enthusiastic trust in their artistic medium is a factor which criticism must recognize in analyzing and evaluating Elizabethan literature, for it had as much to do with determining the temper of this literature as any other influence.

simple homespun vernacular passed from its humble abode to dwell in the gorgeous palace of its literature.

[95] *Grammatica Anglicana*, 1594. Greaves says that not one in a thousand is as much interested in the purity of the language as in eloquence and rhetorical power, and that men are more valued for their knowledge of rhetoric than of grammar. He points out a number of solecisms of which the best vernacular writers were guilty.

[96] The Elizabethans made a short cut to literature without caring whether their language was ruled or not. It is worth noting that English literature became great with a language the spelling of which was chaotic, the grammar uncertain, and the vocabulary unstandardized, but in the artistic powers of which writers had supreme faith.

CHAPTER VII

THE ANCIENT LANGUAGE, PART I

UNTIL the close of the sixteenth century comments on the English language were concerned largely with its eloquent or uneloquent nature, the inadequacy of its vocabulary, the confusion and illogicality of its spelling, and the lack of grammatical regulation. The historical development of the language received little attention. That it began with Anglo-Saxon, was influenced by the Danish invasions, received many French words after the Conquest, and was further enriched by numbers of borrowed words, especially in the sixteenth century, was known in some quarters; yet with the exception of the copiousness thus secured, the significance of the history of the language was ignored, and the character of its constituent elements for the most part passed unnoticed. The fact that monosyllables were largely of Anglo-Saxon origin was recognized and various opinions of them were expressed, from Lever and Gascoigne, who approved of them, to Robert Greene, who considered them the scandal of the language. In general, however, no particular attention was paid to the complex nature of the vernacular, though of course there was much talk about neologisms.

With the beginning of the seventeenth century, however, the situation underwent a decided change. The antiquarians enter the scene and place a pronounced stress upon the Saxon element. Yet they were indebted to a more or less conscious movement in most of the Germanic countries, a movement slightly prophetic of the Nazis. Its chief characteristic was an opinion which, drawing heavily upon Tacitus, extravagantly praised the Germans and all things German.[1] The history of the Teutons was elabo-

---

[1] See, e.g., the dedication and fols. 11^r and 22^v of *Andreæ Althameri Brenzii Scholia in Cornelium Tacitum Rom. Historicum, De Situ, moribus, populisque Germaniæ*, 1529; Conrad Peutinger's *De Mirandis Germaniæ Antiquitatibus Sermones convivales*, 1530 (1506); and John Thurnmaier's *Annalium Boiorum Libri Septem*, 1554, the author of which asserts (p. 49) that, far from being barbarous, the Germans were equal to the Greeks and Romans. A variorum

Germanists

Babel

rated upon in connection with the origin and dispersal of human races, and their far-flung migrations were pointed out as evidence of great excellence. There was also much linguistic discussion based squarely upon Babelian comparative philology. Human races began with Noah and languages with the Tower of Babel, though some ambitious Germanists thought their nation had missed the latter. Many and long were the treatises on these matters, and intricate and imaginative the theories evolved, but they were always so managed as to redound to Teutonic glory. And more than once the Saxons are singled out as especially blessed with all the virtues attributed to the Germans as a whole.[2]

In the opinion of such a language-conscious age as the Renaissance it was natural that the greatness of the Teutons should be conspicuously manifested in their language. In all works on comparative philology—and they are numerous—the tongue is given a high, if not the highest, place among all others. John Thurnmaier is full of praise of it in general and of the Saxon dialect in particular, which, he attempts to prove, is very similar to Greek, a touchstone of linguistic excellence at this time.[3] In this matter he is closely followed by Conrad Gesner, who cites, in addition to Thurnmaier, John Camerar and Andrew Althamer.[4] But admiration for the German language reached its climax in the work of Joannes Goropius Becanus,[5] who went to such ex-

edition of Tacitus, *C. Cornelii Taciti de Moribus et Populis Germanorum Liber . . . Opera et studio Simonis Fabricii editus,* 1580, containing notes of Fabricius, Krantz, Goropius, and a half-dozen other scholars, reveals clearly how well Tacitus lent himself to the Nordic craze. One of the largest and most ambitious books on the subject, which begins with a complete edition of the *Germania,* is *Philippi Cluverii Germaniæ Antiquæ Libri Tres,* 1616.

[2] See Albert Krantz, *Saxonia,* ed. Nicolas Cisner, 1575 (1520). Cisner's preface discovers a Trojan origin for the Saxons, in general reveals the wide interest in them, and states many theories concerning their origin and abodes. Cf. Philip Cluver's *Germaniæ Antiquæ Libri Tres,* Bk. II, chap. xxi, and G. Fabricius, *Originum illustrissimæ Stirpis Saxonicæ libri septem . . .* 1597.

[3] See his *Annalium Boiorum Libri Septem,* 1554, p. 39.

[4] *Mithridates,* 1555, p. 34.

[5] *Opera Joan. Goropii Becani, Hactenus in lucem non edita,* Antwerp, 1580. John Van Gorp, a Flemish physician, was born at Hilvarenbeek (Brabant) in 1518, and died at Maastricht in 1572. He was physician to Eleanor and Marie of Hungary, sisters of Charles V. After long sojourns in Italy, Spain, and France, he settled at Antwerp, where in 1569 appeared his *Origines Antverpianae,* the first expression of his revolutionary theory. Juste Lipsius

tremes in his linguistic views that even the most ardent Germanophiles for the most part could not follow him all the way, though
they more frequently than not paid earnest consideration to his
opinions. That his work should have been taken as seriously and
quoted as often as it was clearly indicates the high estimation in
which the German language was held, for he claimed nothing
less than that it rather than Hebrew was the first language, the
one spoken in the Garden of Eden, and the one in which the Old
Testament was first composed. Fortunately it escaped the Tower
of Babel, from which Hebrew and all other modern languages
were descended. The fact that such an unorthodox and even
heretical theory should have made the impression it did emphasizes the Teutonic mania.

It is not my intention to go into details regarding the arguments which Goropius advances, but the great stir which his
treatise created justifies a short outline of his ideas.[6] He attempts
a historical approach by claiming that German was the language
which Adam spoke and in which he gave such satisfactory names
to all things that when once the name was known, the nature of
the thing itself was known.[7] The Old Testament was first written in this flawless German tongue, but since God wished "to free
men from the danger of the pride which would be engendered
by a perfect knowledge of religious mysteries," He caused it to
be translated into Hebrew. The author circumvents the difficulty offered by Babel with the assertion that the Cimbrians, or
early Germans, were not at the tower, and so did not assist in
building it. Thus they continued to speak the same language as
before, which came down to modern times, changed only by those

---

thought highly of him though very sceptical of his theory. He has been credited
with being the first to call attention to the great antiquity of the German language. *Dictionnaire des Écrivains Belges Bio-Bibliographie,* 1931, II, 1886.

[6] His theory is elaborately elucidated in a treatise entitled *Hermathena,*
contained in the *Opera.*

[7] In the seventeenth century this was called the natural language and was
widely discussed. Its conception figured in the efforts of the Baconian scientists to invent a language more suited for scientific purposes than established
tongues. See John Wilkins, *An Essay Towards a Real Character and a Philosophical Language,* 1668, and Richard F. Jones, "Science and Language in England of the Mid-Seventeenth Century," *Journal of English and Germanic
Philology,* XXXI (1932), 315-31.

mutations which the passage of time introduced into all languages.[8]

Having cleared the ground in this fashion, he proceeds with his linguistic proofs. Postulating perfection for the first language, he finds this perfection to consist of clarity, brevity, propriety of sound, and significant compounds. Since the purpose of speech is to express the ideas of the mind, the greatest linguistic fault is obscurity, which arises from different meanings being given to the same word or from the ambiguous meanings of words. This thesis enables him to attack the opinion that the Jewish tongue was the first language, since, he asserts, it does not express ideas clearly, because its expressions stand constantly in need of interpretation and because it possesses many homonyms and ambiguous compounds. No language, he declares, is beset with more difficulties, or suffers from more ambiguity or darker obscurity, as may be seen in the many interpretations placed by commentators upon Hebrew writings. The greatest linguistic excellence lies in an abundant vocabulary, but Hebrew is much impoverished because of the necessity of giving many meanings to one word. Furthermore, the composition and structure of the words themselves make for obscurity. Finally, the fact that many Hebrew words have been derived from the Cimbrian language proves that the latter must be the older.

The German tongue, on the other hand, can claim every linguistic virtue. In its early development all words were monosyllables, which were so abundant that all ideas could be expressed without different meanings being given the same word. It surpasses Hebrew in richness of vocabulary, and Latin and Greek in brevity, so that at one and the same time it is the most copious and the briefest of all tongues. Its alphabet contains more letters and diphthongs, from which more combinations, with more distinctions between words, can be formed than is true of any other tongue. The language is brief because of the monosyllabic nature of its primitive words; it is rich because the great number of its characters make possible many monosyllables. He makes something of the fact that, unlike Hebrew, these

[8] See the passage from *Indoscythia* quoted in S. Fabricius' edition of the *Germania*, 1580, pp. 212–15.

Van
Gorp

monosyllables may admit more than three consonants. If words
of more than one syllable are found, they have been produced
by derivation, declension, conjugation, or compounding. In
short, the abundance and succinct brevity of the primitive words
are responsible for that clarity of meaning which raises German
far above Hebrew. He even sees fit to exalt the soft and pleasant
sound of the language, a view that would have startled the English in the latter part of the seventeenth century. Since the German alphabet possesses so many letters, it exercises all the vocal
organs, but the letters cause less fatigue because there are no
rough collisions of letters, vehement breathings, sharp hissing
sounds, and abdominal pronunciations. Extremes are avoided
in all dental, palatal, guttural, and lingual sounds. Because a
German's organs of speech are so profitably exercised by the
variety of his letters, he can with great facility learn a foreign
language, whereas a foreigner learns German with difficulty since
his slight linguistic experience has not taught him to hold a
middle way in his pronunciation. Finally, the greater abundance
of German words furnishes knowledge of more things than is
true of other languages.

He has much more to say, but the above is his main argument,
which, indeed, resolves itself into the simple syllogism that the
first language must have been the most perfect, and since German is superior to all other languages, it must have been the first.
Though he is cited again and again by contemporary and later
philologists, Continental and English, he finds few or none to
accept his theory *in toto*, but he effectively impressed upon his
age a belief in the great antiquity of the German language, a view
supported by most Germanic philologists; and in the Renaissance antiquity was a proof of excellence.[9]

The Continental praise of the German race and language

---

[9] Charles Butler considered Goropius' idea a paradox, and he followed the
age in considering Hebrew the first language: "The Excellencie of a Language
doth consist chiefly in three things [1 Antiquity, 2 Copious Elegancie, and
3 Generalitie:] for the first the Hebrew, for the second the Greek, for the
third the Latin, for all the English is worthily honoured." (*The English
Grammar*, 1633, preface.) In the preface to his *Etymologicon Linguæ Anglicanæ*, 1671, Stephen Skinner adopts a severely critical attitude toward the
extravagant claims of the Germanists, especially Goropius.

English & Saxon

was loudly echoed in England, where there was almost as much interest in comparative philology as in Europe. And in the midst of their praise English writers awoke to a fact which had been only passively perceived before, namely, that they and their language were originally derived from the Saxons, the noblest of Teutonic peoples.

The Elizabethans had been somewhat confused regarding the early history of England, owing largely to British legends, and they certainly took little pride in what they knew about the Saxons. Sir Thomas Smith seems to have felt more interest in, *T. Smith* and to have possessed clearer ideas about, Germanic origins than his contemporaries. He is fond of explaining words by tracing them to their Saxon source;[10] in one passage he speaks of the Saxons as those "from whom our tongue is deriued to this day."[11] In tracing the origin of place names one writer says, "So haue we out of oour antike Saxony (whearvpon our English grewe) this name Adelmton."[12] Puttenham remarks that most of the words in "our naturall and primitiue language of the *Saxon English*" are monosyllables.[13] In 1586 Camden reveals not only his own knowledge of the basis of his mother tongue but also the ignorance of his contemporaries in the explanatory parentheses which he deemed necessary in the phrase "of our ancient language (I meane the Saxon tongue)," and in saying that Saxon in his day had been forgotten.[14] Holinshed suggests that the *Hol.* English nation existed before the Saxons arrived, and he shows *demurs* no kindly feeling for the latter, who, he says, introduced "an hard and rough kinde of speach, god wotte, when our Nation was brought first into acquaintance withall."[15] In a sermon preached at Paul's Cross on May 10, 1579 (pp. 30–31), John Stockwood's etymology is better than his history when he says, "it is without all controuersie that we have this woorde [gospel] as also many

---

[10] *De Repvblica Anglorvm*, 1583 (finished in 1565), pp. 9, 24, 66.

[11] *Ibid.*, p. 9. See *infra*, note 23.

[12] See the printer's preface to William Patten's *The Calender of Scripture*, 1575. Mulcaster also recognized German as the original source of English. *The First Part of the Elementarie*, 1582, p. 88.

[13] *Elizabethan Critical Essays*, ed. G. G. Smith, II, 71.

[14] *Britain*, tr. P. Holland, 1610, p. 199.

[15] *The Firste volume of the Chronicles*, 1577, fol. 5ʳ.

others in our englishe tongue, from the language of the old Saxons, which sometimes possessed this lande." He evidently is not fully aware of the Germanic base of the English people or their language, for he speaks of the word as having been "borrowed" from the Saxons. This expression together with the phrase "which sometimes possessed this lande" shows how far the age was from appreciating the true significance of the Germanic origin of the English people. The activities associated with Bishop Parker called some attention to Anglo-Saxon, but the interest developed was largely of a religious nature. As we move from the sixteenth to the seventeenth century, however, we discover increasing evidence of a clearer view of the beginnings of things. In the preface to a very peculiar book, *Dibre Adam*, 1602, Simon Sturtevant refers to "the first fathers of the Saxons, and founders of our English nation," and in the same year Richard Carew calls Saxon "our natural language."[16] In view of the various opinions expressed in the foregoing quotations, we can understand John Clain's caution when he says, "The English tongue is a mixture of many languages, especially German and French, although it is *believed* that formerly it was altogether German."[17]

When the uncertainty regarding their origin was removed, the English discovered a new basis for national pride. As was to be expected in this golden age of antiquarianism, the antiquarians took the lead in proclaiming the noble descent of the English people, and in substantiating their claims they call again and again upon the Continental Germanists.[18] Richard Verstegan

---

[16] *The Svrvey of Cornwall*, fol. 56ᵛ.

[17] *Historia Britannica*, 1603, p. 6 (my italics).

[18] The two men who, if we may judge by the frequent citations to them, did more than any one else to introduce the Continental admiration of the Germans into England and to point out the significance of the derivation of the English from them were Richard Verstegan (*Restitvtion of Decayed Intelligence*) and William Camden (*Remaines*), both of whose works appeared in 1605. Verstegan is more enthusiastic over the matter, but a comparison of the second edition of the *Remaines* (1614) with the first discloses a distinct rise in Camden's appreciation of the Teutons, which perhaps indicates a general increase in regard for them. The second edition is clearly more eulogistic. For example, a passage in the first issue (p. 13) reads: "This English tongue [is] extracted out of the olde *German*, as most other." The later edition (p. 20) reads: "This English tongue is extracted, as the nation, from the Germans the

deliberately set about to make the English realize their true origin and the honor derived from it. In the process he indulges in an enthusiastic description of the physical and spiritual characteristics of the Saxons, their manners, customs, mode of living, government, society, and the like. He asserts that Englishmen "can lack no honor to be descended of so honorable a race."[19] He upholds the superiority of the Germans on the ground that they were never subdued by the Romans, and that they kept their race and language uncontaminated by others.[20] Following Tacitus, he expatiates upon their bravery, honesty, virtue, endurance, and other qualities which make them true and worthy ancestors of Englishmen. Camden sees the wonderful Providence of God in the migrations of the Angles and Saxons into England.[21] And his admiration of them grew with years. Other antiquarians bear witness to the same effect.[22] Histories begin to show the growing regard for the Germans in emphasizing the Germanic invasions of England and in praising the Saxons.[23] John Hare speaks of the "gloriousness" of the Teutons, "our Mother Nation," and after pointing out the many branches of the race comments thus:

doubtless were all the foresaid limbs of the Teutonick Nations as united most glorious of all now extant in Europe for their morall, and martiall virtues, and preseruing the libertie entire, as also for propagating their language by happie victories in France."

[19] *A Restitvtion of Decayed Intelligence*, 1605, "The Epistle to our Nation." See also chaps. ii and iii. Verstegan's real name was Rowlands, but because of his admiration of the Germans he assumed that of his German grandfather.

[20] *Ibid.*, p. 43.

[21] *Remaines of a Greater Worke, Concerning Britaine*, 1605, p. 9. As has been noted, in the second edition (1614) his praise is much more enthusiastic. He had in his first great work (1586) praised the Saxons. *Britain*, tr. P. Holland, 1610, p. 133.

[22] See Henry Spelman, *Concilia, Decreta, Leges, Constitutiones, In Re Ecclesiarum Orbis Britannici*, 1639, 3 vols. In the dedication to King Charles he gives an enthusiastic account of the progress of Christianity among the Anglo-Saxons, which he views as proof of their virtue. The fact that parts of the Scriptures had been translated into Anglo-Saxon supported the Protestant demand for an English version of the Bible, and so enhanced the value of Old English. Cf. William L'Isle's *A Saxon Treatise Concerning the Old and New Testament*, 1623, preface.

[23] See John Speed, *The History of Great Britaine*, 1611, pp. 283, 287. Richard Broughton speaks warmly of the learning and piety of the Saxons, whom he styles "glorious worthies." *Monastichon Britanicum*, 1655, preface.

John Hare

in the political association of one head and heart, as they are in the naturall ligaments and communion of bloud, lawes, language, and situation, that Empire would not only be the head of the West as now it is, but also able to wrastle with the Orientall Competitor, for the command of the world.[24]

Not only did the English find cause for pride in the fact that they were descended from the noble Teutonic race; they were also, by the testimony of Continental authorities, doubly assured of the greatness of their heritage through their derivation from the noblest branch of the Germans. "Such is the transcendent quality," says John Hare,

of our mother Nation, and in these sundry respects, shee sufficiently appeares to be the cheife and most honourable Nation of Europe; of all which honour of hers, wee are the true inheritors and partakers, either as Members of that body or as children of that mother, we being flesh of her flesh, and bone of her bone, yea of the most ancient and noble of her tribes (according to the Germanes opinion) The Saxon, still retaining the name (with a little metathesis as is before related) of the Patriarch *Askenas*, and this so totally and entirely that whatsoeuer bloud among us is not Teutonick is exotick . . .[25]

The English continue to be acutely aware of their racial origin during the Puritan era; the fact that the Saxons had been described by European authorities as the noblest of Germans intensifies their national pride. After stressing the derivation of the English from the valorous Teutons, one author says,

But more particularly, the English descend from those people of *Germany*, which are called *Saxons*. These by good Authors were esteemed the strongest and valiantest of its Nations, and are reported to have inlarged their bounds further then any other particular Nation did in *Germany*, and carried the terror of their Arms into all parts that lay about them; but especially to have lorded it on the Seas. In a word, they were dreaded for their Arms, and commended for their extraordinary

[24] *St. Edwards Ghost*, 1647, p. 8. Hare says that the Saxons were superior to other Germanic tribes, because they migrated to England, and emigrants are "made up . . . of the floure and choice youth of that Countrey from whence they are transplanted." P. 11.

[25] *Ibid.*, p. 10.

Chastity: so that the English derive from a most noble and pure Fountain, being the off-spring of so valiant and so chast a people.[26]

In a work published after the return of Charles II but for the
most part composed before it, Robert Sheringham bestows great
praise upon the Saxons, defending them against the "calumnies"
of the Greeks and Romans, and proving by the testimony of the
latter that the Saxons were braver, more urbane, more just, and
more religious than other people, and that they were especially
the inventors of the arts.[27]

The worship of the Germans produced a change in some historical attitudes. The "Hunnes and Gothians" had fared rather
badly at the hands of the Elizabethans, who attributed to them
some of the real or fancied evils of the time.[28] Now, however,
the "Barbarians" come into some repute, and their invasions are
considered evidence of their strength, prowess, and valor rather
than of their destructive barbarism.[29] Meric Casaubon has praise
for the invasions of the Huns, Goths, Ostrogoths, Visigoths, and
other Germanic tribes.[30] The Saxon conquest of England takes
on added significance, and the benefits which England received
from it are pointed out with much rejoicing. The upholders of
the Saxons, however, had to combat the theory of British origins
which tradition and earlier histories sanctioned and which
legends made famous. The untiring and truly historical investigations of the antiquarians had unearthed little or no basis for
Brut and King Arthur, but had discovered the significance of the
coming of the Saxons. There is a considerable shift in emphasis

---

[26] Richard Hawkins, *A Discourse of the Nationall Excellencies of England*,
1658, pp. 14–15. Pride in the Saxons and insistence upon the importance of
what they bequeathed to their descendents appears in Francis Whyte's *For the
Sacred Law of the Land*, 1652. We have already noticed that Camden praised
the Saxons as early as 1586.

[27] *De Anglorum Gentis Origine Disceptatio*, Cambridge, 1670, pp. 450 ff.

[28] They found, however, a champion in Samuel Daniel, who in his *Defence of Ryme*, 1603, opposed energetically the prevailing condemnation of
them.

[29] See for example the section in Camden's *Remaines* which deals with
languages. Sheringham (*op. cit.*, pp. 450 ff.) vigorously defends the Goths
against the charge of barbarism. In fact, at a time when "the Gothic" was
becoming anathema, he was its stalwart defender.

[30] *De Quatuor Linguis*, 1650, pp. 133–35.

from the part supposedly played by British factors in English history as revealed by earlier historical works to the part played by the Saxons as stressed by the histories of this period.[31]   Brut and King Arthur are restricted to the purely British past, which, according to Samuel Daniel, had little to do with his England.[32] Drayton correctly records the situation when he says,

> *The* Britaines *chaunt King* Arthurs *glory*
> *The* English *sing their* Saxons *storie.*[33]

The prestige of Troy, to which Brut was related, was a factor still to be reckoned with in any opposition to the British legend. Hare soundly asserts that the Germans who were descended "from the top of Nimrods Tower" were far superior to the nations that sprang from the "conquer'd relicks of ruin'd *Troy*."[34]   But it was Verstegan who gave the first and most important expression to this sentiment. He went to great length to clear up the confusion of ideas regarding English origins, with the idea in mind that there was as great honor in being descended from the Germans as from the Trojans. He was incited to his task

by seeing how diuers of diuers nations did labor to reuyue the old honour and glorie of their own beginings and anceters, and how in so dooing they shewed themselues the moste kynd louers of their naturall friends and countrimen; obseruing their-withall how diuers of our English wryters haue bin as laborious and serious in their discourses of the antiquities of the Britans as yf they properly appertayned vnto Englishmen,

[31] John Twyne, e.g., in a historical treatise on England composed before 1581 places all the emphasis upon British rather than Saxon matters. (*De Rebus Albionicis, Britannicis Atque Anglicis, Commentariorum libri duo*, 1590.) The legends of Brut and the Arthurian romances influenced the earlier chroniclers, but as the antiquarians investigated the past, they discovered the mythical nature of this material at the same time that they realized the importance of the Saxon occupation of England.

[32] Daniel says the Saxons entirely overthrew and obliterated the British, and introduced a new body of people, a new state, and a new government. No longer was the country Britain but "New Saxony." *The Collection of the Historie of England*, 1618, pp. 8–9. See also John Hare's *St. Edwards Ghost*, 1647, p. 10, and Francis Whyte, *For the Sacred Law of the Land*, 1652, pp. 76 ff.

[33] See the Argument to the fourth song of *Poly-Olbion*, 1612.

[34] *St. Edwards Ghost*, p. 4, published in 1647 but composed five years earlier.

which in no wise they do or can do, for that their offsprings and descents
are wholy different.

Disclaiming any design to impugn "the praise of the praise-
woorthy Britans," he points out

that sundry our English wryters are found to stand somuch vpon the
descent of the Britans as yf it were a thing that in deed meerly concerned
the originall and honor of our English nation. Whereby and through
the lack of due distinction between the two nations (an ouersight which
the Britans in their accompt of vs wil neuer comit) our true originall
and honorable antiquitie lieth inuolued and obscured, and wee remayning
ignorant of our own true anceters, vnderstand our descent otherwise
then it is, deeming it enough for vs to heare that *Eneas* and his Troyans
the supposed anceters of king *Brute* and his Britans are largely discoursed of.

After he has commented on some historical mistakes made by
writers who did not keep their racial genealogy straight, he notes
the prevalence of the confusion:

Now albeit that these and many the lyke mistakings may vnto some
seem to bee no matters of any moment, yet are they surely of moment,
for that such defect of due obseuring things anciently appertaining to
nation and nation, and language and language, do breed much confusion,
and are the occasion of inuoluing things in such sorte that oftentymes
that which is atributed to one nation belongeth vnto another. And by
this meanes cometh it to passe, that wee not only fynde Englishmen (and
those no idiots neither) that cannot directly tel from whence Englishmen are descended, and chanceing to speake of the Saxons, do rather
seem to vnderstand them for a kynd of forreyn people, then as their
own true and meer anceters, but euen among English wryters themselues, woords diuers tymes vttred that sauour of reproche vnto their
own anceters the Saxons: for Englishmen cannot but from Saxon originall deryue their descent and offspring, and can lack no honor to be
descended of so honorable a race, and therefore are they more in honor
obliged to know and acknowlege such their own honorable and true
descent.

This then considered, as also how ridiculous it must seem vnto the
posteritie of the Britans, for Englishmen to borrow honor from them,
not needing to borrow it of any in the world, I perswade my self that
such distinctions as I wish were in this nationall case of antiquitie ob-

serued; cannot bee thought friuolous, but both agreable vnto truthe and very requisite. And as for the true originall of Englishmen how honorable in deed it is, I trust the reader wil not bee left vnsatisfied, when he shall haue perused some of the ensuing chapters.[35]

The chief purpose of the antiquarians was, in Hare's words, "to vindicate our own [people], as being a stream of the same [Germans], and to evince the nobility thereof."[36] For this reason the Saxon occupation of England was a tremendously significant historical fact. They are careful to point out the clean sweep which the Germans made of the people inhabiting those parts of England which they occupied: ". . . our Progenitors," says Hare,

Hare

that transplanted themselves from *Germany* hither, did not commixe themselves with the ancient inhabitants of this Countrey the Britaines (as other Colonies did with the Natives in those places where they came) but totally expelling them, they took the sole possession of the Land to themselves, thereby preserving their bloud, lawes, and language, incorrupted.[37]

Whyte vs. Normans

Francis Whyte also speaks approvingly of the thoroughness with which the Saxons eradicated everything British, and established their language, laws, and customs, "our sacred Saxon institutions," which uncontaminated by other influences descended to the English.[38] Imbued as he was with the desire to carry back to a Teutonic source as much of English civilization as he could, he severely criticizes Polydor Virgil and historians who followed him for attributing to the Normans many elements in this civilization which antedated the latter. Whyte furnishes an excellent example of the prevalent Saxon worship. Following Camden, Edward Leigh also points out that the Saxons "valiantly and

[35] *A Restitvtion of Decayed Intelligence*, 1605, "The Epistle to our Nation." That some were not entirely convinced by the antiquarians is made clear by Peter Heylyn, who as late as 1656 speaks of "our Ancestors (whether we look upon them as the *Brittish* or *Saxon* race)." *Observations on the Historie of the Reign of King Charles*, p. 5.

[36] *St. Edwards Ghost*, p. 10.

[37] *Loc. cit.*

[38] *For the Sacred Law of the Land*, 1652, pp. 76 ff. He mentions particularly trial by jury and the Common Law. *Ibid.*, p. 94.

wisely performed here [in England] all the three things, which
imply a full conquest, viz, the alterations of Lawes, Languages
and Attire."[39] In the eyes of the antiquarians the Saxons represented the beginning of all things English.

Just as the Saxonists found it necessary to discover in their
Germanic origin prestige equal to that derived from legends of
Troy and King Arthur, they also were compelled to place a new
interpretation upon other historical matters—the Danish invasions and especially the Norman Conquest. In so doing they
reveal a bitterness that can be explained only on the basis that
they resented the victory gained over the glorious Saxons, even
though by a partly Germanic people, and the introduction of an
alien element into the noble inheritance bequeathed by the
former. In short, the Danes and the Normans dimmed the glory
and interrupted the traditions of their true origin. As one worthy
says, they "unteutonized" the English people. There were
various ways of attacking the problem. One was to minimize the
effect and importance of the invasions. Verstegan insists that
the Normans were very few as compared with the large number
of English, and that many of them returned to France. "Thus,"
he says,

haue I made it plainely appeer (for that some haue inconsiderately be-
lieued the contrarie) that the maine corps and body of the realme, notwithstanding the Norman conquest and the former inuasions of the
Danes, hath stil consisted of the ancient English-Saxon people, wherein
euen vnto this day it doth yet consist. And herrvnto accordeth the name
of Saisson, which the Welsh and Irish nations haue continued to call vs
by, notwithstanding the irruptions of the Danes and Normans.

But even granted that the invasions were significant in their influence, still, he says, the Germanic strain in the people could
not have been seriously contaminated.

And whereas some do call vs a mixed nation by reason of these Danes
and Normannes coming in among vs, I answere (as formerly I haue

[39] *England Described*, 1659, p. 22. Camden had said: "And to the
honour of our projenitors (the English Saxons) be it spoken, their conquest
was more absolute here over the Britains than either of the Francs in France
over the Gauls, or the Goths and Lombards in Italy over the Romans, or of
the Goths, Vandals, and Moors over the antient Spaniards in Spain." See the
section dealing with language in *Remaines*.

noted) that the Danes and Normannes were once one same people with the Germans, as were also the Saxons; and wee not to bee accompted mixed by hauing only some such ioyned vnto vs againe, as sometyme had one same language and one same originall with vs.[40]

Samuel Daniel, who in more than one work showed that he was on the side of the Germans, echoes Verstegan's opinion of the relatively slight influence exerted by the invasions, asserting that "notwithstanding the former Conquest by the *Danes*, and now this by the *Norman* (the solid bodie of the Kingdome, still consisted of the *English*) and the accession of strange people, was but as riuers to the Ocean, that changed not it, but were changed into it."[41] Like many others, he pointed out the lack of success encountered by the Normans in trying to force the French language upon the English. In admiration of his Saxon ancestry, Richard Hawkins likewise insisted that the Normans were too few to introduce an alien element into English blood, "for there are but three or four hundred Gentlemen in the Catalogue of *Battel-Abbey*, on whom the Conqueror bestowed Land in *England*, and probably one half of them did not remain two Ages after, and scarce one quarter of them are remaining at this day." Underestimating, like other antiquarians, the number of French words in the English vocabulary for which the Conquest was ultimately responsible, he discovered in the preservation of the Saxon language additional proof that the number of Danes and Normans in England could never have been considerable.[42]

The effort to minimize the influence of the Normans was not enough for John Hare, who carried antipathy to the French invaders to an incredible extreme. He readily admits, and laments, the introduction of French laws, words, names, titles, and

[40] *A Restitution of Decayed Intelligence*, p. 187. Alexander Gil likewise insisted that the Danish invasions made no impression upon the language, and that William tried without success to impose the French language upon the English people, though among the servants of the court there were many French words. *Logonomia Anglica*, 1619, preface.

[41] *The Collection of the Historie of England*, 1618, p. 37. William L'Isle thanks God "that he that conquered the Land could not so conquer the Language" but it can still be spoken and understood to a certain extent. *A Saxon Treatise*, 1623, preface.

[42] *A Discourse of the Nationall Excellencies of England*, 1658, p. 25.

customs, which, he insists, lie as fetters of domination upon the English, depriving them of their ancient liberty and freedom. He constantly berates his countrymen for remaining in servile captivity for five hundred years. He would gladly have invalidated the historic event, but since the past was beyond his reach, he contented himself with showing how its evil effects might be alleviated if not eliminated. After tracing briefly the glorious history of the Germans in general and the Saxons in particular, he is so impressed with the grandeur of that which the English had received from their Teutonic forbears, especially in respect to "a hopefull Language and happy Lawes," that he indignantly asks,

is it then suitable to the dignity, or tolerable to the Spirit of this our Nation, that after so noble an extraction and descent, such honourable atcheivements performed, so much done and suffered for our Libertie and honour against the most mighty of Monarchies and puissant Nations, and after such Priviledges conferred on us from heaven, wee should have our Spirits so broken and un-Teutonized by one unfortunate Battaile, as for above 500 yeares together and even for eternity, not only to remaine, but contentedly to rest under the disgraceful title of a *Conquered Nation*, and in captivity and vassalage to a forraigne power? . . . if we address a look toward our Lawes, they still scorne to speak otherwise then in the Conquerours Language, and are (if Master *Daniel* and others write true) for the most part his introductions, shutting up the remaining Liberties of our Nation, under the name and notion of franchises, as if we were no further to be accounted free, then enfranchised, that is adopted into the quality of French-men, or made denizens of *France*, whereby the first point that occurs to the Reader of our Lawes, is our shame; if wee survey our Language, we there meet with so much tincture of Normanisme, that some have esteemed it a dialect of the Gallick: if wee contemplate the heraldry and titles of our Nobility, there's scarce any other matter then inventories of forraine villages, that speake them to be not of English bloud; but tell us (as their Ancestors sometimes told King *John*) that their Progenitors conquered this Land by the Sword; and lastly if wee but heare the Royall title rehearsed, we heare it likewise attended with a *post Conquestum*, so that we cannot move with our senses, but we hear the chains of our captivity . . . [which] were more proper to an Asiatick Nation, (those *natis ad servitutem* as *Tully* calls them) then to one of Europe, and to any European then a Teutonick, and indeed to tame Creatures and Cattell then to these that professe themselves free-borne men.[43]

Unlike some, Hare found no comfort in the fact that the Normans were largely a Germanic people, for he considered them "a people compacted of Norwegians and Nuestrians . . . the off-scouring and drosse of the Teutonique and Gallic Nations," an attitude which prophesied certain opinions of our own day. It was through treachery and not by valor, he insists, that the Normans won the victory, and also because the English, being displeased with their king, would not fight. The throne was granted to William only "upon his specious and faire vows and promises to preserve inviolate our Lawes and Liberties," which he did not keep, "so that all the alteration and dishonour that followed, was by his villainous perjuriousnesse and treachery against our Country continued." Otherwise, he never would have ruled the English, "so odious at that time was Title of a Conquered Nation to our Ancestors."

There was a definite purpose in Hare's onslaught upon the Norman Conquest. The spirit of reform burns brightly within him. Toward the end of his treatise he points out clearly the specific changes which he desires. First, William should be shorn of his title "The Conqueror," "imposed on him by Normane arrogance and our servile flattery," and he should either be declared a usurper or be considered king by virtue of King Edward's legacy. In either case, he should no longer stand at the head of kings in the Royal Catalogue. The title to the throne should not be founded upon any pretended conquest, and the ancient English Arms should be restored in the Royal Standard. Again, the nobility of Norman descent should no longer base

---

[43] *St. Edwards Ghost: Or, Anti-Normanisme: Being a patheticall Complaint and Motion in the behalfe of our English Nation against her grand (yet neglected) Grievance, Normanisme,* 1647, pp. 13–14. At the end the small pamphlet is dated 1642, and in the preface Hare says it was written in that year. His diatribe did not pass unnoticed. Early in the next year another Puritan, probably Lilburne or Wildman, who was interested in having English laws in the English language, speaks bitterly of laws written in French as "a Badg of our Slavery to a Norman Conqueror." *A Declaration of some Proceedings of Lt. Col. Iohn Lilburn, And his Associates,"* in *The Leveller Tracts,* 1647–53, ed. William Haller and Godfrey Davies, 1944, p. 109.

the right to their possessions upon their being heirs to any pretended conquerors, but they should repudiate names and titles
brought over from Normandy and assume others more consistent
with the honor of the nation. All Norman laws and customs
should be abolished, and other laws should be expressed only in
English or Latin.[44] All French words should be eliminated and
their place supplied by Saxon or Latin terms. Since those English who were of Norman descent could hardly rid themselves
of their blood, they might consider themselves Norwegians (he
had disparaged them before) and so Germans, thus shaking off
the stigma of "Gallicisme." He assured his countrymen that if
these reforms were introduced, the spirit of nationalism would
flame anew with the ancient Teuton glory.

Some three months later Hare returns to his attack on "1066
and all that" in a pamphlet, the title[45] of which sufficiently indicates its spirit and content. His thesis is simply that so long as the
Conquest is accorded the place it has held in history, the English
are necessarily a subjugated people, and hence possess no rights
whatsoever. Hare's treatises[46] probably created some little stir.
At any rate, they received enough public notice to have their
theme celebrated in a broadside.[47] Echoes of this Germanic hos-

[44] He thinks that Edward III, in decreeing that legal cases should be conducted in English, should be given high praise "for restoring in a good degree
the use and honour of the English tongue formerly exiled by Normanisme into
contempt and obscurity." *St. Edwards Ghost*, p. 21.

[45] *Plaine English To Our wilfull Bearers with Normanisme; Or, Some
Queries Propounded To and concerning the Neglectours of Englands grand
Grievance and complaint lately published under the title of Anti-Normanisme.
Wherein is undeniably demonstrated, that while this Nation remains under
the Title of the (pretended) Conquest, She, and every Member of her are no
other then Slaves properly so called; And moreover, that (while she retains the
same Title) all her and her Representators contending with their Prince for
ungranted priviledges, upon any pretence whatsoever, is unwarrantable and
seditious,* 1647. Thomason has dated it November 4.

[46] In the next year he published a third pamphlet on the same theme:
*Englands Proper and onely way to an Establishment in Honour, Freedome,
Peace and Happinesse. Or, the Normane Yoke Once more uncased,* which adds
nothing to what he has already said. All three pamphlets may be found in
The Harleian Miscellany, 1744, Vols. VI, VIII, IX.

[47] See *Universall Madnesse, or A new merry Letany,* 1647, which appeared
about the same time as *Plaine English,* and which ridicules "the Norman Lawes
and the French Guize."

tility to the Conquest linger on into the next century, though for the most part the Restoration and Enlightenment operated strongly against it.[48]

No part of what the Germans had bequeathed to the English filled the latter with more pride or drew from them more comment and praise than the Anglo-Saxon element in their tongue. The antiquarians and their followers never tire of stressing the fact that the origin of the vernacular was to be found in a branch of the German language, a language so old that it threatened to drive Hebrew from the honor of being the first tongue, and to become that which God Himself used, a language so widespread that vestiges of it, according to some philologists, had appeared in the New World.[49] All the praise which Continental scholars heaped upon German, the English could in their own right claim for their speech.[50] This they were not slow to do. The first sixty years of the seventeenth century witnessed a remarkable interest in Anglo-Saxon; the greatest value was placed upon it, and its study was strongly urged. A lectureship in the tongue was estab-

---

[48] See *The Monthly Miscellany; or Memoirs for the Curious*, 1708, II, 84–90. Lawrence Eachard expresses the typical view of his times in speaking of the Saxons in an uncomplimentary way, and in maintaining that "England in general gain'd great Honour and Advantage by this Conquest." (*The History of England*, 1707, I, 153.) The attitude which we have been tracing was not unknown in the preceding century, though it was little developed then. Soon after Elizabeth's accession to the throne, Bishop Aylmer explained William's victory on the ground that he slipped in through the civil war between two brothers. "He [William] lefte his posteritie to reigne, which were rather by tyme turned to be Englyshe: then the noble Englyshe, to becomme Frenche, as oure tongue and maners at this daye declareth, whiche differeth very lytle from our Auncestors the valyaunt Saxones. We haue a fewe hunting termes and pedlars Frenche in the lousye lawe, brought in by the Normanes, yet remayning: But the language and customes bee Englyshe and Saxonyshe. I can not tell what Frenche bloude is left. But if there be any Frenche hartes, I woulde they hadde to it the Mall Francois." *An Harborowe For Faithfull And Trewe Subiectes, agaynst the late blowne Blaste, concerning the Gouernment of Wemen.* Strasborowe, 1559, sig. Q2[v].

[49] See the twenty-fifth chapter of Abraham van der Mijl's *Lingua Belgica*, 1612.

[50] Casaubon says that it is futile to argue about which is the oldest of the German dialects since they are so closely related that all the praiseworthy qualities of one must be attributed to all. The Saxon tongue, for example, is so close to German that he who knows it knows all dialects. *De Quatuor Linguis*, 1650, pp. 132, 143.

lished at Cambridge,[51] poems were written in it,[52] a lexicon of it was compiled,[53] and it takes its place beside Latin, Greek, and Hebrew, the learned languages.[54] Had not the Restoration, with its own linguistic and critical values, intervened, Old English scholarship might have developed to a very high degree. Enthusiasm for the ancient tongue permeates the treatises which we are considering.

[margin note: Anglo-Saxon studies & poems]

It was this enthusiasm which drove the authors of the treatises discussed above to impress upon the English, certainly more than was necessary, the fact that the authentic base of their tongue was Anglo-Saxon. In the sixteenth century, as we have noted, writers sometimes recognize the relationship between Saxon and the vernacular, but any significance the fact might have was largely lost upon them.[55] The antiquarians, being conversant with the Continental Germanists, were convinced of the great importance of this relationship, and as the first step toward revealing it to their fellow countrymen sought to drive home the fact that the vernacular sprang from German. Early in the seventeenth century statements regarding the origin of the mother tongue became increasingly emphatic. John Clain would go only so far as to say that the English language was believed to have been wholly German in former times,[56] but Richard Carew flatly states

[margin note: R. Carew]

---

[51] This was endowed by Henry Spelman about 1623, and some ten years later one in Arabic was founded by Thomas Adams, an alderman. Abraham Wheloc was the first lecturer in both positions. See the sermon preached by William Sclater at Wheloc's funeral, 1654.

[52] See *Irenodia Cantabrigiensis: Ob paciferum Serenissimi Regis Caroli e Scotia reditum Mense Novembri 1641*, 1641. The volume contains a large number of Latin, some English, and a few Greek poems, as well as two poems in Anglo-Saxon, one by Wheloc.

[53] By Sir Simond D'Ewes, antiquarian (1602–1650). It was never published. See William Dugdale's letters to him, February 27, 1639/40 and March 1639/40, in *Life, Diary, and Correspondence*, ed. William Hamper, 1827, pp. 195–96.

[54] These are the four languages which Meric Casaubon planned to treat in his *De Quatuor Linguis*, 1650. In answer to the attacks which the scientists and pseudo scientists were beginning to make on linguistic study, he tried to persuade his son that the road to learning lay only through languages, and he recommended especially Hebrew, Greek, Latin, and Saxon. *De Verbroum usu*, 1647, dedication.

[55] See *supra*, pp. 219–20.

[56] *Historia Britannica*, 1603, p. 6.

that Saxon is the "naturall language" of England.[57] Marked emphasis upon the fact, however, begins with Verstegan and Camden. The latter asserts that "the English tongue is extracted, as the nation, from the Germans";[58] and the former, that it is acknowledged by all that the Teutonic language is the "grownd of our speech," in spite of much borrowing.[59] Alexander Gil makes the interesting but questionable statement that poets for the sake of rhyme and poetic effect use the Northern dialect, "since it is the most pleasant, the most ancient, and the purest, seeing that it is the closest to the speech of our ancestors."[60] Approaching the matter from a different direction, Charles Butler calls attention to the wide area over which the Germans spread their language, with special emphasis upon England.[61] It was Meric Casaubon, however, who went to the greatest length in impressing upon the English the true source of their tongue. He maintains that the Saxon language is the only true and genuine English, that so far as the vernacular has departed from it, so far has it degenerated from its native purity, and that to explain words and expressions of modern English it is necessary to resort to Saxon origins.[62] Even after all need of mentioning the matter had passed, writers continue the habit and belabor the obvious.[63]

[57] *The Svrvey of Cornwall,* 1602, fol. 56.

[58] *Remaines,* 1605, the section dealing with language. In another passage he speaks of "the old *German* tongue, which vndoubtedly is the matrix and mother of our English." (*Ibid.,* p. 29.) In 1586 he had, somewhat ambiguously, stated that the English had kept the Saxon language uncorrupted after a sort. *Britain,* tr. P. Holland, 1610 (1586), p. 133.

[59] *A Restitvtion of Decayed Intelligence,* 1605, p. 188. The prefatory poems by various men praise Verstegan for demonstrating that Saxon is the origin and basis of modern English.

[60] *Logonomia Anglica,* 1619, p. 18.

[61] *The English Grammar,* 1633, preface.

[62] *De Quatuor Linguis,* 1650, pp. 131–32. Later this sentiment was attributed to Henry Spelman in the editor's preface to the third edition of the *Glossarium Archaiologicum,* 1687.

[63] Edward Phillips maintains that "the Saxon, or German tongue, is the ground-work upon which our language is founded" in spite of "the mighty stream of forraigne words, that hath since *Chaucers* time broke in upon it," and which have "not yet wash't away the root; onely it lies somewhat obscur'd, and overshawdow'd like a Rock or Fountain overgrown with bushes." (*The New World of English Words,* 1658, preface.) As late as 1662, that man of many interests, James Howell, promises that "He who will pry well into the pedigree

Conquest

One reason for this needless repetition was the nationalistic pride derived from the idea.[64] This pride sprang from a conviction of the excellence of Saxon, which as a dialect, and probably the best dialect, of the German tongue possessed all the virtues of the latter. First was the wide area over which the conquering Teutons had carried their language, and in the case of Saxon a special virtue was discovered in the fact that it had not been contaminated by the speech of conquered people. The language of such victorious heroes could not but be fine. Various virtues were noted in the tongue itself, a subject which had been fully developed by Goropius. It was varied, copious, and strong. It possessed in its monosyllables a great linguistic asset, particularly with respect to the ease with which they could form compounds. The characteristic, however, which was perhaps considered more important than all others was its great antiquity.[65] Thus the antiquity of the English language, by virtue of its Germanic inheritance, becomes a strong argument for its excellence. Spelman considered the Saxon the oldest of German dialects and the closest to the Gothic.[66] Casaubon thinks it a most worthy tongue

Spelman

of the *English* Language will find that shee is of *high* Descent, For *shee* hath the *Highdutch* (the most ancient *German* Toung) to her *Gran Mother*, and the *Saxon* (the prime dialect of the Highdutch) to her Mother." *A New English Grammar*, 1662, preface.

[64] Christopher Wase would have the Norman language share with Saxon the honor of being the origin of the English tongue, but he pays special tribute to the Saxons. After noting the wide regions over which the "very brave" Teutons spread, he adds, "Moreover, today the Saxon dialect is said to leave the other German dialects behind by many parasangs." *Dictionarium Minus*, 1662, preface.

[65] As we have already noted, Charles Butler could not accept Goropius' idea that German was the language of Adam and Eve, even though supported by Ortelius, yet he stressed the idea that, being the language of unconquered people, in Germany it had come down from the general confusion with little alteration. *The English Grammar*, 1633, preface.

[66] *Archæologus*, 1626, preface. Antiquarian pursuits compelled Spelman to study Anglo-Saxon, but he came to love it and to lament its neglect. William L'Isle stressed its value to antiquarians. (*A Saxon Treatise*, 1623, preface.) Though L'Isle's interest was nearer to that of the sixteenth century, being motivated by religious considerations, he developed a burning desire to rescue the Saxon tongue from oblivion, and he earnestly advocated its study. An interesting contrast to the sixteenth-century attitude is furnished by Gil, who, as stated above, held that poets should use only the Northern dialect because its closeness to Saxon made it the most pleasant, pure, and ancient of English

because of its antiquity and amplitude.[67] Gil defends the excellence of the vernacular by referring to the antiquity conferred upon it by the Saxon element.[68]

Influenced by the Continental panegyrics on the German people, the antiquarians stressed the Saxon origin of the English people, and expressed great pride in it. This attitude resulted in changed opinions of the Huns and Goths and developed an antagonism to the Norman Conquest. Especially did the antiquarians glory in the Germanic origin of their language, which conferred upon the mother tongue all the virtues found by Continental writers in the German language generally, and in Saxon particularly, and by virtue of which the English could point with great pride to the antiquity of the mother tongue. As will be seen, the strength of this pride is revealed in the extent to which under its influence various linguistic and literary values were changed or modified.

---

dialects. Puttenham, on the other hand, forbade poets the use of any dialect north of the river Trent, for though the Northern was the purest English Saxon, it was not in his eyes equal to the Southern dialect. See *Logonomia Anglica*, preface, and *The Arte of English Poesie*, ed. Willcock and Walker, p. 145.

[67] *De Quatuor Linguis*, pp. 131–32. Mulcaster had noted the antiquity of the English language derived from its Germanic origin. See the *Elementarie*, p. 88.

[68] *Logonomia Anglica*, 1619, preface. John Wallis considered the Teutonic language older than Latin, since, he says, the latter had taken a number of words from the former, and since Greek words common to both came into the German tongue without passing through Latin. (*Grammatica Linguæ Anglicanæ*, 1653, p. 126.) By the time of the Restoration this conception of the English language had become well enough established to prompt William Somner to remark that he hoped no one would expect him to lengthen his preface for the sake of expatiating upon the utility, amplitude, and antiquity of the Saxon language, since very many learned men had done so, and especially Meric Casaubon. *Dictionarium-Saxonico-Latino-Anglicum*, 1659, preface.

Chapter VIII

THE ANCIENT LANGUAGE, PART II

HE history of ideas generally reveals that when a thought trend develops unusual enthusiasm it begins to influence other movements, even to the extent of modifying or reversing dominant patterns. We have already noticed how changes in historical attitudes and interpretations were effected by the Continental Germanophiles. In the same way pride in the Germanic element of the language produced a change in the attitude toward monosyllables. That there was a great number of them in the English tongue and that they comprised in large part the Saxon element was known to the sixteenth century. As we have seen, Gascoigne advocated their use from a patriotic motive,[1] and Lever approved of them because they lent themselves readily to his plan of augmenting the English vocabulary, but in the sixteenth century as well as in the next the attitude toward them was frequently critical, particularly with respect to poetry. Those who opposed the adoption of classical principles of prosody offered as one of their chief arguments the unsuitability of monosyllables for classical feet.[2] Nash considered them "the only scandal" of the English tongue.[3] Campion called attention to the difficulty he encountered in coupling "my Words and Notes louingly together," since the monosyllables "are so loaded with Consonants as that they will hardly keepe company

---

[1] See *Elizabethan Critical Essays*, ed. G. G. Smith, I. 51. The next year he suggests one of the charges brought against monosyllables when he says (*The Steele Glas*, 1576, sig. H1ᵛ),

> That *Grammer* grudge not at our English tong,
> Bycause it stands by *Monosyllaba*,
> And cannot be declined as others are.

See the preceding chapter, p. 199, for a more extended account of the sixteenth-century attitude toward monosyllables.

[2] Cf. Gil, *Logonomia Anglica*, 1619, pp. 133 ff.

[3] See the preface to the second edition of *Christs Teares Ouer Ierusalem*, 1594.

with swift Notes, or giue the Vowel conuenient liberty."[4] Gil also thought that they tend to clog metrical movement, for he upheld neologizing on the ground that it is necessary to mix polysyllables with native monosyllables so as to obviate the "heaviness or slowness" produced by the latter.[5] Other critics likewise considered them rough and antagonistic to metrical fluency, a typical neoclassical view.[6] Finally, Thomas Dekker insinuates the belief that monosyllables are incompatible with eloquence, and that in the early days when the mother tongue consisted largely of them, the language was poor.[7]

This skeptical view of the worth of short words could not but be modified by the new pride in the Saxon component of the native tongue, now largely represented by monosyllables. Verstegan attempts to make plain the origin and growth of language according to Nature and God's divine plan, a plan seemingly concerned only with the Teutonic race.

This our ancient language [German] consisted moste at the first with woords of monosillable, each having his own proper signification, as by instinct of God and nature they first were receaued and vnderstood, but heer of grew this benefit, that by apt ioyning together of two or three of these woords of one sillable, new woords of more diuersity of sence and signification were stil made and composed, according as the vse of them for the more ful and perfect expressing of the composers meanings did requyre. By which meanes it grew vnto that copiousness and perfection, that diuers beeing very well learned in other tounges, have much admyred this, when they haue not bin able to fynde any one vsuall woord in any language, for the which they could not giue the like in this, in thesame very true nature, and the sence.[8]

---

[4] *Two Bookes of Ayres,* 1610, preface.   [5] *Logonomia Anglica,* preface.

[6] Cf., e.g., James Howell, *Instructions for Forreine Travell,* 1642, p. 155. One of the reasons which Richard Flecknoe gives for the unpopularity of English on the Continent is "it's many *monosyllables,* and short *snapping* words (deriv'd from the *Dutch*) which renders the sound *harsh* and *unpleasant* unto *Strangers* ears, accustomed unto words of greater length . . . They by reason of their unaptnesse to mixe, making so many breaches in speaking, as renders this Language *ragged* and disjoynted." He recognizes, however, the power of English "to containe and comprize more words and matter in one *verse* (by reason of the shortnesse of its words) then any other *Language.*" *Miscellania,* 1653, p. 105.

[7] See the first chapter of *Lanthorne and Candle-light,* 1609.

[8] *A Restitvtion of Decayed Intelligence,* 1605, pp. 189–90. In another

Words of one syllable were considered the basis of the German language, and so of Saxon. Goropius had made much of their brevity and power of expression. Camden likewise, though considering them unsuited to poetry, praised them for their terseness and ability to express more matter in shorter space than any other tongue.[9] But the facility with which they could be combined to form compounds and thus further the development of a tongue also attracted attention, as the quotation from Verstegan makes plain. Edward Phillips considers it remarkable that though most of the Saxon words in the vernacular were one syllable,

neverthelesse, the things that are understood by them, are as significantly express't, as the same things in other tongues, are by words of two, or more syllables . . . a matter of no small advantage: for if that sentence be judged most praise-worthy, that containeth most matter in fewest words: why may we not commend that word, which consisting of fewest syllables, is yet of as great force, as if it had more. No lesse considerable is the proper and most pertinent signification of some words, which are produced by the coalition, or clapping together of two of these monosyllables into one, as the word *Wisdom*.[10]

Gil maintains that short words by virtue of their compounding value are very serviceable to learned men who can best express their thoughts in long words,[11] and Howell declares that the multiplicity of monosyllables in German, even though more "knotted" with consonants than is true of any other tongue, makes it a fullmouthed, masculine speech, a linguistic virtue in which Saxon necessarily participates.[12] Monosyllables are in

passage he carries his idea further, and has monosyllables put into men's mouth by God at the Tower of Babel, "but by ioyning two woords or more together, that were distinct monosillables before, a new composed woord and therewithal a new sence was at once framed." *Ibid.*, p. 242.

[9] *Remaines*, 1605, p. 21.

[10] *The New World of English Words*, 1662 (1658), preface. John Wallis comments upon the monosyllabic nature of the Saxon element in the vernacular, and elaborates upon the expressive power of monosyllables and their facility for compounding. *Grammatica Linguæ Anglicanæ*, 1653, p. 123.

[11] *Logonomia Anglica*, preface. That interesting schoolmaster, Sir Balthazar Gerbier, expresses the opinion that his native tongue "hath a great advantage in monosyllables, the learned doe make themselves marvellous well to bee vnderstood in the same." *Interpreter of the Academie for forrain languages*, 1649, p. 38.

[12] *Instructions for Forreine Travell*, 1642, p. 155.

themselves peculiarly effective, and in combination they lead to the greatest abundance of expressions.

The admirers of Saxon words, however, are not content with these arguments; they go further and in the face of contrary opinion contend that words of one syllable are especially fitted for English verse. Granted that they do prevent the employment of classical metrical feet, a practice which Daniel in his *Defence of Ryme* had seriously wounded and which Gil all but killed, still they are particularly adapted to rhyme. That ardent believer in the vernacular, George Chapman, in the preface to his translation of Homer (1610?) attributes the superiority of English verse to the fact that

> Our Monosyllables, so kindly fall
> And meete, opposde in rime, as they did kisse,

a sentiment echoed some years later by John Beaumont, who declares

> The relish of the Muse consists in rime,
> One verse must meete another like a chime.
> Our Saxon shortnesse hath peculiar grace
> In choise of words, fit for the ending place,
> Which leaue impression in the mind as well
> As closing sounds, or some delightfull bell.[18]

But the age was not content with merely stating the aptitude of Saxon words for rhyme. An attempt was made to prove by example that monosyllables may be used in poetry. Dr. William Loe, at one time prebendary of Gloucester, and later pastor of the English church at Hamburg, was willing to show the world the power of monosyllables in verse. "I have presumed," he says,

to metaphrase some passages of Dauid psalmes as an Essay to knowe whether we might expresse our harts to god in our holy soliloquies by monasillables in our owne mother tongue, or no. It being a receaued opinion amongst many of those who seeme rather to be iuditious, then caprichious, that heretofore our english tongue in the true idiome thereof consisted altogether of Monasillables, untill it came to blended, and

---

[18] "To his Late Maiesty, Concerning the True Forme of English Poetry" in *Bosworth-field*, 1629, p. 109. Puttenham had expressed the same idea much earlier. *Elizabethan Critical Essays*, ed. Smith, II, 80.

mingled with commixture of Exotique languages. And I my selfe haue
seene all the lord prayer vsed in the tyme of John Wickleefe to be expressed in words of one sillable.[14]

He is not unsuccessful in his attempt, for his translations are
direct and childlike in simplicity of thought and purity of feeling, and at times reveal depths of tranquil emotion suggestive
of Wordsworth.

Even more extensively did enthusiasm for the Saxon element in the language influence other linguistic views inherited
from the Elizabethans, particularly views concerning the ways
in which the native vocabulary might be enriched—neologizing,
reviving, compounding. As one might well surmise, neologizing
fares poorly, the others well. The virtue of compounding grows
much brighter because of the adaptability of Saxon words to the
process, an adaptability stressed by the antiquarians with tireless
enthusiasm. Revival also begins to be more widely noticed, generally in connection with efforts to discredit words borrowed
from other languages. In his attempt to discount the Norman
invasion, Verstegan expressed the belief that words derived from
that source were not as many as generally thought. Yet he shows
a distinct dislike for those which did come into the language, and
he openly opposes the whole practice of neologizing. "Since the
tyme of *Chaucer*," he says, "more Latin and French, hath bin
mingled with our toung then left out of it, but of late wee haue
falne to such borrowing of woords from Latin, French, and
other toungs, that it had bin beyond all stay . . ." Some, he
admits, think this practice improves the vernacular, but foreigners point to it in vilifying the language.

For myne own part I hold them deceaued that think our speech bettered by the aboundance of our dayly borrowed woords, for they beeing
of an other nature and not originally belonging to our language, do not
neither can they in our toung, beare their natural and true deryvations;
and therefore as wel may we fetch woords from the Ethiopians, or East
or West Indians, and thrust them into our language and baptise all by
the name of English, as those which wee dayly take from the Latin, or
the languages thereon depending . . .

[14] *Songs of Sion*, 1620, second dedication.

It is quite possible that Verstegan sincerely believed that the vernacular was discredited by calling to its aid other words, and that he felt a dislike of pedantic expressions such as were conspicuous in the sixteenth century, but what he resented most was the introduction of an inferior alloy into the Germanic metal, and the suggestion that his mother tongue with its store of Saxon words to draw upon was found wanting. "But doubtless," he says,

yf our selues pleased to vse the treasurie of our own toung, wee should as litle need to borrow woords, from any language, extrauagant from ours, as any such borroweth from vs: our toung in it selfe beeing sufficient and copious enough, without this dayly borrowing from somany as take scorne to borrow any from vs.

That what he had in mind was principally the sufficiency of the Saxon element is indicated by his printing thirty-two pages of words of that tongue, which in some cases are followed by the usurping French word, and which are introduced for the purpose of

explaining a number of our moste ancient English woords, some by their modern ortography, others by shewing, (with the signification of them) what French woords wee haue taken in steed of them, as also such as wee have not left of, but stil vse for choise, though wee haue borrowed woords in French to lyke sence.

At the end of his glossary Verstegan definitely advocates the revival of old Anglo-Saxon terms to meet present needs, but it is significant that he thought wise to address his remarks to poets. The problem of augmenting the language by restoring obsolete terms had by now been for the most part restricted to poetic diction. It is possible, however, that he thought of poetry as introducing, not monopolizing, ancient words.

I could heerin haue enlarged myself very much, and peraduenture haue much pleasured some of our English poets, with great choise of our own ancient woords, which as occasion requyred they might, with more reason renew and bring in vse again (by som-what facillitating yf need were the ortography) then to become the borrowers and perpetual debters of such languages as wil not bee beholding to vs for somuch as a woord, and when wee haue gotten from them as many woords as wee wil, they can neuer carry a true correspondence vnto ours, they beeing of other nature and originall.[15]

This is a far cry from Pettie's and Mulcaster's enthusiastic advocacy of borrowing and from the general approval of the practice in the late sixteenth century.

Camden is somewhat inconsistent in his opinion of neologizing. In one passage he admits that the English, like other tongues, had been changed through the introduction of words from other nations such as the Danes and Normans, and he asserts that since learning came into England during the reign of Henry VIII the vernacular "hath been beautified and enriched out of other good tongues, partly by enfranchising and endenizing strange words, partly by refining and mollifying olde words, partly by implanting new wordes with artificiall composition . . . so that our tongue is (and I doubt not but hath beene) as copious, pithie, and significant as any other tongue in *Europe.*"[16] He maintains that admixture is no disgrace to English, since it is common to all European languages, and since in spite of the various invasions of the island it is no more pronounced in his mother tongue than in others, notwithstanding Conrad Gesner had considered English the most mixed and corrupt of all languages. On the other hand, he evidently believes that the ability of a language to resist neologisms is a virtue. He minimizes the linguistic effect of the Norman invasion by maintaining that in spite of the efforts of the conquerors to suppress English for three centuries, few French words were introduced except some terms of hunting, hawking, and dicing, "whenas wee within these 60. yeares have incorporated so many Latine and French [words], as the third part of our tongue consisteth now in them." The English, he says, somewhat inconsistently, have kept their Saxon tongue uncorrupted "after a sort," and

[15] For these references and quotations see that section in *A Restitvtion of Decayed Intelligence*, 1605, pp. 182–240, entitled "Of *the Great Antiquitie of our Ancient English Tongue*; and of the proprietie, worthiness, and amplitude therof. With an explanation of sundry our most ancient English words." It will repay reading in full. The quotations are found on pp. 204, 206, 240.

[16] *Remaines*, 1605, p. 20. Camden here enumerates the three processes by which the sixteenth century sought to enlarge its vocabulary.

he takes pride in the fact that there are few borrowed terms in the Lord's Prayer. "Our Ancestors steadfastness in esteeming and retaining their own tongue" meets with his hearty approval, and he admires the Saxons for so completely conquering the inhabitants of England that no British or Latin words entered their language. "Great, verily, was the glory of our own tongue before the *Norman* Conquest in this, that the olde *English* could expresse most aptly, all the conceiptes of the minde in their owne tongue without borrowing from any." Caught in the eddy created by the meeting of two thought currents, he is whirled around and around.[17]

William L'Isle reveals something of Camden's inconsistency. Though he asks, "what Englishman of vnderstanding is there, but may be delighted, to see the prety shifts our tongue made with her owne store, in all parts of learning, when they scorned to borrow words of another," he believes that through the liberty of borrowing, a liberty enjoyed by other nations,

our language is improued aboue all others now spoken by any nation, and become the fairest, the nimblest, the fullest; most apt to vary the phrase, most ready to receiue good composition, most adorned with sweet words and sentences, with witty quips and ouer-ruling Prouerbs: yea able to

[17] See *Remaines*, pp. 14, 18, 20–22. In the second edition of Camden's work, 1614, was published Richard Carew's "Epistle on the Excellency of the English Tongue," addressed to W. C. For the date of this essay, G. G. Smith (*Elizabethan Critical Essays*, II, 285) suggests 1595–96, without evidence and without giving any reasons. It was inspired by Henri Estienne's treatise on the French language. One might conjecture that it also owes some of its inspiration to the first edition of Camden's *Remaines*, 1605. Carew himself was an antiquary, and there are clear manifestations of the antiquarian attitude in the treatise: "The grounde of our owne [language] apperteyneth to the old Saxon, little differing from the present low Dutch, because they more than any of their neighbours haue hitherto preserued that speach from any greate forrayne mixture." He expressly praises the monosyllables "in our natiue Saxon language" for their significance, and shows their facility in compounding, "a peculiar grace." In pointing out the Saxon nature of English surnames he seems to follow Verstegan. In the manner of Camden he defends the mixed nature of the English tongue against foreign criticism, and praises the copiousness gained by borrowing. He lists the qualities of Italian, French, and Spanish, and shows how words taken from them are improved when introduced into English, a method of approach characteristic of the first half of the seventeenth century. I suggest that the date of composition of the work falls between 1605 and 1614.

expresse any hard conceit whatsoeuer with great dexterity: waighty in
weighty matters, merry in merry, braue in braue.

Impressed with the excellence of current English and cognizant
of the part generally conceded to have been played in this excellence by borrowed terms, he was hardly in a position to denounce
neologizing, no matter how great his love for Saxon. Recognizing the progress which the vernacular had made, he is even
coerced to speak of the Saxon tongue as "these oueraged and out
worne dialects" and "the mean and rude beginnings of our
tongue," toward which the English people should maintain an
affectionate attitude "notwithstanding the perfection it [the lan-
guage] is now come to." Unlike some, he disclaims any desire
to call again "this old garbe [Saxon] into use," yet he concedes
something to the antiquarian hostility to borrowing when he
adds: "but to hold where we are without borrowing when we need
not." He manifests a sterner attitude toward loan words when
he speaks of the fustian and "inkehorne termes" of the Catholic
translations of the Bible, with which he contrasts the purity of
Saxon translations. There are Anglo-Saxon equivalents, he says,
for such words as "Trinity," "Incarnation," and "Resurrection,"
and though he does not advocate the revival of these equivalents,
he implies such a desire. He certainly does wish to pay due hom-
age to the sufficiency of Old English and "to stop the base and
beggerly course of borrowing when we need not." L'Isle is trying to reconcile confidence in the progress and excellence of his
mother tongue with love of its Saxon origin.[18]

John Selden reveals just as truly though not as clearly as
some other antiquarians an appreciation of the linguistic purity
of earlier days. In his *Table Talk*, composed during the last

[18] *A Saxon Treatise Concerning the Old and New Testament*, 1623, preface. L'Isle says that "perfection starts not vp suddenly with invention, but
growes by certaine degrees; and these long after their beginning, for better
proceeding in the sequels, we need and desire sometimes to review, and call
to minde: not vnlike the men, who, borne first in small, solitary and poore
villages, and after by fortune, force and vertue, attaining the highest degree
of honour and Empire, haue yet an earnest desire, yea and great pleasure take,
to visit the meane places againe, from whence they had their beginning. And
why should we not beare the like affection to the meane and rude beginnings
of our tongue, notwithstanding the perfection it is now come to."

twenty years of his life and recorded by his amanuensis, Richard
Milward, he says,

If you looke upon the Language spoken in the Saxon time, and the
Language spoken now, you will find the difference to be just, as if a Man
had a Cloake that hee wore plaine in Queene Eliz: Dayes, and since has
putt here a peece of redd and there a peece of blew, here a peece of
Greene, and there a peece of Orange Tawny. Wee borrow words from
the *ffrench, Italian, Latine,* as every pedantick man pleases.

Wee have more words than notions, halfe a douzen words for the
same thing . . .[19]

How far we have come from Ralph Lever's dictum that there
were in his day more things than words to express them!

Alexander Gil, who was much influenced by the antiquarians,
maintains a severely critical attitude toward neologozing, though
he disclaims any desire to repudiate all borrowed expressions.
His avowed purpose is to restrain the license of those who avoid
the use of familiar Saxon words in order to introduce obscure
foreign terms. His high regard for the Germanic element in
the vernacular makes him prefer compounding to neologizing,

. . . since very many of our words are monosyllables, and freely lend
themselves to compounding, for this reason the learned study much more
eagerly and more fruitfully how they may express their thoughts by apt
compounding of native words, and from its own material render the
language very rich and copious even to the extent of luxury . . .
rather then soil the native beauty with foreign rouge.[20]

He does not stop, however, with compounding, but goes so far
as to suggest that old words might well be revived. In speaking
of the figure barbaralexis, he says that if he should commend the
practice of borrowing pursued by many for the sake of eloquence,

I fear lest I would fix the mark of barbarism upon my ancestors, who
never did or thought of such a thing, and their language, which I have

---

[19] *Table Talk of John Selden,* ed. Sir Frederick Pollock, 1927, pp. 67–68.
In his preface to Michael Drayton's *Poly-Olbion,* 1612, Selden speaks of the
favor shown old words in his own day, for which, he suggests, the antiquarians
are responsible, and like many other archaists he calls for support upon Quintilian, who held that old words confer a certain majesty, not unmixed with
delight, upon an oration.

[20] *Logonomia Anglica,* 1619, p. 27.

highly praised for its sweetness and abundance, I would disparage as ugly, unpolished, and barren. Wherefore, to dissociate myself from this word-filching, I shall deliver what the most famous orators thought, who illuminate Roman eloquence with precepts and examples.

After quoting what Cicero and Quintilian say in respect to clearness and the use of intelligible language, he notes especially the latter's view of archaisms:

Moreover, he [Quintilian] praises the use of words brought from antiquity, since they bring to a discourse majesty not without pleasure. For they both possess the authority of antiquity and produce a charm similar to novelty. If this is true, even those obsolete terms which appear, *of yor*, and *Febus welked in the West*. He waxed *wud*, and *youd*, and others similar to these sometimes effect a charm: moreover that stolen offspring, *pondering*, *perpending*, and *revoluting*, will always stand fixed in *Barbaralexis*.[21]

The desire for eloquence and display of learning, says Gil, has caused many to impose strange terms on the English language to such a degree that the English might well seem not to have descended from the Angles and Saxons, so much of whose language they have deserted for foreign terms such as *common*, *vices*, *malice*, *virtue*, etc.

But indeed why have you ejected those words of the race which our ancestors enjoyed. O you English, you I appeal to, in whose veins flows that ancestral blood; retain, retain what hitherto remains of your native tongue, and follow in the footprints of your ancestors. Or will you whose forebears despised the Roman arms make your language a Roman province.

Although critical of English dialects, he permits poets to use the Northern because, being nearest to the speech of the Saxons, it is sweeter, more nearly pure, and more ancient. He takes pleasure in citing Verstegan as regards the Saxon origin of English surnames, and he tries further to mitigate the curse of borrowing by insistence upon the theory that some words common to both French and English do not represent borrowing but are derived

---

[21] *Ibid.*, p. 97. The reference in the last sentence is to the horrible example of neologizing given by Thomas Wilson, whom he mentions in his preface. See Wilson's *Arte of Rhetorique*, ed. G. H. Mair, p. 163.

from the same German word, and that the Latin language itself took some words from the Saxon tongue: *vinum* from *wine*; *vastus* from *waste*; *via* from *way*; and *vado* from *wade*.[22] Entertaining a high regard for the vernacular of his day,[23] and perceiving how words of foreign origin were woven into its very texture, he necessarily at times felt compelled to modify an opinion dear to his heart; yet his admiration of Old English makes him strong for compounding, and even revival, and inspires the suggestion that neologizing had served its turn in the development of the language and should be supplanted by the other two processes.[24]

One of the chief objections to borrowing, an objection maintained by Gil, was based not so much upon the fear of obscurity or dislike of vanity characteristic of the preceding century as upon resentment that foreign terms supplanted and drove out superior Saxon words. As late as the Restoration, when the pendulum of popular favor was swinging from Germanic to French words, Stephen Skinner complains that "we have lost innumerable words of German Stock partly through injury of time and partly by the vicious zeal of innovating."[25] He not only resents the expulsion of native by alien words, he also regrets the changes that have been introduced into the Saxon element:

Thus we say *Beholding* and *Beseech*, which our ancestors much more correctly pronounced *Beholden* and *Beseek*. Thus in a much better fashion the Anglo-Saxons formed the past passive participle by *ge*, and the Old English by *y* or *i*, in the manner of the Greeks, which we have rejected; thus the Anglo-Saxons distinguished their infinitive by the ending

[22] *Logonomia Anglica*, preface.

[23] He says no language is more polished, more ornate, more suited to expressing all the thoughts of the mind, or more pleasing than English. *Ibid.*, dedication.

[24] In the dedication to King James, Gil is especially severe in criticism of French legal terms, which he styles, in a manner prophetic of Hare, "marks of servitude burned into the English reputation."

[25] *Etymologicon Linguæ Anglicanæ*, 1671, preface. Since Skinner died in 1667, the preface may not be dated later than that year. It might be noted that he ardently advocated the study of English in place of the ancient and modern languages.

With an air of disgust, John Wallis speaks of the "great hodgepodge of French words" which had driven "many native words into exile and oblivion." *Grammatica Linguæ Anglicanæ*, 1653, p. 123.

an, which we today do by that equivocal article Tò placed before the verb and often even omitted.

He passes to a more important complaint, in which some of us even today may concur:

This is that utterly absurd kakozelia which has forced old elegant and emphatic words to pass into desuetude, and much less elegant foreign expressions to be borrowed from Latin and French. Hence for the old Anglo-Saxon *Heretoga,* to which the Greek στϱατηγὸς corresponds we have substituted Tò *Duke* (*i.e.*) Leader in general and for the significant AS. word Belaf we have from a Latin source elected into our language *Remainder, Rest,* and *Residue.*[26]

Love for the Saxon tongue did not move John Hare to frown upon neologizing so much as did an insane hatred of all French elements in English civilization. In fact, he seems to approve of words borrowed from the learned languages. Yet we find in him the same praise of the Teutonic peoples that characterized the antiquarians, introduced, to be sure, to emphasize the evil of which the Normans were guilty in conquering the Anglo-Saxons. He extols the Saxon dialect, which, though a primitive tongue, was most fruitful in significant and well-sounding words, and which possessed a facility for compounding far superior to that of Latin and the languages derived from it. Nor in his eyes was its least virtue the fact that it could be understood by any Englishman without the help of a dictionary or a knowledge of several other languages, "which now is requisite to him that will rightly understand or speak even usual English."[27] We are not surprised, then, to find, among the various reforms which he advocated and which looked toward the complete abolition of all reminders of the Conquest, one proposing

That our Language be cleared of the Normane and French invasion upon it, and depravation of it, by purging it of all words and termes of that descent, supplying it from the old Saxon and the learned tongues, and otherwise correcting it, whereby it may be advanced to the quality

[26] *Etymologicon Linguæ Anglicanæ,* "Canones Etymologici," sig. D3ᵛ. John Davies advocated the use of old words to make up the deficiencies of modern languages. *Antiquæ Linguæ Britannicæ Dictionarium,* 1632, preface.

[27] *St. Edwards Ghost,* 1647, p. 12. He is very critical of the retention of French words in English laws.

of an honourable and sufficient Language, then which there is scarce a greater point in a Nations honour and happinesse.[28]

In general, the antiquarians and those inspired by them advocated compounding and the revival, to a certain extent, of ancient words to supply the deficiency created by the proposed abolition of loan words. There is one writer, however, who not only ignores the first but is somewhat critical of the second, not because of a low opinion of Saxon but because of the strangeness of archaisms, though he thinks the latter are at that superior to foreign expressions. Yet he suggests a substitution for borrowing which is close enough to reviving, and which certainly testifies to his regard for the Germanic element in his mother tongue. After acknowledging that the Saxon, like other Teutonic dialects, is harsh and ill-sounding, Francis Whyte says,

but this Excellency it has . . . that it borrowes lesse, and is more copious, and significant then others, which I thinke might yet be showne; for though time as it uses has made its alterations, there are words enough of use still to expresse our selves in, without raising from the dead any of those which have been buried long agoe and where there can be no progression, I know no reason why it should not be as lawfull to restore some of the softest of our own to their birthright, and honours which would quickly bee as familiar to us, as to take in from *France* and Italy, strangers every day. I make a question, excepting the Teutonick, whether any language of the West, without being beholding to the Greeke or Latin, can in their owne Idiome express, *Creator, Saviour, Redeemer, Spirit, Trinity, Majesty, Divinity, Eucharist, Baptisme, Crosse* . . .

and he extends the list to include thirty-five other terms of religious signification, for which he is expressly indebted to L'Isle. He also follows the latter, and others, too, in pointing out that the Lord's Prayer, the Ten Commandments, and the Apostle's Creed contain scarcely any borrowed terms.[29] Whyte evidently believed in the adequacy of the Saxon vocabulary to meet English needs, but he drew back from the uncouth appearance of words revived after centuries of neglect. Since the need created by the abandonment of loan words could be met only by

---

[28] *St. Edwards Ghost*, p. 20.
[29] *For the Sacred Law of the Land*, 1652, pp. 216 ff.

additional terms of Saxon origin, it was necessary to solve the dilemma in some way. This he would do by a scheme described in his preface.

I have spoke a little in some of the leafes beneath of the fulnesse of our Saxon English Tongue, of its goodness and worth; I will shew here (that I may not seem to talk only) how easily we may utter our thoughts and wills, the drift of our minds, without borrowing of our neighbours, and without going about, nay, and often without waking the sleepie grave, and breathing life again into words hundred of yeers agone and dead and forgotten. We need not delve for buried gold, nor look back for words frightfully old (as they may goe at the first sight) such as would be dreadfull in their rising. Were we but ready in the speeches of the sundry Shires, Towns, Boroughs, and Thorps of our Land, of the West and North, (from whose broad mouthes (as they are thought) we may gather enough though what we gather thus is wronged in them every day more than other;) if all these were brought into one heap, and rightly laid together, we should finde our selves rich within our selves, without taking upon trust.

Whyte appears to think that the fact that an old word is used in some northern or western district, even though in a corrupt form, justifies its being given wider circulation in quarters in which it might look as weird as one that had not been used for a millennium. The Saxon craze led its victims into all kinds of paradoxical situations.[30]

There was more than a superficial sympathy between the antiquarians and the scientists, as may be seen in the fact that some of the former were members of the Royal Society (e.g., Ashmole and Charleton), and that some of the papers published in the *Philosophical Transactions* were on antiquarian topics. They both possessed the same type of intellectual curiosity and were indefatigable searchers after truth. It is not strange, then, to find a number of the experimentalists expressing linguistic views quite similar to those propounded by the antiquarians.

[30] The description which Samuel Butler gives of an antiquary is germane to our discussion: "He has a great Veneration for Words that are stricken in Years, and are grown so aged, that they have out-lived their Employments— These he uses with a Respect agreeable to their Antiquity, and the good Services they have done." *Characters and Passages from Note-Books*, ed. A. R. Waller, 1908, p. 42.

John Wallis, professor of geometry at Oxford, who wrote what
has been called the first philosophical grammar of the English
tongue,[31] disapproved the inordinate number of foreign expressions which had been mixed with native words since the Norman
Conquest, but which, he was careful to explain, did not indicate

> that the English language is in itself sterile, for it is in itself abundantly
> full of words and elegant expressions, and (if you please) copious to the
> extent of luxury, for there is no lack in it which would prevent us from
> expressing by its own resources, significantly and emphatically, the most
> subtle ideas, as clearly appears from the poems of Spenser alone, whose
> style is terse, polished, and copious, and at the same time is pure and little
> adulterated with foreign ornaments; but partly because the language
> can scarcely avoid borrowed terms because of commerce and especially
> the frequent marriages in royal families; partly because that excessive
> affectation of innovating (at least in this last cenutry) has incited in
> many such an inordinate itch of seeking foreign words beyond necessity,
> that men think nothing can be said elegantly or with emphasis, which
> does not smack of a certain unfamiliar and foreign sound.[32]

Though Wallis does not suggest that old words be revived, his
evident approval of them and his condemnation of neologizing
have prepared him to do so. Evelyn, likewise, looked upon borrowed words as an unnecessary, impertinent, and frothy addition to, rather than a solid improvement of, the vernacular, and
he holds that

> those who are a little conversant in the Saxon writers clearly discovered,
> by what they find innovated or now grown obsolete, that we have lost
> more than we have gain'd; and as to terms of useful arts in particular,
> forgotten and lost a world of most apt and proper expressions which our
> forefathers made use of, and without being oblig'd to other nations.[33]

[31] *Grammatica Linguæ Anglicanæ, cui præfigitur de loquela Tractatus
Grammatico-Physicus,* 1653.

[32] *Ibid.,* preface.

[33] *Miscellaneous Writings,* ed. William Upcott, 1825, p. 353. In his
letter to Peter Wyche (June 20, 1665) Evelyn advocates the revival of old
words, the dropping of which had rendered the vernacular barren in places,
and also the introduction of some French words for which there were no
English equivalents. (*Critical Essays of the Seventeenth Century,* ed. J. E.
Spingarn, II, 313.) Elias Ashmole declares that "Old words *have strong* Emphasis," and he is severely critical of those displeased by them. (*Theatrum
Chemicum Britannicum,* 1652, "Prolegmena.") In the demand for a simple,

The whole proposal to substitute Anglo-Saxon words for neologisms was much more paradoxical in this period than was the opposition to borrowing in the preceding century,[34] and necessarily failed to make any great headway. The idea of progress, which was beginning to take form, demanded that the earlier stages in the development of anything must of necessity be cruder than later stages. And the widespread confidence in the quality of current English, inherited without loss from the Elizabethans, demanded acquiescence in the process by which this excellence was in large part achieved. We have already seen how these two factors modified William L'Isle's linguistic views. Another example of their continued operation as late as the Restoration is furnished by the antiquarian Robert Sheringham, who intended to write, if he did not actually write, a treatise on the antiquity, progress, and excellence of the English language. The purpose he had in mind was to answer those who criticized the mother tongue because it had departed too widely from its

plain style, which became an important element in the program of the new science, the experimental scientists conducted an energetic campaign against the use of "hard" words, or neologisms, in favor of the language of "Artizans, Countrymen, and Merchants," and so may be accounted critics of borrowing if not Saxonists. Joseph Glanvill, however, refuses to condemn all words borrowed from the learned and modern languages on the ground that English is a mixed speech, and he holds that when foreign terms have been received into good usage, they may properly be used, "but to affect outlandish words that have not yet receiv'd the publick stamp, and especially to do it when the ordinary *English* will represent the thing as well,—These are the hard words I condemn." (*Critical Essays of the Seventeenth Century*, II, 273–74.) Glanvill even attacks the practice of one, Nathaniel Fairfax, an ardent supporter of the new science and the Royal Society, who in a weird book entitled *A Treatise of the Bulk and Selvedge of the World* (1674) sought, in the manner of Lever, to replace all borrowed terms by words of English composition, such as *all-placeness* for *immensity*, *all-timeness* for *eternity*, *thorowfareness* for *penetrability*, and the like. For a possible relationship between the regard for Anglo-Saxon and the emphasis which the scientists placed upon simple terms, see an interesting article by Miss Rosemond Tuve, "Ancients, Moderns, and Saxons," *Journal of English Literary History*, VI (1939), 165–90.

[34] The sixteenth-century opposition to borrowed words, which pursued a much less conspicuous path through the last quarter of the century, appears in this period, and at times we find displeasure with the vanity revealed in neologisms and also moral distrust of eloquent writing, without any predilection for Saxonism. Cf. James Cleland's book, the English title of which is *The Institution of a Young Noble Man*, 1607, pp. 154, 185.

Robt.
Sheringham

ancient purity through the practice of borrowing, the fundamental antiquarian view. He considers the language of his day
second to none in copiousness, richness, force, power, and
significant words. English prose writers yield nothing to the
Greek and Romans in beauty of discourse, and the poets, especially dramatists, are equally excellent. This excellence, he insists, has been reached through change and consequent progress,
and only the ignorant are opposed to the practice of neologizing,
the most important means of linguistic mutation. Arts and
sciences improve with time, and so language in its progress from
rude beginnings becomes purified, a fact he thinks clearly sub-
stantiated by the history of the classical tongues. Yet he is one
with his fellow antiquarians in his high regard for the Saxons,
and he attempts to reconcile his idea of progress with this admiration by insisting that the excellence of the vernacular can be
appreciated only through a knowledge of its origin. He holds to
the last his approval of borrowed words. This attitude permits
him to assert, in the face of all earlier antiquarians, that the Saxon
was not a pure tongue, but contained a large number of Greek,
Armenian, Turkish, and Persian words, a fact which, he says, he
will discuss in his history of the language.[35] Would that he had
published it!

Edward Phillips, Milton's nephew, deliberately refuses, in
the preface to his dictionary,[36] to try to reconcile belief in neolo-

[35] See the preface and pages 358–59 of *De Anglorum Gentis Origine
Disceptatio*, 1670. Another clear example of the part played by the incipient
idea of progress in determining the attitude toward neologizing is furnished by
James Howell, who says, "Touching the refinings, interpolations and enrich-
ments which the English Toung hath receavd from time to time, it is to be
considered that *Languages* as well as other notions of the mind use to proceed
to perfection by certain degrees . . . Now the English came to that perfection, and fullnes that she is now arrivd unto, by adopting to herself the choicest,
best sounding, and significanst words of other languages, which in tract of time
were enfranchizd, and made free denizons as it were of *England* . . . By
these applications and borrowings of choice exotic words the English may be
sayed to be one of the most copious languages on earth, nor in point of native
eloquence as for Allegories, Tropes, Agnominations, Metaphors, and the constant poursuit of them doth she yield to any, as also for soundness and strength
of poeticall fancyes . . ." *Lexicon Tetraglotton*, 1660, preface. Cf. his
Instructions for Forreine Travell, 1642, sect. xii, and the preface to his *New
English Grammar*, 1662.
[36] *The New World of English Words*, 1658.

E. Phillips

gizing with love of Anglo-Saxon. There are various opinions, he observes, regarding the question, "Whether this innovation of words, deprave, or inrich our English tongue," but he contents himself with stating the arguments on both sides with, however, an obvious leaning toward borrowed terms. He makes what had now become an obvious statement, that "the Saxon, or German, tongue is the ground-work upon which our Language is founded." Pointing out that foreign words must inevitably drive out peculiarly significant expressions of Saxon origin, he refers to Camden in citing *eordswela* as superior to *fertility*, and he expresses the opinion that *deny* is no more effective than *gainsay*, *resist* than *withstand*, *interior* than *inward*. It is true that large numbers of loan words are found in the vernacular, but

almost all the chief material words, and those which are oftnest used in the most familiar, and vulgar discourse, are all, either meer Dutch, or palpably derived from the Dutch. For example, the most primitive and uncompounded words, appellatives, the names of natural things, animals, vegetals, as *Earth, Heaven, Winde, Oak, Man, Bird, Stone*, etc., words that imply a relation, as *Father, Brother, Son, Daughter*; Pronouns, and Monosyllable Verbs, as *Mine, Thine, This, What*; *Love, Give*, besides all our numerals, particles, conjunctions, and the like.[37]

In true antiquarian fashion, he stresses the great antiquity of the German language, the wide area over which it was spread by the conquering Teutons, and the fact that it remained in Germany for a long time uncorrupted by other tongues. All this he says in honor of the Saxon dialect. On the other hand, he asserts that there are "divers Latin words" just as significant, in their etymological meanings, as Saxon terms, e.g., *intricate* and *insinuation*. In the spirit of the Restoration, he makes clear the benefit which borrowed terms, especially French, have conferred upon the vernacular:

. . . these forrainers instead of detracting ought from our tongue, add copiousness and variety to it. Now whether they add, or take from the ornament of it, it is rather to be inferred to sense and fancy, than to be disputed by arguments. That they come for the most part from a language, as civil as the Nation wherein it was first spoken, I suppose is without controversie; and being of a soft and eeven sound, nothing savouring

[37] See *supra*, pp. 248–50.

of harshnesse, or Barbarism, they must needs mollifie the tongue with which they incorporate, and to which though of a different nature, they are made fit and adapted by long use.[38] In fine, let a man compare the best English now written, with that which was written three or four ages ago, and if he be not a doater upon Antiquity, he will judge ours much more smooth, and grateful to the ear: for my part, that which some attributed to *Spencer* as his greatest praise, namely his frequent use of obsolete expressions, I account the greatest blemish to his Poem, otherwise most excellent; it being an equall vice to adhere obstinately to old words, and fondly to affect new ones.[39]

[38] The Restoration looked upon the Germanic element in the language as essentially harsh and rough, a characteristic which, in its eyes, was greatly modified by the introduction of fluent French words. In another passage Phillips is even more explicit when, in speaking of the refinement which a language undergoes, he says, "much more will the alteration that is made by the interspersion of forrein words, especially coming from the more Southerly and civil Climats, conduce to the sweetning and smoothing of those harsh and rough accents, which are peculiar to the most Northerly Countries." James Howell, likewise, holds that borrowed French words "hath not onely enrich'd, but civiliz'd and smooth'd Her [English language] with many thousand of words deriv'd from the *Latin*." (*A New English Grammar*, 1662, preface.) In his *Proposal* concerning the English tongue (1712), Swift interprets the tendency to shorten words as "a tendency to lapse into the barbarity of those northern nations, from whom we are descended, and whose languages labour all under the same defect." For the high value placed upon the French language in the Restoration see the preface to Guy Miege's *New Dictionary. French and English*, 1677.

[39] This last sentence contains a fling at the antiquarians as well as at Spenser. Just as Chaucer was reprehended by the former, as will be seen, for using so many French words, so Spenser was praised by them for his use of archaisms, many of which were Saxon in origin. (See the quotation from John Wallis on p. 252.) Partly in revolt against antiquarian Saxonism, Davenant set the fashion of criticizing Spenser's diction, and the Restoration continued the attitude. (See *Critical Essays of the Seventeenth Century*, ed. Spingarn, II, 6, 271; III, 27; and *Essays or Moral Discourses on Several Subjects. Written by a Person of Honour*, 1671, pp. 117–18.) Though Davenant in 1650 speaks of the poet's obsolete language as "the most vulgar accusation" directed against him, and though Ben Jonson's belief that in affecting the ancients Spenser wrote no language may have influenced the tribe of Ben, the main opposition to the poet's language developed in the Restoration. In the preface to his heroic poem *The Brittish Princes* (1669), which contains a foreword by Hobbes, Edward Howard, though agreeing with Hobbes's metallic conception of language, insisted that authors show enough respect to the vernacular not to use obsolete words, "which render even Wit barbarous." He accuses Spenser either of singularity or of a desire to avoid neologisms and "to honor the Dialects of ages past." He points out, however, that both archaisms and neologisms could have been avoided "if our native words and Dialects, had been better culti-

French

Even if confidence in the vernacular and belief in progress had not operated against the antiquarians, the quixotic idea of making modern English purely Saxon in nature would have been thwarted by the very nature of the Restoration when things French became all the fashion and many Gallicisms were introduced into the language, and when Anglo-Saxon (being viewed from the vantage ground of the self-esteem of neoclassicism) was held in small respect. The powerful influence from across the Channel had so determined social manners and standards, ideas of conversation, and theories of poetry that the importation of French words was inevitable and the limitations of the Saxon part of the vernacular obvious. Poetry demanded a facility and fluency which did not permit that "ten low words oft creep in one dull line." This new spirit influenced the antiquarians themselves. In the preface to his *Dictionarium Minus* (1662), Christopher Wase ascribed the origin of the English language equally to the Saxons and the Normans. He fully appreciates the antiquity and diffusion of the Germanic dialects, he emphasizes the superiority of Saxon over the others, and he is one with the Saxonists in his praise of it. Yet his admiration does not blind him to the virtues of French, which, he says, "being apt for compounding, rich in figures of derivation, amplified by orators, and refined by critics, joined its ancestral riches with the Saxon tongue." In this way the English vocabulary was remarkably enriched and its supply of synonyms greatly increased. The vernacular is great and copious because it stands at the crossroads of the two most celebrated tongues.[40]

ten low words

vated for use than a perpetual transplanting so many from forreign soils." The attribution of an antiquarian motive to Spenser indicates the strong impact that the Saxonists had made upon the century, and the inability to find any other motive suggests the blindness of the Restoration to the poetic power of archaisms. Similar evidence of antiquarian influences is furnished by a "Person of Quality," who may be the same as the "Person of Honour" mentioned above, and who turned the first book of *The Faerie Queene* into heroic couplets and modernized its language in order to see the poem "genuinely and succinctly convey'd by the Purity of our Tongue." He can interpret Spenser's using a diction "no less unintelligible at this Day, than the obsoletest of our English or Saxon Dialect," only as "a design to restore Saxon." *Spencer Redivivus*, 1687, preface.

[40] The same desire to give equal honors to Anglo-Saxon and Norman French is found in James Howell, *Proverbs*, 1659, "To the Philologer"; *Lexicon*

Yet even in the Restoration the voice of the antiquarian was not entirely stilled, but occasionally was raised in protest against admiration of the French language and against importation of its words. In a letter addressed to Sir T. L., an anonymous author struck out against those who "undervalue its [the nation's] ancient and unaffected language," when

Anon.

> our Ancestors understood themselves as well as we do, and spoke as much to the content and pleasure of those they entertain'd; who yet larded not their Discourses with ends of *French*; they were careful of the true glory of *English* men, to justifie the Dominion of their Language, equal to the dominion of their *Seas*.

He was particularly perturbed by the influence which the Restoration wits in their aping of French manners, dress, and language might exert upon the youth of the land. It is better, he says, to let the French dominate fashions in dress

> than our Language; because these are to be altered by time, whilst the other should be left pure and unblemisht to posterity: from whom we betray the glory of our Fathers. This ought to be the principle concernment of the wits; because as they guide the inclinations of the youth, so they are capable of delivering themselves sweetly and pleasantly, in the native beauties of our Language; and can render their conceptions lovely, without the paint and imbellishments of *France*: 'tis they must rescue our captived Language from the Fetters of that Tongue.[41]

Tetraglotton, 1660, "To the tru Philologer"; and *A New English Grammar*, 1662, preface.

[41] *Remarques on the Humours and Conversation of the Town*, 1673, pp. 95, 99. How out of tune this sentiment was with the prevailing temper of the period is revealed by an indignant opponent of "the old Dotage of keeping to our first Language, which was Teutonick," who pointed out that no Germanic dialect had continued pure to his time, that the composition of the English language was a *fait accompli*, and that this language as spoken in London, with its infusion of Gallic terms, was the best tongue in the world. The Saxon language was a primitive language consisting mostly of monosyllables which could satisfy the needs of a barbarous age, but which, even with the aid of compounding, could not meet the demands of more enlightened times without the assistance of borrowed words. *Remarks upon Remarques, or, A Vindication of the Conversations of the Town*, 1673, pp. 90–96.

Another exponent of the antiquarian point of view in the Restoration was John Webb, who, in speaking of linguistic changes introduced by neologizing, says, "And we need not go far for Example. For with us our selves, by this means chiefly, the *Saxon* Tongue, since the time of the *Normans* is utterly lost.

Such was the difficulty which the Saxonists encountered in their attack on neologizing and in their complete or partial desire to revive old words. A firmly based confidence in the excellence of English,[42] an inescapable realization of the great contribution made to this excellence by loan words, and the incipient idea of progress furnished an obstacle which could not be surmounted. Toward the end of the period French influence began to be felt, an influence which in the Restoration swept all before it. Yet the antiquarian point of view had been presented with enough vigor frequently to modify enthusiasm for borrowing, and, at times, to inspire apology for it. Peter Heylyn takes Hamon L'Estrange severely to task for his "new minted termes," allowing only "such words, as either are originally of an English stock, or by continuall usage, and long tract of time, are become naturall and familiar to an English eare."[43] Though Heylyn's opinion was partly determined by the antiquarian attitude, he was far from fully subscribing to the latter, believing that "the affectation of new words never heard before, and of old words, worne out of use by long tract of time . . . [are] equally faulty and ridiculous."[44] An anonymous translator finds it necessary to defend his use of borrowed terms,[45] and Walter Charleton goes to

Insomuch that what by *Latinizing, Italianizing, Frenchizing,* and [as we must have it called forsooth] *Refinizing,* or rather *Non-Sencizing* our old Language is so corrupted and changed, that we are so far from *Saxonizing* as we have scarcely one significant word of our *Mother* speech left." *An Historical Essay Endeavoring a Probability That the Language of the Empire of China is the Primitive Language,* 1669, p. 40.

[42] Besides the various expressions of this confidence already noticed in this chapter, we may cite *Critical Essays of the Seventeenth Century,* ed. Spingarn, I, 79, 107; Carlo Pasquale's *False Complaints,* tr. Covell, 1605, dedication; John Davies (of Hereford), *Scourge of Folly,* 1611, pp. 248–49; Joseph Hall, *Some Few of Davids Psalmes Metaphrased,* 1617, dedication; John Wodroephe, *The Spared Hovres of a Sovldier in His Travels,* 1623, p. 427; *Cyrupædia,* tr. Philemon Holland, 1632, prefatory poems by Farnaby, Lathom, and Heywood; *Campian Englished,* 1632, p. 25; *The Academy of Complements,* 1640, preface; *Vindex Anglicus: Or the Perfection of the English Language defended and asserted,* 1644 (*Harleian Miscellany,* 1744, II, 33), the author of which is obviously indebted to Richard Carew; Richard Flecknoe, *Miscellania,* 1653, pp. 100–101.

[43] *Observations on the Historie of the Reign of King Charles,* 1656, p. 2.

[44] *Extraneus Vapulans,* 1656, p. 36.

[45] George Bate, *A Compendious Narrative of the Late Troubles in England,* 1652, preface.

considerable lengths to answer the charge of neologizing brought against him, holding that it is no crime to follow "those Worthies, who have infinitely both enriched and ennobled our Language, by admitting and naturalizing thousands of forraigne Words, providently brought home from the *Greek, Roman, Italian,* and *French* Oratories."[46] Though Thomas Blount thinks that borrowed terms have "infinitely enriched and enobled our Language," yet he complains that the vernacular "daily changes habit; every fantastical *Traveller,* and home-bred *Sciolist* being at liberty, as to antiquate, and decry the old, so to coyn and innovate new Words."[47] The antiquarians, rather than the sixteenth-century critics of neologizing, determined the attitude toward the practice during this period.

One result of antiquarian hostility to neologizing is revealed in a changed attitude toward Chaucer, who was, for the most part, dear to the Elizabethans. This critical view was strangely contradictory to the praise accorded Spenser for reviving old words, frequently Chaucerian. To Verstegan "the morning star of song" was no "well of English undefiled," for the simple reason that he deigned to use so many expressions of French extraction. After stating that the Normans could not conquer the Anglo-Saxon tongue, though they mingled many of their own words with it, he remarks,

> Some few ages after came the Poet *Geffrey Chaucer,* who writing his poesies in English, is of some called the first illuminator of the English toung: of their opinion I am not (though I reuerence *Chaucer* as an excellent poet for his tyme) He was indeed a great mingler of English with French, vnto which language by lyke for that hee was descended of French or rather wallon race, hee caried a great affection.[48]

Though no other antiquarians followed him in this interesting explanation of Chaucer's use of French terms, numerous others expressed the same opinion of the poet. William L'Isle discovers another motive for Chaucer's linguistic sin, when, in speaking of the change that befalls all languages, he says,

[46] See the preface to his translation of Paracelsus' *Deliramenta Catarrhi,* 1650.

[47] *Glossographia,* 1656, preface. Blount was himself an antiquarian.

[48] *A Restitvtion of Decayed Intelligence,* 1605, pp. 203–4.

Tully himself scarce vnderstood the Latine that *Lælius* spoke; nor wee *Chaucers* English; nor hee, that was spoken before the conquest. If hee did, hee would neuer haue borrowed so many words from abroad, hauing enough and better at home, except it were to please the Prince and Nobles, then all Normanizing, a fine point of Court-rhetoricke for those daies.[49]

Gil

Alexander Gil strongly reprehends the "itch" of neologizing, which he ascribes in part to the fact that Chaucer, "infausto omine," employed French and Latin words in his famous poetry.[50] Skinner is more incensed than all others because of the injury done the vernacular by the poet, who, he says, "pessimo exemplo," corrupted the purity of his mother tongue by bringing "whole cartloads" of words from France into English previously corrupted by the Norman Conquest, thus destroying its native grace and "smearing rouge over its natural colors and putting a mask over its true face."[51]

One way of expressing the virtue of the English language, not particularly important but probably worth mentioning because it was congenial to the interest in comparative philology out of which the worship of Anglo-Saxon in some measure grew, lay in comparison with other languages. The qualities of Italian, French, Spanish, and other tongues are severally listed, and as a climax the combined virtues or superior virtues are ascribed to English. Though refusing to say that the latter is as sacred as Hebrew or as learned as Greek, Camden maintains that it is "as fluent as the Latine, as courteous as the *Spanish*, as courtlike as the French, and as amorous as the *Italian*, as some Italianated amorous have confessed."[52] Gil claims that in English some

qualities

---

[49] *A Saxon Treatise Concerning the Old and New Testament*, 1623, preface.

[50] *Logonomia Anglica*, 1619, preface.

[51] *Etymologicon Linguæ Anglicanæ*, 1671, preface. It is worth remarking that this view of Chaucer's language lingered far into the Restoration. The anonymous author of *Friendly Advice to the Correctour of the English Press at Oxford*, 1682, p. 9, condemns Chaucer for using so many Latin and French terms "to the loss of as many, and as significant Teutonic words, and to the corruption of our Mother tongue; as *Verstegan* hath observed, and proved against Chaucer. Yet is this brave Author more excusable than many of his age, as using the liberty of innovating chiefly in Poetry, where it was evermore allowed, than in Prose, wherein he is much more sparing of forrein words."

[52] *Remaines*, 1605, p. 20.

monosyllables consist only of consonants, a characteristic of no other language, and that no modern vernacular is more polished, more ornate, more suited to expressing all the thoughts of the mind, or more pleasing.[53] Characterizing Italian as pleasant without sinews, French delicate but overnice, Spanish majestical but fulsome, Dutch manlike but very harsh, Richard Carew expresses the belief that in words borrowed from these languages the English tongue gives consonantal strength to the Italian, full sound of words to the French, variety of terminations to the Spanish, and more vowels to the Dutch.[54] One of the prefatory poems in James Howell's *Lexicon Tetraglotton* (1660) concludes:

> The smooth *Italian*, and the nimble *Frank*,
> The long-lunged *Spanish* march all in a rank,
> The *English* head's them, so commands the Van
> And reason good in this Meridian.
> But *Spain* brings up the Rear, because we know
> Her Counsels are so long, and pace so slow.

Whereas copiousness was the greatest virtue of the mother tongue to the Elizabethans, in the seventeenth century an equally important mark of superiority was its strength, derived from its Germanic ancestry, the harshness of which had been modified.[55]

---

[53] *Logonomia Anglica*, 1619, dedication and p. 18.

[54] *Elizabethan Critical Essays*, ed. Smith, II, 292–93. Cf. *Vindex Anglicus*, 1644, in *The Harleian Miscellany*, 1744, II, 35; and Peter Heylyn, *Microcosmvs*, 1621, p. 248.

[55] In a poem prefixed to his dictionary, Howell writes:

> France, Italy and Spain, ye sisters three
> Whose *Toungs* are branches of the *Latian* tree,
> To perfect your *odd* Number, be not shy
> To take a *Fourth* to your society,
> That high *Teutonick* Dialect which bold
> *Hengistus* with his *Saxons* brought of old
> Among the *Brittains*, when by *Knife* and *Sword*
> He first of *England* did *create* the *Word*;
> Nor is't a small advantage to admit
> So *Male a speech* to mix with you, and knitt,
> Who by her *Consonants* and tougher strains
> Will bring more *Arteries* 'mong your *soft* veins,
> For of all toungs Dutch hath most nerves and bones,
> Except the *Pole*, who hurls his *words* like stones.

This conception of English permeates even the Restoration, and incites as inveterate a lover of French criticism as Rymer to maintain the superiority of English over other languages in the writing of tragedy.[56]

There was a far more important linguistic attitude than the one just discussed, which dominated the seventeenth century and extended far into the eighteenth, and which the antiquarians did much to promote. In the midst of varying and sometimes contradictory views of the mother tongue, the conviction of the instability of modern languages remained fixed and unchanged. *Bacon* Bacon expressed the belief that the latter would play the bankrupt with books, and this fear, together with a desire for a larger audience rather than scorn of his mother tongue, turned him from English to Latin. Somewhat later Edmund Waller, in a poem which received wide notice, warned poets to write in the classical languages if they desired literary immortality.[57] Hobbes

---

> Some Feign that when our *Protoplastick* sire
> Lost *Paradis* by Heavens provoked ire,
> He in *Italian* tempted was, in *French*
> He fell a begging pardon, but from thence
> He was thrust out in high *Teuton* Toung,
> Whence *English* (though much *polishd* since) is sprung.
> This Book is then an inlaid piece of *Art*,
> *English* the knots which strengthen every part.

The episode of Paradise was one of the popular *facetiae* of the period. Rymer holds that English has retained the strength but softened the harshness of German. "The *German* still continues rude and unpolisht, not yet filed and civiliz'd by the commerce and intermixture with strangers to that smoothness and humanity which the *English* may boast of." *Critical Essays of the Seventeenth Century*, ed. Spingarn, II, 166.

[56] *Critical Essays of the Seventeenth Century*, II, 186. Roscommon contrasts the energy of English to the thinness of French. *Ibid.*, II, 298.

[57] "Of English Verse," written sometime before the middle of the century, three stanzas of which read:

> But who can hope his lines should long
> Last in a daily changing tongue?
> While they are new, envy prevails;
> And as that dies, our language fails.
>
> Poets that lasting marble seek,
> Must carve in Latin, or in Greek;

assured Davenant that *Gondibert* "would last as long as either the *Æneid* or *Iliad*, but for one Disadvantage . . . The languages of the *Greeks* and *Romans* . . . have put off flesh and blood, and are becom immutable, which none of the modern tongues are like to be,"[58] Sir William Temple speaks as if scoring a point when he bases the superiority of ancient writings over modern on the mutability of the languages in which the latter are written.[59] And Pope echoes Waller in the *Essay on Criticism*:

> Our sons their fathers' failing language see,
> And such as Chaucer is, shall Dryden be.

Throughout the neoclassical period one hears innumerable murmurs of this complaint.

> We wri e in sand, our language grows,
> And, like the tide, our work o'erflows.

> Chaucer his sense can only boast;
> The glory of his numbers lost!
> Years have defaced his matchless strain;
> And yet he did not sing in vain.

Thomas Birch says that Robert Boyle did not have time to study ancient poetry, and refused to study English poems because "they could not be certain of a lasting applause, the changes of our language being so great and sudden that the rarest poems within few years will pass as obsolete." *Boyle's Works*, ed. Birch, 1744, I, 9.

[58] *Critical Essays of the Seventeenth Century*, II, 65. Dryden expresses the belief that only the instability of modern languages prevents the possibility of the future producing as great poets as antiquity can boast. *Essays*, ed. W. P. Ker, II, 25.

[59] *Critical Essays of the Seventeenth Century*, III, 63. Consciousness of the instability of the vernacular permeated the century more than we realize, and frequently finds half-hidden and not easily recognized expression. In the preface to *Pseudodoxia Epidemica*, Sir Thomas Browne, though stating that if neologizing continues, readers will have to learn Latin to understand English, defends his neologisms, and speaks of their "conserving influence," as if, being Latin words, they would not share the fate of native terms. John Milton tells of fixing "all the industry and art I could unite to the adorning of my native tongue," even if "I were certain to write as men buy Leases, for three lives and downward." (*Critical Essays of the Seventeenth Century*, I, 195.) Richard Flecknoe advocates the "Learned and Erudite" style rather than the vulgar, "or that of the Time," because it is "cast in the *Latine mould*, which never varies: whilst that of the Time changes perpetually, according to the various humors of the Time." (*Miscellania*, 1653, p. 78.) Other expressions of the idea of linguistic mutabilty are found in Samuel Purchas, *Purchas his*

The mutability of living languages, being an obvious phenomenon, had attracted attention as far back as Horace.[60] Chaucer himself says, "Ye knowe ek that in forme of speche is change,"[61] and in the Elizabethan age the fact did not escape notice.[62] But it was in the seventeenth century that the attitude

Pilgrim, 1619, p. 534; John Davies, *Antiquæ Linguæ Britannicæ Dictionarium,* 1632, preface; Thomas Fuller, *The Church-History of Britain,* 1655, Bk. II, cent. vii, pp. 65–66; John Webb, *An Historical Essay,* 1669, pp. 39–40; and S. C., *Fanaticism Fanatically imputed to the Catholic Church,* 1672, pp. 149–50. This last treatise argues that the Scriptures should be kept in Latin, an immortal language, rather than in modern tongues, which are subject to corruption and change. Chaucer's *Troilus and Criseyde,* and Spenser's *Shepheardes Calender* were translated into Latin by Sir Francis Kynaston and Theodore Bathurst, respectively, to save them from an oblivion produced by a changing language. See the dedication to *Amorum Troili et Creseidæ Libri duo priores Anglico-Latine,* 1635, and *Calendarium Pastorale,* 1653.

[60] *Ars Poetica,* ll. 60–72. These verses were sometimes quoted in the sixteenth century, and appear again and again in the seventeenth, especially in the Restoration. See, e.g., *Elizabethan Critical Essays,* ed. Smith, II, 153; John Selden, *Jani Anglorum Facies altera,* 1610, p. 67; Peter Heylyn, *Observations on the Historie of the Reign of King Charles,* 1656, p. 7; Thomas Blount, *Glossographia,* 1656, preface; John Wilkins, *Essay Towards a Real Character and a Philosophical Language,* 1668, p. 8; Edward Howard, *The Brittish Princes,* 1669, preface; Robert Sheringham, *De Anglorum Gentis Origine,* 1670, preface; *Friendly Advice to the Correctour of the English Press at Oxford,* 1682, p. 2; Theodore Bathurst, *Calendarium Pastorale,* dedication.

[61] *Troilus and Criseyde,* II, 22.

[62] Like the author mentioned in note 59, Nicholas Sanders opposed the translation of the Bible into English on the ground that it should not be entrusted to a changing tongue but should be preserved in Latin, an unchanging and universal language. (*Nicola Sanderi Sacræ Theologicæ Professoris Tres Orationes in scholis Publicis Louanii Habitæ,* Antwerp, 1566, fols. 56–57.) G. Delamothe and one F. B. both called attention to the cycle of growth, perfection, and decay through which languages pass. The first points to the Latin tongue, which reached its highest development in the Augustan age, as an example (*The French Alphabet,* 1595–96, p. 118), and the latter contrasts Latin and living languages in this respect, with the appropriate quotation from Horace (see F. B.'s letter to Speght, prefixed to the latter's edition of Chaucer, 1598). Mulcaster believed that in his own day English had reached its perfection, from which it was bound to decline (*The Elementarie,* 1582, p. 178). Believing that the mother tongue had already reached its highest development, John Palsgrave and William Bullokar both held forth the possibility of fixing it at this point, the first by his method of teaching Latin, and the second by his grammar and dictionary. In his dedication to Henry VIII of *The Comedye of Acolastus,* 1540, Palsgrave says "the englyshe tonge, which vnder your graces prosperouse reygne is comme to the hygheste perfection that euer hytherto it

became so strong and persistent as to make a definite contribution to the character of the period. Logically it could have dampened the artistic enthusiasm and undermined the conviction of literary immortality which were characteristic of the Elizabethans, though obviously there were more important factors involved in the restraint of the creative spirit in the neoclassical age. Whether historically it did exert influence in this direction is another matter. In the seventeenth and eighteenth centuries, however, it led to very definite demands that the language be fixed, demands that resulted in Dr. Johnson's dictionary.

More than any others the antiquarians impressed belief in the inevitability of linguistic change upon the age. The wide interest in comparative philology of the Babelian variety, the more restricted and more intense interest in the position of the German tongue in this field, and especially the antiquarian concern with Old English could not but focus attention upon the problem. In studying past English civilization, the antiquarians were compelled to use documents written in the language of the various periods, and thus they could not fail to note the changes that time had produced in the mother tongue. Verstegan comments at some length upon the mutations which the German dialects underwent, the alterations of Latin which resulted in the romance languages, and the dialectal differences to be found in the vernacular of his own day.[63] In the same year Camden called attention to the way his mother tongue had varied since Saxon times.

---

was, shoulde by this occasion remayne more stedy and parmanent in his endurance not onely by the well kepynge of his perfection alredy obteyned, but also haue a great occasion to come to his most hyghest estate, and there, by that meanes long to be preserved." Bullokar says that "whereas men be of opinion that our language is at this present time in perfect and sensible vse: my opinion is, that it is the great goodness of God, if the same be now staied in that perfectnes, which may continue as long as letters shall endure: whereas before time (through the vnperfect writing and printing thereof) the same is changed (more or less) in euerie two or three ages." See the last section of *A short Introduction*, 1580.

[63] *A Restitvtion of Decayed Intelligence*, pp. 194–206. To illustrate the last he offers (p. 195) a sentence as spoken in London: "I would eat more cheese yf I had it"; and follows it up with the versions proper to Northern and Western dialects. This illustration proved popular with later commentators on the language.

But that you may seeme [*sic*] how powerable time is in altering tongues as all things else, I will set downe the Lords Prayer as it was translated in sundrie ages, that you may see by what degrees our tongue is risen, and thereby coniecture how in time it may alter and fall againe.[64]

William L'Isle was impressed by the fact that few understood Old English "so much is our speech chaunged from the vse of that time, wherin *Elfrike* liued,"[65] and Selden warns "our quaint Masters of Expression" not to scorn the English of Robert of Gloucester, since linguistic change may in the future make their own verses ridiculous.[66] Robert Sheringham not only notes the great changes which the vernacular had experienced; he also defends mutation on the ground that progress is possible only through change.[67]

The same attitudes may be traced through others associated with the antiquarians or influenced by them. Alexander Gil, though defending the reputation of English against the usual foreign charge of corruption produced by neologizing, concedes and laments the inevitability of change.[68] Stephen Skinner calls poignant attention to the "small portion of our old language, [which] like a few planks from a great shipwreck, has come down to our hands,"[69] and he discusses at length the principle of alteration of tongues.[70] With the typical conservatism of a lawyer, Francis Whyte opposed the movement for introducing new legal terms for old on the ground that the new would soon be old.[71] John Wilkins, who touched his age at many points,

---

[64] *Remaines*, 1605, p. 15. He dates the versions *c.* 700, 900, 1080, and the time of Richard II. This illustration also proved popular with the later writers. See the end of L'Isle's *A Saxon Treatise*, 1623; John Wilkins' *Essay*, 1668, p. 8; James Howell's *Proverbs*, 1659, "To the Philologer."

[65] *A Saxon Treatise*, 1623, sig. T[v].

[66] *Jani Anglorum Facies altera*, 1610, p. 67.

[67] *De Anglorum Gentis Origine Disceptatio*, 1670, preface.

[68] *Logonomia Anglica*, 1619, preface.

[69] *Etymologicon Linguæ Anglicanæ*, 1671, author's preface.

[70] *Ibid.*, "Prolegomena Etymologica," sig. V[v]: "Enimvero ut omnia humana, ita maxime omnium Linguæ in fluxu sunt, perpetuis mutationibus obnoxiæ imo ausim dicere nullum annum elabi, quin aliquid in singulis Linguis, Viris attentis, sed non nisi attentis, observabile varietur." Because custom rather than intelligence determined change, he considered the latter almost synonymous with corruption. In this respect he resembles Wilkins.

[71] "Time is followed at the heels by corruption, and ere our descendent

thought that his century had done more to change the vernacular than any other period.[72]

The conception of the changing nature of languages was the only attitude fostered by the antiquarians which continued unabated or, as in this case, grew more pronounced in the neoclassical period. The attitude toward it and explanations of it, however, were varied. With their love of the ancient Germanic tongue, and their dislike of its corruption through the introduction of borrowed terms, the antiquarians could not but lament this instability, and they lent support to the conservative view that it represented the curse of God placed upon man at the Tower of Babel, and was also an example of human inconstancy and the perpetual study of novelty.[73] The Renaissance effort

Babel

shall make up what we shall leave imperfect (if our change be not disliked and changed by them) they that shall invent the last terms, perhaps without some key or other, wil not be able to understand the first. The length and change of time will make the next as obscure as these; if we look upon our own language not so far back as Robert of Gloucester, and others of the most ancient English writers, if Sir *Geofry Chaucer*, and *John* of *Lidgate* be compared, who calls him master, and betwixt whom there are not many yeeres, it may be seen how quickly it altered, as since the raigne of *King Henry* the eight, we know it has sufficiently changed again. It was the observation of the illustrious Viscount, that books writ in modern Tongues could not be long lived: he expresses it in the terms for bankrupts, *cito decocturos*, they would quickly break (which was the reason why he caused the most excellent piece, his Augmentation of Sciences to be translated into Latine) etc. So that I cannot yet finde why the antiquity of our termes should be a cause of change. It is ridiculous to think otherwise." *For the Sacred Law of the Land*, 1652, p. 222. Cf. William Fulbeck, *A Direction or Preparatiue to the study of the Lawe*, 1600, fols. 20, 21; and Sir John Davies, *Le Primer Report des Cases et Matters en Ley*, 1628 (in *Complete Prose Works*, ed. A. B. Grosart, I, 256–57).

[72] "Since Learning began to flourish in our Nation, there have been more than ordinary Changes introduced in our Language: partly by new artificial *Compositions*; partly by *enfranchising* strange forein words, for their elegance and significancy, which now makes one third part of our Language; and partly by *refining* and *mollifying* old words, for the more easie and graceful sound: by which means this last Century may be conjectured to have made a greater change in our Tongue, then any of the former, as to the addition of new words." He goes on to say that in a long lapse of time a language may be entirely lost through mutation, "For every *change* is a *gradual corruption*." (*An Essay*, 1668, p. 8.) Wilkins attributes linguistic change to the three methods advocated by the Elizabethans for enlarging their vocabulary.

[73] In the preface to *Antiquæ Linguæ Britannicæ*, 1632 (1621), John Davies insists that the curse of Babel was responsible for linguistic change. Cf. Christopher Wase, *Dictionarium Minus*, 1662, preface. E. Ashmole,

at orthographic reformation, which continued in a minor key throughout the age of Dryden and Pope, considered bad spelling one cause of alteration in languages. Bacon, Waller, Hobbes, Temple, Pope, and others saw in the law of linguistic change despair of literary immortality, and for this reason an inherent inferiority of modern tongues to the classical languages. There is also a suggestion of the theory of nature's decay in Wilkins' idea, shared to a certain extent by Skinner and Whyte, that every change is a corruption, a strange opinion to be held by one of the leaders of the new scientific movement. On the other hand, the idea of progress made its influence felt in some instances, and was strong enough to compel even the antiquarian Sheringham to see only improvement as a result of linguistic alteration. The idea of "circular" or rhythmic movement, which in the seventeenth century mediated between the conception of progress and that of nature's decay, is found as early as Richard Mulcaster and as late as Leonard Welsted.[74] For this view the ages of Demosthenes and Cicero furnished excellent support. In fact, the varied opinions of linguistic mutation present an excellent example of the intricate and complex nature of the history of ideas. The antiquarian love for Old English, the theory of nature's degeneration, the conception of progress, the cyclic idea, and the neologizing movement all play their part in determining the pattern of thought concerning the changing nature of modern languages.

The antiquarians made a definite and lasting impression upon ideas of the vernacular. By putting the proper emphasis upon the Germanic origins of the English people, they established the whole historical perspective in the later Renaissance. Thus they made possible a more accurate view of the past history of the English language and they established a pride in the Saxon

Theatrum Chemicum Britannicum, 1652, "Prolegomena"; and Edward Leigh, *A Treatise of Religion and Learning*, 1656, chap. vi.

[74] Cf. *The Elementarie*, 1582, pp. 178 ff., and *Critical Essays of the Eighteenth Century*, ed. W. H. Durham, p. 360. The author of *Vindex Anglicus*, 1644, seems to waver between the conception of change as an instrument of progress and as a factor in rhythmic progress. See *The Harleian Miscellany*, 1744, II, 34, 36. In the next chapter this matter will be discussed again with respect to George Snell.

element which has come down to our own day, and which at the time did much to stimulate the study of Anglo-Saxon and to inspire antiquarian investigations. Professor Roberta Brinkley, however, has attempted to show that the revival of interest in Anglo-Saxon "and the development of an appreciation of the language itself . . . had its beginning in the defense of the people against the Divine Right claimed by the king and broadened out into other fields in which the practical need for research threw the inquiries back upon Saxon Documents."[75] This thesis seems untenable not only because of the lack of positive evidence but also because it goes against known facts. An examination of Camden's *Remaines* and Verstegan's *Restitvtion of Decayed Intelligence*, composed before the strife between King and Parliament arose, will convince any careful reader that the Saxon craze and the demand for the study of the Saxon language began with these two books. Furthermore, the way in which the Saxons are discussed, especially by Verstegan, in relationship to the whole German race indicates that it was the Germanic movement on the Continent which inspired interest in the Saxons. Saxon merit was derived from Teutonic excellence, and Anglo-Saxon was a great and ancient language by virtue of being a German dialect. The numerous references to Continental writers found in works by antiquarians and those influenced by the antiquarians show how well informed the latter were in regard to the Germanophile writings across the Channel.

In other respects the antiquarians were too much at odds with their age to change traditional linguistic views. Their praise of the Saxon language introduced a primitivistic element which ran counter to the beginning of the idea of progress and to the strong confidence in the excellence of modern English. They somewhat modified the attitude toward neologizing but could not change

[75] *Arthurian Legend in the Seventeenth Century* ("Johns Hopkins Monographs in Literary History," III), 1932, p. 53. On a later page she repeats the idea: "The reign of James I became a period of vital interest in all things Saxon, through the desperate need of defending by Saxon law the rights of Parliament against the claim of Divine Right. The study of the Saxon language enforced by the practical need of reading the Saxon documents developed rapidly and the language became of interest *per se*." (*Ibid.*, pp. 87–88.) Professor Douglas Bush has followed Miss Brinkley in this error. See *English Literature in the Earlier 17th Century, 1600–1660,* 1945, p. 215.

the practice. Their effort to revive old words in place of neologisms made little headway in the first half of the century and died a natural death in the second. The antiquarians, however, exerted a distinct influence on all students of the mother tongue. As the century advances the writers of English grammars and compilers of English dictionaries do not often lose sight of the Saxon origin of the mother tongue. But even while the antiquarian movement was in full swing, there were developing other attitudes toward the English tongue which laid the foundation for the position occupied by the language today.

CHAPTER IX

THE RULED LANGUAGE

As interesting as the views of the antiquarians are, they do not represent the most important linguistic attitude of the period. The antiquarians were responsible for a pride in the Saxon element of the English language, they established the true origin of the vernacular, and they called attention to its history, but their program was not such as to secure its triumph over the classical languages. We must look elsewhere for the influences which laid the basis for this triumph, though many years, even centuries, passed before it was fully realized.

The Elizabethans had discovered once and for all the artistic power of the vernacular and had freed native writers from a crippling sense of inferiority, for which the classical languages and the classicists were largely responsible. Yet much remained to be done if the mother tongue was to acquire other functions performed by Latin, which throughout the long years of the past had almost monopolized the religious, scholastic, and professional worlds. English had to be equipped with those aids, such as grammars and dictionaries, which had helped make the classical languages effective, and its advocates had to insist long and loudly upon its use before conservative inertia or prejudice would give way. Toward the end of the period in which we are interested plenty of this shouting is heard. The first and perhaps greatest need which the vernacular felt at this time was dictionaries. The development of the language through the sixteenth century had swelled its vocabulary by at least one-third with words taken from other languages, Latin especially, and the seventeenth century continued the practice of borrowing, though in a somewhat different spirit.[1] Many of these terms had not

---

[1] The Elizabethans borrowed from necessity, vanity, or sheer exuberance. One senses a different spirit, something akin to the metaphysical, a seeking for the strange and out of the way, perhaps a striving for certain imaginative or sound effects, in the borrowing of men like Burton, Donne, Taylor, and Browne.

been used so frequently as to be easily understood by the reading public. They were often the expression of individual learning or individualistic whim. A few years before the Restoration as educated a person as Thomas Blount says that though he had read widely in the best English histories and knew some Greek, Latin, French, and other languages, "I was often gravelled in English Books; that is, I encountered such words, as I either not at all, or not throughly understood."[2] To render knowledge of the mother tongue independent of other languages and thus to make it self-sufficient, dictionaries were very essential. So great was the specific need of lexicons to explain borrowed terms that it overshadowed their other functions, and though sometimes attention was paid to orthography and derivation, by far the greater stress was on definitions. Therefore, it was natural and perhaps fortunate that these compilations were confined to "hard" words, though in the eyes of the modern lexicographer they were for this reason deficient.[3]

Not only were the authors of these works interested in neologisms in general; they were especially careful to include definitions of what the Elizabethans called "terms of Art," that is, technical expressions peculiar to learning, science, trades, or arts, and some even included words that were "hard" because obsolete. John Bullokar covers the ground well when he speaks of

the great store of strange words, our speech doth borrow, not only from the Latine and Greeke, (and some from the ancient Hebrew) but also from forraine vulgar Languages round about vs: beside sundry olde words now growne out of vse, and diuers termes of art, proper to the learned in Logicke, Philosophy, Law, Physicke, Astronomie, etc. yea, and Diuinite it selfe, best knowen to the seuerall professors thereof. And herein I hope such learned will deeme no wrong offered to themselues or dishonour to Learning, in that I open the signification of such words, to the capacitie of the ignorant, whereby they may conceiue and vse them as well as those which haue bestowed long study in the languages; for considering it is familiar among best writers to usurpe

[2] *Glossographia*, 1656, preface. He asserts that few without a dictionary can understand ordinary English books, and finding no "significant" dictionaries in existence, "though now many make it their study to be learned in our own Language," he determined to compile one.

[3] See Sir James A. H. Murray, *Evolution of English Lexicography*, 1900.

strange words, (and sometime necessary by reason our speech is not sufficiently furnished with apt termes to expresse all meanings) I suppose withall their desire is that they should be vnderstood, which I . . . haue endeavored by this Booke, though not exquisitely, yet (I trust) in some reasonable measure to performe.[4]

[4] *An English Expositor: Teaching the Interpretation of the hardest words vsed in our Language*, 1616, preface. Other dictionaries were: Robert Cawdrey, *A Table Alphabeticall, conteyning and teaching the true writing, and vnderstanding of hard vsuall English wordes, borrowed from the Hebrew, Greeke, Latine, or French*, etc. *With the interpretation thereof by plaine English wordes* . . . 1604; Henry Cockeram, *The English Dictionarie or An Interpreter of Hard English Words: Enabling as well Ladies and Gentlewomen, young Schollers, Clarkes, Merchants; as also Strangers of any Nation, to the vnderstanding of the more difficult Authors already printed in our Language, and the more speedy attaining of an elegant perfection of the English tongue, both in reading, speaking, and writing*, 1623; Thomas Blount, *Glossographia: or a Dictionary, Interpreting all such Hard Words, Whether Hebrew, Greek, Latin, Italian, Spanish, French, Teutonick, Belgick, British or Saxon as are now used in our refined English tongue. Also the Termes of Divinity, Law, Physick, Mathematicks, Heraldry, Anatomy, War, Musick, Architecture* . . . *Very useful for all such as desire to understand what they read*, 1656; Edward Phillips, *The New World of English Words: Or, a General Dictionary: Containing the Interpretations of such hard words as are derived from other Languages; whether Hebrew, Arabick, Syriack, Greek, Latin, Italian, French, Spanish, British, Dutch, Saxon*, etc. *their Etymologies, and perfect Definitions: Together with All those Terms that relate to the Arts and Sciences* . . . 1658. (For a discussion of these dictionaries see *The English Dictionary from Cawdrey to Johnson, 1604–1755*, by D. T. Starnes and Gertrude E. Noyes, 1946.) There were also dictionaries defining terms peculiar to specific fields or vocations: Thomas Wilson, *A Christian Dictionarie, Opening the signification of the chiefe wordes dispersed generally through Holie Scriptures of the Old and New Testament* . . . 1612; Captain John Smith, *A Sea Grammar*, 1627; Sir Henry Manwayring, *The Sea-Mans Dictionary*, 1644. There were several dictionaries of legal terms, made necessary by the change in language: John Cowell's *Interpreter*, 1607; Edward Leigh's *Philologicall Commentary*, 1652; Thomas Blount's *Nomolexicon*, 1670; and Edward Phillips' *Nomothetes*, 1670. In addition there were treatises, which, though not cast in the form of dictionaries, obviously were written for the same purpose, as well as works which contain glossaries of the hard words used in them, such as Henry More's *Platonicall Song of the Soul*, 1642. In somewhat the same manner as Puttenham, John Smith defines rhetorical figures of speech, with special reference to the Bible, in *The Mysteries of Rhetorique Vnvail'd*, 1657; and John Prideaux, Bishop of Worcester, pursues the same purpose in *Sacred Eloquence*, 1659. The need of explaining scientific and technological terms is revealed by John Tradescant's *Musæum Tradescantium*, 1656, and, later, by John Ray's excellent *A Collection of English Words, not generally used*, 1674. At the end of his incredible *Trissotetras; or a most exquisite table for Resolving all manner of Tri-*

The compilers of these dictionaries maintain varied attitudes toward the words they are explaining. Cawdrey condemns them in a manner popular a half-century before,[5] and even near the time of the Restoration Blount is severely critical of them.[6] Yet one of the purposes of Cawdrey's work, as stated in the title, is to enable women and "other vnskilfull persons" to use aptly "many hard English wordes, which they shall heare or read in Scriptures, Sermons, or elsewhere." Cockeram likewise devotes a section of his lexicon to this purpose.[7] One might ascribe Blount's dislike of loan words to the influence of the antiquarians, especially since for the first time Saxon appears among the languages mentioned in the title, but such an influence was not exerted upon Phillips, who also included Saxon in the languages considered, and who in addition made use of and praised the antiquarians.[8]

angles, 1645, Sir Thomas Urquhart thoughtfully adds "A Lexicidion of some of the hardest words that occurre in the discourse of this institution *Trigonometricall.*"

There were polyglot dictionaries: Randle Cotgrave, *A Dictionarie of the French and English Tonges,* 1611; Edmund Rive, *An Heptaglottologie,* 1618; John Minsheu, *The Guide into the tongues,* 1617; and James Howell, *Lexicon Tetraglotton,* 1660. Minsheu tells us that his ambitious work cost him twenty years of labor and all his money, quite a credible statement since the volume includes English, British, Low Dutch, High Dutch, French, Italian, Spanish, Portuguese, Latin, Greek, and Hebrew. His etymologies, upon which he laid great emphasis, were not very successful.

[5] He holds that preachers and others who address unlearned audiences should not seek to be "fine or curious," but should use plain language. He condemns those who employ such "outlandish" English that they seem to have forgotten their mother tongue, and others who "pouder" their conversation "with ouer-sea language." "Doth any wise man think," he says in the preface to his *Table Alphabeticall,* "that wit resteth in strange words," and not in wholesome matter properly expressed? If the "follie" of "affected Rhetorique" continues, two kinds of English will be established: learned, or court, English; and rude, or country, English. (Cf. Thomas Wilson, *Arte of Rhetorique,* ed. Mair, pp. 163–64.) The principles for the use of words which he lays down demand that they be idiomatic, plain, appropriate, and figurative.

[6] See the preface to *Glossographia,* 1656. He quotes Seneca against the use of far-fetched words, and condemns the condition which justifies his book.

[7] "The second Booke contains the vulgar words, which whensoeuer any desirous of a more curious explanation by a more refined and elegant speech shall looke into, he shall there receiue the exact and ample word to expresse the same." Cockeram is more consistent than Cawdrey in this matter, for he considered neologisms "the choisest words themselves now in use, wherewith our Language is inriched and become so copious."

[8] The antiquarians, however, made some impressions upon Phillips, as is re-

Phillips' purpose was not only to furnish an aid in the understanding of spoken and written English; he also hoped to do something toward refining the language, a design which, partly inspired by the French Academy, was pursued throughout the Restoration and the greater part of the eighteenth century.[9] Both Blount and Phillips, who wrote on the eve of the Restoration, introduce some interesting innovations. Blount cites authorities for some of his words, a practice which Phillips thinks should be followed only when "long custom" has not sufficiently authorized the word.[10] In order to make their works more authoritative, both lexicographers secured the services of specialists in the various fields from which their words were taken, and in later editions, published after the founding of the Royal Society, they engaged its members to define scientific terms.

These dictionaries represented an attempt to meet the most immediate need of those using the vernacular. Without them the mother tongue would have lost in utility, and in dignity, too, since its significance would in large part have remained dependent

---

vealed by his cautious treatment of old words: "I . . . have stript away those obsolete termes that have defaced our language, not degrading [it] too much from its primitive integrity, nor declining what with judgment I might insert." He also says that though foreign terms exceed in number the Saxon words in the vernacular, the latter are more essential than, and not so remote as, the former. In fact, they form the foundation of the language, and the others only the superstructure. See the preface and the dedication to the two universities of *The New World of English Words*, 1658.

[9] He is not backward in proclaiming the virtues of his work in this respect. "I have illustrated and refined it [the language], instated it in its proper majesty, rendred it admirably useful for all persons on all occasions, worthy of the greatest Masters of Rhetoricians, and the tongues of our Vernaculous Oratours." In reading the "best Authors" for words to define, he distinguished between "what words are natural, and legitimate and what spurious or forc'st," and he marked those he could not recommend. *Ibid.*, dedication and preface.

[10] *The Glossographia* contains reference to Taylor, Fuller, Bacon, and Browne. It approaches a glossary of pre-Restoration prose. Both Blount and Phillips refer to Chaucer and consider archaisms proper material for their work. *The New World of English Words* emphasizes the need of reading "ancient Records and Manuscripts . . . the Works of our ancient poets . . . as also some of our more Modern Poets, as *Spencer*, *Sidny*, *Draiton*, *Daniel*, with our Reformers of the Scene, *Johnson*, *Shakesphear*, *Beaumont* and *Fletcher*, and among the renowned Antiquaries, *Cambden*, *Lambard*, *Spelman*, *Selden*, and divers others." *Ibid.*, dedication.

upon a knowledge of other languages.[11] Though they recorded many words which did not survive, they helped to fix others securely in the vernacular, and, in Phillips' work, sought to establish the principles of authority so necessary for the effective use and stability of a tongue. Finally, they reveal a desire to survey and take stock of the remarkable growth of the language during the preceding century, and to mold it into a more effective instrument.

The same desire is apparent in the various grammatical treatises on the English language which were published during the fifty years preceding the Restoration. Before they are considered, however, it is well to notice the change in opinions concerning the teaching of Latin, which resulted in a widened use of English and an increased regard for its importance. In respect to Latin the dominant pedogogical opinion was that "there should be a North-West passage found for the attaining"[12] of it, so as to avoid afflicting students with unnecessary difficulty and to save time, too much of which would otherwise be spent on the mere preparation of tools, for such was the rising attitude toward linguistic study. The chief purpose of the educational reformers was to change the traditional method of teaching Latin grammar as an art in itself, detached from its manifestation in literature and demanding of its learners interminable and uninspiring drudgery, into the practice of teaching grammar as revealed in written works. Additional means for making the learning of Latin easier were suggested, but the main proposal demanded that only enough time be spent on the study of grammar to enable a student to begin to read authors, in whom "customary" rather than "art" grammar would be found.[13] Though discon-

---

[11] Edmund Rive says, "it is impossible for an English person throughly to vnderstand his own language, to speake or write it rightly, without the skill of Latine." *An Heptaglottologie*, 1618, p. 27.

[12] T. C., *Morall Discourses and Essays, upon Severall Select Subjects*, 1655, p. 60.

[13] The problem involved here was essentially the same as that found in the controversies over the spelling of English and the introduction of classical prosody into English poetry. It is not strange then to find Joseph Webbe, the chief English exponent of the new way of teaching Latin, referring to Mulcaster's defense of custom in the orthographical movement. (*An Appeale to Truth*, 1622, p. 44.) Later the neoclassical critics developed the same concep-

tent over the amount of time spent on learning grammar is voiced in the sixteenth century,[14] and though the most complete expression of the proposed reform in England is to be found in the works of Dr. Joseph Webbe,[15] published before Comenius' influence had been felt, it was the latter who became the chief support of the movement.[16] Under his influence the Puritans conducted an energetic offensive against the grueling method of grammatical instruction which had too often obtained in the past.

In this pedagogical attack it was inevitable that the prestige of Latin should suffer somewhat, for the critical attitude contained an inescapable implication that Latin was not worth so much trouble, an implication which later led to vehement assertions of its inutility. There was, however, another element in the attempt at educational reform which touched the vernacular even more closely, and that was the insistence that Latin grammars should be written and taught in English. In the sixteenth century and even earlier, grammars and grammatical works of various kinds had appeared in the vernacular,[17] but from the time of Henry VIII to the end of the century Lily's, or the official, grammar was written in Latin.[18] Though it is quite possible that

tion of literary types that the Latin grammarians had of grammar, and fashioned and studied abstract forms too much divorced from literature itself.

[14] Among others, by Sir Thomas Elyot and Roger Ascham. Cf. Foster Watson, *The English Grammar Schools to 1660*, 1908, pp. 262–64.

[15] *An Appeale to Truth, In the Controuersie between Art, and Vse; About the best and most expedient Course in Languages. To be read Fasting; For the greater benefit of the deluded innocencie of our owne and other Nations,* 1622; and *A Petition to the High Court of Parliament, In the behalfe of Ancient and authentic Authors, For the vniuersall and perpetuall good of euery man and his posteritie,* 1623. Webbe makes a clear distinction between "Grammar Latin" and "Authors Latin." (*An Appeale,* p. 14.) He was much indebted to Vives; and indeed, though Comenius furnished the chief pedagogical inspiration to the Puritans, the impulses of Vives' thought continued to be felt.

[16] In the preface to *Methodi Practicæ Specimen,* 1660, Christopher Wase speaks of "that great Regulator of School-Policy, who hath much matured the Learning of Tongues, the Reverend and Singularly Ingenious Comenius"; and in the preface to Comenius' *Vestibulum,* 1640, Hezekiah Woodward says that Comenius "Hath said al."

[17] See Foster Watson, *English Grammar Schools,* pp. 233–37, 257, 295. In 1590 John Stockwood published *A Plaine and Easie Laying open of the meaning and vnderstanding of the Rules of Construction in the English Accidence.*

[18] The first part called "The English Introduction," which named and

grammar was never presented in Latin as much in England as on the Continent,[19] yet since it was illegal to use any textbook other than Lily's, the educational reformers must have had a just grievance, which Comenius' influence intensified. The seventeenth century set about changing this situation, and by the time of the Restoration, Lily's grammar had been entirely rendered in English and had been reinforced by supplementary and auxiliary works, all in English. The vernacular had become the medium through which Latin was to be taught.[20] In this way the mother tongue appropriated another function which had in part been performed by Latin, and in doing so increased its prestige at the expense of the latter.

That its prestige and importance were increasing is revealed in no way more impressively than in the insistence that the classical languages should be learned through English and not English through them, that knowledge of English must precede their study. Here also Comenius' influence was strong,[21] though Brinsley's espousal of the view antedates it.[22] Hezekiah Woodward asserts that "The Master must make the Mother-tongue, I mean that, wherein the childe is daily versed and understands, a precognition to that tongue he understands not; it is the onely ready means to informe a childes understanding in both, and to speed his course."[23] In a treatise published by Samuel Hartlib, John

defined the eight parts of speech, was in English, but the grammar proper, *Brevissima Institutio seu Ratio Grammatices cognoscendae*, was in Latin. See Watson, *op. cit.*, p. 295.

[19] See M. W. Keatinge in his translation of Comenius' *Great Didactic*, 1896, p. 109. Keatinge calls the *Brevissima Institutio* a "Latin appendix."

[20] See Watson, *op. cit.*, pp. 266–72.

[21] See *The Great Didactic*, tr. M.W. Keatinge, pp. 357–58.

[22] See *Ludus Literarius*, chap. iii, "How the Schollar may be taught to reade English speedily, to fit him the sooner and better for the Grammar schoole."

[23] *A Childes Patrimony*, 1640, p. 160. John Hewes believed so strongly that the chief difficulty in learning Latin was ignorance of the mother tongue that before launching on his Latin grammar proper, he introduced a few pages of succinct grammatical explanations of English, and he continued to discuss the two languages together, pointing out their dissimilarities. He says that he "made an exact Suruey (as the time hath yeelded me) of the *English* Tongue, as the same may for the vse of all the parts of Speech in Composition best conduce or accord with *Latines*; and so haue I made as a *posteriori* the English tongue for those that are English, the first ground-worke to the Latine." See

Dury maintains that the first reform for the advancement of learning is "a direction for their own mother tongue, to know the true properties thereof; for it is to be the rule of understanding all other tongues."[24] Joshua Poole is more explicit:

My drift and scope therefore is, to have a child, so well verst in his Mothers toungue, before he meddle with Latine, that when he comes to the construing of a Latine Author, he shall from the signification of his words in construing, be in some good measure able to tell distinctly what part of Speech every word is, though he be not able to parse, varie, or give any other account of one word in his lesson; and when he is put to translation, or making of Latine, he shall know from his English both what part of Speech every word is, And what Syntaxis, or ordering it should have in Latine, though in the mean time he never heard of one Latine word: And this I conceive may be in an indifferent manner effected by the Rules of this book, and the Praxis of them, according to these following directions.[25]

---

the preface to *A Perfect Svrvey of the English Tongve, Taken According to the Vse And Analogie of the Latine. And serueth for the more plaine exposition of the Grammaticall Rules and Precepts, collected by Lillie, and for the more certaine Translation of the English tongue into Latine,* 1624.

[24] *A Motion Tending to the Pvblick Good of this Age, and of Posteritie . . . Shewing briefly, What a Publik good is, and how by the best means of Reformation in Learning and Religion it may be advanced to some perfection,* 1642, sig. Civ. Cf. Dury's letter to Sir Cheney Culpeper, January 6, 1642, quoted in R. F. Young's *Comenius in England,* 1932, p. 74, where the same sentiment is expressed in the same words.

[25] *The English Accidence. Or a short and easy way for the more speedy attaining to the Latine Tongue,* 1655, preface. A knowledge of English grammar as an essential prerequisite for the learning of Latin came to be stressed so much that it is offered as one important purpose of grammars concerned only with the vernacular. The most extended comment on the importance of a knowledge of the vernacular for the learning of Latin is found in the preface to *A New English-Grammar,* 1655, by J. Wharton, who says that his treatise will be "especially profitable for the youth of this Nation immediately before their Entrance into the Rudiments of the Latine tongue: becaus the knowledg of their mother-tongue is most necessarie, both for the understanding of what they hear or read therein, as also the expressing of their conceit, in what they understand: And it is as commendable to give a warrantable rule or reason of their own, as of a forrein tongue. Besides they will more easily comprehend the Rules and Terms of Art in that tongue, wherein they have been accustomed from their infancie, then in the Latine, whereof they are altogether ignorant. Lastly it will bee a notable Preparative to the learning of the Latine, or any other Grammatized language; becaus the Rules in *this,* for the most part may bee applied unto

The attitude continues unabated in the Restoration. Elisha Coles insists that a good foundation in English is essential to instruction in Latin, and he differs from another view, to which he refers, in making English rather than Latin the common base for the study of all other languages.[26]

Again and again in these treatises on the teaching of Latin, English comes in for special attention, not only as a foundation for the learning of other languages but also as an object of study worthy in itself and demanding attention. If one person was more responsible for this attitude than another, it was Robert Brinsley, whose *Ludus Literarius* (1612), exerted wide influence long before Comenius made any impression in England. Yet even before Brinsley published his treatise, an anonymous writer issued a translation of Cicero's letters in order to help children "attaine a variety and copy [abundance] of words and phrases, and in time to a laudable propriety, and purity of writing and speaking the English tongue." He does not hesitate to assert that "the Idiomes, proprieties, and elegancies, peculiar to this tongue [English] are as much, and as constantly by the Maister to be shewed, taught, inculcated, exercised, and learned, as the Latinismes, Grecismes, Hebraismes, and so forth."[27] But it was Brinsley who made the most earnest and influential appeal for the grammatical study of English. In fact, he demands that

that. Moreover by them also, that are already entred into the Latine-tongue, it may profitably bee learned upon the By, without any hinderance to their other proceedings."

[26] *Syncrisis, Or, The Most Natural and easie method of learning Latin: By comparing it with English,* 1675. As early as 1580 William Bullokar had expressed his opinion on the necessity of learning English before Latin, and toward this end he composed an English grammar, which, he claimed, when once learned would give children a mastery over "Latine and other ruled languages." He insisted that "among our nation" a knowledge of English "must be the foundation to such as desire farder learning, for that our owne language serueth euery mans turne in euery estate and dealing." But his was a voice crying in the wilderness. See *"The commodities of the amendment of ortographie for Inglish speech,"* found at the end of *A short Introduction,* 1580, and *Bullokars Booke at large,* 1580, p. 14.

[27] *Certaine Epistles of Tully Verbally Translated: Together with a short Treatise: containing an order of instructing Youth in Grammar, and withal the use and benefite of verball Translations,* 1611, sig A4ᵛ. The work is dedicated to the Merchant Taylors. The author says at the end of his work that he had communicated his ideas to Brinsley.

in the teaching of Latin, instruction in the vernacular should be of equal importance. Not only should children not be admitted to the grammar school until they are well grounded in English, they should continue to read English as well as Latin, and should improve as much in it as in the latter. Brinsley laments "That there is no care had in respect, to traine vp schollars so as they may be able to expresse their minds purely and readily in our owne tongue, and to increase in the practice of it, as well as in Latine or Greeke; whereas our chiefe indeuour should bee for it." He advocates the constant reading of English works, the daily use of Lily's rules, continual practice of English grammatical translations, lessons in writing and spelling in order that students "may goe thus forward, not onely in reading English perfitly, but also in the propertie, puritie and copie of our English tongue." All this is to be done in the grammar school which Latin had hitherto monopolized.[28] The interests of the mother tongue are being guarded as carefully as those of Latin.

Brinsley's influence was later reinforced by Comenius, who insisted on the study of the mother tongue and considered its interests of no less value than those of the learned tongues.[29] The insistence that it was just as important for a child to learn his native tongue grammatically as to learn the classical languages, that his knowledge of it should develop *pari passu* with his study of Latin, continues to grow until it reaches a climax in the Puritan era and clamors at the gates of the universities themselves. In the preface to his *Phraseologia Puerilis, Anglo-Latine* (1638), John Clarke is as considerate of the vernacular as of the language for which his book was ostensibly composed, and the

---

[28] *Ludus Literarius*, 1612, p. 22. Brinsley continued throughout his life to press his idea that in the grammar school children should "grow in our owne English tongue." (*A Consolation For Our Grammar Schooles*, 1622, p. 54.) In a work published shortly after the *Ludus* he insists that grammar, propriety, and purity should be studied in both tongues together, and that care should be taken "Least whil'st wee seeke to get Grammar and Latine, wee lose purity or propriety in our owne tongue, and bring in barbarisme in steade thereof." *Corderius Dialogves Translated Grammatically*, 1636 (1614). Cf. *Ouids Metamorphosis Translated Grammatically, and also according to the propriety of our English tongue* (translated by Brinsley), 1618, preface. English was telling Latin in no uncertain terms to move over and make room.

[29] See especially his *Janua Linguarum Reserata*, 1631.

next year an anonymous Latin grammarian holds that English must be regarded as much as Latin.[30] In an augmented edition of one of Comenius' works, John Robotham asserts with impatience that "it is meer follie, to be curious and expert in *forrein* cunning, and be a stranger *at home*: and it should be the care of every teacher, as well to accustome a child betimes to the practice of *good English* as of *good Latin*."[31]

Since for most purposes other than literary or social Latin had for centuries been used, and since it had been held in such respect and reverence that it thrust far in the background consideration of modern tongues, it stood as the principal bar to recognition of the vernacular. Therefore, it is in connection with its study that the claims of English are most frequently heard and effectively pressed. The point was reached when any treatise on Latin was more often than not attended by insistence that the vernacular also must be considered. The recognition of the importance of the mother tongue and the desire to see it regulated and stabilized find clear expression also in the various grammars of English and the grammatical treatises on it which were published during this period, and which, together with the dictionaries already considered, represent the progress toward a "ruled" language made by English before the Restoration. The Elizabethans had sought to make their language eloquent rather than grammatical; in fact, Sidney thought it was better for not being subject to grammatical regulation, and Mulcaster expressed doubt that it could be confined within strict limits.[32] The seventeenth century accepted the characterization

---

[30] *Hermes Anglo-latinus: Or, Directions for young Latinists to speake Latine purely*, 1639.

[31] *Janua Linguarum Reserata*, 1643, "To the Reader." At the time of the Restoration Charles Hoole was demanding that students write English as well as Latin poetry: "Let them procure some pretty delightful and honest English Poems, by perusal whereof they may become acquainted with the Harmony of English Poesie." *A New Discovery Of the Old Art of Teaching Schoole*, 1660, p. 158.

[32] See *Elizabethan Critical Essays*, ed. G. G. Smith, I, 204, and *The First Part of the Elementarie*, p. 181. Richard Carew mentions, as one of the virtues of English, that since the latter is not loaded with declensions, inflections, and variations, it needs only "a very shorte grammar." (*Elizabethan Critical Essays*, II, 288.) In the preface to an early English grammar, written under the influence of Ramus, Paul Greaves says that of the many famous writers in the ver-

of the language as eloquent, and set about to make it grammatical.

William Bullokar had called attention to the "unruled" condition of the vernacular, which, in his eyes, rendered it barbarous and inferior to the classical languages, and he had argued earnestly for both a dictionary and a grammar.[33] He spoke of having compiled a dictionary, and he published a *Bref Grammar for English* (1586), probably an abbreviation of a longer treatise, but since it was printed in his unsightly orthography it could hardly have had many readers. Eight years later Paul Greaves published *Grammatica Anglicana*, a more ambitious grammar of the English language written in Latin, not because of any lack of appreciation of the vernacular, which he considered superior to all modern languages, but because he especially wished foreigners to use it. The latter, he thought, would be very grateful to him for being the first to open to them a language closed for so many ages. He was not silent, however, regarding the need which his own countrymen had of it, of whom even the best educated, he says, did not speak or write grammatically. Among the mistakes frequently made by them he mentions such solecisms as double comparatives, lack of agreement between subject and verb, and improper cases of pronouns. Several times he calls attention to his work as being the first grammar to be written on the vernacular. He expresses the hope that its imperfections will incite others to perform the task better.

A number of the grammatical treatises published during this period for the most part merely continue the work of the Eliza-

---

nacular during the latter part of the sixteenth century none had paid any attention to the purity of the tongue. Studious of rhetoric, they ignored grammar, and were interested only in eloquence and rhetorical power. Needless to say, both the literature and the literary history of the period bear him out, especially with respect to the numerous rhetorical treatises written in English and to the almost complete lack of grammars. The discussions of classical prosody and of orthography touch the only aspects of grammar to receive serious attention, and interest in the latter had greatly waned by the end of the century. See *Grammatica Anglicana, præcipue quatenus a Latina differt, ad vnicam P. Rami methodum concinnata. In qua perspicue docetur quicquid ad huius linguæ cognitionem requiritur*, Cambridge, 1594.

[33] See the section at the end of *A short Introduction*, 1580, entitled "The commodities of the amendment of ortographie for Inglish speech."

bethan orthographic reformers,[34] and others, such as Alexander
Gil's *Logonomia Anglica* (1619), Charles Butler's *English
Grammar* (1633), and George Snell's *The Right Teaching of
Useful Knowledg* (1649), devote a disproportionate space to
orthography. Of the various parts of grammar Daines considered orthoepy, orthography, and "etymology" (to which he
assigned the eight parts of speech) "as most necessary and only
absolutely requisite in our English Tongue," but his treatise
handles only the first two, which he considered so interdependent
that one could not be discussed without the other.[35] Orthographic
opinions are not so warm nor are the recommendations made so
radical as in the Elizabethan period; they express more the spirit
of Mulcaster, to whom some of the treatises are indebted, than
of Smith or Hart. More emphasis seems to be placed upon
sounds and the way they are made than was true of the sixteenth-
century reformers.[36] The interest in phonetics reached its climax

[34] Some of these are: Alexander Hume, *Of the Orthographie and Congrui-
ties of the Britan Tongue: A Treates, noe shorter than necessarie for the
Schooles* (composed *c.* 1617) ed. H. B. Wheatley, 1865 (E.E.T.S., No. 5);
Iohn Evans, *The Palace of profitable Pleasure. Contayning and teaching with
ease and delight, whatsoeuer is necessary to bee learned of an English Scoller,*
1621; Simon Daines, *Orthoepia Anglicana,* 1640; *A special help to orthographie,* 1643, *The English Primrose,* 1644, and *The plainest directions for the
true-writing of English, that ever was hitherto publisht,* 1649, all by Richard
Hodges; R. L., *The Schoolmasters Auxiliaries,* 1659; John Brooksbank, *The
Compleat School-Master in Two Books,* 1660. Among his many interests, James
Howell did not accord orthography a low position; he touched upon the matter
in the "To the Intelligent Reader" appended to *Epistolæ Ho-elianæ,* 1645, at
the conclusion of *The Parley of Beasts,* 1660, and in *A New English Grammar,*
1662.

Two years after Greaves published his treatise, Edmund Coote, master of
the free school in St. Edmunds Bury, put forth a simple English grammar entitled *The Englishe Scholemaister teachinge all his schollars, of what age soever
the most easie, short, and perfect order of distinct readinge and true writinge
our English tonge,* 1596.

[35] *Orthoepia Anglicana,* 1640, preface. Just before the Restoration Charles
Hoole laments the poor spelling of students, and for some unaccountable reason attributes it to the fact that "our common Grammar is too much de-
fective in this part, and scholars so little exercised therein." See the second
preface to his translation of Comenius' *Orbis Sensualium Pictus,* 1659.

[36] An interesting example of this stress is seen in Thomas Gataker's *De
Diphthongis sive Bivocalibus,* 1646, a learned study of diphthongs which draws
upon Continental as well as English authorities, and which treats English on the
same level as Latin, Greek, and Hebrew. Gataker was an active member of the
Westminster Assembly.

in a work by John Wallis, entitled *De Loquela, Tractatus Grammatico-Physicus* and prefixed to his *Grammatica Linguæ Anglicanæ* (1653). This is a thoroughly scientific analysis of sounds and the way they are produced by the vocal organs. Earlier attempts had been made to explain sounds in this way, but Wallis rightly considered his work the first important treatment of the problem. Though the subject is naturally wider than the vernacular, his discussion is pointed toward the knowledge and improvement of English. Interest in the problems of English spelling has never died; the simplified speller will be with us always.

The importance of the establishing of grammatical principles for the mother tongue, which would embrace more than orthography, had been stressed by William Bullokar in 1580, and repeated by Paul Greaves fourteen years later, but their countrymen had been too eager to employ the vernacular eloquently to be interested in its grammar. In the seventeenth century, however, the issue is again raised and pursued vigorously enough to yield tangible results in various works.[37] The consideration which inspired their composition was the view that knowledge of the mother tongue should not rest only upon imitation and use, but should, as with the learned tongues, be soundly founded also on rational principles organized into an "art." Only in this way could the language really be learned and understood, not only by foreigners but also by the English themselves. Grammatical regulation was essential to a knowledge of the tongue; it was also necessary if the tongue itself was to be freed from the imputation of barbarism and allowed to take its place among the great languages of the world. The Elizabethans thought that linguistic excellence depended upon a capacity for eloquence, or, in other words, for figures of speech. It is suggestive of the

---

[37] The most important are: Alexander Gil, *Logonomia Anglica*, 1619; Charles Butler, *The English Grammar*, 1633; Ben Jonson, *The English Grammar*, 1640 (composed before 1623); John Wallis, *Grammatica Linguæ Anglicanæ* (dated 1653 on the title page, but Thomason gives November 10, 1652), Oxford; J. Wharton, *A New English-Grammar*, 1655; and in the Restoration, James Howell, *A New English Grammar*, 1662. The fact that Greaves, Gil, and Wallis wrote their grammars in Latin is of little significance, since they were especially interested in assisting foreigners to learn English and in convincing them of its excellence.

change which had occurred that the seventeenth century believed, as Bullokar had earlier pointed out, that a language must be "ruled" in order to be great or effective. Daines realized that grammatical principles were essential to an intelligent understanding of the vernacular, and to "more confidence and delight in our own Tongue."[38] Ben Jonson composed his grammar to develop the wits and advance the knowledge of students, to show the excellence of the language, and thus to free it from the charge of rudeness and barbarousness brought against it by foreigners especially. Wallis was not deterred by the fact that some of his countrymen believed that the vernacular could not be made subject to grammatical regulation, but wrote his treatise to enable foreigners to learn the language more easily and the English to understand it more deeply. Wharton says that his grammar will help foreigners to learn English, and will convince them that the language is not barbarous, confused, and irregular, but orderly, easy, and superior, indeed, to Greek and Latin in that its principles are simpler and less intricate. In addition, Wharton touches upon a reason for the grammatical regulation of the tongue which was to play a large part in the linguistic views of the Restoration and eighteenth century—namely, the need of a grammar to give permanency to a changing language when it has reached the peak of its development.[39] In general, the purpose of these grammars was to render the vernacular more easily learned, better understood, more respected, more effective, and more permanent.

Latin, however, was not entirely content to be pushed aside. When the grammarians proceeded to regulate the vernacular, it was not unnatural that they should accept the former as a model, though the differences between the two languages were apparent,

---

[38] *Orthoepia Anglicana*, 1640, preface.

[39] "Now if any here object, What need a Grammar for that language which all speak by custom, especially for ours which is so easie: To this I answer, Even the same that made the noblest of the Romans, when their tongue was com to the highest pitch, to write somthing of the Grammar thereof, that by Rules and Precepts it may bee made yet more elegant, certain, and permanent. And for this caus *Charls* the Great caused to bee set forth a Grammar for the Teutonick tongue, from which our English at first proceeded." *A New English-Grammar*, preface.

and though they refused to see in this difference evidence of the inferiority of their own tongue. Ben Jonson especially tried to introduce the whole Latin system of conjugations, declensions, and the like, and to force the native tongue to conform to it. Sooner or later a realization of the difference between the two languages and a desire for linguistic independence were sure to change the practice. It fell to the lot of John Wallis, professor of geometry at Oxford and an enthusiastic promoter of the new experimental science, to break away. His *Grammatica Linguæ Anglicanæ* (1653) reveals definitely three points of view: Puritan, antiquarian, and scientific. The very fact that he was interested in the English language and its grammatical regulation to the extent of writing a grammar himself is a result of his Puritan sympathies and affiliations, for by 1640 the Puritans had openly espoused the cause of English and had become the chief advocates of its use and development. Furthermore, his avowed purpose of enabling foreigners to learn English more easily so as to read religious treatises points in the same direction.[40] The influence of the antiquarians is immediately apparent in the opening pages of his preface, in which he says he will trace the origin and progress of the English language.[41] As we have already seen, the antiquarians had laid great emphasis on the Germanic source of the vernacular, and, especially in the case of Camden, had shown its subsequent development by means of versions of the Lord's Prayer written at different times. They had called due attention, often regretfully, to the linguistic significance of the Norman Conquest and the later importation of words, especially from the classical languages. In this way they were the first to suggest an authentic history of the language,[42] and

---

[40] The popularity and admiration of English theological writings on the Continent are remarked in the dedication of John Owen's *Vindiciæ Evangelicæ*, 1655.

[41] The influence of the antiquarians upon Alexander Gil and Charles Butler was strong, especially in respect to their views of the history of the language. Gil considered the Saxon characters far superior to Latin in polish and elegance, and he wished to introduce some of them into the English alphabet.

[42] Clear evidence of the part which the antiquarians played in creating interest in the history of the language is discovered in Robert Sheringham, an excellent antiquary, who speaks as if he had actually written or would soon write a treatise entitled *The Origin, Progress, and Excellence of the English Lan-*

the suggestion finds clear expression in Wallis. He begins with an emphatic assertion that the vernacular is not an offshoot of the ancient British tongue, but that fact does not deter him, being Welsh, from elaborating upon the latter. He next touches upon the Roman conquest, which, he thinks, introduced some words into the language, and the invasion of the Angles and Saxons, who, driving the inhabitants into Cornwall and Wales, kept their own tongue pure and unmixed until the arrival of the Normans. This unhappy event, though it could not destroy the language, modified it considerably by the introduction of usurping French words. He reaches a climax in glowing praise of Anglo-Saxon, concluded by another emphatic assertion that the English tongue is an offshoot of the *ancient* Teutonic language.

But the most important influence playing upon Wallis was that of the new experimental science, for it determined both the theory and the nature of his grammar. One marked tendency throughout the whole of the Renaissance in England was the desire to make an "art" of everything, to coerce into a system of rational principles that which had grown up naturally and even unconsciously, and in most cases the model was furnished by the classics. Notice has already been taken of this attitude in the case of orthography, prosody, and the teaching of Latin.[43] It was inevitable then, that the desire to raise English to the level of a "grammatized" language[44] should result in the same effort to force the mother tongue into a Latin mold. Ben Jonson, poet and classicist, tried to do so; John Wallis, Puritan and scientist, had a different idea. The struggles of the new philosophy to throw off the authority of antiquity gave Wallis both the desire and

guage. It is unfortunate that this first history of the language was either not written or not published. (See *De Anglorum Gentis Origine Disceptatio,* 1670, p. 359. Cf. also Edward Chamberlayne, *Angliæ Notitia,* 1669, pp. 18–20.) Another interesting example of the way in which the antiquarians turned attention to the matter is revealed in Richard Flecknoe's *Miscellania,* 1653 (p. 75), in which a section entitled "A Discourse of Languages" begins a discussion of the English tongue with comments on its origin and constitution. In fact, this method became popular.

[43] Seldom, however, were the results as conspicuous as those that followed the neoclassical effort to make an "art" of literature.

[44] An excellent example of this desire is furnished by Alexander Gil, who was all for an "art" language. See the preface to *Logonomia Anglica.*

sufficient confidence to turn his back, without regret, upon Latin, while the method demanded and followed by the experimental scientists inspired him to seek his data in the vernacular itself, and not try to impose upon the latter a preconceived pattern.[45] In other words, he employed the inductive rather than deductive method. Wallis complains that grammar has been handled in such a way that some consider the mother tongue so confused and erratic that it cannot be reduced to any principles, and that the teaching and learning of it are so difficult and tedious that foreigners especially give up in despair. He pays proper respect to Jonson, Gil, and others, but he strongly condemns their method,

for all bring our English language too much to the Latin norm (because of which almost all who treat of modern languages are in error), and so introduce many useless principles concerning the cases, genders, and declensions of nouns, and the tenses, moods, and conjugations of verbs . . . and many other like things, which are all together alien to our language, and thus the confusion and obscurity they create are greater than the clarification they afford.

And therefore it seemed to me that an entirely new method should be employed by which the nature of our own tongue, no matter how unfamiliar, should be observed rather than the principles of the Latin language, no matter how familiar: in the syntax of nouns all things are established by the aid of prepositions, and in the conjugation of verbs all things are done by the aid of auxiliaries, so that the element which causes great trouble in other languages is achieved in English with the least difficulty . . . there is no reason for introducing the fictitious and inept conglomeration of cases, genders, moods, and tenses beyond all necessity and the essential nature of the language itself.[46]

Wallis oversimplifies the matter somewhat, for he especially desired foreigners to learn the language easily, though he was equally concerned that the English should see more deeply into

[45] Wallis says that he was importuned to publish the "De Loquela," which was prefixed to his grammar, by some of the members of the scientific group which met in Oxford about the middle of the century to carry on experiments. See his *Defence of the Royal Society*, 1678, p. 26.

[46] The second and fourth editions of Wallis' grammar were published at Oxford in 1664 and 1674. A third edition was printed at Hamburg in 1671. The preface, from which the above quotation is taken, appeared for the first time in the edition of 1674, though it probably was written earlier. Other editions appeared in 1688, 1699, 1727, 1731, 1740, and 1745.

its true nature. He also, like others, believed that the simplicity of the grammatical structure of the vernacular was a token of its superiority over other tongues, and he set about diligently to show this simplicity.[47] His reputation and influence were far reaching. Later commentators on the language attributed to him the first thorough and scientific exposition of the way sounds are made by the vocal organs, and also the first attempt to study the structure of the vernacular and to formulate its principles in a manner entirely independent of Latin.[48] Finally, his scientific spirit, as revealed in clarity and directness of expression, intelligent analysis and classification, and authentic inductive method, found the next age congenial.[49]

The effort to render English a ruled tongue through dictionaries and grammars marks as definite a stage in linguistic views as the earlier emphasis upon eloquence. In the sixteenth century William Bullokar and Paul Greaves had insisted upon the need of regulating the vernacular and had made attempts toward that end, but their voices were drowned out by the panegyrics on the literary qualities of the mother tongue. When this latter view was firmly established, it is not strange that attention was directed toward other aspects of English, and that the grammatical problem was approached pedagogically and in connec-

[47] *Op. cit.*, p. 67. Cf. Otto Funke, *Die Frühzeit der englischen Grammatik . . . von Bullokar bis Wallis*, 1941.

[48] An early instance of his influence is probably revealed in J. Wharton's *A New English-Grammar*, 1655, though Wallis is not mentioned. Wharton reveals a tendency to rely on good usage, to reduce actual practice to rules. He reveals accuracy, common sense, and comprehensiveness. His ideas rgarding words derived from Latin are the most complete and sensible of the period. He considered English equal to Greek and superior to Latin in compounding, and "happie above them both in this; not that it cannot bee reduced to any [rules]: but that indeed it needeth little or no Grammar at all. For whereas in the Latine-tongue there are threescore Variations of the Terminations of Nouns, and six hundred of Verbs, and in the Greek, that number almost dubbled; in the English there is little or no variation at all; and therefore needeth not any Declensions of Nouns, any Conjugations of Verbs, any Rules of Concord or Construction, wherein the difficultie of any language doth consist, and which in the Latine and Greek cost much labor and toil." *Ibid.*, preface.

[49] Robert Plat, in *The Natural History of Oxford-Shire* (Oxford, 1677, p. 281) declares that Wallis "first observed and discovered the *Physical* or *Mechanical* formation of all *sounds* in *Speech*." In the preface to his *Grammatica Linguæ Anglicanæ, tripartita*, 1685, C. Cooper praises Wallis for re-

tion with the teaching of Latin. The great amount of time required by the grammatical study of that language could hardly
have failed to bring home to the English the contrasting neglect
of the vernacular, now highly respected. It is remarkable that
the first emphatic demand for its grammatical improvement
should have occurred in grammars of a classical tongue. The authors of these treatises must have possessed an awareness of the
unfortunate state of their own speech incredibly sensitive to linguistic suggestion from any source. Indeed, at times we feel
that the insistence upon a knowledge of English as a prerequisite
to the study of Latin looked less to this purpose than to the improvement of English, and that Latin grammars were written
with as keen a consciousness of the vernacular as of their os-
tensible subject. In short, the mother tongue took attention
away from Latin, and, as in the case of Wallis' grammar, asserted its independence of the latter, an independence which in
the twenty years preceding the Restoration turned into a con-
certed effort to drive the ancient tongue entirely off the boards.

---

moving the useless mass of rules, applicable to Latin rather than to English, and
for adapting the art of grammar to the latter, and he himself follows the same
practice. One M. Lewis, headmaster of a "progressive" school at Tottenham
High Cross, improved somewhat on Wallis' attitude in stating that "Whatever
Tongue hath less Grammar than the English is not intelligible; whatever
hath more is superfluous." (*Grammaticæ Puerilis*, 1674, preface.) In his effort to uphold the superiority of modern achievement to ancient, William
Wotton found good evidence in Wallis. The "Grammar of English," he says,
"is so far our own, that Skill in the Learned Languages is not necessary to comprehend it. *Ben Johnson* was the first Man, that I know of, that did anything
considerable in it: but Lilly's Grammar was his Pattern: and for want of Reflect-
ing upon the Grounds of a Language which he understood as well as any Man
of his Age, he drew it by violence to a dead Language that was of a quite different Make; and so left his work imperfect. After him came Dr. Wallis; who
examined the English Tongue like a Grammarian and a Philosopher [i.e., a
scientist] at once, and showed great Skill in the Business; And of his English
Grammar one may venture to say, That it may be set against any Thing that is
extant of the Ancients of that kind: for, as Sir *William Temple* says upon another Occasion, there is a *Strain of Philosophy, and curious Thought* in his previous *Essay of the Formulation of the Sounds of Letters*; and of *Subtilty* in that
Grammar, in the reducing of our Language under Genuine Rules of Art, that
one would not expect in a Book of that kind." *Reflections on Ancient and
Modern Learning*, 1694, pp. 58–59.

CHAPTER X

THE USEFUL LANGUAGE

T HE recognition of the use and importance of the mother
tongue, revealed in both Latin and English grammars,
and the consequent effort to modify the demands of the
first and to promote the development and independence of
the second were so congenial to the Puritans that though at first
they were by no means the only people interested in the matter,
after 1640, when the influence of both Bacon and Comenius
(who visited England in 1641) became strong, they were by far
the most important advocates of the vernacular. Their views
are most clearly expressed in a series of educational treatises
which reveal more completely perhaps than any other documents the secular spirit of Puritanism. The most comprehensive
of these, as far as the vernacular is concerned, was by George
Snell, archdeacon of Chester and rector of various towns in
Cheshire before being sequestered in 1646.[1] Since it touches most

Geo.
Snell

---

[1] *The Right Teaching of Useful Knowledg to fit Scholars for som honest
Profession, Shewing so much skil as anie man needeth (that is not a Teacher)
in all knowledges, in one schole, in a shorter time in a more plain waie, and for
much less expens than ever hath been used, since of old the Arts were so taught
in the Greek and Romane Empire,* 1649. Biographical data regarding Snell is
meager. A few details are furnished by the account of him in *Alumni
Oxonienses: The Members of the University of Oxford* [Snell was incorporated
there], *1500–1714,* ed. Joseph Foster, 1891. One antiquary says, "Then we
have the smart business man Dr. Snell, who rebuilt the rectory (1632), and
who made so much out of dilapidation claims on the former one, which was
thatched, as to enable him to build a new one. The same Dr. Snell, who was
archdeacon of Chester was a royalist and he had to compound for his estate
during the Commonwealth." (*Journal of Chester Archæological and Historic
Society,* New Series, 1887, I, 64.) From the spirit revealed in the treatise
under discussion we can well understand his business acumen, but his conversion
to Puritanism must have been sincere, for he expresses most of its attitudes.
Furthermore, his preface is addressed to "his verie loving Friends Mr. Durey
and Mr. Hartlib, men notedly known for their earnest endeavours to promote
the welfare of more profitable learning in English Schools." In fact, he says
he was invited to publish his treatise by these two men, both of whom were
dynamic leaders in projected Puritan reforms. However, his approval of the

of the matters discussed in the preceding chapter, an analysis of its contents will furnish a useful summary of what has been said, and also point to future developments.

Snell believed that when a child had learned his primer, he should be conducted to "the Grammar for English . . . so soon as hee shall bee found able for it," for it is easier for the impressionable mind to learn "terms, hard words, rules, and precepts of that speech, which they have used from their cradel; then of the Latine to which they are strangers." Thus they will more easily comprehend and better remember the intricacies of grammar, and be well prepared to pursue the study of Latin and other "Grammatized languages." Furthermore, it should be considered "a verie excellent and useful skil" to be able to justify grammatically one's use of the vernacular. This is the only way, he asserts, "to feed and nourish the natural seeds and inbred principles of right intelligence, and sound understanding." The ability to employ the mother tongue correctly, and to understand wherein the correctness lies, "wil bring great increas of knowledg, and a verie great delight to him that is taught."

It seem's little better then a brutish and reasonless Reason, for a man to bee able to saie no more for the defens and justification of the speech which hee useth, then this, I speak so and so, becaus I hear and see that all others do speak, as I speak, and do write so as I write: and for a truth, this idiotish reason is all the reason that anie man can give, for anie thing that hee writeth, unless by help of a wit more then ordinarie, hee can applie the Rules of his Latine *Grammar*, to maintein the rights of his English speech . . . Surely it is a simple incogitance, and a want of due consideration, to stand perswaded, that it maketh much for a man's perfection to know the causses and rules of the Greek and Latine; and yet to think, that without defect or dammage hee may securely want the rational knowledg of his own natural speech: everie illiterate plowman can allege the constant use and custome of others, to uphold and justifie his own manner of words, pronunciation, and writing: but shall one that hath been bred up at School, bee able to know no better caus, nor to yield stronger reason for the speech which hee useth, then illiterate ones can?

---

study of rhetoric, his respectful attitude toward the universities, and his seeming indifference to or ignorance of Baconian science may be relics of his Royalist days.

He points out that the Romans valued their tongue so much that they made it a "Grammatized and learned language," and caused Palemon and Priscian to cast it into a grammatical mold, all departures from which were to be condemned as barbarous, as "strangers from the Romane State." His countrymen, he says, should imitate them "by all Scholarly exercise and use, till everie learner of the second stage bee made a skilful Grammarian for English." He issues a warning that

The neglect of this teaching of English by Grammar, is the nurs and cherisher of manie and verie hurtful mischiefs, not onely among the common sort of Scholars, but even among them also, who otherwise are famously reputed for learning:

1. Becaus they never studied to know the derivation and proper signification of the English words which they use, but take anie, to which their fancie more then their judgment leadeth; whether for signification proper or improper for their purpose, they know not.

2. Manie that would bee esteemed verie reverend for depth of learning, do not know scientifically with what warrantable letters and syllables they ought to write their own native speech; inasmuch, as they have no precepts of *Grammar* for English, by which they may do it: whence it is, that in Orthographie for writing, som, in som few words, follow the Orthographie of the old Britains; manie, that of the Latines; som that of the Saxons; more are they that imitate the French: and not a few are they that follow their own reasonless fancie.[2]

He realized, however, that something more than a grammar was needed to improve the diction and spelling of vernacular writers. An authoritative dictionary, not containing hard words only, but "a full measure of all sorts of words, as in a common storehous," was required "to make the English tongue a settled, certain and corrected language."[3] He proposes that only words of pleasing sound and "in use among the English" be included, that derivations be plainly given, that clear and complete definitions, embracing the original, derived, and figurative meanings of words, be recorded, and that words borrowed from other languages be properly Anglicized. Though he does not make

[2] *The Right Teaching of Useful Knowledg*, pp. 26–35.

[3] The proposal to refine and fix the vernacular was frequently put forth in the years to come.

clear the source from which authority is to be secured for the lexicon, his words suggest that he had an act of Parliament or a royal edict in mind. For he proposes that from "the date of the edict to ratifie and settle the English language . . . all words, thenceforth to bee used, have onely their metal from the *Lexicon*, and their stamp from the *Grammar*," and that "by authoritie; like that once granted to famous *Priscian*, everie word thenceforth to be used, by anie native of *England*, contrariant to the edict for [the] English language, bee adjudged and condemned for non-English, barbarous, non-significant, and of none effect, and void to all intent and purpose."

The grammar and lexicon would, in Snell's mind, render the mother tongue refined, authoritative, and permanent. They would make it a "wel-turned," "smooth-running," and "choisly significant language," and would enable men to justify their use of it. But the benefit which received the greatest emphasis was the stability of the vernacular. As was noticed in a previous chapter, the mutability of living languages was no idle or academic matter, but a deep-seated conviction which dominated the seventeenth and first half of the eighteenth centuries. Thus we can easily understand why Snell elaborates upon the possibility of fixing the language offered by his proposals.

The language and the writing of it, and the signification of it will bee alwaies undoubted and certain, without variation and change; and held to an immutabilitie; as the Latine now is, by the power of the *Grammar* and *Dictionarie* for Latine . . . The language of our Land thus brought to a fixed and immutable state, it will not as in former ages, so alter out of date and knowledg, but that posteritie may bee abel to read and understand, what was written by their Elders, that lived five hundred years before. . . . Wee shall reap all the same profits and advantages, that wee see the glorious *Romans* have gotten, by the means aforementioned . . . What forced the great Theologues of *England* and the Sages of the Laws not to trust the changabel English, or French-tongue to conserv and inviolately keep their sacred oracles? was it not becaus the English and French, as all other vulgar speech, was alwaie in mutation and change, insomuch that within the space of two hundred years, succeeding posteritie cannot understand that language which their forefathers used . . .[4] Therefore, if the people of *England* will have

[4] In a later passage Snell points out that because of the instability of the

the *maxims* and mysteries of the Laws to bee translated into English; First by effecting such a work as is afore-mentioned, let them prepare such a stanch and lasting vessal as will not loos it self, with the Laws conteined within the space of a few hundred years.

Snell believed that his proposed grammar and lexicon were the instrumentalities by which the language could be stabilized. He says nothing about an organization for refining the language before stabilization, which, owing largely to the influence of the French Academy, was generally advocated by those who later were interested in the refinement and permanence of the vernacular. He does, however, think that in his own day English had reached its highest peak of development, and was therefore ready for fixation.[5] "And above all other," he says, "the present,

vernacular "the wisdom of our Elders did ordain that the private pleadings, recoveries, and judgments concerning particular right, tenure, and inheritance should bee entred and recorded in the unchangabel Latine tongue, that howsoever the language of the Land might bee quite worn out and gon, yet all succeeding heirs, after manie ages might bee abel to know by the Records in Latine, how their tenure and titel, had beginning; and how it hath been conveied down and continued." *The Right Teaching of Useful Knowledg*, pp. 180–81.

[5] Three views of the course followed by things human on this earth struggled for mastery in the seventeenth century. One was the theory of nature's decay, which dominated the latter half of the reign of Elizabeth and the early years of the seventeenth century, and which was held almost exclusively by the conservatives and the admirers of antiquity. It envisaged, of course, a progressive decline in the excellence of all things. Another was the incipient idea of progress, which derived its chief support from the forward-looking spirit of Bacon, and which was largely held by the Baconians or progressives. Then there was a view which mediated between the two by asserting that everything passed through a cycle of youth, development, perfection, and decay. It was given elaborate and influential expression by George Hakewill in *An Apologie of the Power and Providence of God in the Government of the World*, 1627, in which it is termed "circular" progress. Under the name of cyclic or rhythmic progress it has its adherents today. It was largely, though not exclusively, held by the progressives. It was this view that entered most frequently into the ideas of linguistic mutability. L'Isle speaks of the long process by which the English language progressed from its rude Saxon origins to its perfection in his own day. (See *supra*, p. 244.) Francis Gouldman says, "To Languages as well as Dominions (with all other things under the Sun) there is an appointed time: they have had their infancy, foundations and beginning; their growth and increase, in purity and perfection, as also in spreading and

exquisite, and elaborate times of learned eloquence, seem to bee the most advantagious for settling and stateing of our English tongue, as beeing now at the highest perfection for elocution and language, that ever have been, or are like to bee." In order to prove that "wee have as good language at home, as I suppose that of the Latines was," he points out that the languages from which English was derived—British, German, French, and Latin—were more polished than those, with the exception of Greek, which entered into Latin when it was at its peak. "Now out of all the forenamed languages, from which the speech of our Nation is assumed, wee have an abundant election of words, filed and smoothed already to our purpose, which with delightful varietie can make our English as copious as either the Latine

---

propagation; their state of consistency, and their old age, declinings and decays. That thus it pleased the divine providence to deal with *Rome* in her Power and Tongue is abundantly manifest." (*A Copious Dictionary*, 1664, preface.) In the preface to his *English Grammar*, 1688, Guy Miege says, in respect to the mutability of the English tongue, " 'tis well known, that Languages, as States, have their Infancy and Age, their Wax and Wane." In his essay *On Ancient and Modern Learning*, Sir William Temple introduces the idea of cyclic progress, but he did not popularize it, as F. W. Bateson says (*English Poetry and the English Language*, p. 47), for Hakewill had rendered it popular, and by Sir William's time it had become trite; in fact, the book largely responsible for Temple's essay touched upon it. (Thomas Burnet, *The Sacred Theory of the Earth*, 3d ed., 1697, p. 221.) In the light of this theory any attempt to fix the language should occur when the language is at its height. Mulcaster and others had expressed such a view in the sixteenth century (*supra*, p. 165) and Welsted and others were to express it in the eighteenth. (*A Dissertation Concerning the Perfection of the English Language*, 1724, in *Critical Essays of the Eighteenth Century*, ed. W. H. Durham, pp. 356–62.) Since Snell antedates Davenant (*Critical Essays of the Seventeenth Century*, ed. J. E. Spingarn, II, 6) in giving elaborate expression to the idea, Mr. Bateson's ambitious theory (*op. cit.*, pp. 46–47), based largely upon the botanical comparison used by Davenant, seems hardly valid. Needless to say, Latin in the Augustan age furnished an excellent illustration. In a poem prefixed to R. Loveday's translation of a French romance by La Calprenède under the title *Hymen's Præludia: or Love's Master-piece Being the third Part of that so much admired Romance Intituled, Cleopatra*, 1655, R. W. says,

> All Tongues must have their heigh [*sic*] and fall. In *Rome*
> *Tully* made Latin perfect, but its Doome
> Soon follow'd his. *Loveday* has done the same
> For English, whose Beauty will renown his Name.
> The great feare is, that none can tread his Path,
> So that his Lines will be its Epitaph.

or Greek."[6] The emphasis which he places upon the benefit to be derived from a stabilized language reveals how serious was the concern over the changeableness of the vernacular.

Snell's linguistic proposals are included in a larger plan which demanded the establishing of a college in every large town in England. These were to be called rural colleges to distinguish them from "Colleges Academical," or universities, and would be supervised by "a general college," composed of a select faculty to which some able foreigners would be admitted. The general college was especially devised as a teachers' college to train instructors for the other institutions. For the latter Snell proposed two different curricula, one for those students who studied Latin, and one for those who did not, but all pupils were to study English by the aid of the grammar and dictionary discussed above. The nonclassical curriculum contained handwriting and shorthand, arithmetic, good manners and etiquette (upon which much emphasis is placed), physical education, logic, rhetoric, criminal and civil laws, business documents, and vocational guidance. The other included Latin (learned in the easiest way, which would require only one year after the English grammar had been mastered), geometry, cosmography, geography, topography, limning, heraldry, ethics, natural philosophy (to a small extent), metaphysics, history and chronology, natural law, international law, civil law, natural theology, catechism, economics ("how by prudence to maintein a Familie in a happie estate"), political science (much emphasized), and diplomacy. All these subjects, he declares again and again, are to be taught in English, and English only, for "it is more facil for an Englishman, by the eie of reason, to see through the *Medium*, and light of the English tongue; then by the more obscure light of anie forreign language: to learn unknown arts and terms, a speech and language less known then our own doth make the learning by much more obscure and hard."[7]

[6] *The Right Teaching of Useful Knowledg*, pp. 35–49. In addition to his lexicon, he advocated a dictionary of the "hard" words used in special fields. *Ibid.*, pp. 135–36.

[7] *Ibid.*, p. 207. Cf. also pp. 62, 141, 171–79, 316. Snell seems to have had in mind for his schools some such idea as he attributed to the Romans, who, he says, by means of an authoritative lexicon and grammar established

It is rather significant that he should think it necessary to defend the inclusion of Latin by pointing out that it was a "storehous" of divine and human wisdom, that a knowledge of it was necessary for a proper knowledge of English orthography and terms of art, that it was of assistance in learning foreign languages, and that some public offices required it. Though he admits and defends the learned tongue, he is hardly enthusiastic about it, and would not permit much time to be devoted to it,

as if the Scholars, during all the pretious time of their youth, had nothing else to do, but to get the knowledg of the Latine tongue, of which, to saie the best, the learning of it, as of all other tongues, is but to have knowledg of the cask, and vessel, and not of the rich wares that are conteined in them: onely to teach children the use of speech and language, is but to make them emptie nominals, without knowledg of materials, and realities, by which they should bee made more abel and more readie to perform all personal duties, and especially those that pertein to the particular calling, which they intend to practise during all their life.[8]

Here is the touchstone—utility, the value that dominated that period as it does our times. The insistence upon usefulness plays somewhat the same part in determining linguistic attitudes in the seventeenth century that the emphasis upon eloquence played in the sixteenth. As early as 1611 a translator of Cicero maintained the value of his work, not with respect to the study of Latin, but on the ground that its purpose was to teach pupils the proper use of the vernacular,

the very maine end, why more then nine ten parts of children bee set to Schoole. Which seeing it is our naturall tongue, and in any course of

their language on firm grammatical principles, and "The Latine beeing thus made a Grammatical language, elegant, certain, and perfect, above that of rustic Latines, and beeing thus assumed to bee the State-speech of the Romane Empire; hereupon there were Schools set up in everie province and Nation to instruct all the . . . children of the better sort in the . . . Latin tongue; and the Latine beeing thus brought to perfection above all other languages . . ." (*Ibid.*, p. 176.) William Dell seems to have taken his cue from Snell in proposing that schools be erected throughout all England, even in the smaller villages, and that "they first teach them to read their native tongues, which they speak without teaching." "The Right Reformation of Learning," pp. 26–27, in *The Tryal of Spirits*, 1653.

[8] *The Right Teaching of Useful Knowledg*, pp. 184–85.

life afterward altogether in use, ought much more then it is, to bee Grammatically knowne, and after the course here set downe for the Latine, parsed and examined, and in all Schoole exercises . . . daily practised.[9]

Brinsley, likewise, gives utility an important place among the reasons for studying English, one of the purposes which he assigns to the grammar school being to teach children *"To grow in our own English tongue, according to their ages, and growths in other learning: to vtter their minds in the same, both in propriety, and purity; and so to be fitted for diuinity, law, or what other calling or faculty soeuer they shalbe after employed in,"*[10] and in his chief work he justifies his emphasis on the teaching of the vernacular on the ground that the "language which all sorts and conditions of men amongst vs are to haue most vse of, both in speech and writing, is our owne natiue tongue."[11] In the sixteenth century we occasionally hear voices expressing an obvious comment on the practical value of the native tongue, but the age was too much intent on eloquence to grant such a view an important place in the climate of opinion. In the seventeenth, however, "our mother-tongue beeing likely (in the practice) to bee most useful"[12] demands attention more on that score than on others.

The utilitarian spirit permeates Snell's volume. He pays scant respect to the theories and problems of natural history; in

[9] *Certaine Epistles of Tully Verbally Translated*, 1611, sig. A4ᵛ.

[10] *A Consolation for Our Grammar Schooles*, 1622, p. 54.

[11] *Ludus Literarius*, 1612, p. 22.

[12] *Janua Linguarum Reserata*, 1643, "To the Reader." The same sentiment, and in the same words, is expressed by J. Wharton in the preface to his *New English-Grammar*, 1655. Wharton pays his respects to the emphasis formerly placed upon eloquence when he says that "the puritie and Elegancie of our own Language is to bee esteemed a chief part of the honor of our Nation, which wee all ought to our utmost power to advance," but he evidently considered the teaching of English even more necessary because of the fact that "for *one* that is trained up in the Grammar Schools, to any perfection, fit for the Universitie, or any learned Profession, a hundred are taken away before; of whom the most, very shortly after, wholely in a manner forget their Latine; so that if they bee not bettered in the knowledge of their Native Language, their labor and cost is to little or no purpose." How often in our own day have we heard this sentiment!

fact, he stipulates that "becaus this contemplative knowledg, is so far estranged and remote from the practive affairs of a civil vocation, the Solicitor willeth that the rural student do spend verie little time on it." He evidently had not read his Bacon well. He continues: "It is the propertie of true wisdom to look alwaies to the intended end, goodness, and happie state of life which shee desireth to enjoie; and to pass by all things that do not help to attein that happiness," and which may be left to idle minds.[13] We are not surprised to learn that students should pursue only "useful Historie, as may serv to make them more fit to do service in their own Countrie and in their own calling," and that the "reading of Histories onely for delight, talk, and ostentation is a prodigal consumption of precious time."[14] Snell will admit into the curriculum no useless, vain, or unprofitable learning.[15] One of the claims made for the proposed schools is that "the arts and abilities here intended to bee taught in the English onely, do very much prepare and enabel a man for anie profession or calling of a private life."[16] And in this utility "our onely useful tongue" participated.[17] In fact, English and its grammar are the very foundation of his pedagogical proposals.

[13] *The Right Teaching of Useful Knowledg*, pp. 243–44.

[14] *Ibid.*, pp. 256–57.

[15] His favorable attitude toward eloquence and rhetoric, however, is somewhat at variance with this spirit. After speaking of the "sweet allurement, or pleasant delight" of rhetoric, he says: "therefore according to the narrow measure of our cursorie and countrie teaching, som knowledg of the art of Rhetorick, or beautified language and of fair speaking should bee learned in our rural College. 1. That a Scholar may bee abel to speak and write in a more refined and in a more pleasing manner, then an untaught man, and without harsh and fulsome surfeit of the ear," and also to distinguish between true argument and the sophistical "shaddows and colors, popular comparisons, and seducing similitudes," with which demogogic orators mislead ignorant people. (*Ibid.*, pp. 129–30.) One of the sections of his lexicon was to be devoted to a *Florilegium* containing "all the wittie and pleasant expressions which are plentifully extant in the works of our great Predicants, and famous Comedians." He says that if the English valued their speech as much as the Romans did theirs, "England might have such Orators as *Tullie, Hortensius,* and *Demosthenes* were. But such is our own supinitie, and neglect, that it would bee well for us, if wee in this learned age could rightly, use Orthographie, and spel our despised English." *Ibid.*, pp. 47, 207–10.

[16] *Ibid.*, p. 183.

[17] *Ibid.*, p. 317.

Knowledge of English and the giving of all instruction in English would in his judgment greatly cut down the time required to learn anything, and would make possible the comprehensive education which his curricula called for. It was the only language that could be used for his practical, utilitarian type of education.

It was this type of education for which the pedagogical Puritans cried long and loudly. Just as they believed that in religious matters the Anglicans had not revolted far enough from the Catholic church, so they believed that the universities had not changed enough from their medieval character.[18] The changes which they wished to introduce called for the abolition of all remnants of scholastic theology and philosophy, traditional ceremonies, manners, and customs, and, for the most part, humanistic subjects such as classical literature, language, and ethics.[19] There were varying degrees of hostility to established education. The more ignorant and fanatical Puritans wished to abolish all university learning,[20] but others wished to substitute for traditional education scientific, professional, and vocational subjects. Some would leave the universities as they were with the exception that Baconian science was to take the place of the

[18] Cf. especially "An Apologie to the Reader," prefixed to *A Plain and Necessary Confutation of divers gross and Antichristian Errors, Delivered to the University Congregation, the last Commencement, Anno. 1653 by Mr. Sydrach Simpson, Master of Pembroke Hall in Cambridge,* found in William Dell's *The Tryal of Spirits,* 1653. The seriousness with which the Puritans viewed the problem of the reformation of the schools and universities is seen in the minutes of the Council of the House of Commons for September 7, 1650: "When the propositions for reforming schools are presented the council will give them all possible furtherance." The minutes for July 20, 1653, in the *Journal of the House of Commons* (VII, 287), read: "*Resolved,* that a committee be appointed for Advancement of Learning. *Ordered,* that the Committee that brought in this Report for Committees, do name a Committee for this Purpose; and to present it to the House." The next day the members of the committee were presented, and a quorum determined.

[19] John Webster would substitute "practical" Christian ethics for the Aristotelian variety, "set forth as a splendid and beautiful thing, bearing forth the brightness of wit, and vigour of eloquence," for "water is better in an Earthan vessel, than poison in a golden cup." *Academiarum Examen,* 1653, p. 87.

[20] Anthony à Wood says that in 1653 Parliament even "considered among themselves of the suppressing Universities and all Schools of Learning, as heathenish and unnecessary." *History and Antiquities of the University of Oxford,* 1796, p. 657. Cf. pp. 680, 683, 695–97.

traditional natural philosophy.[21]   It was a Philistine age and the
beginning of our own world.   Puritanism conducted an aggressive
campaign against Humanism,[22] and inevitably the classical litera-
tures and languages suffered.   A very critical attitude was maintained toward the study of poetry and rhetoric,[23] and linguistic
study, as an academic discipline, was sternly reprehended.

[21] See especially *Vindiciæ Academiarum*, 1654, by Seth Ward and John
Wilkins.   The more important treatises advocating educational reforms by such
men as Hall, Dury, Hartlib, Petty, Webster, Biggs, and others are discussed,
from the point of view of the new science, by Richard F. Jones in chapter v,
"The Advancement of Learning and Piety," of *Ancients and Moderns* ("Washington University Studies"), 1936.

[22] In "The Right Reformation of Learning, Schooles, and Universities
according to the State of the Gospel, and True Light that shines therein,"
appended to *The Tryal of Spirits*, 1653, William Dell furnishes an excellent
illustration.   Though reluctantly consenting to the teaching of the classical
languages for reasons which will be discussed later, he urges "that in teaching
youth ... *Greek* and *Latin*, such *heathenish Authors*, be most *carefully avoided*,
be their *Language* never so good, whose *writings* are full of the fables, *vanities*,
filthiness, *lasciviousness*, *idolatries*, and *wickedness* of the heathen.   Seeing
usually, whilst *youth* do learn the *Languages* of the *heathen*, they also learn
their *wickedness* in that *Language*; whereas it were far *better* for them to want
their *Language*, then to be possessed with their *wickedness*.   And what should
Christian youth have to do with heathenish *Poets*, who *were* for the most part
the *Devils Prophets*, and delivered forth their *writings* in his *spirit*, and who
through the *smoothness*, *quietness*, and *sweetness* of their *language*, do *insensibly*
instill the *poison* of *lust* and *wickedness* into the hearts of *youth*; whereby their
Education, which ought to *correct* their *natural corruption*, doth exceedingly
increase and *inflame* it.

"Wherefore my *counsel* is that they learn the *Greek* and *Latine Tongues*,
especially from Christians, and so without the *lyes*, *fables*, *follies*, *vanities*,
whoredoms, *lust*, *pride*, *revenge*, etc. of the *heathens*; especially seeing neither
their *words*, nor their *phrases*, are *meet* for *Christians* to take unto their *mouths*:
and most *necessary* it is, that *Christians* should *forget* the names of their *Gods*,
and *Muses*, (which were but *Devils* and *damned Creatures*) and all their
Muthology and *fabulous inventions*, and let them go to *Satan*, from *whence*
they came."

[23] The spirit that attributed uselessness, vanity, and affectation to them
and their study was the same that opposed eloquence in the sixteenth century.
John Webster expresses the typical attitude of the Commonwealth when he
says, "Lastly, for *Rhetorick*, or *Oratory*, *Poesie*, and the like, which serve for
adornation, and are as it were the outward dress, and attire of more solid sciences; first they might tollerably pass, if there were not too much affectation
towards them, and too much pretious time spent about them, while more
excellent and necessary learning lies neglected and passed by: For we do in
these ornamental arts, as people usually do in the world, who take more care
often time about the goods of fortune, then about the good of the body, and

In Puritan eyes a knowledge of Latin gained through difficult grammatical study yielded no profitable returns. "I could never yet," says John Hall, "make so bad an *Idæa* of a true University, as that it should serve for no nobler end, then to nurture a few raw striplings, come out of some miserable Country-school, with a few shreds of Latine, that is as immusicall to a polite ear as the gruntling of a Sow, or the noise of a Saw."[24] John Webster likewise found little "profit or emolument" in the study of Latin and Greek:

The knowledge of Tongues beareth a great nois in the world, and much of our precious time is spent in attaining some smattering and small skill in them, and so we do all *servire duram servitutem* before we arrive at any competent perfection in them, and yet that doth scarcely compensate our great pains; nor when obtained, do they answer our longings, and vast expectations."

After declaring that a man might know the names of all things in all languages and yet possess no more true knowledge than he who knew the English names only, he says,

Now for a Carpenter to spend seven years time about the sharpning and preparing his instruments . . . were ridiculous and wearisome; so for Scholars to spend divers years for some small scantling and smattering in the tongues, having for the most part got no further knowledge, but like Parrats to babble and prattle . . . that whereby the intellect is no way inriched, is but toylsome, and almost lost labour.[25]

A knowledge of Latin was useful only as a key to the learning expressed in it and as a means of communication with other

more nice and precise sollicitousness about fashions and garbs, than either about the body it self or the goods of the mind, regarding the shell more than the kernal, and the shadow more than the Substance." *Academiarum Examen,* 1653, p. 88.

A little later this view of rhetoric was entertained by the experimental scientists, many of whom were Puritans, and reinforced the demand for a simple, plain style, which constituted a most important part of their scientific program. See Richard F. Jones, "Science and English Prose Style in the Third Quarter of the Seventeenth Century," in *PMLA,* XLV (1930), 977–1009.

[24] *An Humble Motion to The Parliament of England Concerning The Advancement of Learning and Reformation of the Universities,* 1649, p. 25. For the attacks on the teaching of the classical languages see chaps. v and vi of Richard F. Jones's *Ancients and Moderns.*

[25] *Academiarum Examen,* p. 21.

(margin note: & divinity)

nations. It was to be learned in the simplest manner and the
shortest time for this purpose.[26] The fact that the Scriptures had
been originally written in Hebrew and Greek, and that commentaries had been written in Latin, forced many Puritans to concede
the need of knowing those languages, but some even denied
this necessity. Seizing upon the prevailing idea of linguistic
mutation, Webster holds that Greek and Hebrew have been so
changed by intermixtures and migrations that a knowledge of
them assists little in understanding the Bible, since it "can but
teach the *Grammatical* construction, signification, and interpretation of words, propriety of phrases, deduction of Etymologies
. . . so . . . he that understands the original tongues, in which
the text was first written, conceives no more of the mind of God
thereby, than he that only can read or hear read the translation
in his Mothers tongue."[27] Others held, with better reason, that
since the Bible had been translated into English, and a great mass
of religious writings had appeared in the vernacular, even a
minister could perform his function without being conversant
with the learned languages. As early as 1616 Charles Richard-
son, a London preacher, expressed the conviction that if ministers

[26] The ways of teaching Latin discussed in the preceding chapter, such as
the use of the vernacular and the learning of grammar directly from authors
rather than as an "art," are advocated in these educational treatises. John
Webster mentions with praise and approval Webbe, Brinsley, and Comenius.

Francis Osborn doubted the value of the long and difficult study of Latin,
"It being likelier to have been the voyce of *Custome* then *Reason* that *Fonted*
a bare *Knowledge* in *Tongues* with the *Title* of *Learning.* In the prosecution
of which the *Spirits* of *Children* are blunted, and *Wit* exchanged for *Insignificant Termes,* and a *Stupid* Ignorance of all things else, under the Tyrannicall
Regiment of an Ignorant *Pedagogue.*" (*A Miscellany of Sundry Essays and
Paradoxes,* 1659, p. 78.) Peter du Moulin (the younger) is also of the opinion
that of "humane sciences the most part hath more luster then price: Learning
in Tongues is a fine Ornament, and of great use, yet not answerable to the
labour and time that it stands in. When we have learned to name heaven and
earth five or six several wayes, we know their natures never the better for that.
A wiseman will rather seeke the use then the luster of languages." (*Of Peace
and Contentment of Minde,* 1657, p. 178.) The emphasis which in the
sixteenth century was frequently placed upon the active and practical in contrast to the contemplative and scholarly, and which persisted in the essayists
of the seventeenth century, was entirely congenial to Puritanism and the new
science.

[27] *Op. cit.,* pp. 6, 7.

"would but diligently studie *English* bookes of *Diuinitie* that are now in print, they might doe much good in Gods Church." He mentions especially the works of Calvin, Willet, Greenham, Perkins, and Dod, as representative of those who had performed "very profitably in handling the controuersies between vs and the *Papists*."[28] In *Considerations Touching The likeliest means to remove Hirelings out of the church* (1659), written in answer to those who considered a university training necessary for a clergyman, John Milton maintained

Milton

> that what learning either human or divine can be necessary to a minister, may as easily and less chargeably [expensively] be had in any private house. How deficient els and to how little purpose are all those piles of sermons, notes, and comments on all parts of the bible, bodies and marrows of divinitie, besides all other sciences, in our English tongue; many of the same books which in Latine they read at the universitie.[29]

If in the general attack on humanistic education Latin suffered both in prestige and use, English profited. It is generally true that as Latin falls in estimation, the vernacular rises. We have already seen how the grammatical teaching of English and the expansion of its use in the lower schools were advocated with increasing emphasis. The Puritans, however, do not stop short of the universities. After criticizing certain methods and customs in the latter, Webster engages in the usual attack on Latin, asserting that

> Their [the universities'] custome is no less worthy of reprehension that in all their exercises they make use of the *Latine* tongue, which though it have custome, and long continuance to plead its justification, and that it is used to bring youth to the ready exercise of it, being of general reception almost through the whole world: yet it is as cleerly answered, that custome without reason and benefit, becomes injurious, and though it make them ready in speaking the *Latine* while they treat of such sub-

---

[28] *A Workman That Needeth Not to Be Ashamed*, 1616, pp. 29–30.

[29] P. 137. The desire to adorn his native tongue was one of the motives inspiring Milton's poetic compositions, and he deliberately refrained from writing one of his prose treatises in Latin, though intended for the learned, because of "the love I beare to my native language to serv it first with what I endeavor." See the end of the dedication of *The Doctrine and Discipline of Divorce* (1644), "To the Parliament of England, with the Assembly."

jects as are usually handled in the *Schools*, yet are they less apt to speak it with facility in negotiations of far greater importance. And in the mean time, the way to attain knowledge is made more difficult, and the time more tedious, and so we almost become strangers to our own mother tongue, loving and liking forein languages, as we do their fashions, better than our own, so that while we improve theirs, our own lies altogether uncultivated, which doubtless would yield as plentiful an harvest as others, if we did as much labour to advance it. . . . And therefore were the *Romans* so careful to propagate their language in other nations . . . And so likewise *Pythagoras*, *Plato*, and *Aristotle* did teach in their own mother tongues, and *Hippocrates*, *Galen*, *Euclide*, and others writ in the vulgar language of their own nation, and yet we neglecting our own, do foolishly admire and entertain that of strangers, which is no lesse a ridiculous than prejudicial custome.[30]

When Webster begins to prescribe remedies for the serious ailments with which in his eyes the universities were afflicted, we are not surprised to find one proposal requiring that "their exercises . . . be in English as well as other tongues, that while they labour to make other languages familiar unto them, they become not altogether strangers unto their own,"[31] and another asking

That care may be had of improving, and advancing our own language, and that arts and sciences may be taught in it, that thereby a more easie and short way may be had to the attaining of all sorts of knowledge: and that thereby after the example of the *Romans* we may labour to propagate it amongst other nations, that they may rather be induced to learn ours, than we theirs, which would be of vast advantage to the Commonwealth, in forrein Negotiations, Trading, Conquest and Acquisitions, and also of much domestick advantage within our own territories. For if we should arrive at any extraordinary height of learning, and knowledge, though we should but speak and write in our own mother tongue, then would other nations be as earnest in learning it, and translating our books, as former ages have been in labouring to attain the language, and translate the books of the *Grœcians* and *Romans*, and we at this day of the *French*, and *Germans*.[32]

---

[30] *Academiarum Examen*, 1653, pp. 92–93. Webster employs the same classical precedent in upholding the study of English that translators used in the sixteenth century to justify their activity.

[31] *Ibid.*, p. 109.

[32] *Ibid.*, pp. 98–99.

The Puritan plea for the improvement of English and for its study and employment in the schools was inspired by several considerations. One was a desire to render the vernacular more effective and to raise it to a higher plane of esteem and dignity. Another was the pedagogical principle that knowledge could be imparted much more rapidly, comprehensively, and efficiently through the mother tongue than through a strange medium. Perhaps the most important consideration sprang from the strong antipathy to linguistic study of the traditional kind (one manifestation of a more comprehensive antihumanistic spirit), which in the case of Latin seemed to be pursued for its own sake, and which possessed no utility in human affairs. By contrast, the usefulness of the vernacular in preparing one for all the walks of life shone all the brighter.[33] On this last consideration the budding experimental science exerted a definite influence, but since the rise of science was so involved with the Puritans, it is difficult to distinguish between the two. All problems of a historical nature become complex when they enter the twenty Puri-

[33] Along with other attitudes characteristic of the Commonwealth, the emphasis upon the vernacular continued strong during the Restoration as may be seen in John Eachard's *The Grounds and Occasions of the Contempt of the Clergy*, 1670, and in a work by Carew Reynell, which both in text and in title support the ideas expressed above. After recommending the promotion of knowledge, Reynell presents his own idea of how it may best be attained:

"To which purpose it were well that the Arts and Sciences were taught in the Mother Tongue, and all manner of Books of use and Learning, in any other Language Translated into our own; and that there were a publick maintenance for Professors, and Scholars that should teach the Sciences in the Mother Tongue; and Accademies erected for that purpose, so should youth quickly improve in Knowledge, and men be fuller of wisdom then at twenty, than now they are at forty years of age. Not that I would have the Languages neglected, but that all may learn those as before. But that the *English* Tongue may be promoted and made excellent, general, and useful in all manner of Knowledge. And young Gentlemen that have a mind to it, may attend the Sciences, without so much trouble, and cracking their brains so many years about Learning the Languages. This would make the generality of the Nation more Wise, Learned, and useful one to another, both to themselves, and Country, and our Language would be popular, and esteemed in all places. For the desire of retaining Languages, is only for the Learning contain'd in them, which if disclosed without them, their extraordinary use ceaseth." *The True English Interest: Or an Account of the Chief National Improvements; in Some Political Observations Demonstrating an Infallible Advance of this Nation to Infinite Wealth and Greatness, Trade and Populacy, with Imployment, and Preferment for all Persons*, 1674, pp. 76–78.

tan years of the seventeenth century, the seminary of modernity in the Anglo-Saxon world. However, the bearing of experimental science upon the thought pattern in which we are interested may be clarified in a few particulars. The very fact that the Baconians were in revolt against antiquity and the traditional science rendered them indifferent or even hostile to Latin and Greek, the languages in which this science was for the most part recorded. Furthermore, their insistence upon a plain and simple medium of communication and upon common words, such as merchants and artisans employed, naturally called for the use of current English.[34] The strong antirhetorical bias thus engendered strengthened the feeling against the classics, with which rhetoric had been closely associated for a long time. Bacon's injunction that the data of science must be gathered directly from nature itself and Comenius' educational principle that a thing should be learned when its name is first taught joined in placing an inordinate emphasis upon material reality which the vernacular alone could adequately express.[35] Finally, the spirit of utility, which science inherited from Bacon, and which rendered it dear to the Puritans, preferred English, the usefulness of which was obvious, to Latin, the inutility of which was being vigorously denounced.

There were two considerations that prevented the complete abandonment of Latin. As one participant in a famous controversy was to remark, Latin would "last longer, and go further" than English.[36] The early scientists, with the exception of Bacon, were not particularly concerned over the instability of the vernacular, though a committee of the Royal Society was later ap-

[34] See Thomas Sprat, *History of the Royal Society*, 1667, pp. 111–13. Another member of the Royal Society says, ". . . 'tis the Profession of the Society to make Mysterious things plain; to explode and disuse all insignificant [nonsignificant] and puzling words." Sir William Petty, *The Discourse Made before the Royal Society The 26. of November, 1674*, dedication.

[35] See the preface to John Wilkins, *Mathematicall Magick. Or, The Wonders That may be performed by Mechanicall Geometry. . . . Not before treated in this language*, 1648. "Other discourses of this kind [i.e., on mechanics], are for the most part large and voluminous, of great price and hardly gotten; and besides, there are not any of them (that I know of) in our vulgar tongue, for which these Mechanicall arts of all others are most proper."

[36] Charles Boyle, *Dr. Bentley's Dissertation on the Epistles of Phalaris and the Fables of Æsop, Examin'd*, 1698, p. 230.

pointed to refine and stabilize it. They were, however, vitally interested in some international medium of communication, rendered all the more essential by Bacon's idea of a universal natural history, which called for data collected over the whole world, and to which his followers heartily subscribed. Latin had served this purpose in the past, and the fact that the scientists sought a substitute for it is indicative of the way it was losing ground. The objection to Latin was partly that too much time was spent upon its study, which could much better be employed upon things,[37] and partly that it was an imperfect medium, a deficiency in which all known tongues participated. And the associations of the old erroneous science ever clung to it. As a result, there was a wide and energetic demand for a universal language, and many were the plans and suggestions offered for one,[38] beginning with

[37] In the Prolegomena to his translation of Arthur Dee's *Fasciculus Chemicus* (1650), Elias Ashmole says that a universal language would remove the curse of Babel's confusion, and that "Our misery now is, we spend a great part of our best and most precious time in learning *one Language*, to understand a *little Matter* (and in how many *Tongues* is it necessary to be perfect, before a man can be *generally knowing*?) whereas, if this invention [universal language] were but compleated, *Arts* would arrive at a high perfection in a little space, and we might reckon upon *more time*, in the short account and measure of our *days*, to be imployed in a *substantial study* of *Matter*."

[38] Some of the proposals for a universal language, besides Wilkins', may be found in: Francis Lodowyk, *A Common Writing: Whereby two, although not understanding one the others Language, yet by the helpe thereof, may communicate their minds one to another. Composed by a Well-willer to Learning,* 1647; William Petty, *The Advice of W. P. to Mr. Samuel Hartlib. For the Advancement of some particular Parts of Learning,* 1648, p. 5; the Prolegomena to Elias Ashmole's translation of Arthur Dee's *Fasciculus Chemicus,* 1650; *The Ground-Work, or Foundation Laid (or so intended) For the Framing of a New Perfect Language: And an Vniversal or common writing. And Presented to the consideration of the Learned By a Well willer to Learning,* 1652; Sir Thomas Urquhart, *Logopandecteision, or an Introduction to the Vniversal Language,* 1653 (which calls for eleven cases, four numbers, eleven genders, ten tenses, and four voices); Cave Beck, *The Universal Character,* 1657; Henry Edmundson, *Lingua Linguarum,* 1658 (the preface to which expresses doubt of the feasibility of such a language); James Howell, *Lexicon Tetraglotton,* 1660, preface; George Dalgarno, *Ars Signorum,* 1661; Somerset, second Marquis of Worcester, *A Century of the Names and Scanthings,* 1663, p. 26. For further discussion of the idea see Otto Funke, *Zum Weltsprachenproblem in England im 17. Jahrhundert (Anglistische Forschungen,* LXIX, 1929), and Richard F. Jones, "Science and Language in England of the Mid-Seventeenth Century," *Journal of English and Germanic Philology,* XXXI (1932), 315–31.

Bacon himself. The matter was of special interest, first, to the group of experimenters who met at Oxford in the middle of the century,[39] and later to the members of the Royal Society. John Wilkins was their leader in promoting the idea. As early as 1641 he expressed interest in it,[40] and on his removal to Oxford, shortly before the middle of the century, he continued his interest, largely in association with Dalgano. This interest finally bore fruit in his ambitious *An Essay Towards a Real Character and a Philosophical Language* (1668), which was really sponsored by the Royal Society and was of much interest to its members.[41] There were other considerations involved in the effort to invent a new language, such as the striving for a more perfect scientific medium of communication than was afforded by any known language, and the desire for a "natural" language, in which words would not be mere counters, but would express the nature of the things signified. Yet the deep underlying motive was to render the use of Latin unnecessary.

The Puritan opposition to learning and the universities was inspired partly by religious and partly by secular convictions. Hostility to scholastic divinity and the belief that the heathenish, or profane, philosophy taught in the schools was inimical to true religion based squarely upon the Scriptures were strong and widespread. There were certainly many learned men among the Puritans, who in the course of argument and controversy could

[39] They were especially interested in George Dalgano's scheme, which was published in 1661 under the title *Ars Signorum*. In a proclamation from Charles II, prefixed to the treatise, it is said that John Wilkins, John Wallis, and Seth Ward (all members of the Oxford group) judged the proposal "to be of singular use, for facilitating the matter of Communication and Intercourse between People of different Languages, and consequently a proper and effectual Means, for advancing all the parts of Real and Useful Knowledge [i.e., experimental science], Civilizing barbarous Nations, Propagating the Gospel, and encreasing Traffique and Commerce." William Petty, another member of the group, reveals interest in a universal language in his *Advice of W. P. to Mr. Samuel Hartlib*, 1648, p. 5.

[40] *Mercury: Or the Secret and Swift Messenger*, chap. xiii.

[41] John Aubrey says that the *Essay* "was his [Wilkins'] darling, and nothing troubled him so much when he dyed, as that he had not completed it; which will now in a yeare more be donne by the care and studies of," among others, Robert Hooke, Francis Lodowyck, and John Ray, all members of the Royal Society. *Brief Lives*, ed. A. Clark, 1898, II, 302.

not have escaped the use of learning and Latin, even if they had wished to do so. Custom and tradition were too strong to be flouted consistently, and the necessity of knowing the learned languages for an understanding of the Bible, if the latter were not equated with the English translation, was too obvious for any of the less fanatical elements to ignore. Yet the spirit of the age was critical of the learning with which was associated so much that it abhorred, and toward the end even influenced Milton to discount it.[42] The fact is apparent, not only in the various treatises which attack learning and the universities[43] but also in serious apologies for the latter by men like Edward Leigh, Thomas Hall, and Edward Waterhouse.[44] Furthermore, the seriousness of the concern over the state of learning and education is clearly revealed in the notice which Parliament took of the matter.[45] Nor should the testimony of contemporary witnesses like Anthony à Wood be disregarded.[46] It is not strange that Latin, which figured so largely in this learning, should suffer and the time spent in studying it should be resented.

To the more fanatical Puritans, Latin, the language of the Vulgate and the Catholic church, was the Language of the Beast. No less a person than Bishop Bramhall states explicitly that the Westminster Assembly took definite action against Latin. In answer to a book that shows how the Puritan espousal of English took firm root in non-Puritan quarters in the Restoration, the Bishop calls the proposal that ministers be trained in the use of English,

A pretty piece of *Reformation* indeed, though he must not think to claim the honour of being its first *Inventor*: for there was a time when those heavenly *Reformers* at *Westminster* voted down Latine for the Language of the *Beast*, and were clearly for throwing the whole practice of

---

[42] See *supra*, p. 307, and George Sensabaugh, "Milton on Learning," *Studies in Philology*, XLIII (1946), 258–72.

[43] See Richard F. Jones, *Ancients and Moderns*, chap. v.

[44] *A Treatise of Religion and Learning, and of Religions and Learned Men*, 1656; *Vindiciæ Literarum, The Schools Guarded*, 1654; *An humble Apologie for Learning and Learned Men*, 1653.

[45] See *supra*, p. 303, n. 18.

[46] See *supra*, p. 303, n. 20.

the *Law* into an *English* Model. In imitation of them the famous Culpepper brought the design to admirable effect in Physic.[47]

That this view of the learned languages was widespread, and also that it found verbal more often than written statement, is confirmed by the frequent attribution of it to various sects and the infrequent expression of it by them. It is also apparent that the opinion was only part, but a very important part, of the general attack on the universities. In a defense of learning and the Anglican clergy against the Puritans, John Gauden holds that the Church of England will not be able to defend itself,

if such *witlesse lack-latin Zelots* can prevail in their absurd desires, and most *fanatick endeavours*; who while they tell their *silly disciples*, (who are rather spectators than hearers of these mens *affected gesticulations*, and ill acted Oratory) That *Latin* and *Greek* are the languages of the Beast; that all books but the Bible, (and as much of that, as they take not to be for their turnes) are *Antichristian* and to be *destroyed*.[48]

Brian Walton attributed the attitude only to the Quakers, "who abhor all Learning, and account that Language [Latin], *the Language of the Beast*,"[49] but an anonymous indignant soul left out few, if any, of the sectaries in his accusation, and gave them instead full publicity in the title of his treatise. "They cry out," he says,

against all humane Learning and Studies, all *Liberal Arts* and *Sciences*, against all Books but the *Bible*, against the *Schools* and *Universities*,

[47] *A Vindication of the Clergy, From the Contempt imposed upon them by the Author of The Grounds and Occasions of the Contempt of the Clergy and Religion. With Some short Reflections upon his Further Observations*, 1672, p. 54. I have not yet discovered in any record of the Assembly that action was taken on Latin, but, as we shall soon see, there is ample evidence supporting the other statements. John Eachard, the author of the book answered, maintained a vigorous attack on the pedantic and vain employment of Latin, and an equally vigorous advocacy of the necessity of prospective ministers' studying English in the schools. His work, however, is only part of a movement toward the stylistic reform of the pulpit carried on by Anglican writers, who strenuously attack rhetorical preaching, with its Latin and Greek quotations, and insist on a plain English style. Cf. Richard F. Jones, "The Attack on Pulpit Eloquence in the Restoration," *Journal of English and Germanic Philology*, XXX (1931), 188–217.

[48] *Hieraspistes: A defence by way of Apology for the Ministry and Ministers of the Church of England*, 1653.

[49] *The Considerator Considered: Or, a brief view of certain Considerations*

as heathenish and *Antichristian* marks of the *Beast,* as deformities and impertinencies (where we have Scripture-light) prejudicial to that immediate Divine teaching to which they pretend, and by which they learn and teach all true Religion, which needs not any of those rags and additional tatters of humane learning.

These witlesse *Lack-Latine* Zealots tell their Proselytes and silly Auditors, that *Latine* and *Greek* are the Languages of the *Beast,* perswade Christians to burne all Books, that they may better understand the Bible.[50]

The antilinguistic spirit of the Puritans, or certainly of very many of them, is pilloried by John Boys in a poem addressed to William Somner, and prefixed to the latter's *Dictionarium Saxonico-Latino-Anglicum* (1659):

> What mean'st thou man? think'st thou thy learned page,
> And worthy pains will relish with this age?
>
> .   .   .   .
>
> Thy Barb'rous *Saxon,* with the heathen *Greek*
> And profane *Latine,* buyers may go seek:
> Together with the *Hebrew,* and the rest,
> Which are the language of that *Romish* beast.[51]

The secular convictions supporting the criticism of traditional learning may be traced to the materialistic nature of Puritanism, as far as the latter can be considered homogeneous, and to the influence of Bacon.[52] In a very worldly way, the Puritans were interested in the practical and useful, in what would increase

upon the *Biblia Polyglotta,* the *Prolegomena and Appendix thereof,* 1659, pp. 21–22. Walton had obviously read Gauden's book.

[50] *A Breife Description or Character Of the Religion and Manners of the Phanatiques In Generall. Scil. Anabaptists, Independents, Brownists, Enthusiasts, Levellers, Quakers, Seekers, Fift-Monarchy-Men, and Dippers,* 1660, p. 27.

[51] The poem was reprinted in Boys's *Æneas His Descent into Hell,* 1661, p. 230. It is worthy of note that for the second time Anglo-Saxon is ranked with the learned tongues. (Cf. Meric Casaubon, *De Quatuor Linguis,* 1650.) The same arguments which in our own day have been used *ad nauseam* against the study of the classics and the same that have been used in defense of them are found in this period.

[52] The discussion of this aspect of our problem presupposes the reader's familiarity with Richard F. Jones's *Ancients and Moderns,* especially chaps. v, viii, ix.

their worldly goods and creature comforts, and in whatever instrumentalities or machinery would make for this end. Thus they developed a Philistine character which was critical of humanistic subjects such as ethics, poetry, oratory, and, especially, linguistic study. As we have seen, they insisted upon an education scientific, practical, and vocational in nature, and their scientific interests frequently did not extend beyond technology. The utilitarian character of Baconian science and the promise it held out for earthly benefits rendered it very attractive to them. So the study of languages, and especially of Latin, was not considered a commendable discipline, but only a means of acquiring tools, by which desirable knowledge might be gained. When the possibility of the vernacular's containing such knowledge was envisaged, even this function of Latin was removed, and the latter was branded as pedantic and useless, an attitude largely responsible for the low state to which the classics have fallen today. As Latin falls, English rises. In a practical world, the vernacular is the useful language; it is the means of communication in the multifarious activities which support a materialistic civilization.[53] Therefore, its study, use, and improvement become of great importance, while the study of ancient and, at times, even of modern languages, is tabooed.[54]

As we have noted, the Puritans tried as far as possible to free the study of divinity from the necessity of a knowledge of Latin, Greek, and Hebrew. They made similar attempts in respect to

[53] Compare the title of Reynell's book and the quotation from the latter given in note 33.

[54] It is with pride and almost affection that we watch the rise of the mother tongue from its humble position at the beginning to its lofty estate at the end of the sixteenth century, but its progress through this period gives us pause. In his answer to Eachard, Bishop Bramhall recognizes the relationship between the former's espousal of English and the earlier Puritan predilection for it. In refuting the reasons advanced by Eachard for the study of English, he says, "The first is, That the Language learned *Men* must live by, is the *English*, there being no use of *Latine* in the Country, but only to *chequer Sermons*. . . . Bate me an Ace, quoth *Bolton!* The Language *Plum-sellers* indeed and *Cheesmongers* live by, is the *English*, and 'tis enough for them to read English Histories, Romances and Plays, if not too much. But hath the *Parson* no more use for *Latine?* Hath he none but the *Assemblies* Notes and *English Divines* to consult?" *A Vindication of the Clergy*, 1672, p. 53; Bramhall's *Vindication of Himself*, 1672, p. 89.

matters connected with the two other learned professions, law and medicine. The most active in behalf of the latter was Nicholas Culpeper, not the most worthy of advocates, who published a number of medical books in English,[55] in each of which he inveighs against the shrouding of scientific knowledge in unfamiliar languages, and introduces the same reasons that the educators of the unlatined had employed a hundred years before. He also makes good use of the example offered by the English translation of the Bible, ascribing to the writers of medical works in Latin the same motive of self-interest that he attributes to the Catholic oppositon to scriptural translations.

It was, however, in respect to law that the Puritans were most insistent upon the use of English, and with good reason. With Crown and Parliament struggling to maintain their prerogatives against each other, there was a diligent searching of the past to find a legal basis for their respective claims, and with the hazards that individuals ran in those troubled times, a knowledge of law was certainly a desideratum. Thus laws written in English would serve both a political and a private purpose. One of the published petitions to Parliament, composed presumably by Lilburne, requested

That considering it a Badg of our Slavery to a Norman Conqueror, to have our Laws in the French Tongue, and it is little lesse than brutish vassalage to be bound to walk by Laws which the People cannot know, that therefore all the Laws and Customes of this Realm be immediately written in our Mothers Tongue without any abreviations of words, and the most known vulgar hand, *viz.*, Roman or Secretary, and that Writs, Processes, and Enroulments, be issued forth, entered or inrouled in English, and such manner of writing as aforesaid.[56]

[55] E.g., *A Physicall Directory or A translation of the London Dispensatory Made by the Colledge of Physicians in London*, 1649; *A Directory for Midwives or A Guide for Women*, 1651; *Culpeper's School of Physick*, 1660 (the preface, signed by R. W., is dated December 15, 1658). Culpeper created sufficient stir to be mentioned by Bishop Bramhall a dozen or more years later in the passage quoted above. R. W. says that *"the late famous Mr. Noy of Lincolns Inne"* tried unsuccessfully to persuade his fellow lawyers "to have the Law turned into English."

[56] *A Declaration Of some Proceedings of L^t. Col. Iohn Lilburn, And his Associates*, 1647, p. 29. See *The Leveller Tracts*, ed. William Haller and Godfrey Davies, 1944, p. 109.

Lilburne's petition, probably reinforced by other expressions of similar views,[57] must have prevailed, for within two or three years Parliament passed, on November 22, 1650, a very comprehensive act:

The Parliament have thought fit to Declare and enact, and be it Declared and enacted by this present Parliament, and by the Authority of the same, That all the Report Books of the resolutions of Judges, and other Books of the Law of England, shall be translated in the English Tongue: And from and after the First of January, 1650, all Report Books of the resolutions of Judges, and all other Books of the Law which shall be Printed, shall be in the English Tongue.

And be it further Enacted by the Authority aforesaid, That from and after the first Return of Easter Term, which shall be in the year One thousand six hundred fifty and one, All Writs, Proces and Inquisitions, Certificates; and all Patents, Commissions, Records, Judgements, Statutes, Recognizances, Rolls, Entries, and Proceedings of Courts Leet, Courts Baron, and Customary Courts, and all Proceedings whatsoever in any Courts of Justice within this Commonwealth, and which concerns the Law, and Administration of Justice, shall be in the English Tongue onely, and not in Latine or French, or any other Language than English, Any Law, Custom or Usage heretofore to the contrary notwithstanding. And that the same, and every of them, shall be written in an ordinary, usual and legible Hand and Character, and not in any Hand commonly called Court-hand. [Penalty: £20 fine.]

On April 9, 1651, a supplementary act was passed calling for the translation into English "of all Writs, Proces and Returns thereof, and of all Patents, Commissions, and all Proceedings whatsoever in any Courts of Justice within this Commonwealth of England, and which concerns the Law and Administration of Justice." And in an act for bringing in public revenues, passed June 21, 1654, it was stated that Latin must be changed to English in the "Tallies."[58]

[57] Cf. John Jones, *Jurors Judges of Law and Fact*, 1650, p. 76. Jones inveighs against the use of "Pedlers French and Law-Latin, the very disguises of the Law." He asks if "Quelquechose Latin were banished, and the Law rendred in English (as Scriptures are which were hidden from us by Prelats as our Laws by Lawyers) would not all learning, and argumentations in Law be as necessarie for the continual preservation of mens lives and estates, and therefore continued in English as Sermons in Pulpits, and disputes in Schools and Universities, requisit for the salvation of our souls are?"

[58] *Act and Ordinances of the Interregum, 1642–1660*, 1911, II, 455–56,

The Puritans had taken such a definite stand on the teaching and employment of English in the schools, had inveighed so loudly against the learned language in respect to religion, and had so stoutly insisted upon the use of the vernacular in matters pertaining to law and medicine that a predilection for the mother tongue became inseparably associated with them. John Boys elucidates this association by presenting the vernacular itself as a Puritan:

> Our *Mother-tongue* well nos'd, with a wry face,
> And eyes inverted now hath chiefest grace.[59]

And satire, which, for the most part, selects as its victim only the notorious or well known, busied itself with this aspect of Puritanism. In 1659 a satirical catalogue of fictitious books was published by Sir John Birkenhead with such items as "An Act for turning all Lawes into *English,* with a short Abridgement for such new Lawyers as cannot write and read," and "An Act forbidding any more to put Greek or Latin Titles to their books, unlesse such person as can spell English."[60] Indignation sometimes supplants satire, as when Richard Whitlock, in "Learnings Apology," an attack on the Puritans for rejecting classical ornamentation in their sermons, exclaims, "If a man cloath his discourse in a Language that is not second hand English, or but one degree above the offensiveness of Caterwauling, why he is affected."[61] A number of years later Bishop Bramhall sarcastically grants a

510–11, 918. The first act may also be found in William Hughes's *Exact Abridgment of Publick Acts and Ordinances of Parliament, Made from the year 1640 to the year 1656,* 1657, No. DLII. This act soon produced results, for in the next year appeared *The Institutes of the Lawes of England, Digested into the Method of the Civill or Imperiall Institutions . . . Written in Latin by John Cowel . . . And Translated into English, According to the Act of Parliament, for the Benefit of all.* By W. G., 1651. That all did not approve this act is made clear by *The Unhappy Marks-man: or, Twenty three Queries Offered To the Consideration of the People of These Nations,* 1659, p. 3.

[59] See a poem prefixed to William Somner's *Dictionarium,* 1659.

[60] *Pauls Churchyard. Libri Theologici, Politici, Historici, Nundinis Paulinus (una cum Templo) prostant venales. Juxta seriem Alphabeti Democratici. Done into English for the Assembly of Divines,* Classis II, item 21, and Classis VI, item 137.

[61] ΖΩΟΤΟΜΙΑ, *or Observations on the Present Manners of the English,* 1652, p. 143.

minister the right to use classical quotations "to distinguish him from a Gifted Brother in a Conventicle who talks all of his own head in homespun English."[62]

No other justification for the general association of the Puritans with the English language, an association so pronounced as to render the linguistic aspect of Puritanism significant, need be sought than is found in the "spiritual verses" of James Hunt, a collection of wretched poems written near the beginning of the twenty years of Puritan domination. As the scientists held the classical languages responsible for the old science recorded in them, so Hunt attributes to them the false doctrines of the prelates:

> For you have so many false and corruptible doctrines raisde,
> By your Latine tongue, and your Greeke phrase;
> That now I trust in the living God,
> The plaine English tongue will win the praise;
> For the powerfull God that made the skies,
> Hath chosen the weake things of the world
> To confound the famous Universities.
> Again, our glorious God, from whence all true wisdom doth
>   arise,
> Hath chosen the foolish things of the world to confound the
>   wisdome of the wise.

In his excitement he seems to consider the vernacular both weak and foolish, but he means that it appears so only when judged by earthly, not heavenly, standards. He foresees a glorious mission for his mother tongue in becoming the universal language, for which there was a rising demand.[63]

---

[62] *A Vindication of the Clergy*, 1672, p. 64. He says that in the days of Cromwell, "to make a Through-Reformation, the *Independents, Anabaptists, Antinomists*, and other Factions, set up publick Schools in St. Pauls, . . . wherein they frequently held *Declamations* and *Disputations* in their *Mother-Tongue*, to train up the Old and gain New Proselytes." (*Ibid.*, p. 54.) In any popular movement like the puritanic upheaval, the vernacular is, for obvious reasons, necessary, but much more was involved in the linguistic attitude.

[63] The fact that there was at this time a movement on foot, in which John Dury participated, for the unification of all protestant churches furnishes Hunt an opportunity to make English the language of the whole body.

But master Lawyer, you may think this is an il sound,
To tell us our craftie kingdome will goe downe,
But I would intreate you not to think so,
For I am your friend and not your foe;
For I shall sing you a pleasant song,
You may be Schoolmasters to teach other Nations the
    English tongue,
For God will gather all Nations into Religion one;
So by degrees all shall be taught the English tongue;
For the Word which proceedeth from the God of peace,
Doth plainly say, that *tongues shall cease*: 1 Cor. 13.
But Lord Bishops and deep Doctors which Schollership so
    much adore,
You may perceive this being so, your Universities will
    grow poor,
But the children of God shall glorifie his name therefore,
For they shall plainly understand, they are thetosels of
    the whore;
For henceforth no man shall need the Universities,
For to learn the wisedom of the wise;
For there are very few mysteries in the Gospel that be so
    strong
But they may be unfolded by the plaine true English tongue.[64]

As a climax he suggests that Latin and Greek are the languages of the natural, or carnal, man, and therefore English is the tongue of the regenerated soul.[65]

    The distinction thus drawn between Latin and the vernacular, only one manifestation of the clash between Puritanism and

[64] See the first poem of *These Spiritval Verses of Iames Hunt, Concerning the Down-fall of the Ceremonies. Whereby the Bishops and their Clergie have made, as it were, a trade to blinde and deceive the Children of God, whom Christ Jesus hath redeemed from the bondage of Hell and corruption, by his suffering upon the Crosse, and the power of his Resurrection,* 1642. Hunt was an insignificant and ignorant Puritan, but he reveals an attitude of considerable importance, even though he gives it narrow and illiterate expression.

[65] *The Spirituall Verses and Prose of James Hunt: Concerning The Advancement of Christ his glorious and Triumphing Church,* 1642, p. 3. Had Hunt not despised Latin, he might have found support for his linguistic religion in Goropius, who made the German tongue the language of Paradise before the Fall. Nor must we forget that in 1560 Thomas Becon interpreted "Gods Blessed Word" entirely in terms of the English translation.

Humanism which played a great part in the literary history of
the seventeenth century, was a clear survival of the antirhetorical
spirit prominent during the first three quarters of the sixteenth
century. The Elizabethan insistence upon eloquence had merely
forced this attitude underground. In other respects views of
the mother tongue underwent great change. The conception
of it as an uneloquent, humble medium of instruction for the
unlearned, inadequate in its vocabulary, chaotic in its spelling,
and grammatically unregulated, dominated the first three quarters of the century. During this time there was genuine interest in remedying these defects by increasing the vocabulary
with borrowed, compounded, or revived words, and by the introduction of phonetic spelling. Few attempts, however, seem to
have been made to render the speech eloquent; in fact, a strong
antirhetorical spirit vigorously opposed one way in which to
secure eloquence, namely, by borrowing from the classical languages. These early attempts toward grammatical improvement
gave way in the second half of Elizabeth's reign to the pursuit
of eloquence. Imbued with a strong faith in the literary potentialities of the mother tongue, writers insisted on its rhetorical
rather than grammatical development. To this firm faith in the
eloquence of the vernacular the antiquarians added a pride in
the Saxon element, and this somewhat contradictory combination represented the normal pre-Restoration view.

A more important development in the attitude toward the
native tongue is seen in the seventeenth-century revival of the
attempt to introduce grammatical regulations into the language.
And it is in connection with grammatical considerations that English begins to oppose Latin. The Elizabethans emulated the
classics and at times asserted the equality of their own language
and literature with those of antiquity, but they did not attempt
to supplant the latter. In the next century, however, beginning
cautiously with the idea that too much time is devoted to the
study of Latin grammar, believers in the vernacular proceed step
by step to show that English should be used in the study of Latin,
that its interests are always to be regarded in the study of Latin,
and that it is as worthy of grammatical regulation as Latin, and
should be regulated. They turned their faces away from the elo-

quence of English to its development into an efficient medium of communication. Whereas the Elizabethans seemed to think the vernacular was destined only for literary purposes, their successors in the next centuries, and especially the Puritans, developed a more comprehensive view of its uses, and laid great stress upon its utility. The Elizabethans had demonstrated the potentialities of the language for great literature; the seventeenth century insisted upon its development and adequacy for all nonartistic purposes. Finally, the advancing scientific movement of the Puritan era, together with the materialistic nature of Puritanism itself, created an attitude hostile to Humanism and its classical foundation but much enamored of the mother tongue. As the classes which this attitude dominated grew strong socially, economically, and politically, it, too, prospered until now it reigns supreme over a scientific world, from which Latin, Greek, and the classical spirit have all but disappeared. And if we listen historically to the voices around us, we can detect in them unmistakable echoes of an earlier day.

INDEX

The titles of an author's work appear under his name and are followed by the pertinent page references, but general references to an author containing no mention of his works follow immediately the author's name. The titles of translations are listed under the names of the authors of the originals, but the names of translators are entered separately without reference to translations. Exceptions have been made in the case of Caxton, Lydgate, and Pynson. Modern editions of earlier works have been omitted, and modern editors likewise have been left out except when they play some part in the discussion.